NEIL RATTIGAN

IMAGES OF AUSTRALIA

100 Films of the New Australian Cinema

SOUTHERN METHODIST UNIVERSITY PRESS   DALLAS

The author gratefully acknowledges the
cooperation of the National Film and
Sound Archive of Australia in locating
and selecting still photographs, and in
particular the invaluable and cheerful
help of Meg Labrum, Film/TV
Documentation Officer.

Library of Congress Cataloging-in-
Publication Data
Rattigan, Neil, 1946–
  Images of Australia : 100 films of the
new Australian cinema / Neil Rattigan. —
1st ed.
    p. cm.
  Includes bibliographical references
and index.
  ISBN 0-87074-312-0 (hdcvr) —
ISBN 0-87074-313-9 (pbk)
  1. Motion pictures—Australia.
2. Australia in motion pictures.
3. National characteristics, Australian, in
motion pictures. 4. Motion pictures—
Social aspects—Australia. I. Title.
PN1993.5.A8R36 1991
791.43'6294—dc20 90-52662

For my parents,

FLORENCE AND CLIFFORD,

and in memory of BARBARA

Contents

PART I. CONTEXTS

Introduction

There is an irresistible symmetry in considering 1970 the beginning of the renaissance of Australian cinema, the start of a new decade thus heralding the start of a revitalization of consistent feature film production in Australia and the appearance of a new if modest movement in world cinema. Some sociocultural historians are fond of using the concept of the "moment" as a key factor in cultural analysis, and 1970 is as good (and true) a point as any other to locate the moment of the rebirth of Australian cinema.

This notion of a moment does not suggest that this rebirth of cinematic production was accomplished instantaneously without a gestation period and birth pains. Feature films that could be designated as Australian (as opposed to films that were simply made in Australia) were made in the 1960s. Some of the individuals who were to be prominent in the New Australian Cinema as it gained momentum were already active before 1970. But Australian film production was as spasmodic and as rare in the years immediately prior to 1970 as it had been throughout the two previous decades. Equally, from 1970 until 1975, feature film production was both infrequent (although numerically greater than at any time in the previous twenty years) and uneven, with few films of this period receiving much attention. Nonetheless, there was an easily observable movement in the early 1970s not only toward increased production within Australia, but toward films that were Australian in both origin and content. Credence can thus be given to accepting 1970 as the moment of the New Australian Cinema.

As the use of terms such as "renaissance," "rebirth," and "revitalization" implies, the production of feature films in Australia had existed prior to 1970. Although it is true to an extent that the New Australian Cinema seemed to be unaware of or uninterested in any sense of historical continuity (which is odd, given its predilection for finding the material for many of its narratives in history), there is some value in locating the New Australian Cinema within the broader historical view of motion picture production in Australia.

What follows does little more than sketch the outline of the history of cinema in Australia. Readers are referred to the select bibliography at the back of this volume for sources of more detailed histories.

The Historical Context

The history of cinema in Australia is nearly as long as the history of cinema elsewhere in the world. The first footage was shot and commercially exhibited in Australia (which was not a single nation but a collection of self-governing colonies of Britain at the time) in late 1896, just over twelve months after the first public screening in the world had taken place in Paris.[1] This footage, taken around Sydney, was shot by a cameraman in the employ of the Lumière brothers of France, who were pioneering the spread of cinema worldwide—not through some form of evangelical zeal to introduce the new technology but to obtain footage for their own exhibition purposes. The earliest extant footage shot in Australia is of a horse race, the 1896 Melbourne Cup—a national sporting and cultural event of such significance that it has been recorded on film or videotape every year since.

Feature filmmaking (as distinct from the shooting of "actualities") also began in Australia at a very early date. It is sometimes claimed that the world's first feature-length narrative fictional film was made in Australia: *The Story of the Kelly Gang* in 1905. Whether this claim can be supported or not, it is clear that this film, with a running time of over an hour, was longer than any story film being made at that time—or for some years hence—in the United States. The novelty value of the cinema and the lack of competition from overseas meant that a reasonably healthy production industry grew alongside the exhibition industry and (later) the distribution industry during the first decade and a half of this century.

Film production continued at a high level in Australia until World War I, and the peak in the number of productions in 1911 and 1912 was not equaled again until the mid-1970s. The effect of the increasing dominance of Hollywood in world cinema was progressively felt by Australian producers from about 1918. Production then began to decline at an increasing rate during and immediately following World War I. Film exhibition, however, flourished during the early decades of this century and indeed well into the 1950s.

The production side of Australian cinema began to suffer first through Australia's homegrown distributor/exhibitor monopoly (Australasian Films and Union Theatres, known as the "Combine") and later as a result of the growth of distributors (including the Combine) owned or part-owned by or contractually bound to overseas interests (American or British). In general, distributors showed less and less interest in (and sometimes outright hostility toward) the locally produced film.

The lessened demand for Australian films cannot be totally explained by reference to the commercial preferences and trade practices of distributors (which included block booking, contracts with overseas distributors, and so on), nor by the fact that exhibitors also revealed a preference for imported, particularly American, films. The reasons for decreased demand for Australian productions must also include audience response to the stereotyped, clichéd nature of their storylines (obsession with bushrangers, for example), and their failure to measure up technically and aesthetically to the competing Hollywood product.

By the mid-1920s, the production situation was sufficiently grim to bring about a Royal Commission of Inquiry into the Film Industry. Exhibition and distribution were, in fact, flourishing although also revealing the usual oligopolistic capitalist tendencies toward amalgamation, outright purchase, growth of cinema chains that reduced competition, and consolidation of distribution outlets into three or four major distributors closely tied to overseas interests. From a confusing and conflicting mountain of evidence, the Royal Commission made certain recommendations, particularly in regard to the introduction of quotas to ensure release for Australian films. Most of these recommendations were ignored or proved incapable of being put into practice.

In the late 1920s, the arrival of sound threatened to reduce a largely moribund film production industry to total inertia, mainly as the result of the high cost of reequipping an undercapitalized industry for the new technology of the synchronized sound film. Added to this were the problems in obtaining the necessary equipment from overseas, given the demands that Hollywood and other large film producers were making on the limited suppliers at the same time and the exercise of patent restraints that prevented, or made difficult, the spread of sound recording technology.[2]

After 1930, feature filmmaking in Australia was, with the exception of sporadic independent attempts (Charles Chauvel is an important example), virtually conducted solely by two "studio-type" organizations: FT Films based in Melbourne and Cinesound (a wholly owned subsid-

iary of the Combine) based in Sydney. FT films folded in 1934 following the death of its owner and head of production, Frank Thring, Sr.,
but not before making a series of feature films that had some success on
the local market and in Britain. There was one other attempt to create
a studio organization: National Studios made two films in 1936, both of
which failed to attract a profitable audience, and then folded.

Cinesound, under the control of Ken G. Hall (director, producer,
and studio boss) made its first film in 1932 (*On Our Selection*) and
continued to produce films throughout the 1930s (some fourteen in
all) while also producing a regular weekly newsreel. Cinesound had
little difficulty in placing its films in cinemas: it was owned by one of the
largest distribution and exhibition organizations. Its two or three films
per year were generally low-budget productions, but they were also
films that were quintessentially Australian in plot and theme as well as
location (e.g., the *Dad and Dave* series, which centered on the doings of
a farming family, or films with titles that indicated quite clearly where
their stories were placed, like *Orphans of the Wilderness, Tall Timbers,* or
The Squatter's Daughter).

Subsequent to World War II, during which feature filmmaking pe-
tered out, Cinesound ceased all feature film production after a change
in top management at Australasian Films and a joint venture production with Columbia Pictures (*Smithy,* 1946). The company continued to
make newsreels for some years until the arrival of television reduced
the demand for even this modest form of local production.[3]

The period from the end of World War II until the beginning of the
1970s is a barren one as far as indigenous production is concerned.
Exhibition was also affected by the worldwide downturn in cinema
attendance that accompanied the spread of television, although cinema attendance still remained at a fairly high level, given the small
Australian population. Despite sporadic attempts to make feature films
in Australia from 1946 onward, there was no consistency in production: very seldom were more than two or three made in any one year.
Overseas companies occasionally visited to make films that had varying
degrees of Australian contributions and settings.

An Australian company, Southern International, attempted a continuous but well-spaced flow of films in the 1950s but could manage no
more than a handful altogether. By 1960, virtually all activity had
ceased; no more than ten feature films (including overseas productions) were made between 1960 and 1969. In the thirty years since the

beginning of World War II, Australians—audiences, distributors, and exhibitors—had largely forgotten that Australian films were even a possibility beyond a rare novelty.

The rebirth of the Australian film production industry that took place in the 1970s had its gestation period in the late 1960s with a series of initiatives, not always coordinated, that came from within the industry (which now included television) and from outside it. Quite unrelated political motives may account for some of the interest taken at the level of the federal government. These various factors coincided with a gradual awakening of Australian nationalism (which was to culminate in the early 1980s and which, arguably, was partly the consequence of the very films it encouraged in the first instance).

It seems apparent that it was a combination of all these various contributing factors—the artistic and intellectual atmosphere that argued for the "respectability" of Australian culture and encouraged its examination and artistic production, economic interest, political motives—that led to active intervention by both federal and state governments (for example, through the various bodies, committees, and boards that culminated in the Australian Film Commission; the South Australian Film Corporation; the establishment of the Australian Film and Television School, etc.). But as the experience of the past had shown, an ability and a willingness to produce films were not enough. The production of the first feature films of the 1970s coincided, fortuitously, with a downturn in the supply of films from overseas. There was a simultaneous (but causally unrelated) increased acceptance of Australian films by audiences—partly evidenced by the popularity of locally produced serial dramas on television. The financial success of a number of these early films and the artistic and critical success of Australian films both at home and overseas confirmed the decisions being made at governmental levels and encouraged the increased production of films.

The 1970s became the most exciting period of film production in Australia since the first decade and a half of the century. Not surprisingly, the revitalized production industry took a little while to find its sense of direction.[4] The first few years of the 1970s were largely ones of experimentation and of developing skills, knowledge, and competencies. Films were made on what would now be seen as minuscule budgets and tended to be the result of more enthusiasm than know-how.

The mid-1970s were a period of consolidation and of less undisciplined enthusiasm, arguably of a greater impetus toward ideas of commercial appeal than upon "putting Australia on the screen." Such experimentation as took place was more a matter of testing the water to see what was box office and what would gain both audience and critical approval. By 1976, with the Australian cultural revival in full swing, it was apparent that the now confident film production industry had found its material and its themes within examinations of Australia itself, especially in its mythical dimensions.

The period 1975–1982 has proved to be the most fertile in the New Australian Cinema to date, not merely in terms of the number of productions, but in quality as well. Many of the best-known films of the New Australian Cinema were made during these years, such as *Picnic at Hanging Rock, Breaker Morant, Mad Max,* and *Gallipoli.* Not only spectacular productions but many of the best of the more modest, more personal films of the New Australian Cinema were produced then, among them *Newsfront, Mouth to Mouth,* and *Caddie.* Films from this period are already being given classic status.

The middle years of the 1980s saw something of a return to the situation in the early 1970s. Rather as if the mythic Australian themes had been exhausted, new filmmakers were looking for new directions. There was more experimentation, more searching for new images and themes, and new methods of financing feature film production led to internationalization of films and attempts to produce genre films that owed more to Hollywood models than to Australian cultural identity. Then, in 1987, film production dropped alarmingly—at least in part as a consequence of the stock market collapse of late that year. But growing dissatisfaction within the industry and within the government with the method of encouraging investment in local film production (the 10BA provisions) led to strong indications that the tax concessions so offered would shortly be withdrawn.

The high level of production in the first half of the 1980s was partly the inevitable result of the success of earlier films—success in both box-office and critical terms as well as the sheer excitement of actually making films—and partly the result of particular initiatives by the federal government to encourage private investment in feature film production. This encouragement took the form of especially favorable tax concessions for capital expenditure on film production. Initially these concessions were 150% of capital expenditures written off in the first year and an exemption on income tax on net earnings of 50%. This became known as 10BA financing after the section in the relevant tax act.

During the period 1980–1988, these provisions were varied in a number of ways, most notably by a progressive reduction in the write-off and exemption percentages. In 1988, with increasing pressure from the treasury, which claimed that the loss of tax revenue was higher than expected and too high to be maintained (an economically arguable position), criticism within the industry and the media that many film budgets were being inflated to allow producers, accountants, lawyers, and other consultants to rip off overly large fees, and a high degree of critical dissatisfaction with the quality and type of film being produced, the 10BA provisions were removed.

Government support, absolutely essential in a national economy as limited as Australia's, was maintained in the form of a Film Finance Corporation, a wholly owned government body provided with funds from the federal government budget for an initial four years ($A70 million the first year). Commencing in early 1989, the Film Finance Corporation was to have a commercial focus and to provide funds fully or partially to finance productions initiated by outside producers. The hidden agenda of the Film Finance Corporation seemed to be an attempt to reimpose a form of direction upon the Australian cinema, to bring it back to a state in which it was more fundamentally concerned with providing films along the lines of those of the 1975–1982 period: "putting Australia on the screen" *and* encouraging the production of quality films (as opposed to films ostensibly made simply for tax-saving purposes). There seems to have been an undercurrent of feeling that Australian films were becoming too international (i.e., Americanized) under the "freedom" of 10BA. Film investment decision by committee seems a dubious proposition, although the scheme has not yet been fully implemented. Nonetheless, funding decisions have been made and support for a variety of projects, feature films, documentaries, and television series has been publicly announced. A slightly disturbing aspect of the feature film support is that more than half the projects will have foreign actors in main roles—a slightly different form of internationalism may be taking place within the Australian film industry. Whether this means that the New Australian Cinema will, in times to come, be seen to fit historically (and rather neatly) into a twenty-year era (1970–1990), with Australian film in the 1990s and beyond taking a significantly different shape under a clearly changing set of conditions, remains to be seen. Two decades may well be quite enough time for the appellation "new" to have outlived its appropriateness. The effect of the new financing arrangements and a fresh influx of talent into the industry will become clearer when the production slump of the late 1980s is reversed and corporation-supported films appear in sufficient numbers on the screens.

Despite fluctuations in the economic fortunes of Australian films, film production has continued without interruption since 1970. In that time well over 350 feature films have been made in Australia (estimates vary according to differing definitions of "feature film"). Some but not all have been sold overseas; since the mid-1970s, when there was an Australian presence at the Cannes Film Festival for the first time, overseas sales in many markets other than the North American market have been an increasing trend. Many films from 1980 on were made with an eye to overseas sales to recoup ever-increasing budgets, a source of considerable industry controversy. Some films have received critical acclaim outside Australia, and some of the better-known talents of the Australian cinema (notably directors and actors) have been tempted to the United States. As the New Australian Cinema moves toward the end of its second decade, although it is still heavily dependent on government assistance in some form, it remains in a very healthy state.

It is my intention, in the pages that follow, to explore this development, this renaissance of Australian film production, not from an industry or production point of view, still less from a historical perspective, but through examination of the films themselves—or at least some of them—as representations of Australian culture: in other words, as images of Australia.

The Cultural Context

Understanding how films (or any popular cultural commodity) may represent the culture from which they arise requires some understanding of that culture itself. Before discussing the films themselves, it will be useful to outline the parameters of Australian culture. In the relatively brief discussion that follows, I do not wish to suggest that Australian culture is rudimentary, homogeneous, and monolithic, but a general simplification of its historical and social bases will help contextualize the films of the New Australian Cinema.

As is well known, the first European settlements on the continent of Australia were, and remained for some time, penal settlements of Britain; the first settlers were convicts and their warders. Australia as it is presently constituted—post-Europeanized Australia—had its beginning as part of the aftermath of three "revolutions": the English Industrial Revolution, the American Revolution (the War of Independence), and the French Revolution.[5] A certain tendency toward a secular, democratic cultural temper might well be expected to have existed from the outset beyond that inherent in the social origins and (lack of) social power of the early (reluctant) colonists. While not really a product or even a consequence of the Enlightenment (the Age of Reason) in any direct sense, Australian culture nonetheless evolved from a background that included it, and equally importantly from a climate of European thought that was to embrace (however controversially) Darwinism and especially the concepts embodied in what came to be known as Social Darwinism.[6] It is also apparent that the fundamental structures of Australian culture were in place before the Age of Marx. The collectivity that is an important part of Australian identity has rather less basis in socialism than it does in the celebrated mythic cultural perception of getting (or demanding) a "fair go."

Darwinism, however, was a two-edged sword for Australian culture: it was a rationale (in a way) for dispatching the "unfit" of English society (and its "colony," Ireland) to a distant land where they might survive or not, according to whatever bastardized view of survival of the fittest the English ruling class subscribed to. Survival of the fittest also took the form of justifying the dispossession and genocide by commission or by omission (mainly the latter) of the native people of Australia. But the potent myth of "mateship"—collectivity as essential for survival—is in clear contradiction to the concept of survival of the fittest at its simplest level.

There is a fundamental schizophrenia that runs through Australian culture. Present-day culture is the legatee of the processes of both colonizing and colonization. Australia was a colony in the same way America had been and Canada was, although different from either.

Nonetheless, as the result of being and perceiving themselves to be members of a colonized society—and a dispossessed and despised one because of the penal origins of most of the colonists—Australians developed a culture based upon the rejection of much of the dominant colonizing culture of England. Thus, while there was continuity of many of the ideological state apparatuses of England—legal system, Westminster system of government, public administration, education, church, and so forth—a cultural identity developed (which would become in turn a *national* identity) based upon the denial (as much as possible) of class distinction, based upon ideas of egalitarianism, collectivism, and the distinctly Australian mythos of mateship. These ideals were not universal, of course: they did not extend to the aboriginal population in any way, shape, or form, and they did not really apply to women except in certain circumstances. They were, however, cultural perceptions that developed "from below" and might have taken the form, had they ever coalesced sufficiently, of a radical political doctrine.

The early and lasting perceptions of Australian cultural identity proved to have sufficient cultural potency to ensure their adoption (with suitable modification to remove their most radical implications) by the conservative classes as *the* dominant images of national identity.

Australia is one of the few nation-states that has no land border with any other—and is certainly the biggest such nation-state. It did not become a nation as such until the first year of this century, and its history—its white history at least—extends back barely more than a hundred years before that. Australian history can make no claims beyond that time span to a culture developed within its own geographic boundaries. Its cultural origins, for the most part British (dominant English culture and Irish, Scottish, and Welsh subcultures), are nonetheless confused. The strong sense of Australianness that developed was partly a consequence of the rejection by the embryonic country of much that the dominant English culture stood for—especially by people of Irish and Scottish origin who were already "precolonized" by the English in any case. Also, since the mid-point of the twentieth century, immigration to Australia has added a diversity of cultures (still European for the most part) to the social mix. Finally, perhaps obviously enough, the population is made up of an increasing proportion of those who were born in Australia and whose immediate ancestors were also born there.

Australians thought of themselves as Australians before the nation-state achieved formal political existence—in no small part because of the dispossession and rejection many of the early settlers (whether convict or immigrant) felt. On the other hand, the independence achieved by Australia and Australians or granted by their colonizing rulers was unusual. A precedent of sorts existed in the case of Canada, but most of the British Empire existed as subject states. The extent to which Australians and English at the time perceived the relative political independence of Australia as *de facto* recognition of cultural independence is difficult to gauge; in any case, such cultural independence was at best marginal. That margin, however, is where notions and perceptions of Australian national/cultural identity formed and flourished—and where the myths of Australianness that prevail mostly originated.

Culture, Ideology, and Australian Identity

In a study of Australia carried out a few years prior to the Australian cultural renaissance of the 1970s,[7] Russel Ward (a preeminent scholar of Australian cultural history) reinforced the view that Australian culture derived from "difference":

> A recognizably distinct and distinctive Australian culture developed from 1788 onward, and the differences between it and its British prototype became increasingly evident during the nineteenth century to visitors if not always to Australians themselves. These characteristic differences sprang from two main sources: first, from the strange new environment and the struggle of the immigrants to adapt themselves to it and, second, from the fact that the emigrants came in disproportionately large numbers from certain parts of Britain and certain classes of British society.[8]

The question of the relation of cultural myths to historical and/or contemporary reality is a vexing one in the Australian context: Australian history, being both short (two hundred years) and more or less a matter of record (documents, public and private, were not only kept but are mostly available), seems to lie ready to be dissected in order to locate the precise origins of the images of Australianness that prevail. A certain caution, however, must be maintained in claiming too close an equation between apparently unassailable historical "facts" and the shape of Australian images of identity. Indeed, a certain caution must also be maintained to avoid falling into a sub-Darwinian fallacy that sees cultural identity as "evolving" progressively in response to a pre-scribed set of conditions (social, natural, historical).

In the specific instance of film as an indicator of cultural perceptions, there is difficulty in discerning where reality and ideology part com-pany in this construction of Australian national identity because of the emphasis given to naturalness or realism in Australian cinema. The very concepts "naturalism" and "realism" connote a lack of media-tion—they consist of *reflections* of what *is*. The power of the "everyday" to be a vehicle for, indeed to *be*, cultural myth is shown in the pages of Fiske, Hodge, and Turner's *Myths of Oz*, a revealing examination of the mythic dimensions of selected aspects of Australian ordinariness: "The Pub," "The Beach," "The Australian Accent," "Shopping," and so forth.[9]

Bearing these caveats in mind, it is possible to suggest certain factors that are responsible in some measure for the shape of Australian images of national identity. Isolation—in almost all senses, not merely the geographic (although that is important)—is one of these. This sense that Australian society is removed from its social origins—ini-tially, at least, as a deliberate act of explusion, later by choice—leads to a historically based acute sense of rejection of the Eurocentric cultures from which most Australians are descended. This in turn has made Australian culture keenly aware of its need to differentiate itself from seemingly comparable cultures—those in which it has origins and those that might seem for sociohistorical reasons to be similar, such as the United States and Canada and, to a lesser extent, New Zealand.

The titles of two recent books dealing with Australian culture are revealing: *Inventing Australia* and *Constructing a Culture*.[10] The implica-tion of these two titles is apparent: Australian culture is not a trans-posed version of an older culture (or mixture of such cultures) but has been actively and systematically created, for complex reasons but pri-marily to meet a perceived social demand for a new culture for a new land. The first hundred years of relative isolation of Australia from direct contact with Europe (requests for instructions to the center of control, Whitehall and Westminster, could take up to a year to be answered) meant that Australian culture had a chance to consolidate before the twentieth century and its technologies of global cultural communication (the cinema, radio, television) arrived, with the consequent possibilities of a new form of cultural imperialism.

Few cultures are encased in armor to withstand the encroachment of more powerful cultures, and fewer still are set in concrete, resistant to the eroding and shaping winds of change—and this is particularly true of Australian culture. The process of "inventing Australia" is dynamic and continuing. For if there is one distinguishing feature about Australian culture, it is a never-ending demand that it serve a defining, descriptive role. This is the factor of uncertainty.

Australians, in the cultural sense, are continually asking the question "Who are we?" In view of the youthfulness of Australia as a nation and as a distinct culture, it is not surprising that it experiences an "adolescent identity crisis"—exacerbated by the (apparently) continually changing nature of its demographics. What is important here is that of all the possible answers to the question only a restricted number of answers have been demonstrated to be culturally acceptable. The New Australian Cinema demonstrates in film after film this peculiarly Australian obsession, in some more flagrantly than in others. Even films that deal with situations involving the life of immigrants (meaning, of course, non-Anglocentric ethnics) have tended to construct their narratives around problems caused by an overt or covert clash between the culture the immigrant comes from and clings to and Australian culture. Of course, the same preoccupation with asking and usually answering this question is present (with various degrees of subtlety) in Australian television (particularly soap opera but also in the miniseries, which have boomed in production since 1980) and in Australian literature and theater as well.

It would be ridiculous to suggest that films (or any other popular culture texts) may be reduced to one simple set of meanings, and it is not my intention to do so. But I do contend that Australian films of the past two decades, in the many aspects of Australian existence that they present and also in those that they ignore, have always found themselves—sometimes deliberately, sometimes inadvertently—concerned with this fundamental cultural preoccupation: "Who are we?"

At various times, and to meet the demands of varied narratives, the answer to the question will be slightly different; it is never a sufficient answer or a complete definition. The answer never satisfies; the question has to be repeated again and again. It is even arguable that, historically speaking, the question will not always seem to be particularly culturally important.[11] But on the evidence of the New Australian Cinema alone, the question became prominent in the early 1970s and has remained high on the cultural agenda since.

The consistent and dominant image of Australian cultural identity promulgated by cinema (and by television) since the 1970s is one that has been derived from an image that gained cultural predominance in the last decade of the nineteenth century. Quite simply, this image states that the Australian character is formed by the experience of the Australian environment (especially as that environment is "felt" in the interior, in the bush) and of man's (the gender is deliberate) responses to these experiences. These experiences have given rise to a set of perceptions, of myths, around the notions of egalitarianism, mateship, and collectivization in a loose populist sense. These experiences give rise to the myth of the "battler" defined by his refusal to give in to conditions that are, nevertheless, overpowering. The rejection of the old, decadent and/or corrupt cultures of Europe leads to a valorization of the ordinary and a celebration of the vulgar, especially through the image of the ocker (e.g., Paul Hogan/*Crocodile Dundee*). The image is of a white male, nearly always Anglo-Celtic (but not rigidly so), down-to-earth, unsophisticated, democratic, and unimpressed by authority.[12] This representative "true" Australian derives his characteristics from previous (alleged) firsthand experience of the bush, and these characteristics (by various mechanisms) become the mythic characteristics of the Australian national character.

The Australian landscape, as many films directly demonstrate, has enormous mythical power.[13] It is a significant factor in aiding the claims for an essential difference between Australian-*man* and English-*man*— a particularly potent demonstration of the power of nature over nurture, environment over culture—except, of course, that in the fullness of time the changes wrought become enculturated and do not have to be lived directly by each succeeding generation. So the bush, for all its geographical and ecological actuality, becomes the mythic forming factor that separates the experience of Australia and the fact of being Australian from the rest of the world (but especially from the European world). The national and cultural origins of white people in Australia are, so the myth of the bush insists, less important than experiences of the environment and men's responses to those experiences. This myth is directly demonstrable in a number of films of the New Australian Cinema: for example, *Sunday Too Far Away, Gallipoli, Razorback, Picnic at Hanging Rock, Burke and Wills, The Irishman,* and *Crocodile Dundee*—and it underlies many more.

Most films take the dominant myths of Australian identity for granted. But that is the function of myth: to offer highly structured ways of seeing as natural and commonsense, through a highly organized and selected set of images. It is from this selected set of images that may or may not have any direct relationship with a historical or contemporary reality that a mythology is created and maintained, and it is through this mythology that the New Australian Cinema (in particular, but also television drama) offers its images of Australia.

Of course, Australian cinema draws upon the "reality" of contemporary Australia: a highly suburbanized, predominantly Anglo-Celtic (but with a high percentage of other ethnic groups), English-speaking, Western, twentieth-century, postindustrial, late-capitalistic, postcolonial culture. This makes it even more significant that

> the particularities of the 1890s version of nationalism have outlasted most of the political and social conditions which produced them, without losing their potential for carrying important cultural meanings or evoking myth. Indeed the legend of the nineties is still the dominant nationalist myth, its centrality revealed by yet another maturing art form—the cinema—turning to the images of an apparently anachronistic version of national identity as the appropriate mode through which to project nationalism.[14]

The Australian Cinema and Australianness

Why should the New Australian Cinema have been overwhelmingly concerned with producing films so centered in a restricted set of images of Australianness?

In a conference paper Australian film historian Tom O'Regan makes a case for seeing, within a discourse during the mid-1970s about what the New Australian Cinema *ought* to be, a nexus coming into existence between concepts of quality cinema defined in a specifically Australian way and ideas of commercial appeal defined according to Hollywood conventions. His argument, then, is that the Australianness of these films was not so much the result of an ideological (or cultural) determination but the result of particular production strategies that received approval from government agencies that felt they had a stake in the matter. Further, this was often achieved in the face of considerable opposition to any emphasis on explicit Australianness in locally produced films. His concern is to implicate ideologies of national identity in conditions of film production practice in Australia: "With [a] shift away from TV to the more marginal zone of the cinema, problems [of commercial appeal] facing the independent production industry shifted, but its ideological mission remained constant: to inscribe its historical spectator, a bourgeois audience, within Australian-produced culture and cultural production."[15]

O'Regan points to a frequent claim that can be summarized as being centered on an apparent tautology: Australian cinema must be Australian. The quarters from which this claim is made are quite varied, and so are the reasons: the antidote to cultural imperialism; encouragement of a local industry for economic reasons (i.e., employment and/or profit from capital investment); Australians yearning to see themselves on Australian screens; showing Australia to Australians, and so on. This idea that Australian cinema must be Australian is promulgated upon a set of assumptions about how the cinema ought to function as a cultural industry in the national context, what it ought to be doing, and how it ought to be doing it.

> The supposition that there can be true or false fictions about Australia relies on values that are deeply rooted in our film culture—that film must strive for verisimilitude, that there is a "real" Australia which can be faithfully and neutrally mediated by the camera. Films are assumed to replicate this reality; the pleasure they give is a sense of recognition, a heightened awareness of what is already known. These are the defensive aesthetic values of a provincial culture that has undoubtedly been starved of the sight of its "self" on stage and screen. . . . Self-recognition through realism has been an important element of an attempt to create and consume local imagery. . . .[16]

Even while this argument sees deliberate production of a certain type of Australianism, for reasons located within an ideology of how cinema constructs its meanings, the demand for Australian identity is not seen to have an overt ideological purpose other than that of official and unofficial bodies responding to a perceived demand in a time of heightened national/cultural awareness.

The problematic of Australianness and its relationship as a concept to the very development of the New Australian Cinema, its place within the discourse of an Australian film industry (which in turn legitimized the very notion of the New Australian Cinema), and its various (if restricted) manifestations within the narratives of the films themselves have been rehearsed in a number of forums (which have tended to inform each other quite directly). The analyses of this problematic of the relationship of Australianness and industry have taken a number of approaches:

1. Discussion of the relationship between the structure of the industry (meaning both producers and the trade—distributors and exhibitors—although the idea of the industry often covers only the producers) and notions of "cultural exactitude."[17]
2. Discussion of the tug-of-war that has existed both within and outside the industry proper between the proponents of quality cinema (based on Australianness as the criterion and definition of quality) and commercial appeal (based on notions of internationalism or dominant Hollywood form).
3. Examination of the nature and substance of the involvement of government funding bodies and how ideas of Australianism and the need to promote or encourage it have influenced decisions and policy.

Each of these approaches has, explicitly or implicitly, seen its central focus as being determined by the Australianism in the Australian film industry and New Australian Cinema. They point to the way in which the notion of Australianism has been activated as a support for various positions in relation to the idea of an indigenous film production industry and the way that industry ought to function. The notion has entered into the discourse of the Australian film industry almost as a given condition: an Australian film industry must, by definition, make Australian films. What is less clear is just how and why certain definitions of what Australianism constitutes at the level of manifest content of film texts came to be adopted, retained, and reproduced.

Dermody and Jacka have explained how their examination of the activities of the Australian Film Commission (AFC)—which played a dominant role in encouraging film production from the mid-1970s in a number of ways, including direct investment—led them to conclude that the policy of the AFC was to have no policy at all.[18] Their summation of the position of the AFC (and other bodies like it, including the various state government film bodies) may seem to indicate a lack of a *declared* interest on the part of official and influential government bodies in the form that Australianism took in films. In practice, however, the films made under the direct auspices of the AFC and those made as a result of the success of these AFC films demonstrate quite clearly a construction of Australianness along the lines already indicated. Thus, Australianness was of primary importance, even if there was no openly declared policy of what this was understood to be. This was justified in various ways—often along the rather vague lines of opposing the (assumed) cultural imperialism represented by the dominance of American cultural productions in Australian cinemas and on Australian television screens.

It appears that the AFC and other bodies were without any sense of direction and certainly free of any deliberate intention to foster a particular set of images of Australianness. At the same time, however, it seems that the AFC and others felt they could recognize Australianness when it manifested itself in scripts and production proposals and, of course, in the films that resulted (when they did). In order to do so, the AFC would need to have recourse to some already existing perceptions of what Australianness might be. Since the cultural/nationalist revival of the 1970s, of which the AFC was an obvious manifestation in itself, arose from a period in which Australian culture had been especially devalued, it can hardly be surprising if it (like other cultural institutions and popular and "high" culture forms) turned to the only established myths of national identity that had substantial dominance and widespread acceptance in the past: the Australian legend as formulated in the 1890s (which had given Australia the powerful images of the Anzacs and Gallipoli and a sense of destiny before and especially during World War I).

It is a rather large step to suggest anything particularly duplicitous in the establishment (even if by trial and error) of a surprisingly rigid set of images of Australian cultural identity within the films fostered, sponsored, and/or invested in by the AFC (which Dermody and Jacka have named the "AFC-Genre"). The same set of images can often be seen operating in films not made under the AFC umbrella—although these may well have been encouraged to take this particular approach because of the signal success of AFC films. Again, not *all* Australian films of the period subscribe to this set of perceptions—but, it needs to be stated, most do in one way or another.

It is rather more difficult to analyze what part the broader Australian culture may have had in shaping the perceptions of Australia that appeared in films and on television screens. In other words, what was the audience doing? How did anyone know an Australian audience for these films existed? Examinations of contemporaneous developments in local television production seem to indicate that "the return of audience to Australian films was preceded by a popular and emphatic move on prime-time television to Australian drama."[19] At least one writer on Australian cinema in the 1970s (John Hinde) has gone further to suggest that audiences are essential in the development of a true national cinema. Dermody and Jacka summarize his position in this regard: "The classical seminal audience is drawn from a population which has been culturally or economically displaced, and which needs mediating fictions to help recover lost or alienated traditions, social equilibrium, histories of its own."[20]

The great "Who are we?" cultural obsession is implicit in this structuring of the national cinema audience. Even so, the notion that the audience itself sets up a demand, a "feedback loop" that encourages further reproductions of its own culture by its own filmmakers, is an appealing one, and it can be given further substance in the particular context of Australian filmmaking in the 1970s by reference to two factors previously mentioned. One of these is Australian culture's need consistently to ask itself questions about its very identity and consistently to answer itself, as a consequence of the perceptions of the environment discussed earlier, the isolation from its cultural origins (partly imposed externally, partly self-imposed), and its geographic uncertainty. It needs to be borne in mind that white Australian culture never, at the bottom line, truly *believes* it actually belongs in Australia. Despite the manifest irreversibility of history (even history as comparatively recent as that of white colonization of Australia), the liberal humanism of the twentieth century ensures that Australian culture is never truly at peace with being the inheritor of a nation gained by one group of dispossessed dispossessing the members of a prior culture.

The other factor is the cultural condition of Australianism immediately prior to this nationalist revival of the 1970s. Post–World War II Australia, especially in the 1950s and 1960s, was a place of dull conformity, arguably as a result of an unbroken two decades of nearly somnolent Conservative political rule, which deliberately played down "extreme" Australianism. Thus Donald Horne, a perceptive leftist social critic, was able to claim in 1964 in his influential book *The Lucky Country*:[21] ". . . Australian nationalism—once so strong—is now so hesitant that it no longer achieves self-definition. No-one any longer tells Australians who they are, nor do they seem to care. . . . Australia seems to have lost both its sense of direction and its sense of a future."

With the benefit of hindsight, it is now possible to see that Horne, writing when he did, was describing the nadir of Australian culture in this century and that the enthusiasm with which a cultural revival—of which the New Australian Cinema was a highly visible and dominant part—was embraced a few years later reflects an inevitable if not entirely foreseen rediscovered sense of national identity. In a revised edition of his book, in 1971, Horne was able to see that "Australians are confidently 'becoming themselves.'" He felt that the process did not involve "going back to the old rural ethos," a view that films a few years in the future (like *My Brilliant Career, Sunday Too Far Away, The Irishman,* etc.) would contradict. But he did recognize that "certain selected parts of the old ways [were] spreading pervasively through urban life." The New Australian Cinema has played no small part in the pervasive spread and no small part in determining that it was indeed a selection of the "old ways" that so spread.

This is explicable in the light of the lack of anything remotely recent to turn to for confirmation of cultural identity. A war in which old alliances were broken in favor of new—turning away from Britain toward the United States—and twenty years of the "cultural cringe" and political conservatism had created a void. The old images of national identity seemed to flow in to fill the vacuum quite naturally. Just as apparently natural was the fact that Australian film should turn to attempting to place the genuinely Australian on screens; it need not have done so and occasionally, with films like the *Mad Max* trilogy or

Roadgames (1981), has not done so. But as Dermody and Jacka point out, "There is always *some* sense that the pursuit of that national obsession as a primary object for Australian film is a symptom of persisting cultural insecurity, provincial anxiety."[22]

The cultural insecurity has been enhanced, so to speak, by the changes in white Australia's cultural origins. The period of postwar conservatism, in which Australianness was deemphasized or rendered virtually "speechless," was also a period in which large-scale immigration from non-English-speaking countries occurred for the first time. In terms of numbers at least, the Anglo-Celtic ethnic majority in the Australian population was considerably reduced. Australian cities became cosmopolitan. In keeping with the essentially tolerant character of Australian society—which may well be the product of a mixture of relative well-being, a hedonist indolence, and cultural "memories" of a disadvantaged and dispossessed colonized origin—adjustments were made to these changes without fuss. It is reasonable to assume, however, that at least part of the impetus for more demonstrations of Australianness in the cinema and for the reproduction of dominant images of national identity from a more mono-ethnic past is a direct consequence of a threat to the "Australian way of life" that was perceived to exist, if in unarticulated form, during the quiescent period of the 1950s and 1960s. Therefore, "it is not really paradoxical that the intensifying multi-culturalism of Australia has propelled a relatively old, unproblematic, pre-multi-cultural image of the native Australian into prominence for proud display—just when the vehicles, television and especially film, were conveniently at hand."[23]

The Dominant Myths of Australian National Identity

As indicated above, to understand Australian culture, three principles must constantly be held in mind: isolation, uncertainty, and ecology. Isolation (both within Australia and from the mother cultures of Europe) and uncertainty (the "Who are we?" question at the base of so many Australian narratives) have already been discussed.

The films dealt with in this book (and many others) represent in one form or another answers to the questions founded in these "principles"

raised by the culture. It may not have been the intention of the makers
to provide answers to these questions: they may not have been fully
aware of the questions, let alone that aspects of their films were answers. This is the "naturalizing" effect of culture: cultural perceptions
can become commonsense ways of understanding and structuring
experience. It is natural in this sense, therefore, to construct narratives
and characterizations within films in a way that is informed by the sense
of the cultural perceptions of Australia and Australianness. The same
is true of any text that is produced in and from any culture (including,
of course, this book as well); but Australian films, at least, seldom take
cultural identity *for granted* in the way American cinema takes Ameri-
canness, by and large, for granted. No matter how commonsense the
rendering of Australia may seem to be in any Australian film, there is
always another level at which the film says, "This is what we are—this is
what Australia is" or asks, "Is this what we are? Is this what Australia
is?"

The cultural image of Australia is not a monolithic mythic image. It
is surprisingly complex, or at least flexible; Australianness can be
defined in a number of different ways according to occasion and circumstance. The films of the New Australian Cinema have made only a
limited choice from within the wide spectrum of Australian cultural
identity.

All cultures construct their own myths and are also constructed in
part by their own myths. Frequently the narrative forms that myths
adopt become detached from the culture or from the cultural reasons
that initially created them; but irrespective of whether they have lost
their cultural context or not, myths are traditionally assumed to be the
discourses of explanation on the way in which a culture organizes
meaning. Because myths are primarily ideological in function, they
are, within the cultures to which they are specific and peculiar, "trans-
parent" or "natural" or the "commonsense way of looking at things,"
and not likely to be perceived as myths at all. It is also true that myths
are sometimes deliberately created. As Richard White has pointed out,
"Most new nations go through the formality of inventing a national
image, but Australia has long supported a whole industry of image-
makers to tell us what we are."[24] Australian filmmakers are often
members of that "industry of image-makers." But it is also true that
some of these images, deliberately fostered at one time or another for

different reasons, become the naturalized perception of the way Australia actually "is." They have become part of the cultural mythology of Australia. These myths have coalesced into a dynamic and complex image of what it is, and what it means, to be Australian, and what Australia itself is.

THE BUSH

There is one overriding myth that defines and underlies all attempts to create and maintain a perception of what Australia is: the myth of the bush. The bush, sometimes called the outback, is that great expanse of the continent, thousands of miles in any direction, that lies beyond the cities that cling to the coastline.

The bush, in this mythic sense, is more than simply the ecologically verifiable natural condition of the geography of Australia. Much has been made of the "reverence . . . of the landscape" in recent Australian films;[25] inescapably, a large number of films have relied upon natural appearance to present the landscape as no more than exotic, sometimes unworldly, background. This unmediated verisimilitude is deceiving. The fact that the bush consists of wildly diverse geography and botany is immaterial. While these different geographic conditions provide different "real" images, mythically all these landscapes coalesce into the bush and thus share its mythic qualities.

The enduring and perhaps paramount image is of the desert, seen again and again in Australian films, although not necessarily in a greater proportion than other aspects of the "real" bush. The desert landscape is at once more alien and yet more Australian than greener, more vegetated landscapes—more cinematic, more photogenic, and more mythic. The power of the landscape has been irresistible both for the long-term inhabitants—the aborigines—and for the more recently arrived Europeans. The bush seems to both cultures to be eternal, and eternally unyielding.

The legends that arise out of the "sur-myth" of the bush seldom totally accept its indomitable nature or, when they do, they also construct the culture-heroes of the legends as being what they are as a direct consequence of the struggle that the bush imposes. The nature of the Australian landscape itself is the primary determining factor from which the other determinants follow. "Both the strangeness or

special character of the land and the conflict between man and land
have been central to the Australian imagination and major inspirations
for the creative artist."[26]

So the bush, for all its geographical and ecological actuality, becomes
the mythic forming factor that separates Australia, the experience of
Australia, and the fact of being Australian from the rest of the world
(especially the European world). The national and cultural origins of
the early white settlers and those who followed and have continued to
follow are, so the myth insists, less important than the experience of
the environment and people's responses to those experiences. Moreover, these experiences and responses and their results are organized
into three subsidiary mythic legends, each of which builds upon this
basic structure of the effect of the bush upon those who venture into it,
each in turn (they are roughly historically chronological) building
upon the preceding one without ever totally subsuming it but altering
it in the process. These three are the legend of the bushman, the
legend of the pioneer, and the Anzac legend. While in total these three
legends, together with the "subversive" image offered by the ocker, add
up to a cumulative image of what it is to be an Australian, they nonetheless exist sufficiently autonomously to be examined as distinct myths
in their own right with their own cultural validity—bearing in mind
that cultural myths are not concerned with what is real but with what is
taken to be real.

THE LEGEND OF THE BUSHMAN

The legend of the bushman is an expansion of this emphasis on the
bush; it provides the myth of the bush with the foundations of a
narrative structure by providing a generalized set of situations and,
more importantly, a conflict and a protagonist. The protagonist was, of
course, European man; the conflict pitted him against the environment. The outcome, whether that protagonist was defeated or triumphant, was that he became a "new man," an Australian. Although the
majority of people have lived in the settlements clinging to the coasts
from the very outset of European settlement of Australia, the image of
the Australian as defined by the legend of the bushman very rapidly
became the cultural perception held in common by those who did have
some experience of the actual conditions that created such an individual (in reality and romance) and by those who did not.

Although the ideal figure of the bushman is drawn from the "facts" of the bush worker in Australia in the early nineteenth century, the bushman is largely a mythical creature who needs to be considered not as the average Australian but as the typical one—and typical in this mythic sense has taken on some of the connotations of ideal.

Historically, the bushman legend is formed by the conditions of life in the colonies—especially life outside the towns and embryonic cities in the pastoral areas. The prototype for the typical Australian was the bush worker in the pastoral industry, and the bush worker is still a narratively potent figure. The bush conditions beyond the coast and the towns were harsh and inhospitable, lonely and remote. The ability merely to survive in these conditions led to the characteristics of the legendary bushman and enhanced the mythic status of the bush.

This image is deeply ingrained in the Australian consciousness; it is one of the most powerful ideologies of being Australian. The image carries through, is the basic structure of, the legend of the pioneer and the Anzac legend. Those concerned with promoting the mythical elements of the bushman saw the life of the pastoral worker as one of "manly independence," with a healthy disregard for authority as a consequence. This attitude could also be perceived as one of insolent insubordination, an appreciation that resurfaces throughout the changes that the different legends work on this seminal material—by which manly independence taken too far becomes antisocial, and its perpetrators become larrikins and ockers rather than heroic bushmen.

It is (or was) a lifestyle that is both seminomadic and male-group-oriented. The individuals within this group have a great sharing of common goals and of common experiences. They see their interests as best served by the group, and they see themselves as separate from the rest of society. This group orientation gives rise to the significant aspect that is dwelt upon in all the Australian legends: mateship.

Mateship is a contradictory concept. On the one hand, its presence and its importance in the myths would seem to be a contradiction to the myth of individuality. On the other hand, it can also be seen, when "taken too far," to be culturally undesirable—as is often the case with the larrikin and the ocker. Yet it is the single most important mythic element in the cultural identity of Australia. Mateship allows emotional release and emotional commitment: the commitment to mates overrides all other considerations. It also lies at the bottom of the much-vaunted Australian egalitarianism. The environment and the sense of group identity lead to an emphasis on physical prowess and physical endurance as two important characteristics by which men are judged as men and mates.

It may seem, then, that the legend of the bushman is solidly based in historical actuality, but myths are not necessarily dependent upon historical reality, although they may frequently be distorted reflections of some aspects of that reality.

THE LEGEND OF THE PIONEER

The legend of the pioneer places its emphasis upon those who settled the land rather than those who roamed its wide expanses. Thus it has a place for both the "squatters"[27] and the small landholders ("cockies")—in other words, for owners and employers as well as workers—men and, for the first time, women who came to the bush but who settled in one place. Even more than the legend of the bushman, the legend of the pioneer is a heroic myth. The bushman mythos emphasizes the concepts of mateship and the group and defines the individual within those confining terms. The pioneer mythos emphasizes the individual, despite the fact that it lumps together a diverse body of people under the general heading "pioneers." Here again there is a clear emphasis on egalitarianism. Pioneers—wealthy squatters, struggling farmers, small-town storekeepers, and so forth—are all equal.

The bush still retains the central place that it held in the formation of the legend of the bushman. But instead of emphasizing the way in which individuals have had to adapt to the environment, the legend of the pioneer offers the myth of taming the environment—or at least attempting to, frequently with only marginal success if at all. Together with the myth-heroic task of taming the land is the corollary: that the pioneers were working and dying not for themselves but for posterity, for the future generations of Australians. This ideology embodies a reverence for the past. Thus the nostalgic quality of the legend of the bushman becomes more pronounced in the legend of the pioneer—indeed, is positively celebrated in the creation of a "golden age" for Australia.

The image of the pioneer that this golden age produced lingered and took on most of the qualities of the "redundant" myth-hero, the bushman, giving them instead to the owner/employer or to the small (nonemploying) landowner. Thus is created a new Australian image, powerful because it is "natural"—that is, a reflection and a product of "how things were."

The legend of the pioneer does differ from the legend of the bushman in another significant way: it permits a place for women in its mythology. Women are almost totally absent from the legend of the bushman, their place, or rather their function in a social sense, being taken by other male companions: by mates. The legend of the pioneer grants considerable status, frequently even pride of place in its various narratives, to women.

The pioneer took on the attributes of the bushman—the essential elements of the myth—but transformed them to include the dominant economic and political classes within the overall ideals of egalitarianism. The bush was now, mythically, the great leveler.

The legend of the pioneer in common with the legend of the bushman is of course nationalistic. The need is for myths that create national heroes who will, by being both ideal and typical, make Australia unique and distinct from the rest of the world. The need is for national symbols—particularly in the absence of clearly heroic historical individuals—so that the pioneer in abstract becomes the symbol of Australia and Australianness (and the pioneer in "narrative concreteness" signifies those symbolic qualities). Heroic status is given to ordinary people who are acting in heroic circumstances.

THE ANZAC LEGEND

The legend of the bushman and the legend of the pioneer are not promulgated upon any one specific incident, historical or fanciful; the scope for variation in the narratives is quite large because of the lack of a single legend that fully contains all the essential elements. The more rigid Anzac legend is a culmination of the legends of the bushman and pioneer, forged together into one overriding mythic identity as a result of cultural and ideological perceptions and desires coinciding with a readily documented historical event.

The Anzac legend, in part, represents the development of a national tradition from a historical event and as such differs from the previous, more diffusely inspired legends. This historical event itself involved very few Australians. It was, however, the landing of Australian soldiers on the beaches of the Gallipoli Peninsula on April 25, 1916, and actions in the succeeding nine months that formed the focus for the legend—and provided it with narrative shape. The legend is, however, much broader than these limited events, which simply provide the instigating factor.

The reason why this limited action in a remote corner of a much wider, more globally significant conflict should have gained this significance in Australian culture goes back to the attempts in the early days of colonization to argue that the Australian experience would (and did) create a race of people who could stand proudly among the nations of the world without being considered, or considering themselves, to be inferior—a "degeneration" of the original European stock.

The significance that Australia has always placed upon the events of Gallipoli and the Anzac experience in general was a claim that it conferred nationhood upon Australia through warfare. Despite the legal status of Australia as one nation since federation some fourteen years previously, Australia, in cultural perception, only gained full nationhood through the actions of its soldiers in World War I.

The historical context, the connection between the Anzac legend and actual events, should not be overstressed. The historical circumstances (as they were reported or recorded) provided a way to bring completely into the dominant culture all those things that the legend of the bushman seemed to symbolize, to deradicalize them and transform them into a more conservative ideology of Australian cultural identity. The historical facts of Gallipoli and the Anzacs provided an opportunity to bring the ordinary Australian into the dominant cultural perceptions—an important aspect of the legend that enables it to survive the historical fact that the Anzac in the trenches could also be, would have to become, the "digger" in civvy street.

At, or through, Gallipoli the legend of the bushman, however, ran up against a conservative ideology in the emphasis on the empire that the conduct of World War I demanded. So the radical bushman legend was altered to one of empire conservatism. Loyalty, the great mythic quality of the bushman, was given a new hierarchy: loyalty was first to the empire, and then to Australia and to one's mates. Empire loyalty has since been effectively removed from the Anzac legend as the cultural ideology of Australia has progressively exorcised its cultural dependence on Britain. The qualities of the Anzacs, their personal codes and behavior, were closely associated with those attributed to the bush-men: resourcefulness, initiative, capacity for endurance, reliability, courage, and (most importantly) mateship. The Anzac legend is two-fold, and its second part might almost be given a new title, the "digger legend," if it was not for the fact that the two are really just one. It is useful to separate the two: the distinction is that the Anzac is the digger in uniform—or, more accurately, the digger is the Anzac in civilian clothes.

For the legend to have proper cultural value it must encompass the essential Australian male as a civilian. The Anzac image needed trans-lation out of the precise historical circumstances of World War I to the more diffuse cultural circumstances of everyday Australian existence. The mythical qualities of the Anzac were too culturally valued, too entrenched to be abandoned just because the war was over. The war provided the final structure for the myth of Australian identity, and the mythic figure of the Anzac becomes for our purposes the more gener-alized figure of the digger. It is impossible to call any Australian male an Anzac who was not in fact a member of the first Australian Imperial Forces, but any Australian male can be called digger.

The Anzac legend is in its pristine form inseparably associated with a specific narrative that is further (and confusedly) linked with actual historical occurrences. This is not to say that the image of the Austra-lian soldier that is at the core of the Anzac legend cannot be applied in a more general way as an overall cultural perception of the Australian soldier. The qualities that the Anzac legend in its narrative form as-cribes to soldiers (warriors) are the mythic dimension that is applied to the Australian male in general.

THE OCKER IMAGE

To understand the ocker, one needs to realize that, although the no-menclature is relatively recent, the "type" is much older; one will need a passing acquaintance with the ocker's ancestor, the larrikin (and also, of course, with his "country cousin," the bushman).

The term "larrikin" is culturally specific to Australia, even if the type is not. Its meaning appears deceptively simple: "a young street rowdy";[28] that is to say, the larrikin, historically specific to the period around the turn of the century, was a delinquent, maybe even a minor criminal. But the wider cultural implications of the term are suggested in a second meaning that evolved from the first: "In a more favorable sense, as though referring to authentically Australian characteristics of non-conformism, irreverence, impudence."[29]

The ocker, because he has no historical specificity, is more complex and more diffuse in meaning. *The Macquarie Dictionary* offers:

1. The archetypal uncultivated Australian working man.
2. A boorish, uncouth chauvinistic Australian.
3. An Australian male displaying qualities considered to be typically Australian, as good humour, helpfulness and resourcefulness.

The heroic legends outlined above are all concerned with creating a romantic if abstract figure who is the essential Australian—the "dinkum Aussie." An aspect of these legends that the myths do not emphasize but that the various narratives woven around the structures of the legends reveal is that these are usually defeated figures. But underlying these three heroic legends is an "underbelly," a mythic structure that is manifest more as a series of images than as a legend, with a hero who is less easily defeated but less ideologically acceptable at the same time.

This is the ironic hero of a line of development that begins with the convict and the bushranger, continues with the subversive figure of the larrikin, and culminates in the contemporary figure of the ocker. Each of these terms represents a slight move up the ladder of social acceptability and respectability. The convict is, by definition, a lawbreaker; the larrikin is more akin to a delinquent, possibly a lawbreaker but seldom a hardened criminal as such; the ocker is an ordinary member of the community but distinguished by a number of less desirable social traits: drinking, swearing, noisy vulgarity.

Convicts, bushrangers, and larrikins represent some real challenges, even threats, to the validity of the myths of Australian national identity. Clearly they represent the unacceptable face of the bushman, the pioneer, and the Anzac. They display many of the attributes of the bushman—frequently those that are undervalued or treated as absences in the legends: philistinism, inherent vulgarity or crudeness, anti-intellectualism, and especially the consequences of lack of proper respect for authority, which if taken too far is insolence or even revolution.

These traits culminate in the ocker, perhaps not a pretty image but clearly socially acceptable at least to the extent of being noncriminal: ". . . the figure of the ocker originated as a satire on Australian boorishness, but became an affectionate tribute to the national identity."[30]

The ocker passed with ease from the intelligentsia (who maintained elitist snobbery about the cultural myths of Australia) to the "people," who were always quick to catch at a subversive method of utilizing the dominant myths. But the curious paradox was that the dominant myth of Australianness remained understood and was even enhanced by this apparently unorthodox (and potentially radical/revolutionary) embracing of what was intended to be ridicule of the extremes of the contemporary Australian image. The work of the image-makers was again confounded by the deeply entrenched nature of cultural myth. The ocker contains nearly all the attributes that have been seen as those of the bushman on his way to becoming the digger and beyond. In his most extreme form, the ocker is a clown—but clowns are not creatures culturally apart.

The ocker image celebrates the rejection of many dominant or middle-class values. The emphasis is on vulgarity and philistinism, aggression, and latent hostility. Hostility masquerades in the ocker as mateship, as openness and honesty, for the ocker attacks anything that is phony. With the ocker, the maleness, the male dominance, of the other legends becomes licensed male chauvinism. There is, in the ocker image, a great irreverence for everything.

The ocker reemphasizes the lack of idealized individual heroes in Australian culture and the lack of happy endings in Australian narratives. The clowns, the low mimetic heroes, are the appropriate ones for Australia.

America in the New Australian Cinema

While many Australian films reveal an acute awareness of England and are concerned with throwing overboard the English cultural and historical baggage once so essential to Australian cultural ideology, there is a notable absence from films of the New Australian Cinema of any *direct* awareness of the United States—in the sense of references to America, settings there, or the presence of Americans (as Americans) in narratives.

It is clear on the other hand that in an *indirect* way the New Australian Cinema is only too well aware of the United States. First, the dominant aesthetics of the films of the New Australian Cinema are informed, shaped, and structured by both classic Hollywood cinematic conventions and contemporary American film practices—perhaps more by the former than by the latter. Second, since the New Australian Cinema established itself it has maintained at least one eye on the North American market as a source of sales.

This has naturally led to debate in Australia about the concept of internationalization of films. To what extent (if at all) should Australian films attempt to mute or deny their Australianness, to aim for a sort of mid-Pacific feel in story, themes, even locations, in order to attract sales to distributors in the United States? The debate, at least as it refers to the marketing of Australian films, remains unresolved but seems to have polarized around two opposite positions that claim that films should either retain and indeed emphasize their Australianness with a view to gaining distribution in Europe (where it is said their Australianness makes them attractive) and limited "art-house" release in America or attempt an international (i.e., nonculturally specific but heavily Americanized) "feel" in order to be offered for major commercial distribution in the United States. It is reasonable to presume that both types of films will continue to be made—as will films that do not seem to consider either polar position as exclusive or essential.

My claim that the United States is an absence in the New Australian Cinema must, of course, be modified to recognize the predominance of America as a location and as a narrative function in the two *Crocodile Dundee* films and a brief location in some others. The presence of Americans in some films must also be registered (e.g., *Death of a Soldier, Rebel, The Man from Snowy River,* and a few others). The actual representations of Americans in these films is determined by certain stereotyped cultural views, but in general they reflect the ambivalence Australia feels toward the United States and lack the extremes that Australian culture manifests toward England and the English.

Death of a Soldier is unique in that it is "about" Americans in Australia during World War II and is based upon actual events of U.S. military and Australian civil history. *Rebel* is a fictional narrative also concerned to some extent with American servicemen stationed in Australia during the same war. Films such as *The Odd Angry Shot* (Australian soldiers in Vietnam) and *Phar Lap* (a historically existing racehorse from Australia that died in the United States) of necessity have some American characters. Whether a major character in *Phar Lap* must be an American is a moot point. The same may be said of one of the characters in *The Year of Living Dangerously*.

Two films that offer interesting insights into the ambivalence Australia has toward America are *Undercover* and *The Coca-Cola Kid*. Both narratives postulate the arrival of an American expert to help run Australian businesses (or, in *The Coca-Cola Kid*, the Australian end of an American business), using the traditional boy meets girl dramatic formula to set up conflicts between the brash American and the more down-to-earth Australian girl. Both conclude with the Americans being won over to an Australian point of view, partly by the girl and partly by the realization that Australian culture is more life-enhancing than American culture. But before these conclusions are reached, in each case a certain admiration is expressed for American culture through the recognition of the dynamism of the Americans.

There is very little that is vehemently anti-American in the New Australian Cinema. Certain exceptions do exist, although their anti-Americanism is much more a matter of interpretation than is the more obvious anti-Englishness of many other films. For example, it may be significant that in *Dead Calm* (1989) the narrative revolves around two very pleasant, harmless Australians being menaced by an *American* psychopath. But the fact of the third character (the psychopath) being American may be explained by production exigencies rather than by cultural perceptions. This may well be the explanation for Americans turning up in other films where no Americans logically need to be: for instance, *The Last Wave*, *Attack Force Z*, or *The Man from Snowy River*.

Equally, there is very little that is distinctly positive in representations of America and Americans in the New Australian Cinema—other than the celebrated instance of *Crocodile Dundee*. In view of the apparent need to sell films in the American market, this absence or extremely muted presence may seem odd; but culturally Australians have enormous difficulty trying to obsequiously curry favor whether in personal one-to-one relationships or in the larger politico-economic spheres. Toadyism is contrary to Australia's mythic egalitarianism and works against any sense of the "fair go syndrome"—Australia's version of liberty, equality, and fraternity, according to Donald Horne.

The Structure of This Book

It is necessary to provide a word or two about the structure of this book. The decision to organize this book around separate entries for individual films was prompted by my experiences as both film scholar and film teacher in trying to find critical analysis of an individual film. I found myself having to resort to flicking back and forth from the index to the text, gleaning a comment here or a reference there. This is especially true of Australian films because of the dearth of written material on the Australian cinema in general and the New Australian Cinema in particular (which was especially true when I began to write the entries in this book but is marginally less so now). My own experience in attempting to write on the Australian cinema led me to conclude that a book that provides easily accessible information on the films themselves was needed. I do not pretend that this book is a definitive reference for Australian cinema, but I do humbly hope that it will help fill a very real gap.

There was another reason for writing this book with separate entries for individual films. I subscribe to the belief that the films themselves remain the core and single most important aspect of the study of cinema. This may seem so self-evident that it is absurd to mention it. But the fact is that the films themselves are frequently lost in much writing on the cinema. This may be understandable when the emphasis is upon, say, an industrial history of the (or a) cinema; but when the writing is sociological, or cultural, or analytical in principle, I cannot help but feel that the films themselves deserve some primacy beyond providing examples. As a corollary to this, it is also true that, when film titles are mentioned as examples for arguments in many texts, it is sometimes difficult for a reader who does not know the film in question to know whether the argument is justified by the film itself. A book that deals with the films themselves may help rectify this.

It is inevitable, then, that there is a certain amount of repetition: each entry is self-sufficient (but not exhaustive) and indeed was written to be read that way. The discussion frequently makes the same points in relation to separate films or requires reiteration of arguments when analyzing a number of films individually. This does not mean that I have omitted cross-references to other films that are comparable or stand in contradistinction in some way.[31] But while I hope that the book as a whole offers a useful (if far from comprehensive) insight into the New Australian Cinema, it is also my intention that readers should be able to use the book as a reference source on individual Australian films of the past twenty years and that it may therefore be "dipped into" to locate comments on any particular film that may be of interest.

The book has entries for only 100 of the feature films produced in Australia since 1970. Some comments on how the films were selected need to be made at this point. My initial definition of a "feature film" was a film of narrative fiction over eighty minutes in length. This meant that I eliminated documentaries from consideration from the outset. I have also ignored animated films and those that I consider to be exploitative pornography (hard or soft core). Even with the application of these negative criteria, there were many more films than this book could encompass. The selection of the 100 titles in the book was made according to one or more of the following criteria:

1. Films that reflect or represent in their narrative content, story-lines, or thematic concerns aspects of Australian cultural myths of national identity.

2. Films that reflect or represent in their narrative content, story-lines, setting, or thematic concerns aspects of contemporary Australian life, social conditions, or preoccupations.

3. Films that reflect, represent, or give importance to the Australian landscape, especially through the landscape's effect on or determination of the content of the narrative and storyline.

4. Films that reflect, represent, or are structured around aspects of Australian history.

5. Films that have made a significant contribution to the New Australian Cinema both at home and abroad.

In nearly every case there is much more that could be said about the selected films. I have tried to restrict my comments to three main approaches. First, as the title of the book implies, the way in which the individual film is an "image of Australia" with particular but not slavish reference to the dominant myths of Australian identity. Second, I have endeavored to locate each film in relation to the body of films of the New Australian Cinema in general. And third, I have tried to give some critical reaction to the film as a piece of cinema, in its own right. In this last regard, my comments may seem rather severe on occasion, for although I consider myself to be an enthusiastic supporter of Australian film—to the point of sometimes illogical prejudice in their favor—I do neither the readers of this book nor the makers of films in Australia any service by turning a blind eye to imperfections and inadequacies in individual films. I have tried, however, to assess the New Australian Cinema and its productions in their own terms.

Finally, in the matter of the format of the entries themselves, I have included production credits only for the major production/creative roles. I have ignored producer credits that carry the qualifier "executive," "associate," or "co-." The descriptions "art director" and "production designer" are used as the individual films use them, but "director of photography" is used even where the credit on the film is sometimes "lighting cameraman" or simply "cinematographer." The "sound" credit generally means the sound recordist rather than the sound editor (if these were separate individuals). The cast entry is restricted to principal characters, and I have taken it upon myself to decide who is a principal character. The story summary, too, is my own summary of the film's narrative and plot and provides only the simplest outline of stories that take an hour and a half or more in the cinema.

Australian cinema, in the years covered in these pages, has produced perhaps only a handful of truly significant films—but, proportionally, has any other national cinema (including the American) done any better? The New Australian Cinema has produced less than a handful of stars: preeminently Mel Gibson, but also Judy Davis, Sam Neill, Bryan Brown, and now, perhaps, Paul Hogan. It has certainly produced a number of recognized world-class directors: Peter Weir, Fred Schepisi, Bruce Beresford, George Miller, Paul Cox, Gillian Armstrong; and a few others who have found work in Hollywood if not critical recognition: Richard Franklin, Simon Wincer, Carl Schultz. As yet, seemingly, the New Australian Cinema has produced no cinema writers whose credentials are considered sufficient to earn them international recognition. But, important as the New Australian Cinema has been within Australia (for complex reasons), it has also moved out of its early perceived position as a merely interesting corner of international cinema. In these pages are found the films that helped it to do so, along with many films that might well have been equally valuable in creating the positive image of the New Australian Cinema abroad had

they been more widely distributed or more widely seen. Who knows?
With the ever-increasing availability of films on videotape for domestic
viewing, perhaps they still might be.

Notes

1. There is some dispute over this being the first film actually *shown:* a Melbourne man is recorded to have shown films as part of a vaudeville program as
early as August 1896. These would have been imported films and thus signaled,
unknowingly, an irreversible trend in importing films, a practice that would
cause problems for indigenous production for the next eighty or ninety years.

2. Nonetheless, one of the interesting sidelights of the history of Australian
film at this time was the manufacture from scratch of sound recording equipment by Australian technicians.

3. Phillip Noyce's film *Newsfront* is based upon this latter period of Cinesound's operations and provides a fascinating insight into the production of
films in Australia in the decade that followed World War II—and also shows
that not all those involved in the New Australian Cinema are ignorant of the
history of Australian film.

4. The term "industry" is used advisedly here: film production throughout
the 1970s and 1980s was organized more along the lines of a cottage industry
(despite the amount of money spent, especially in the heady days of 10BA)
than according to modern industrial practice. It did not and still does not
compare with the studio-based Hollywood model in almost any regard. That
film production will become a "nationalized" government-controlled industry
is a distinct possibility once the effect of the Film Finance Corporation is felt
further into the 1990s.

5. To be strictly accurate chronologically, the first English settlement on the
continent that was to become the nation-state of Australia took place slightly
before the French Revolution, in January 1788.

6. The significance of Darwin to burgeoning Australian culture can be
gauged from the fact that Australia's northernmost city, the capital of the
Northern Territory, is named Darwin, whereas most other capital cities of
Australia are named after (aristocratic) English statesmen (Sydney, Brisbane,
Melbourne, Hobart), with Adelaide named after the wife of King William IV,
and Perth rather prosaically named after a town in Scotland associated with the
first governor of the Swan River Colony, William Stirling. However, the first,
failed attempt to settle the northern coast of Australia was near the present
Darwin; in keeping with tradition, it was named Palmerston.

7. The 1960s saw a tremendous upsurge of interest in examining Australia
in many different ways from both within and outside the country. Published
works "explaining" Australia ranged from the purely dilettante tourist view,

through the journalistic, to the scholarly. These works tended to show an extraordinary consistency in their view of what Australia was—although their attitudes to that revelation differed quite a bit.

8. Russel Ward, "The Social Fabric," in A. L. McLeod (ed.), *The Pattern of Australian Culture*, p. 14.

9. John Fiske, Bob Hodge, and Graeme Turner, *Myths of Oz: Reading Australian Popular Culture* (1987).

10. Richard White, *Inventing Australia: Images and Identity 1688–1980;* Verity Burgmann and Jenny Lee (eds.), *Constructing a Culture* (Ringwood, Victoria: Penguin, 1988).

11. During the long reign of conservative governments in Australia from 1949 to 1972, especially under the Anglocentric prime minister Robert Menzies, Australian culture was considered at best an embarrassment, at worst a barely mentionable entity of inexcusable vulgarity—although some vague sense of an "Australian way of life" (a suntanned version of England) was maintained for political purposes, to be trotted out as an explanation of why Australia was what it was under the conservatives. The distaste for Australianism, however, extended to any suggestions that Australians could produce "high" culture—many initiatives to encourage the arts were stifled by deliberate government policy, often at the behest of Menzies. Following his retirement, the succeeding conservative governments began to loosen up considerably in their attitudes toward fostering Australian culture. The process was greatly speeded up by the reformist Labor government under Gough Whitlam in 1972–1975.

12. A far more complete description, in fact a catalogue, of the attributes of this mythical Australian may be found in Russel Ward's seminal work, *The Australian Legend.*

13. It has the same power for the aboriginal culture as well—perhaps even more so.

14. Graeme Turner, "Our 'Dubious Heritage': Nationalism and Contemporary Australian Film," *Overlander* 91 (1983): 38.

15. Tom O'Regan, "A Fine Cultural Romance: The Seventies Feature Film," unpublished paper.

16. Tim Rowse and Albert Moran, "'Peculiarly Australian'—The Political Construction of Cultural Identity," in Sol Encel and Lois Bryson (eds.), *Australian Society: Introductory Essays*, p. 239.

17. The term is used by Susan Dermody and Elizabeth Jacka in *The Screening of Australia, Volume 1* (p. 37), although they have taken it from critic and filmmaker Bob Ellis.

18. Ibid., pp. 27ff.

19. Ibid., p. 22.

20. Ibid., p. 34.

21. Horne's title was meant as sarcasm; however, it was adopted literally.

22. Dermody and Jacka, *The Screening of Australia, Volume 1*, p. 37.

23. Ibid., p. 43.

24. White, *Inventing Australia,* p. viii.

25. Ross Gibson, "Landscape in Australian Feature Films," *Framework* 22/23 (1983): 48.

26. Geoffrey Searle, *From Deserts the Prophets Come* (Melbourne: Heinemann, 1973), p. 14.

27. "Squatter: A pastoral magnate . . . regarded as one of the privileged or affluent" (G. A. Wilkes, *A Dictionary of Australian Colloquialisms* [Sydney: Fontana, 1978]).

28. Ibid.

29. Ibid.

30. White, *Inventing Australia,* p. 170.

31. When I refer to an Australian film that does not have a separate entry, the title is followed by the date of release. For foreign films, the title is followed by the country of origin and date of release. Films without a date have their own entry herein.

PART II. TEXTS

The Adventures of Barry McKenzie 1972

Director: Bruce Beresford.

Producer: Phillip Adams.

Screenplay: Bruce Beresford, Barry
   Humphries.

Director of Photography: Don McAlpine.

Editor: John Scott.

Production Designer: John Stoddart.

Music: Peter Best.

Sound: Tony Hide.

Cast: Barry Crocker (Barry McKenzie);
   Barry Humphries (Aunt Edna, Hoot,
   de Lamphrey); Paul Bertram (Curly);
   Avice Landon (Mrs. Gort); Dennis
   Price (Mr. Gort); Jenny Tomasin (Sarah
   Gort).

Production Company: Longford
   Productions.

Running Time: 114 mins.

STORY

Barry McKenzie, all-Australian boy, receives an inheritance with the
proviso that he must visit England. His Aunt Edna Everage, all-
Australian housewife, goes with him. During a beery reunion with his
mate Curly, he is prevailed upon to appear in a new cigarette campaign. His attempts at intercourse with the female model are thwarted
by the jealous director. Visiting with the Gorts, a middle-class suburban
family, Barry is matched with their unattractive daughter and forced to
flee. Later Barry's rendition of an "authentic Australian folk-tune"
leads to a riot. After confusion in a gay bar, he becomes the target of an
insistent police detective. Barry is interviewed on a television program
about expatriates. After his drunken mates wreck the studio, Edna
decides it is time she and Barry went home.

COMMENT

Even a lengthy plot summary could not do justice to the inventiveness
and the pace of the plot of *The Adventures of Barry McKenzie*. The film
piles joke upon joke, gag upon gag—mostly verbal humor but often
visual as well. Given the part played in the production by Barry Humphries, this blend of vulgarity, satire, ridicule, double entendre, and
pure linguistic inventiveness (especially when referring to bodily functions) is hardly surprising. What is surprising is the sheer audacity of
the film's material and the sheer confidence with which it was made.

At the time, what was to become known as the Australian film

The Adventures of Barry McKenzie. National Film and Sound Archive/Phillip Adams.

renaissance had hardly begun and was still several years away from
critical and commercial recognition and continuity of production.
Barry Humphries had been known in Australia and Britain for many
years and was recognized as Australia's leading satirist—on the stage.
His creation Edna Everage had not attained "mega-stardom" (still an
ordinary "Mrs."), although she had appeared in an early film, *The
Naked Bunyip* (1970). Bruce Beresford had been involved in a number
of films (in various capacities), but these were mostly short documentaries; *The Adventures of Barry McKenzie* was his first feature film. Yet this
film shows a sureness of touch and a confidence with narrative material
that few Australian feature films were to demonstrate for some years to
come. The grasp of cinema that Beresford has demonstrated in over
ten feature films is evident here even though the sheer weight of
incidents threatens to overburden the film. Hardly any conceivable
target, Australian or English, escapes the satirical eye of the film,
although perhaps the "poms" get the worst of it overall.

The attacks that the film makes on aspects of Australian society and
culture are, however, tinged with a greater degree of affection than the

attacks on English targets. Beer-swilling yobbos are rather more sentimentalized than are rapacious or perverted Englishmen/women. This
same degree of sentimentalization is not noticeably present in the
sequel, *Barry McKenzie Holds His Own*. The love/hate attitude that the
film (or, more specifically, Barry Humphries as the prime instigator
and creator of the two films) has toward "Bazza" himself is paralleled by
the love/hate attitude toward the English, not so much through Bazza
(who remains rabidly anti-pom, although he softens just for a second at
the very end) but in the structure, incidents, and situations of the
narrative. In this the film reflects a deep-seated cultural confusion in
Australia; the attitudes and contradictions inherent in Barry McKenzie's position are inherent in many Australians, especially those of
Anglo-Saxon or Anglo-Celtic descent. Although, as the 1970s moved
into the 1980s, the nationalistic revival within Australia—fed by the
increasing sense of multiculturalism—saw the fading of these remaining cultural links with Britain, the rejection of Englishness was nowhere near complete in 1972 when this film was made. In any case,
Humphries (not so much through this film but in other ways) is clearly
an anglophile.

Barry McKenzie may be the ocker par excellence, but he also has
something of the folk-hero in his naive makeup. Innocent to the point
of near imbecility, in his history here he is still close to the honest bush
type set upon by the cunning, rapacious, mendacious, and often perverted city dwellers. As such he is a figure that strikes a chord in most
Australians' consciousness. Of course, McKenzie is not a bushman in
the Australian sense—he is a city dweller (as are most Australians)—
but in this instance the opposition bush/city within the Australian
context is precisely paralleled by an opposition Australia/England.

Thus McKenzie is very much an Australian hero, taking on the poms
and, if not exactly victorious, at least showing what he is made of (quite
literally) in defeat. McKenzie's status as a hero seemed unlikely at the
time the film was made. Indeed, much of the initial reaction to the film
was a mixture of embarrassment and outrage. But the groundswell of
Australian nationalism in the 1970s and early 1980s raised the ocker to
near apotheosis—a trajectory completed with *Crocodile Dundee*.

Although Barry McKenzie as ocker hero slightly predates the full
blooming of the ocker in Australian popular mythology, and although
the ocker's status was cheapened somewhat by some films that followed

(particularly the *Alvin Purple* films), he remains one of the most complete renderings of the ocker-as-clown on film. The film itself retains its potency; its hero may be gauche, but the film itself is not.

Alvin Purple | 1973

Director: Tim Burstall.

Producer: Tim Burstall.

Screenplay: Alan Hopgood.

Director of Photography: Robin Copping.

Editor: Edward McQueen-Mason.

Production Designer: Leslie Binns.

Music: Brian Cadd.

Sound: John Phillips.

Cast: Graeme Blundell (Alvin); Elli MacClure (Tina); Penne Hackforth-Jones (Liz); George Whaley (McBurney); Alan Finney (Spike); Jill Forster (Mrs. Horwood); Noel Ferrier (judge).

Production Company: Hexagon.

Running Time: 95 minutes.

STORY

Despite his rather unprepossessing appearance and character, Alvin Purple has proved to be intensely sexually attractive to women since his school days. Equally, he has found it impossible to resist women's lures. A friend, hoping to profit from Alvin's "gifts," employs him as a water-bed installer and Alvin finds himself consistently having to make love to the women in whose homes he installs the beds. Alvin's unique abilities are put to work as a "sex therapist" for a psychiatrist, Dr. McBurney, but another psychiatrist, Liz Short, finds out and blackmails Alvin into providing her with endless favors. Alvin is prosecuted for incitement to adultery but is acquitted. To escape the snares of the world, he takes a job as gardener in a convent.

COMMENT

It is difficult not to be embarrassed by some of the early films of the Australian film revival. Some of these films embarrass through being incompetently made—or, perhaps more fairly, by being made by people inexperienced in many aspects of feature film production, especially writing but also directing and acting. *The Adventures of Barry*

McKenzie (which predates *Alvin Purple* by a year) embarrasses because, despite its caricature and exaggeration, it depicts Australians as they are (an image not popular at the time but since increased in cultural value). *Alvin Purple* embarrasses more because of the stunning lack of subtlety and wit in its attempts at constructing an "adult sex comedy."

Alvin Purple was not director Tim Burstall's first film (*2000 Weeks* [1968] and *Stork* [1971] predate it), so what might have passed or been excused as inexperience in another director could not be so easily excused in Burstall. With this and succeeding films, Burstall was to display a cavalier disregard for inventiveness and subtlety in favor of a rather insulting commitment to commercialism justified as "giving the public what it wants." In a number of his later films, notably in *The Last of the Knucklemen* and *Kangaroo,* Burstall almost perversely disregards opportunities that seem to demand specifically Australian perceptions to inform the narratives—the nexus of landscape with action and characterization in particular. It seems that Burstall wants to make Australian films that deny being Australian.

The initial sexually oriented jokes in *Alvin Purple* are basically a seemingly endless stream of heterosexual couplings that gradually run down to a scene of homophobic panic. It is demonstrable that homophobia is widespread in Australian society due, it is occasionally surmised, to the alleged homoerotic underpinning of the essential cultural concept of mateship.

The humor of *Alvin Purple* is little more than adolescent and is perhaps only explicable in view of the then recently relaxed (late 1971) Australian film censorship system, whereby an "R" rating was made available for "adult only" material.

There are vague suggestions of a plot worth following, but these suggestions are barely raised before they are flung aside for a bit more nudity, sexual coupling, and double entendre—making sure that this last is understood by invariably displaying an awareness of the double meaning through characters' reactions. There have been suggestions of comparisons with the British *Carry On* films of the 1950s and 1960s, but *Alvin Purple* cannot manage the "saucy postcard" style of those films let alone the quite genuinely funny ensemble acting of the *Carry On* team.

Toward the conclusion, with Alvin's trial, the film staggers from farce to pathos, with neither approach integrated in more than the most tangential manner with the slim narrative, and then abandons both for near-slapstick chases highly reminiscent of the British television's *Benny Hill Show*. (This is even more true of the sequences of the adolescent Alvin pursued by hordes of schoolgirls.) *Alvin Purple* has been described as an ocker comedy, but there seems little that is especially ockerish about Alvin. The prurience of the sex comedy is not particularly Australian, although it may have reflected in a distorted way the sense of sexual (and general cultural) awakening of the time.

While the films that followed in the flowering of the Australian cinema in the 1970s made use of the traditional view of Australian heroes as being in some manner associated with or placed in the bush, with the corollary that urban males could not be heroes, few films of either bush or city have postulated such an ineffectual protagonist. Alvin is not an antihero as such; he is a nonhero. As a joke, the concept of a completely personalityless nonentity as a source of extraordinary sexual magnetism is a very thin frame upon which to hang a whole movie narrative.

But, if nothing else, *Alvin Purple* did demonstrate quite clearly that Australian films could find favor with an audience and make money at the box office. It undoubtedly encouraged the still-embryonic film revival to continue growing. Few of the immediately subsequent Australian productions (save the sequel, *Alvin Rides Again* [1964]) chose to follow the blatantly clichéd furrow *Alvin Purple* plowed, and Australian film became, in fact, much more introspective in its search for subjects.

The early 1970s were, of course, a time of discovery, learning, and experimentation for the newly developing Australian cinema, and producers were still uncertain of what to make and how to make it. Unlike other early 1970s films (including *The Adventures of Barry McKenzie*, to which it would seem to have superficial links), *Alvin Purple* does not stand the test of time.

Annie's Coming Out (USA: *Test of Love*) 1984

Director: Gil Brealey.

Producer: Don Murray.

Screenplay: John Patterson, Chris Borthwick.

Director of Photography: Mick Von Bornemann.

Editor: Lindsay Frazer.

Production Designer: Robbie Perkins.

Music: Simon Walker.

Sound: Rodney Simmons.

Cast: Angela Punch McGregor (Jessica); Tina Arhondis (Annie); Drew Forsythe (David); Wallas Eaton (Dr. Rowell); Simon Chilvers (Metcalfe); Monica Maughan (Vera Peters).

Production Company: Film Australia.

Running Time: 96 minutes.

STORY

Jessica Hathaway gets a job as an educational therapist at a Melbourne hospital for the profoundly retarded. She begins to realize that many of the patients are not simply the "vegetables" the medical staff assumes. She is attracted to one in particular, Annie O'Farrell, who has been in the institution for eleven years. Jessica discovers that although Annie is profoundly physically disabled, she is really intellectually normal. She takes Annie home with her and becomes totally obsessed, much to the annoyance of her boyfriend David. When the authorities refuse to believe Jessica, she seeks help from the news media, and legal assistance. At a hearing, it is determined that Annie is capable of desiring freedom and communicating that desire. Annie's "coming out" provides hope for other inmates in her situation.

COMMENT

Films based upon fact or upon biographical histories of actual individuals form a substantial part of the output of the New Australian Cinema. These range from the highly romanticized *We of the Never Never* through *Caddie* to the more socially realist *Cathy's Child*. All of these films, and others of the same type, are to a greater or lesser extent fictionalized: their factual or biographical bases are subordinated to fictional narrative conventions. There are few films of the New Australian Cinema that consider their factual material sufficiently important to utilize documentary conventions rather than those of the dramatic film. *Strikebound* and *Death of a Soldier* occasionally come close, although they more closely approximate certain British television docudramas (e.g., Ken Loach's *Days of Hope*). *Annie's Coming Out* also utilizes some of these docudrama techniques; it seems to be a documentary using fictional film techniques. This is the direct consequence of the unavoidable poignancy and inescapable seriousness of its material, despite the fact that there have been some deliberate attempts at fictionalizing through the changing of names. (None of the principals has the same name as the individuals upon whose history the film is based.)

In order to condense what was in reality a long time in the life of Annie O'Farrell (in reality Annie McDonald) and to explain both her background and her condition, the film occasionally has to resort to what in an ordinary fictional narrative would be dismissed as over-simplification or gross exaggeration. Nonetheless, it is fair to say that the film avoids sacrificing veracity for the sake of explanation, even at the risk of confusing its audience. To an extent, then, the film has to lose a certain amount of audience identification in order to make its point. It must also, for the purpose of clarity and narrative economy, focus more directly on Jessica than on Annie. This is partly redressed by allowing Annie a voice-over narration ("legitimized" by the real Annie's commentary, which functions in the same way in the book written by her and the real-life Jessica, Rosemary Crossley). Inevitably, however, the narrative structure of the film becomes Jessica's fight for justice for Annie rather than their joint efforts to secure Annie's re-lease. This does not distract from the film, although it does tend to give it a more conventional fictional gloss.

Discussion of, say, the acting performances (remarkable in some instances), or comment on the scriptwriting seems both superfluous and irrelevant. Nonetheless, it is possible to commend the director on the handling of highly sensitive and emotionally charged material.

Curiously, *Annie's Coming Out* bears some resemblances to *Careful, He Might Hear You*—certainly in the later stages, where the story in both films becomes a fight for possession of a child (bearing in mind, how-ever, that Annie O'Farrell is actually a legal adult). Both films position their audiences in respect to the desired outcome of the battle and clearly delineate the opposing camps in terms of good and bad.

In *Careful, He Might Hear You*, the members of the family PS might join are not drawn in fully and inescapably attractive terms. In this film, there is a danger that Annie's allies will be too clearly "on the side of the angels"; this is not redressed by making David, Jessica's lover, less sympathetic and less believing than Jessica or by making Jessica single-mindedly obsessive. Again, this delineation of good and bad needs to be tempered by the fact that *Annie's Coming Out* is based on reality: no doubt the institution and its administration were as ghastly and inhuman as they are in the film.

Other than its historical and cinematic setting, there is nothing about *Annie's Coming Out* that is specifically Australian: Australia has no monopoly on dehumanized and dehumanizing bureaucratic institutions. Although the concept of the "fair go" has great ideological potency and it is possible that Australians might be more outraged than other more "objective" cultures over the denial by authority of Annie's right to a fair go, it is claiming too much to assert that Australians have a culturally determined higher sense of moral outrage than other cultures. The fair go principle is a culturally specific moral or ethical philosophy certainly, but other cultures have moral standpoints that reflect their ideologies. Overall, ethical specificity aside, *Annie's Coming Out* is a film too important to ignore in any survey of the New Australian Cinema.

Attack Force Z | 1982

Director: Tim Burstall.

Producer: Lee Robinson.

Screenplay: Roger Marshall.

Director of Photography: Lin Hung-Chung.

Editor: David Stiven.

Production Designer: Bernard Hides.

Music: Eric Jupp.

Sound: Don Connolly, Tim Lloyd.

Cast: John Phillip Law (Veitch); Mel Gibson (Kelly); Sam Neill (Costello); Chris Haywood (Bird); John Waters (King).

Production Company: John McCallum Productions/Central Motion Picture Corporation.

Running Time: 110 minutes.

STORY

World War II: five members of the Special Z force unit, led by Captain Kelly, land on an island occupied by the Japanese. Their mission is to rescue an American diplomat and a high-ranking Japanese government official. After making unexpected contact with the local resistance, they locate the plane but not the survivors. In searching for them, they succeed instead in stirring up and killing a large number of

Japanese. Their efforts to escape with the official and his American escort bring about a premature armed uprising by the population. In a fight against overwhelming odds, all the members of the unit save Kelly are killed; although Kelly gets off the island with the diplomat, he finds the diplomat has been killed by a stray bullet.

COMMENT

Attack Force Z is a film that deals, ostensibly, with Australian involvement in World War II. As such it might be expected to throw some interesting light on the national myth of Australians as warriors, through its very placement in a historical setting that has been largely ignored by Australian cinema but is considerably less remote than the Boer War and World War I.

It turns out, however, that *Attack Force Z*'s narrative structure and its character construction owe little or nothing to Australian cultural myths. Its narrative structure and characterization are determined by other conventions, notably the conventions of the war movie genre—or, perhaps more accurately, of a subgenre within that all-encompassing genre: the "behind-enemy-lines" formula of the type typified by *The Guns of Navarone* (Britain, 1961) or more analogously (given the plot) *Ill Met by Moonlight* (Britain, 1956). It makes claims to a sort of historical accuracy: a caption before the film commences states that the film is "honest" and "accurate." This can only suggest either that real life is even more like the movies than most imagine or that in recollection and personal narration there is a tendency to describe experiences in the narrative formulas of popular culture. What is of immediate importance is that the conventions of the genre are clearly at odds with or override any coding that the Australian myths might bring to the narrative. There are few specifically Australian cultural references (other than the occasional use of language in a specifically Australian way); in particular, there is an absence of any Australian cultural references that might disrupt or be contradictory to the dominant conventions of the genre. *The Odd Angry Shot* could never be this type of film, or vice versa.

By concentrating upon a small group of men in an elite unit, *Attack Force Z* might have offered an interesting comparison with *The Odd Angry Shot*—but it in fact offers only contrast. The failure of the unit, or more notably the failure of their leader, Captain Kelly, is about the most Australian cultural convention the film has to offer; as such, it is somewhat at odds with the conventions of the genre—which usually allow for success although not without cost.

Defeat and failure run like indestructible threads through nearly all Australian narratives, especially those that touch most closely on its cultural mythology. So it would seem that even as "un-Australian" a narrative film as *Attack Force Z* cannot, in the final moments, deny this cultural imperative. Captain Kelly is left alone on a Chinese fishing boat with a dead Japanese diplomat, with his team all dead on the island—little wonder that he sinks to the deck holding his head in his hands. This final aspect of defeat is quintessentially Australian because it is arbitrary—or, more accurately, it is fate. Having fought bravely and tenaciously against overwhelming odds, having used all the skills and ability that he has, Kelly is finally defeated by a stray bullet. The defeat, the failure, is undeserved. It is not even narratively necessary; the conventions of the formula would suggest otherwise. But it is inevitable. It is the defeat and failure that is prominent in Australian mythology, that has worked its way into the mythology from the bush.

Kelly is an Australian in charge of a disparate group: two Australians, a New Zealander, an Englishman, and a Dutchman. *Attack Force Z* uses the generic conventions of intragroup disharmony and conflict particularly between Kelly and Veitch, the Dutchman, although the reasons are never spelled out narratively. (It is asking too much of the film to see this as a metaphor for contemporary Australian multiculturalism.) This conflict between Kelly and Veitch could have been located within the Australian mythology of mateship. After all, a New Zealander and an Englishman are close enough surrogates for Australians; it is conceivable they could be taken on as mates. A Dutchman who talks with an American accent is irredeemably alien. An early incident in which a wounded member of the unit, King, is shot by a comrade to prevent his becoming a prisoner would seem to suggest something akin to mateship operating in the narrative. But King is "finished off" to save the others. This not only violates the code of mateship, but also suggests that military objectives are capable of claiming a higher loyalty than the demands of mateship. This is not a questioning of mateship but a denial of it. Its narrative purpose is to give the mission importance in the story as it unfolds. Its conventional generic coding overrules any Australian cultural codes that might compete for consideration.

There is little that reflects Australian myths in *Attack Force Z*. These are the comic-book heroics of the genre rather than the more muted heroics of "true" Australians as evidenced by *Gallipoli, The Odd Angry Shot,* and *Breaker Morant.*

Barry McKenzie Holds His Own 1974

Director: Bruce Beresford.
Producer: Bruce Beresford.
Screenplay: Barry Humphries, Bruce Beresford.
Director of Photography: Don McAlpine.
Editor: William Anderson, John Scott.
Production Designer: John Stoddart.
Music: Peter Best.
Sound: Les Bone.

Cast: Barry Crocker (Barry, Kevin); Barry Humphries (Edna, de Lamphrey, Manton, Englishman); Donald Pleasence (Count Plasma); Dick Bentley (Col the Frog); Ed Devereaux (Sir Alex).
Production Company: Reg Grundy Productions.
Running Time: 96 minutes.

STORY

Barry McKenzie and Aunt Edna Everage, traveling back to Australia, fall in with some of Barry's drunken mates. In Paris, Edna is mistaken for the queen of England and kidnapped by the agents of Eric, Count Plasma, minister of culture for the now communist Transylvania. Barry is smuggled back into England and organizes through the Australian High Commission and the British Foreign Office a commando-style raid on Transylvania with a group of young Australians. Plasma discovers that Edna is not the queen and attaches her to his labor-saving blood-draining machine. He is overcome by a cross made of beer cans wielded by the Reverend Kevin, Barry's twin brother, and Edna is rescued. Edna and Barry return to a hero's welcome in Sydney, and the prime minister, Gough Whitlam, tells Edna she has been made a Dame.

COMMENT

More than a decade later it is difficult not to be disappointed by the second in the *Barry McKenzie* series. Certainly *Barry McKenzie Holds His Own* enjoyed a much larger budget than *The Adventures of Barry McKen-*

zie, and that is obvious in both the quality of the production and the presence of not a few well-known (and expensive) faces—even though most of them are in cameo roles. *The Adventures of Barry McKenzie* may have been cheap, even crude (in production terms), but it had the advantage of being fresh, even new. *Barry McKenzie Holds His Own,* on the other hand, is better quality (in production terms—thanks to the larger budget), but it is fairly stale overall. Most of what it has to say was already said in the earlier film, which seemed both shocking and extremely funny because what it said had seldom been said before—and certainly never in such language. It is perhaps both inevitable and understandable that a sequel should be largely based upon those things that are perceived as making the original a success. In this case it was presumed that the success of *The Adventures of Barry McKenzie* was built upon extremely colorful descriptions of physiological and sexual functions, demonstration of the same, use of the linguistically inventive insult, and the overall narrative structure of the adventures of the "innocent" Australian abroad. And those presumptions were justified.

There can be no doubting Barry Humphries' continued success either in inventing fascinating euphemisms for urination, regurgitation, and the sex act or in making use of Australian idiomatic speech with telling accuracy. He does his best to revitalize the inventive Australian vulgarity of *The Adventures of Barry McKenzie* with new metaphors for these basic biological functions and his ability to find or invent descriptive terms never fails to produce admiration. But it all becomes a bit too much: there is a sense of cataloguing rather than integrating.

There can be little doubt, either, that some of the targets well deserve his satire; unlike *The Adventures of Barry McKenzie,* this time around Australia is on the receiving end of most of the blasts. But while satire appears to be on the makers' minds at first, the need for (or demands of) a plot seems to get in the way of the satire. This is also true of the later Humphries film *Les Patterson Saves the World* (1987), an abysmal flop.

Even granted a satiric purpose, most of the ridiculing of things Australian (or otherwise) serves not so much as satire but as a source of comedy of a much broader farcical and slapstick style. Beresford's contributions to this seem less obvious than in *The Adventures of Barry McKenzie* and his other later films. The passing parodies of horror, war, and kung fu films are not taken up by Beresford as opportunities to add cinematic or directorial comedy to a script that relies heavily upon the dialogue, situation, and caricature of Humphries.

Thus it is that *Barry McKenzie Holds His Own* not only tends to turn into a repeat of *The Adventures of Barry McKenzie* (with a modicum more plot) but within itself relies upon repetition of gags: constant fountains of foaming lager, several scenes of "chundering," the running gag of Plasma thinking Edna is the queen of England, and so on. The formula is the same as before but more so: more beer, more vomit, more dog turds on the footpaths, and more sexual possibilities that do not come to fruition for Bazza. Bazza's sexual innocence in *The Adventures of Barry McKenzie* has become sexual moronity.

Barry McKenzie Holds His Own is not informed by even a grudging affection for England and the English. England is simply the butt for a lot of jokes that derive from its attitudes, circumstances, and environment. Even so, the film is on weaker ground when dealing with the French—presumably because Australia lacks any fully formed cultural attitudes (or prejudices) toward the French, having only a very small set of stereotyped images (oversexed, eating snails and frogs' legs, etc.). Such images are borrowed from English cultural attitudes to the French. Because of this the Paris sequences lack the bite of the English sequences and turn the film into a series of situations that are comic because they are farcical rather than because they are satirical.

It cannot be said *Barry McKenzie Holds His Own* is not a funny film. But it is a disappointment after *The Adventures of Barry McKenzie*. Here Barry McKenzie has lost a great deal of his cultural relevance and, as such, the end of the film notwithstanding, much of his claim to be an authentic Australian hero.

Blue Fin 1979

Director: Carl Schultz.

Producer: Hal McElroy.

Screenplay: Sonia Borg.

Director of Photography: Geoffrey Burton.

Editor: Rod Adamson.

Art Direction: David Copping.

Music: Michael Carlos.

Sound: Don Connolly.

Cast: Greg Rowe (Snook); Hardy Kruger (Pascoe); Elspeth Ballantyne (Mother); Liddy Clark (Ruth); John Jarratt (Sam); Hugh Keays-Byrne (Stan); Ralph Cotterill (Herbie).

Production Company: South Australian Film Corporation.

Running Time: 95 minutes.

STORY

Snook lives in the remote fishing community of Streaky Bay. He aspires
to be a tuna fisherman like his father, Bill Pascoe, but seems unable to
win his father's approval for anything he does. Snook and some school
friends disrupt the annual Tuna Fisherman's Ball by crowning a fish as
"Miss Tuna." His sister's fiancé Sam is lost at sea when another boat
disappears. Snook's father has no option but to take him on the next
fishing trip. All goes well until the *Blue Fin* is struck by a water spout.
All the crew are lost, save Snook and Bill. Bill is badly hurt, and the
boat considerably damaged and in danger of sinking. Single-handedly,
Snook manages to repair and restart the engine and bring the *Blue Fin*
back to Streaky Bay.

COMMENT

There have been a number of occasions in the New Australian Cinema
where a successful film has spawned another film that, while not exactly a sequel to the first, is sufficiently similar (with a continuity of
creative personnel) to describe the films as "stable mates." *Moving Out*
and *Street Hero* fall into this loose category, as do *Fatty Finn* and *Ginger
Meggs*, *The Man from Snowy River* (which had its own sequel in 1988)
and *Phar Lap*, the *Mad Max* films, and especially *Storm Boy* and *Blue Fin*.
In the case of the last two, the description is apposite because both films
emanate from the same production company, the South Australian
Film Corporation. That being so, it is not surprising that the two films
should share cinematographer, art director, composer, and so on. But
they also share the main actor (Greg Rowe) and the same scriptwriter
(Sonia Borg) and are derived from books by the same author, Colin
Theile. It seems inarguable that *Blue Fin* was produced in order to try
to recapture the success (box-office success, that is) of *Storm Boy*. Rec-
ords seem to suggest that it did not. Neither was it the equal of *Storm
Boy* as a work of cinema. To what extent this is a consequence of a new
director and a new producer and to what extent a consequence of a less
involving story is a matter of conjecture.

In terms of narrative, *Blue Fin* seems to fall somewhere between the
two early South Australian Film Corporation successes: *Storm Boy*—a
boy growing up desperately needing and trying to gain his father's

Blue Fin. National Film and Sound Archive/South Australian Film Corporation.

approval and love—and *Sunday Too Far Away*—a group of men going about their specialized and demanding work. But the mix does not quite seem to work. Unlike the men in *Sunday Too Far Away,* the group of men in this film do not seem to be sufficiently differentiated (or their characters are not sufficiently developed) and their work, exciting as it is, seems less vital than that of the shearers. Despite Snook's obsession to become a tuna fisherman, the film gives little indication of quite why and how such a life should appeal to the boy. And given the profligate way the narrative kills off the crew of the *Blue Fin,* for the purpose of isolating Snook in order to permit him to prove himself, it is difficult to form a strong attachment to or interest in the men as a group.

On the other hand, the narrative focus on Snook tends to be presented in a way that borders on children's story cliché, particularly the manner in which his father disregards him. In short, it lacks motive: why is Snook so determined to be a fisherman? Is it hero worship of his father? Or is it that he is determined to prove his father wrong in his assessment of Snook as "useless"? Is it simply the romance of the deepsea fishing life? The film is noncommittal; other than the initiating role Snook takes in the prank with the tuna at the ball, little time is spent developing his character beyond this simple question of whether he will get the chance to prove himself.

Blue Fin reveals its Australianness (other than through accent and location, etc.) in two ways. First, it is concerned with the basically malignant qualities of natural conditions, especially storms, thus tending to add credence to the view that the sea that surrounds Australia is as dangerous as the bush that composes most of its interior. (Of course, it is recognized that, in general, cultures that come into physical contact with the sea tend to have a very wary attitude toward it.) Second, *Blue Fin* continues the usual mixture of affection and disdain for the inhabitants of remote country towns and especially for their unsophisticated rustic rituals—the dance in *Blue Fin* is easily the satiric equivalent of the dance in *The Cars That Ate Paris* and *Newsfront* and is seen primarily as a comic device rather than an occasion of community celebration and confirmation (unlike the rare instance of Fordian community "ritual" in the dance in *Dusty*).

As a children's film, *Blue Fin* does have some merit. In many respects, it is similar to a whole host of "growing up" films in the New Australian Cinema (*The Getting of Wisdom, The Irishman, My Brilliant Career,* etc.), but it lacks the metaphoric implications of those other films—there is little sense that the narrative journey that Snook undergoes has references beyond that character's own fictional history.

BMX Bandits 1983

Director: Brian Trenchard-Smith.

Producer: Tom Broadbridge, Paul Davies.

Screenplay: Patrick Edgeworth, Russell Hagg.

Director of Photography: John Seale.

Editor: Alan Lake.

Production Designer: Ross Major.

Music: Colin Stead, Frank Strangio.

Sound: Ken Hammond.

Cast: David Argue (Whitey); John Ley (Moustache); Brian Marshall (Boss); Angelo d'Angelo (PJ); James Lugton (Goose); Nicole Kidman (Judy); Bill Grady (sergeant).

Production Company: BMX Bandits.

Running Time: 90 minutes.

STORY

After an accident in which their BMX bicycles are damaged, PJ and Goose meet Judy, who is working during her holidays to buy her own BMX and is unfairly blamed for the accident. The three find a cache of smuggled two-way radios; not realizing they are intended for a payroll robbery by gangleader Boss, they decide to sell the radios to pay for repairs to their bicycles. Two of Boss's henchmen are soon on their trail. Judy is caught and threatened with torture to reveal the whereabouts of the radios. She is rescued by PJ and Goose. Their story of being chased is believed by the police, who tell them there is a reward for the capture of the two. PJ, Goose, and Judy decide the reward money would pay for a much-needed BMX track. With the help of all the local kids, they capture the whole gang.

COMMENT

From the outset, the New Australian Cinema has always included one or two films in any given year specifically produced with an audience of children in mind. Many of these have been animated films; others have been adaptations from best-selling children's authors. In this last category especially notable are the three films made from novels by Colin Theile, *Storm Boy, Blue Fin,* and *The Fire in the Stone* (1984). And there were the two films taken from 1930s newspaper comic strips, *Fatty Finn* and *Ginger Meggs.* However, no distinctively Australian style of children's films has developed, no narrative structure that can truly be said to be a consequence of specifically Australian concerns. Stories for children's films tend to be indigenous only to the extent that they take place in distinctly Australian locations, particularly the bush and, in the case of *BMX Bandits*, the beach and harbor suburbs of Sydney. There is a tendency to rely upon the setting to provide cultural recognition for the audience. In their narratives they do not differ greatly from conventional children's stories—on the screen or in literature.

Of these films, *BMX Bandits* is possibly the closest to an Australian children's film (although *The Fire in the Stone* occasionally utilizes its unique setting in the opal fields to suggest something more than a conventional narrative in an exotic but Australian setting). *BMX Bandits* is one of the few children's films that does not rely for its narrative center point upon an Oedipal conflict between father and son (the basis of all the Theile adaptations, for example, and with modifications also of *Fatty Finn* and *Ginger Meggs*). Indeed, the parents of the main protagonists are conspicuously absent from *BMX Bandits*.

More important than this, however, is the characterization of the three kids, PJ, Goose, and Judy. Instead of simply being precocious (a conventional requirement of most children's narratives), these three are constructed along lines that owe not a little to a (positive) larrikin image. The three have no compunction about selling the radios they happen across—and the audience is not encouraged to see anything wrong in this either. It is simply good old Aussie initiative. There is no place for "Famous Five" moralizing (that is, suitable for children) in *BMX Bandits*. The three main characters are constantly given to "one-liners," jokes, or wisecracks that are quite in keeping with the way in which the Australian sense of humor frequently manifests itself: deadpan exaggeration, a sense of seeing a tangential and funny construction of events. This sometimes seems a little forced and a little tedious, but it is an aspect of characterization that is perhaps only matched in Australian children's films by *Fatty Finn*. The two bumbling crooks in *BMX Bandits,* Whitey and Moustache, are rather representative larrikins as well.

In most other narrative aspects, *BMX Bandits* is conventional. It is structured around simple dichotomies of "good" and "bad"—although the moral shadings are, as suggested, less rigid than one might expect. Moral shadings often are in Australian culture. The narrative finds the adult world (represented here simply by the gang of criminals and by the police, with very few other sustained characterizations save for the pompous shopping mall manager) always less flexible than that of the kids and as usual easily outwitted.

BMX Bandits is slightly unusual, then, not in finding a new narrative structure but in being one of the few children's films that is strictly for children. It does not, in other words, have one eye on a possible adult audience, as is the case with *Storm Boy* and the other Theile adaptation films. It does not patronize children, a charge that can be leveled at many other children's films. This may well be because the makers have actually hit upon a subject that is of intrinsic interest to children (rather than one they think they can interest children in) and that subject is quite simply BMX bicycles.

BMX Bandits is, in fact, the *Mad Max* of the two-wheeler—not in its hero-mythic structure but in its concern with showing vehicles (in this case, obviously, a special species of bicycle) in high-speed stunts. Much of the narrative (if not all of it) is structured around chases, cars pursuing bicycles and vice versa, with the aim of displaying the possibilities for spectacular stunts on the BMX. (These are so spectacular that the film carries a warning to others not to attempt them.) *BMX Bandits* is made up of terrific action sequences excitingly photographed that are easily the two-wheeled, human-powered equivalent of most of the opening action scenes in *Mad Max*.

Breaker Morant | 1980

Director: Bruce Beresford.
Producer: Matt Carroll.
Screenplay: Bruce Beresford, Jonathan
  Hardy, David Stevens.
Director of Photography: Don McAlpine.
Editor: William Anderson.
Art Director: David Copping.
Music: Phil Cunneen (Arranger).
Sound: Gary Wilkins.
Cast: Edward Woodward (Morant); Jack
Thompson (Thomas); Bryan Brown
(Handcock); John Waters (Taylor);
Charles Tingwell (Denny); Terry
Donovan (Hunt); Alan Cassell
(Kitchener); Lewis Fitz-Gerald
(Witton); Rod Mullinar (Bolton).
Production Company: South Australian
  Film Corporation.
Running Time: 104 minutes.

STORY

The Boer War, South Africa, 1901: three Australians, members of the Bush Veldt Carabineers (an irregular unit of the British Army), Harry

"Breaker" Morant, Peter Handcock, and George Witton, are court-martialed for shooting Boer prisoners and a German missionary. An inexperienced country solicitor, Major Thomas, is given the task of defending the three men—unaware that British High Command has determined on a guilty sentence as an act of appeasement to bring an end to the war. Major Thomas puts up a spirited defense, and through a series of flashbacks the circumstances of the killing of the prisoners are revealed. Witton is sentenced to life imprisonment, and Morant and Handcock are executed.

COMMENT

Breaker Morant is without doubt Bruce Beresford's finest Australian film and may well rank as one of the very best Australian films of the past nineteen years. Beresford has displayed his talents as a filmmaker in a variety of films that ranged from the rather slight (*Puberty Blues*) through the distinctly commercial (*Money Movers* [1979]) and biblical epic (*King David* [USA, 1985]) to the dramatic intensity of this film. Throughout, Beresford has shown that, irrespective of the subject (or indeed the budget), he has the ability to make a work of cinema out of the most diverse material.

There is no doubt that part of *Breaker Morant*'s success (beyond its sheer competence as a film) is that it touched upon a particularly sensitive cultural nerve in Australia at the time of its release. A renewed sense of cultural identity was gaining momentum in the late 1970s, and the creation in *Breaker Morant* of a cultural hero—actually two, Morant himself and the even more "dinkum Aussie," Handcock—virtually being persecuted for being Australian was timely. Much is made of the fact that the so-called crimes with which the men were charged arose as a consequence of their being Australians: that is, their alleged actions are frequently attributed to various Australian qualities (lack of discipline, insubordination, etc.). This was even more ironic given that Morant was in fact an Englishman—who had "learnt all Australia's bad habits." It is as much Australia (or rather Australianness) that is on trial in *Breaker Morant* as the three individuals.

The film is thus anti-English inasmuch as the English within its narrative are anti-Australian. Australianness is consistently presented in a favorable light, even when being decried by others within the narrative diegesis. Handcock, the most Australian of the three, is also the most attractive, more because of his larrikin personality than his physical attributes. The British duplicity only serves further to reinforce the positive results of a new culture being born from the old in the sun-drenched conditions of Australia. Australianness is thus confirmed as much by what it is as by what it is not in *Breaker Morant*. What is also uniquely Australian is the fact that the protagonists are defeated, overwhelmed by events and circumstances difficult for them to understand and impossible for them to withstand. An American drama would, one suspects, have had the central characters survive, be set free. Fatalism in the face of unarticulated but inevitable defeat is part of the Australian cultural identity. Morant himself has taken on enough of that identity to refuse the offer of assistance to escape when it is made to him.

Of course, if it were only this emphasis on demonstrating aspects of Australian character and a sort of muted jingoism, *Breaker Morant* would not have found the approval it has with overseas audiences as well as with domestic ones. In essence, the film is one of a tried and true formula—the courtroom drama—and as such is an expertly crafted example. Many such films, though, while insisting (at least initially) that circumstances and evidence are stacked against the defendant(s)— invariably the sympathetic figures of the narrative—in the end have the defendant(s) being vindicated. But there are a smaller number (not infrequently based on historical circumstances, as is *Breaker Morant*) in which the defendants are not freed. Such films are, of course, examinations of injustice and duplicity, and the central figures are no less (and often more) the objects of audience sympathy and identification than in the other type. *Breaker Morant* is one of the latter and has been compared, not unreasonably or unfavorably, with Stanley Kubrick's *Paths of Glory* (USA, 1957) and Joseph Losey's *King and Country* (Britain, 1964). *Breaker Morant* differs from these two earlier films in one important aspect: the defendants (or Morant, and Handcock to a lesser extent) did in fact carry out the acts of which they stand accused. Thus the power of the film is in Beresford's handling of the material, which ensures that the audience is moved by the plight of the men and the duplicity of the British High Command that leads to their execution. To this is added the manner in which the film makes a matter of military discipline and political intrigue a question of national and patriotic examination.

Gallipoli, ostensibly a quite different film, takes many of these questions of national identity much further.

Breaker Morant is one of the most complete and satisfying films of the Australian film revival. It is an excellent work of cinema. And, perhaps as importantly, it is uniquely Australian in its thematic concerns.

Break of Day | 1977

Director: Ken Hannam.
Producer: Patricia Lovell.
Screenplay: Cliff Green.
Director of Photography: Russell Boyd.
Editor: Max Lemon.
Production Designer: Wendy Dickson.
Music: George Dreyfus.
Sound: Don Connolly, Greg Bell.

Cast: Sara Kestelman (Alice); Andrew MacFarlane (Tom); Ingrid Mason (Beth); John Bell (Arthur); Tony Barry (Joe); Ben Gabriel (Evans); Eileen Chapman (Susan).
Production Company: Clare Beach Films.
Running Time: 97 minutes.

STORY

Returned wounded Anzac Tom Cooper finds life in a small town in the Australian bush difficult after World War I and becomes increasingly withdrawn. He meets Alice, a "bohemian" painter, and is fascinated by her sophistication and openness. Although Tom is already married, they become lovers. At the town's Anzac Day celebrations, Tom seems strangely remote and declines to reminisce with other returned soldiers. His affair with Alice leads to further estrangement from the townspeople. On the day of the annual picnic and cricket match, Tom, at first separate from the townspeople, joins with them to help win the cricket match, which ends in a brawl. Later, drunk, he relives the trauma of the landing at Gallipoli, where he shot himself in the foot. He returns home and later, reconciled with his wife and new child, watches Alice leave town.

COMMENT

Even a brief summary makes it sounds as if there is rather more to *Break of Day* than there actually is. It must be admitted that, at the time the film was written and produced, film production in Australia was reveling in the reflected glory of its first international recognition but was still taking uneasy steps toward a fully competent industry. Many of this film's faults might be put down to immaturity—despite the previous involvement of producer, director, and writer, separately, in two of the most critically successful films to that time (*Sunday Too Far Away* and *Picnic at Hanging Rock*).

As a story of illicit love, it lacks passion. While Tom may be handsome enough to attract Alice's sexual attention, he lacks any indication of fire or emotion. This is, it is true, a traditional image of the Australian male; the New Australian Cinema has few instances of fiery lovers among its heroes. While Alice may be sufficiently fascinating (as a reasonably liberated woman—for the times), it is difficult to see why Tom is attracted to her except as a more exciting alternative to his mousy, almost personalityless wife and his dull bourgeois existence.

It may be that the sheer tedium of small-town existence has worn Tom down to a state of passive acceptance. While on one hand small country towns are the last resting place of "true" Australian virtues, they are usually and contradictorily presented negatively—as boring, conservative, hidebound, behind the times. This one is no different— yet the film directs us to approve of Tom's decision to stay.

Alternatively, Tom's impassivity may be explained by the dread secret that he carries with him. But the secret, when revealed, for all its cultural reverberations (an Anzac who was a coward!) falls flat: it simply fails to carry the dramatic weight it has been given. (This imbalance between narrative enigma, the drama it carries, and its eventual revelation is also true of writer Cliff Green's next script, *Summerfield* [1977], also directed by Ken Hannam.)

Despite the film's constant reference to Anzacs—a statue of a soldier is raised as a memorial, an Anzac Day ceremony takes place, old soldiers reminisce in the pub, Tom has flashback memories of the landings—the discovery that, far from being a hero, Tom wounded himself to avoid fighting fails to shock. It does explain his self-imposed isolation from the rest of the people of the town and perhaps explains his general surliness. But since the film does not suggest that Tom is (or is thought to be) a hero, the revelation that he is not is hardly climactic and comes too late in the story to work as a useful (if overly obvious) piece of psychological insight. More to the point, Tom's curious (in the Australian context) disinclination to be a mate seems a more likely reason for his alienation. His status as a sort of inside-outsider is reduced by the arrival of the real outsiders, one of whom, in a telling sequence (a personal attack on Tom), assails the mateship/Anzac myth. This attack, however, lacks iconoclastic clout: Tom is already outside the cultural centrality offered by the myth and turns out not to be a "real" Anzac at all.

Nonetheless, even if Tom's status as a *true* Anzac is not the real issue in terms of narrative construction, the fact that he is or was an Anzac does provide the film with an opportunity to question the Anzac myth—whether it intends to or not. It does so in two ways: first, by the delayed revelation that Tom's injury is self-inflicted, and second, by the challenge flung out by the "citified" Arthur questioning Tom's assumption that he represents the true Anzac type and that Arthur by inference does not. Because of Tom's demonstrated cowardice (which remains his secret within the narrative), the challenge is not to the status of the "true" Australian but to his status as a warrior-hero. But by making Tom atypical—his outsider status in the community at large—*Break of Day* obfuscates the questioning of the myth. Also, Tom (comparable to Frank Dunne in *Gallipoli*) ultimately carries out an act of redemption on the playing field.

Even with this muted questioning of an essential Australian myth, *Break of Day* makes an interesting comparison with *Wake in Fright*. Both films exist to some extent as premature interrogations of Australian cultural mythology, in that later films such as *Gallipoli* were to offer uncritical views of that mythology as if for the first time.

As an examination of country life in rural Australia, albeit set in 1920, *Break of Day* demonstrates little more than tedium and petty-mindedness—although in this respect it is in keeping with quite a few recent films and reflects a cultural attitude toward small rural communities that is reiterated time and again in the Australian film.

Burke and Wills 1985

Director: Graeme Clifford.

Producer: Graeme Clifford, John Sexton.

Screenplay: Michael Thomas.

Director of Photography: Russell Boyd.

Editor: Tim Wellburn.

Production Design: Ross Major.

Music: Peter Sculthorpe.

Sound: Syd Butterworth.

Cast: Jack Thompson (Burke); Nigel Havers (Wills); Greta Scacchi (Julia); Matthew Fargher (King); Ralph Cotterill (Gray); Drew Forsythe (Brahe); Hugh Keays-Byrne (Kyte). Production Company: Hoyts/Edgley. Running Time: 140 minutes.

STORY

An expedition designed to cross Australia from south to north in 1860 led by Robert O'Hara Burke leaves Melbourne but moves so slowly that Burke is able to travel back to Melbourne to romance Julia Matthews and return unnoticed. Burke divides the party in the interest of speed at the edge of the desert and again at Cooper's Creek. With William Wills and two others, King and Gray, Burke sets out in a mad dash across the most inhospitable terrain to the sea. The terrible conditions encountered cause the small party to take longer than expected, and those waiting at Cooper's Creek leave—a few hours ahead of Burke, Wills, and King's return. Burke and Wills die in the desert. King is saved by aborigines and found by a rescue party months later.

COMMENT

The real star of *Burke and Wills* is, as Russell Boyd's widescreen panoramic and sensuously awesome cinematography demonstrates beyond debate, the Australian landscape. This film is the culmination, indeed the celebration, of a decade's obsession in Australian film with the bush. More than simply a panegyric to the unique photogenic (and thereby commercial) properties of the bush, *Burke and Wills* lays bare the very basic clay from which the concept of Australianness is formed: beneath all perceptions, images, and symbols of the bush is an atavistic fear, long forgotten in Europe and even in North America, of untrammeled nature. In Australia, the human obsession with controlling nature with culture collapses in the face of a nature that is perceived to be immutable.

There are three films of the New Australian Cinema that examine the bush in this way, as the central inspiring and structuring device in the narrative: *Picnic at Hanging Rock*, *Razorback*, and *Burke and Wills*. Each takes as a given the fundamental perception that the bush is inimical to the existence of white humans. *Burke and Wills*, for all its epic scale, is the one of the trio most concerned with the *reality* of the bush, in two ways. First, with the deliberate intention of outdoing all previous representations of the Australian landscape, this film is concerned with making full cinematic use of the awesome geography of Australia, in particular, the desert. Second, it demonstrates the reality of the destructive essence of the bush by showing men going to their death in, and largely because of, the bush itself. The extent to which ignorance and incompetence, greed and negligence, may have contributed to the deaths of Burke, Wills, and Gray, while given some importance (mainly through the parallel narrative of individuals in Melbourne), is rendered secondary through the dominance of the *mise-en-scène* by landscape. This understanding of the nature of the bush is given the stamp of authenticity by being based upon a historically documented set of actions and individuals.

Like *Picnic at Hanging Rock, Burke and Wills* takes the dominant naturalistic approach of the New Australian Cinema to the images of the bush, which seem to be as unmediated as the camera will allow. Even in this, certain culturally determined ways of seeing the bush affect the construction. Unlike *Picnic at Hanging Rock, Burke and Wills* imparts no spiritual or metaphysical quality to the bush and the sacrifice it extracts. The film is literal or, more accurately, it is completely constructed by the naturalized perceptions of what the bush is, what it looks like, and what it is capable of.

Several other aspects of *Burke and Wills* draw it toward a mythic centrality in the Australian context. The real Robert O'Hara Burke and William Wills, their activities and their fate, were the staple of Australian schoolbook history. Explorers have failed, however, to become convincing folk/cultural heroes, probably for the very reasons that *Burke and Wills* reveals: Burke and Wills were intruders and outsiders, both to the bush (which the myth insists all whites are) and also to Australia: one was Irish, the other English. They are mythic in the sense that they are examples of outsiders "who didn't know any better."

Burke and Wills reaches toward mythic centrality in another way, in that the protagonists fail in the face of the implacability of the Australian environment. Whether Burke and Wills can be counted as "dinkum Aussies" in any sense is immaterial in this perception. Australian narratives, particularly those of and in the bush, are narratives of defeat and failure. *Burke and Wills* makes full use of the epic qualities of a historical failure to create cinematic mythology. If the film does not succeed, it is less a failure to capture its material mythically than an inevitable failure to find adequate drama. The action fails to capture the imagination; the landscape cannot of itself carry the entire load. What is missing is any idea of mateship. In almost complete contrast to *Gallipoli,* wherein the mateship of Archy and Frank is forged in adversity (crossing an admittedly much smaller piece of desert), this film offers no such coming together of Burke and Wills or of other members of the expedition. This serves to enhance their status as outsiders; the failure to become mates is a failure to become "Australianized."

Despite the deprivation and terror (human and environmental) it depicts, *Burke and Wills* is the glossiest film of the New Australian Cinema to date. It attempts to raise the actions of the human participants to epic mythic level but reveals their inadequacy to support such a heavy cultural demand. The epic scale of the cinematography gives grandeur to the bush but reduces human beings to insignificant dots in the landscape.

Caddie 1976

Director: Donald Crombie.
Producer: Anthony Buckley.
Screenplay: Joan Long.
Director of Photography: Peter James.
Editor: Tim Wellburn.
Art Direction: Owen Williams.
Music: Peter Flynn.
Sound: Desmond Bone, Sara Bennett.

Cast: Helen Morse (Caddie); Takis Emmanuel (Peter); Jack Thompson (Ted); Jacki Weaver (Josie); Drew Forsythe (Sonny); Ron Blanchard (Bill); Melissa Jaffer (Leslie).
Production Company: Anthony Buckley Productions.
Running Time: 107 minutes.

STORY

Sydney, the 1920s: Mrs. Marsh takes her two small children and leaves her comfortable suburban home and philandering husband. Work is hard to obtain but she is eventually employed as a barmaid. She is given the name Caddie by Ted, a womanizing bookmaker. As the economic depression deepens, she loses her job and is forced to place her children in different homes. She is frequently out of work. A brief moment of happiness occurs after she meets Peter, a Greek immigrant with his own clothing business, but he is called back to Greece. Caddie rents a home and brings her children back to live with her, but the strain of making ends meet undermines her health. She is nursed by two brothers, Sonny and Bill. Things look up when another S.P. bookie takes Caddie on to collect bets on commission.

COMMENT

Caddie quickly achieved something akin to classic status upon its release in 1976, a status that has been confirmed since. This is only partly derived from the cinematic qualities of the film—although it "looks good" cinematographically, in strictly narrative terms, it is an episodic film that provides very little in the way of characterization beyond Caddie herself. More important in granting it classic standing, it was seen as a film that was essentially Australian and had most of the characteristics that were to become identified with popular and successful films in the first decade of the New Australian Cinema: period reconstruction, strong central character, nostalgia, "literariness" (it was based on an autobiography), and references to dominant cultural myths (in this case, the myth of the battler winning despite odds).

Caddie was an extremely timely production. It came immediately upon the heels of the two notable early successes of the New Australian Cinema, *Sunday Too Far Away* and *Picnic at Hanging Rock*. It was also a thoroughly competent piece of cinema, notable as such in light of the confident but frequently crude (in aesthetic and production terms) earlier films. And, of course, it was thoroughly Australian. *Caddie* was one of the films that demonstrated a certainty on the part of its makers that Australian material, settings, and mythology make good films.

The film's classic status is also due to its being one of the first films of the New Australian Cinema to offer a strong female protagonist. Despite the apparently masculine ethos of Australian culture, Australian narratives (both literary and cinematic) are by no means as patriarchal as, say, American narratives. In the Australian cinema, female protagonists are easily the equal of male protagonists (although this equality is demonstrated in separate narratives). *Caddie* was the first film really to provide such a narrative and may be said to offer a pattern for many of the films that followed.

In so doing, *Caddie* did not challenge prevailing cultural assumptions. Caddie herself is a "woman of the city": her existence, her narrative journey, her dramatic conflicts are all placed within its environment. As such, she does not present a direct challenge to masculine images of Australia, which are nearly always constructed within the setting of the bush. Like the hero/heroines of nearly all Australian cinematic narratives, Caddie is in conflict with the conditions of her existence. She is not in conflict with men or indeed in conflict with a totally male-dominated society. Many of the dramatic conflicts in the narrative are between Caddie and other women. Men are sometimes helpful, sometimes chauvinistic, but so are women. For every man who calls Caddie "just a bloody barmaid," there is a woman who says the same thing. Egalitarianism takes a few knocks along the way.

What aids *Caddie* in its classic status is the way in which the narrative structures itself around the battle for survival against conditions that are largely beyond the control (and frequently beyond the comprehension) of the protagonist. Such conditions allow the emergence of qualities that are considered to be typically Australian: mateship/fellowship, humor in adversity, tenaciousness, and so forth. The mythic significance of the battle for survival (usually at its most obvious in the setting of the bush) is why so few Australian films deal with the matter of personal relationships—or even bother with them. Australian films, by and large, are uneasy with personal relationships, with internally rather than externally imposed conflict. *Caddie* is no different in this.

Caddie also started, or at least continued, the vogue for period reconstruction in the New Australian Cinema. At the time, this seemed exciting; in later viewings, the plethora of period touches, particularly the endless stream of vintage cars, horse-drawn vehicles, and trams, seem a little wearying. Unlike some later films, however, *Caddie* carries its period with integrity—and this is not justified simply by being based on actual biography and historical events; it helps structure the narrative.

As with many classics (be they film or any other cultural artifacts), taken in isolation and objectively, it is not always apparent why this film should be accorded that status. *Caddie*, for all its intrinsic interest and value as a film, is perhaps more important for the way in which it encapsulates most of the concerns of the New Australian Cinema as they were to be revealed in the films that followed in the next four years.

Careful, He Might Hear You 1984

Director: Carl Schultz.

Producer: Jill Robb.

Screenplay: Michael Jenkins.

Director of Photography: John Seale.

Editor: Richard Francis-Bruce.

Production Designer: John Stoddart.

Music: Ray Cook.

Sound: Syd Butterworth.

Cast: Wendy Hughes (Vanessa); Robyn Nevin (Lila); Nicholas Gledhill (PS); John Hargreaves (Logan); Peter Whitford (George); Geraldine Turner (Vere); Isabelle Anderson (Agnes).

Production Company: Syme International.

Running Time: 110 minutes.

STORY

Sydney, the 1920s: six-year-old PS's life with his Aunt Lila and Uncle George is disrupted by the return from England of Vanessa, Lila's sister. As joint guardian of PS, Vanessa now wishes to claim him. PS does not want to live with Vanessa, but her wealth and self-confidence wear down the asthmatic Lila. Vanessa's plans to get PS's father, Logan, to agree to her adopting PS fail when Logan meets the boy but refuses to agree. Vanessa successfully petitions the courts for full-time guardianship. PS makes life miserable for Vanessa and she eventually recognizes she cannot buy his affection. On her way to tell Lila that she is giving up PS, Vanessa drowns in a ferry accident. PS demands to know his real name. It is William, and he insists that he be called Bill in the future.

COMMENT

On the face of it, *Careful, He Might Hear You* seemed a new departure for the New Australian Cinema. "Tearjerkers" or highly emotionally charged melodramas are rather rare in recent Australian production, although there were a few under the 10BA conditions. In keeping with their cultural perceptions, Australians make tough films about tough people. Films that deliberately "tug at the heart strings," especially ones that use children as their emotion-releasing focuses, are few and far between—and where they do exist have seldom been particularly successful.

The unabashed paperback romanticism of *Winds of Jarrah* (1983) and

Careful, He Might Hear You. National Film and Sound Archive/Syme International
Productions.

The Umbrella Woman (1988) may imply the possibility of a change of
attitude; but the cultural image of Australia as a land and a society that
has no time and no place for sentimentality is perhaps too deeply
entrenched to permit a sustained radical departure. Insensitivity, fre-

quently disguised as crudity or vulgarity, is a cultural trait. *Careful, He Might Hear You* succeeds in challenging this because it is an exceptionally well-made film and, equally importantly, because it operates within culturally acceptable perceptions that are familiar and mythologically significant.

While appearing to be a departure, the narrative of *Careful, He Might Hear You* is actually constructed around three recurring themes of the New Australian Cinema: growing up, loss of innocence, and the search for identity. *Careful, He Might Hear You* utilizes the theme of growing up a little differently from other comparable films: its protagonist is only six years old, whereas most of the others are adolescents bordering on adulthood. But PS has little in common with other child-heroes such as Ginger Meggs or Fatty Finn—who are really adults in the guise of children. That is, they are considerably wiser and more capable than the adults in their world. PS is and remains a child.

The idea of loss of innocence (or in some cases, the threat to the retention of innocence) is explored directly or peripherally in so many productions as to make it arguably the dominant cultural theme of the New Australian Cinema and the dominant theme of Australian culture. The idea of innocence is central to the polar opposition of bush and city. But the notion of innocent/corrupted is also structured around an antinomy of Australia/Europe (new culture/old culture), and this opposition strongly informs much of the narrative structure of *Careful, He Might Hear You*—although the loss of innocence in the film is not closely connected with the presence of this dichotomy within the narrative. The loss of innocence is individual and not metonymic. It is the narrative journey of the protagonist, PS.

There can be no doubt that PS's personal history involves a loss of innocence, for he has not only to defy Vanessa's plans for him but also to suggest a degree of independence from the loving but oppressive Lila and George. This rebellion is narratively located in PS's search for identity—another obsessive Australian concern. But the need to discover his identity only comes late in his personal history. It does, however, bring the film thematically full circle. The discovery of his identity (his real name, Bill) is confirmation of his starting to grow not so much *up* as *away*.

It is ironic that it is Vanessa who "bequeaths" him the determination to discover who he is. First, Vanessa has been cast throughout in the

role of the villain (the wicked witch). Here the film touches upon the
Australia/Europe opposition; more specifically, this opposition is basically anti-English. Vanessa, although Australian, has been anglicized.
This is as great a sin as her wealth. Whatever her intentions and
motives (which are never fully revealed) she has many counts against
her, but the desire to take PS to England is the most damning. Second,
it is ironic that Vanessa should point the way to his independence
because, despite the fact that PS's life is dominated by females, it is
Logan, his father, who has the most effect. Logan is a transitory and
ineffectual figure, yet it is his exhortation to PS not to do anything he
doesn't want to do that leads to PS's first loss of innocence—his rebellion against these women who threaten to tear him apart. This
advice from Logan is very much within the Australian cultural myth of
"manly independence"; and although Logan is a worthless drifter and
drunkard (not necessarily conditions for cultural disapprobation in the
Australian ethos), he is by far the most significant figure in PS's growing up. George, the only other male figure of any importance in PS's
life, is shown to be especially powerless.

Few films of the New Australian Cinema show such a complete
integration of Australian cultural perceptions (and obsessions) into a
structured narrative: they exist as unspoken cultural foundations upon
which the superstructure of the film is built.

The Cars That Ate Paris 1974

Director: Peter Weir.
Producer: Hal McElroy, Jim McElroy.
Screenplay: Peter Weir, Keith Gow, Piers
  Davies.
Director of Photography: John McLean.
Editor: Wayne Le Clos.
Art Director: David Copping.
Music: Bruce Smeaton.

Sound: Michael Midlam, Ken Hammond.
Cast: Terry Camilleri (Arthur); John
  Meillon (Mayor); Melissa Jaffer (Beth);
  Kevin Miles (Doctor); Max Gillies
  (Metcalf); Bruce Spence (Charlie);
  Chris Haywood (Darryl).
Production Company: Salt Pan Films.
Running Time: 91 minutes.

STORY

Arthur and George Waldo are involved in a horrendous car accident
close to the small township of Paris. George is killed. Arthur's fear of

driving becomes overpowering and he is unable to leave Paris when given the opportunity to drive away. He is "adopted" by the mayor. He learns that the town lives by deliberately wrecking cars and scavenging the wrecks. Survivors are handed over to the local doctor for "medical" experiments. Arthur is made parking inspector, a position that furthers the antagonism between the elders and the young people. The conflict comes to a head on the night of the Pioneers' Ball. A battle is waged between the youth and the older townsfolk, during which Arthur finds the will to drive again. The wrecked town is abandoned and Arthur drives out past the fleeing survivors.

COMMENT

For all its interest in the macabre and the inexplicable, *The Cars That Ate Paris* is atypical of Peter Weir's output. Two elements absent from Weir's other films, comedy (as distinct from humor) and parody, are dominant in this film. The comedy is distinctly black for the most part—and thus quite different from the ocker humor of *Gallipoli,* which is derived from writer David Williamson's insightful creation of the essential Australian character. The use of black comedy in *The Cars That Ate Paris* undermines the menace of the quite horrific situation of the narrative. On the other hand, menace is quite clearly a Weir trademark, one that is dominant in *Picnic at Hanging Rock, The Last Wave, The Plumber,* and even Weir's 1985 American feature, *Witness.*

The combination of black comedy and a self-reflexive consciousness of cinematic aesthetics in *The Cars That Ate Paris* tends to suggest a lack of certainty on Weir's part, a sense that he was unable to commit himself fully to a film that directly challenged a number of cherished Australian cultural perceptions: one, old and established—the bush/ small country town as the repository of all that is good, moral, life-confirming (especially as opposed to the city)—and one more recent— the Australians' materialistic love affair with the motor car. Weir was probably right in this tentativeness. As the films of the New Australian Cinema were to demonstrate (and Weir himself was to confirm with *Gallipoli*), Australia was in a mood in the late 1970s for confirming rather than questioning its cultural mythology. Although *The Cars That Ate Paris* was a sugar-coated pill, its box-office failure may have been because its sugar coating was not thick enough.

On the other hand, there is a narrative confusion that threatens the diegesis of *The Cars That Ate Paris.* The sense of indefinable malevolence that is the linchpin of later films by Weir runs foul of the lightness of tone of this film—its *mise-en-scène,* with the exception of the final sequences of destruction, is nearly always in bright sunlight. The feeling of menace that can still be wrought despite (or perhaps because of) this sunlight that *Picnic at Hanging Rock* demonstrated is not present here. As a view of the hidden horrors of remote and small-town existence, *The Cars That Ate Paris* is comparable with *Wake in Fright;* but where *Wake in Fright* reveals men and women who are totally brutalized or, at best, dehumanized by living in such a community, *The Cars That Ate Paris* does not go quite that far. The inhabitants of Paris may seem sinister and the manner of their economic existence may seem barbarous, but they themselves are not barbarian.

The narrative stability of *The Cars That Ate Paris* is also affected (as in *The Last Wave*) by consisting of two strong plot strands that compete with each other while seeming to be complementary. The "secret" of Paris—its communal survival built upon car-wrecking and the corollary of the doctor's Frankensteinian medical experiments—offers one strong narrative. But so does the narrative conflict between the generations that is simmering within Paris's tiny confines and explodes into the apocalyptic climax. Each of these narratives is only slightly connected with the other, so the film seems ultimately to fall into two parts; although the climax can be seen to be intellectually appropriate, it seems somewhat arbitrary narratively.

The view of small-town Australia in this film is not unique in the New Australian Cinema, which is slightly schizophrenic about small towns. Films like *The Cars That Ate Paris* and *Wake in Fright* with their far from flattering, indeed quite horrific, views of life in remote communities are balanced by more romantic views offered by *The Irishman* or *The Mango Tree.* Towns, as cultural transition points between the bush and the city (polar opposites in the dominant Australian mythology) are bound to produce conflicting cultural perceptions. Small towns seldom become metaphors or metonyms for either the bush or the city; they are usually given narrative positions of their own, and this is true of *The Cars That Ate Paris.* Paris itself may live by preying upon outsiders (presumably city folk), but it seems to be totally self-contained (despite the implications that Arthur Waldo's power in the community comes from the fear that he may go outside to report what he knows). If metaphoric status can be granted to this film, it is arguable that Paris is a metaphor for Australia itself—especially in its insularity, its insistence on community consensus, and its dependence upon the (feared) outside for its economic well-being.

Cathy's Child 1979

Director: Don Crombie.

Producer: Errol Sullivan, Pom Oliver.

Screenplay: Ken Quinnell.

Director of Photography: Gary Hansen.

Editor: Tim Wellburn.

Art Director: Ross Major.

Music: William Motzing.

Sound: Tim Lloyd.

Cast: Michelle Fawdon (Cathy Baikas); Alan Cassell (Dick Wordley); Bryan Brown (Paul Nicholson); Willie Fennell (Consul); Arthur Dignam (Minister).

Production Company: C. B. Films.

Running Time: 90 minutes.

STORY

Cathy Baikas, the Maltese-born wife of a Greek immigrant, comes to *The Sun,* a newspaper in Sydney, to ask for help in getting back her small daughter who has been taken out of Australia by her estranged husband. Dick Wordley, a journalist on the "Hotline" column of the paper, reluctantly takes up Cathy's case. Impressed with Cathy's courage and determination, Wordley pursues leads and hints beyond the value of the story as news. Despite the fact that a number of laws have been broken by Cathy's husband in leaving with the child, the government seems unable to act. At last, learning where the child is, Cathy manages to get to Greece and, with the help of her husband's family and the Australian consul, regains her child and returns to Sydney.

COMMENT

Despite the male orientation of *The Irishman,* Donald Crombie's reputation in the New Australian Cinema is very much that of what would have been known as a "woman's director" in the Hollywood of the 1940s. His first success as a commercial feature film director was *Caddie;* he subsequently made *Cathy's Child, The Killing of Angel Street,* and *Kitty and the Bagman.* Not only does each of these films feature a woman as a central character, but two (*Caddie* and *Cathy's Child*) are based upon fact, and *The Killing of Angel Street* is based, albeit loosely, upon incidents taken from life. The same is claimed, less convincingly, for *Kitty and the Bagman*. More than this, each film offers a narrative that has a woman protagonist forced to face circumstances and events initially beyond her control (or seemingly so), thus having to draw upon hidden reserves of strength. Not that these films are feminist texts—or not completely so. Although all the women concerned go through a process of growth and maturity—particularly marked in the case of Cathy Baikas—they do not do so in spite of men. In nearly every instance they are both hindered and helped by men. There is, however, a sense in which each of these individual women establishes a more defined place in society for herself.

Comparisons between *Cathy's Child* and *Caddie* are perhaps inevitable. Certain circumstances of both characters and events are very similar. Both Cathy and Caddie are mothers struggling to bring up their children by themselves. Both are initially uncertain but go through a journey of discovery, of themselves and of the world outside. Both films contain a clash of Australian and Greek cultures—central to *Cathy's Child*. These cultural clashes or, perhaps more fairly, cultural meetings are largely depicted in family terms—attitudes toward as well as responsibilities and duties of the family.

One of the most significant social features of post–World War II Australia has been the degree of non-English-speaking immigration. The New Australian Cinema has not explored themes arising from this to any great extent but has expended quite a bit of its energy in interpreting and reiterating the dominant myths of its culture—which may in itself be seen as an ideologically determined response to a population that is not as culturally familiar with these myths as a fully native-born one might be. The particular situation of immigrants in Australia (other than English immigrants, who are a special case) has, however, been explored in *Moving Out, Kostas* (released almost simultaneously with *Cathy's Child*), *Silver City,* and *Promised Woman* (1975).

Cathy's Child differs from these other films in that it does not center its narrative on the problematic of assimilation or upon the difficulties caused by the clash of the old (alien) culture with the new (Australian) culture. It does, however, offer insight into the social reality of the questions of nationality, citizenship, and loyalty that a multiracial society raises. Cathy is herself Maltese and thus a British subject; her husband is a naturalized Australian but clearly both considers himself and is considered by the Greek government to be Greek. The children are, legally at least, Australian. The film reveals without emphasis or particularly overt comment the almost parallel worlds of the "native" Australian (represented by Wordley and the newspaper office in general) and the "new" Australian (the Greek and Italian subculture that seems to exist within its own rules).

Unlike *Kostas* or *Moving Out*, *Cathy's Child* is not primarily a documentation of the immigrant experience in Australia. Its story is a more basic human interest story that, while based upon an actual incident, takes on something of the crusading newspaper genre formula in its structure. Although there is a strong sense that Cathy becomes more Australian— changing from a timid if determined outsider at the beginning to a confident, tough, and optimistic "Aussie battler" by the conclusion— this is not the film's basic narrative premise.

Like so many Australian productions, *Cathy's Child* is a film that is thematically concerned with a seemingly helpless individual's battle against apparently overwhelming odds. This film is not unusual in that it has a central protagonist who is a woman or that it is basically a "city" film. It is a little unusual in that it is contemporary in setting (although in the context of a narrative featuring a female protagonist this is not remarkable), but it stands apart in that it allows the female protagonist a final and unambiguous success. *Caddie*, by comparison, offers no such certainty even if it does confirm hope and a certain sense of optimism. *Cathy's Child* deserves to be better known than it is.

The Chain Reaction 1980

Director: Ian Barry.
Producer: David Elfick.
Screenplay: Ian Barry.
Director of Photography: Russell Boyd.
Editor: Tim Welburn.
Art Direction: Graham Walker.
Music: Andrew Thomas Witton.
Sound: Lloyd Carrick.
Cast: Steve Bisley (Larry); Arna-Maria Winchester (Carmen); Ross Thompson (Heinrich); Ralph Cotterill (Gray); Hugh Keays-Byrne (Eagle); Richard Moir (Piggott); Patrick Ward (Oates).
Production Company: Palm Beach Pictures.
Running Time: 92 minutes.

STORY

During an earthquake, Heinrich, a scientist at the WALDO radioactive waste refinery, is fatally contaminated attempting to prevent a spill. Learning that the multinational company's bosses are planning a cover-up, the dying Heinrich escapes from the establishment and flees as far as the isolated Paradise Valley. Larry, an ex–racing driver, and his wife Carmen, spending a weekend in a cottage at Paradise Valley, find and look after Heinrich. They too become contaminated from the radioactive waters of the river into which the spill has seeped. A team from WALDO, headed by the sinister Gray, tries to prevent Heinrich from contacting the outside world. Heinrich dies, but despite Gray's murderous efforts the news media are successfully alerted by Larry.

COMMENT

It is arguable that the years 1979–1982 were the most fertile in the New Australian Cinema to date—not in terms of the number of films produced but in terms of the variety of material and the sheer exuberance of many of the productions. The rather tentative beginnings of the New Australian Cinema were over and a period that history may well decide is notable only for its lack of truly memorable films was just around the corner.

The Chain Reaction is an excellent example of the films of the 1979–1982 period precisely because it was not a prestige production (or a period piece) along the lines of Gallipoli or Breaker Morant. It might, in the context of another national film industry, be considered to be a run-of-the-mill production. Apparently costing less than half a million Australian dollars to make, The Chain Reaction demonstrates the enthusiasm of its makers—an enthusiasm for making films rather than simply making money (or writing it off for tax purposes as the late abuses of the 10BA system permitted the unscrupulous to do).

It is perhaps inevitable that The Chain Reaction should be compared with Mad Max. Certainly, this film features a number of actors who also had prominent roles in Mad Max, and Mad Max's director, George Miller, is credited as associate producer and supervised the shooting of the two spectacular car chase sequences. Although an action film, and a very good one, The Chain Reaction is a film with a message as well.

The future, especially a nuclear future (or rather nuclear nonfuture), has not received much attention in the New Australian Cinema—unsurprisingly, perhaps, given its tendency to overemphasize the past. *One Night Stand* is the only other film that contemplates the consequences of nuclear madness for Australia, but it does so in terms of nuclear war. *The Chain Reaction* is concerned with the so-called peaceful use of nuclear energy and the very real dangers that waste products offer to the present and the future. This has some topicality, but nuclear energy is not used in Australia for the production of electricity; although there is talk of refining uranium prior to export, this does not yet take place. To this extent, then, *The Chain Reaction* is fantasy or, if it is addressing or utilizing matters of some actuality, the Australian setting is irrelevant. (It is explained by suggesting that WALDO recycles nuclear waste in secret.)

The Chain Reaction is no illustrated lecture; it is not even explanatory or informative in the way of, say, *The China Syndrome* (USA, 1979). Instead, it allows the results to speak for themselves—at least as manifest through the rapid deterioration of Heinrich and thus the presumed fate of Carmen and Larry as well. In a way, *The Chain Reaction* is comparable with a later American film, *Silkwood* (USA, 1983): it shows both the effect of radiation poisoning and, more significantly, the consequent attempts to cover up and deny those effects by those who derive economic advantage from the use of nuclear products.

While staying within the parameters of the recognizable formula of an action film, *The Chain Reaction* manages to combine action with message extremely well. The nightmare quality of the film is due to the consequences of nuclear accident and attempted coverup, and that point is never permitted to be lost sight of throughout. Like the later *One Night Stand*, although in a totally different context, the narrative of *The Chain Reaction* depends upon ordinary (and ignorant) people slowly becoming aware of the consequences, in first a personal then a global way, of nuclear madness. Like the four young people in *One Night Stand*, the innocent bystanders of this film are powerless to deal with the nuclear threat. But, unlike the people in the later film, they are capable of fighting back against those who would not even permit them to protest their own destruction. This provides the basic excitement of this action-packed film—but also its final irony: escape from "Pluto's men" (as the minions of WALDO are called) may permit exposure of the coverup and announcement of the danger to the outside world, but Larry and Carmen are already doomed by the radiation within them.

The Chant of Jimmie Blacksmith 1978

Director: Fred Schepisi.

Producer: Fred Schepisi.

Screenplay: Fred Schepisi, from the novel by Thomas Keneally.

Director of Photography: Ian Baker.

Editor: Brian Kavanagh.

Production Designer: Wendy Dickson.

Music: Bruce Smeaton.

Sound: Bob Allen.

Cast: Tommy Lewis (Jimmy); Freddy Reynolds (Mort); Ray Barrett (Farrell); Jack Thompson (Neville); Angela Punch (Gilda); Steve Dodds (Tabidgi); Peter Carroll (McCready); Don Crosby (Newby).

Production Company: The Film House.

Running Time: 124 minutes.

STORY

Jimmie Blacksmith, a half-caste aboriginal, is torn between the black world of his mother's family and the white world of the Reverend Neville. Jimmie finds that the only work he can get is building fences for farmers—who then cheat him on the price. He marries a dimwitted white girl, Gilda, believing her to be pregnant with his child. While he is working for the Newby family, the racist Newby women try to disrupt his marriage. Jimmie's pent-up frustration explodes and with his uncle Tabidgi, Jimmie attacks and kills the Newby women and their governess. Jimmie and his brother Mort go on the run from the police posse, taking as hostage a local schoolteacher, McCready. McCready talks Jimmie into leaving Mort, but Mort is killed taking the sick McCready to a settlement. Jimmie is wounded and then captured.

COMMENT

The Chant of Jimmie Blacksmith is a sprawling, complex, and ultimately overambitious epic film. The most expensive film of the New Australian Cinema at the time (though still made very cheaply at $A1.2 million), the film broke the bonds of genteel period reconstruction that had characterized the New Australian Cinema to that time.

The Chant of Jimmie Blacksmith. National Film and Sound Archive/Fred Schepisi.

The Chant of Jimmie Blacksmith deals with an important but seldom discussed aspect of Australian history: the relationship of the European to the aboriginal. Few films of the New Australian Cinema even recognize the existence of aboriginals, let alone treat them as a social topic. This film chooses to do so through the narrative device of a central character who is placed in the crux of the opposition black/white (by being half-caste) and is thus caught between two mutually noncomprehending cultures. This cultural alienation is superbly captured in the opening sequences, where Jimmie's aboriginal initiation rituals are contrasted with the Reverend Neville's condescending patronage.

The problem of the development of this theme is that, beyond the few scenes in which Jimmie lives with the Nevilles, it is clear both to Jimmie and to the audience that he can never be, by his own or by others' (black or white) perceptions, anything other than aboriginal. The destruction of the false hope of passage into the dominant white culture that has been engendered by Neville provides only part of the reason for Jimmie's homicidal passion. The rest is simply because Jimmie is an individual who is wronged, oppressed, patronized, cheated, and disregarded irrespective of his parentage. The two themes are indivisibly bound but occasionally confused.

It must nonetheless be recognized that, in keeping with so many films of the New Australian Cinema, *The Chant of Jimmie Blacksmith* is an aesthetically visual film. But, more than many of its contemporary films, it combines its impressive cinematography of the Australian landscape (frequently seen in mist and early morning haze) with thematic intent. This is especially so in the isolation of (aboriginal) character in the landscape contrasted with the cluttered, claustrophobic, and sterile interiors of whites' homes and buildings.

Schepisi's script has a tendency to pontificate occasionally but also has many moments of remarkable and simple lucidity—such as Tabidgi's statement to the court after being found guilty of murder. Overall, *The Chant of Jimmie Blacksmith* is a rather extraordinary mixture of sledge-hammer didacticism and kid-glove observation and understatement, a mixture that makes the film both demanding and disappointing.

It is not unreasonable, then, to suggest that the film was ill-timed in the sense of being premature: the New Australian Cinema (and by extension Australian audiences still coming to terms with seeing their own films) was not ready for a film that was clearly so bitter and recriminatory about Australia's past (especially when set at the culturally sensitive historical moment of federation in 1901). It was also ill-timed in that it misjudged the cultural revival that was gaining strength in Australia: the time was not yet ripe to suggest that something was rotten at the core of Australian society when that core itself still needed to be rediscovered.

By contrast, a film like *My Brilliant Career,* released a year later, was clearly more in tune with contemporary perceptions, and a film like *Breaker Morant,* two years later, could reflect bitterness and betrayal in its narrative and its themes far better because it was (white) Australians being betrayed by outsiders. In the dominant ideological perceptions, Jimmie Blacksmith was an outsider; no matter how much sympathy his plight engendered, and how justified his actions, cultural perceptions beyond the diegesis of *The Chant of Jimmie Blacksmith* controlled how the character of Jimmie would be received.

If this film had been made in the 1980s, when the novelty of seeing Australia on the screen had worn off, when more experience and maturity had been achieved in film production, and when greater demands for integrity rather than simply representation were made of the New Australian Cinema, *The Chant of Jimmie Blacksmith* might have proved to have been a film as important as *Breaker Morant, My Brilliant Career,* and *Gallipoli* in speaking to Australians, meaningfully and significantly, of themselves. As it is, it is a film that is important but fails to impress its importance on the audience—or, indeed, upon subsequent filmmakers. The theme of aboriginal cultural existence within the greater context of Australian culture has not provided the inspiration for more than a handful of films: *The Last Wave* two years before this film; *The Wrong Side of the Road* (1981), *Short Changed* (1986), *The Fringe Dwellers* and (perhaps) *Manganinnie.*

The City's Edge 1983

Director: Ken Quinnell.

Producer: Pom Oliver, Errol Sullivan.

Screenplay: Robert J. Merritt, Ken Quinnell.

Director of Photography: Louis Irving.

Editor: Gregory Robert.

Art Director: Robert Dein.

Music: Chris Neal.

Sound: Noel Quinn.

Cast: Tommy Lewis (Jack); Hugo Weaving (Andy); Katrina Foster (Laura); Mark Lee (Jim); Ralph Cotterill (Horrie); Martin Harris (Webster); Fredric Abbott (Lloyd).

Production Company: CB Films.

Running Time: 90 minutes.

STORY

Andy White arrives in Sydney from the country and finds rooms at a rundown house in an outer beach suburb. He quickly meets the other inhabitants: the vaguely threatening aboriginal Jack; the drug addict Jim; the bitter cripple Horrie. Andy meets Jim's sister Laura and they become lovers. Laura's neurotic behavior leads to their breaking up. After an evening drinking, Andy and Jack are attacked by thugs, one of whom is killed by Jack in self-defense. Andy attempts a reconciliation with Laura, and she admits her erratic behavior is a result of having an abortion at age sixteen and that the child was Jim's. Jim, hearing this for the first time, takes an overdose and is killed when he falls under a train. Jack returns to the boarding house and assumes the police are there for him. He is killed in a shootout with the police.

COMMENT

Life on the fringes of society has provided material for a number of productions of the New Australian Cinema. Most, however, have tended to fall within a category that has been labeled social realism: *Moving Out, Mouth to Mouth, Hard Knocks,* and so forth. The milieu of *The City's Edge* is the same as in these films; its particular mode, however, is melodrama. Realism extends no further than location and initial characterization. *The City's Edge* is not concerned, as are the films mentioned above, with documenting existence on the social fringe. It is a romantic narrative, a story of a love affair between two troubled people. A certain element of social comment does intrude through the character of the aboriginal, Jack Collins. This particular aspect of the film occasionally suggests a subplot or a subsidiary theme being explored. But if the Jack Collins character is intended to provide an examination of racial attitudes in Australia, then it lacks both clarity of focus and coherence.

Lack of coherence characterizes the entire film, which is not so much episodic as spasmodic. The greater part of the film relies upon an elliptical editing style and a faith in narrative ambiguity not merely to add tension but also to add depth or meaning. There is a structure of deliberate obscurity in the overall approach; dialogue sequences are frequently ambivalent or oblique. But to what purpose? All narratives, fictional or otherwise, are structured around unresolved but to-be-resolved enigmas, but a narrative that is totally enigmatic without concomitant resolution, or enigmatic simply for the sake of being so, is in some difficulties. Such a film defies audience anticipation and forces the audience at the same time to seek alternative meanings or thematic explanations—to ask, in other words, what the film is about. Narrative obscurity can also lead to thematic obscurity as well. But in *The City's Edge* the most real consequence of the ambiguity of action, character, and dialogue is only to disguise the lack of any other meaning. This is not a film with a discernible message—and certainly not with a message more important than its narrative.

The latter half of the film does fall into a much more usual cinematic narrative form. The fractured approach of the first half of the film cannot be maintained when the film actually has a continuous story to cope with. In retrospect, this tends to make the fragmented obliqueness of the earlier part seem not so much simply arbitrary as a deliberate attempt to disguise the paucity of the narrative material. But, given that the majority of the productions of the New Australian Cinema slavishly follow cinematic narrative traditions with continuity of action and character dominating aesthetics, *The City's Edge* at least offers a challenge to the "normal."

It is a little surprising, then, that the film was directed (and co-written) by Ken Quinnell, whose previous work included the script for *Cathy's Child,* a straightforward narrative film in the social realist tradition—although the realist/romantic unevenness of *Hoodwink* (also written by Quinnell) should have provided some hint to a potential for peripatetic directorial style. *The City's Edge,* despite its obvious location shooting, has a much more theatrical quality to it, most notably in the dialogue.

Overall, *The City's Edge*'s most conspicuous achievement is its unrelievedly negative view of urban life. This should perhaps not be surprising, given the dominant cultural mythology of Australia, emphasizing the bush over the city, which is almost always negatively perceived. But, although many films of the New Australian Cinema that have urban settings hardly paint a pretty picture, most do allow a certain grudging positive attitude. Protagonists of city narratives (often women) frequently achieve triumph over odds in ways that are seldom attained by protagonists (usually male) in bush narratives. Positive (happy) endings are more prevalent in city films. *The City's Edge* does not offer any such optimism; it is inescapably dark and pessimistic.

Yet it is also interesting because its protagonist is male. As other entries in these pages note, the usual protagonist of the city films is a woman (e.g., *Caddie, Cathy's Child, The Killing of Angel Street, Heatwave*). This may account for the downbeat ending—Australian narrative heroes are heroes in defeat. *The City's Edge,* however, is so confused and confusing a film that confident assertion about its meaning, even within the context of this approach, is at best provisional.

The Clinic 1984

Director: David Stevens.

Producer: Robert Le Tet, Bob Weis.

Screenplay: Greg Millin.

Director of Photography: Ian Baker.

Editor: Edward McQueen-Mason.

Production Designer: Tracy Watt.

Music: Redmond Symons.

Sound: John Rowley.

Cast: Chris Haywood (Eric); Simon
   Burke (Paul); Gerda Nicholson (Linda);
   Rona McCleod (Carol); Suzanne
   Roylance (Patty); Pat Evison (Helda).

Production Company: The Film House–
   Generation Films.

Running Time: 90 minutes.

STORY

Another ordinary day at a public VD clinic: Dr. Eric Linden arrives for work the worse for wear from the night before. An arrogant and homophobic medical student, Paul, is placed with Eric to observe. Dr. Carol Young is pregnant but has left her husband; he is trying to patch things up with endless roses. Organized chaos reigns as a steady stream of patients, new and regular, young and old, men and women, straight and gay, confused and confident, come in for treatment. Helda, the motherly counselor, tries to cope with people's ignorance about VD but is driven too far when one patient commits suicide after being fired from his job. Paul is at first disgusted when he learns that Eric is gay, but later comes to respect him and the work he does. A maniac leaves a bomb—which turns out to be a hoax. Patients and staff mingle on the footpath outside the clinic.

COMMENT

Sophistication is not a term that would usually be used in relation to Australian comedies. The New Australian Cinema commenced with broad, farcical, vulgar ocker comedy: *The Adventures of Barry McKenzie* (and its sequel), *Alvin Purple* (and its sequels), *Petersen*, and so forth. Despite (or perhaps because of) the much-vaunted (but nonetheless genuine) Australian sense of humor, full-fledged comedies have not proved to be a high proportion of the New Australian Cinema's output or to be among its most successful, noteworthy, or critically acclaimed productions—until *Crocodile Dundee*, of course. Even with this exception, it is still fair to say that some of the most ill-conceived and ill-executed films of the New Australian Cinema have been essays into the field of comedy. These infrequent and often failed comic films have for the most part retained the broad crudity of the ocker—indeed, ockerism provides humor in many films that are not comedies per se.

The Clinic is of a different order from most of the film comedies that have preceded it. It studiously avoids the possibility of vulgarity, which is even more remarkable given that its narrative is almost totally structured by the everyday activities of a VD clinic, offering innumerable possibilities for double entendre, scatological humor, and plain vulgarity. *The Clinic,* while remaining a very funny film, does not suggest that its subject matter, the treatment of venereal disease, is in itself a subject for comedy. It was produced before the even less amusing facts of AIDS became well known. The comedy arises from the multitude of characters who inhabit its narrative; the humor is related to situation, to action and reaction on a human level. If anything, the film may be said to have quite a serious intent, an educational role in teaching about venereal disease and its treatment.

Of considerable merit is the way in which the film has been constructed. Lacking a strong single narrative thread, it is linked by one or two consistent histories: Eric and the gradual revelation (for the audience) that he is gay; the enigma of Paul's reactions to events at the clinic; Dr. Young's pregnancy and the campaign of roses; and so on. But the film really consists of a series of vignettes, most of which are fragmented and scattered throughout the film's running time rather than presented one at a time. This provides the film with pace and interest. Pace is important: with the benefit of hindsight, it is possible to argue that the time-space continuum is not merely somewhat jumbled but in fact quite impossible. For all of that, it is undeniable that the film, in structure at least, frequently resembles a Direct Cinema documentary.

As well as offering a valuable and enlightening view of VD and its treatment, *The Clinic* also offers an extremely sympathetic (and equally enlightening) view of gay men. In a society as homophobic as Australia's—Australians, in cultural terms, are as aggressive toward gays as people anywhere in the Western world (witness the many jokes on the subject in the *Barry McKenzie* films)—*The Clinic* is quite a courageous production. Homosexuality is almost a taboo subject in Australian mythology because of the strength of the mateship ethos: denial of any sexual implications takes the ironic form of accusing of being "queer" anyone who does not conform to group norms. *The Clinic* offers a positive view of gay men through the character of Eric (the central character—if the film can be said to have one), through showing Paul's homophobia to be part of his bigotry, arrogance, and ignorance, and through several basically comic but unstereotyped characters. It goes almost without saying that gay men are few and far between in other films in the New Australian Cinema; when permitted an appearance, they are usually either threats to Australian manhood or stereotyped "raging queens."

The Clinic rushes in where angels fear to tread and creates both interest and comedy in two taboo areas: VD and homosexuality. It satirizes, although not with viciousness, both ignorance and prejudice on both these counts, and it sugars the pill with remarkable success. A problem with Australian comedy films has tended to be their self-consciousness, a sort of "look how funny we are being by poking fun at ourselves" attitude. *The Clinic* is almost totally devoid of this coyness. It is a delightful film that mixes humor with humanity without ever overreaching with the former or oversentimentalizing with the latter.

The Club 1980

Director: Bruce Beresford.
Producer: Matt Carroll.
Screenplay: David Williamson.
Director of Photography: Don McAlpine.
Editor: William Anderson.
Art Director: David Copping.
Music: Mike Brady.
Sound: Gary Wilkins.

Cast: Graham Kennedy (Ted); Jack Thompson (Laurie); Alan Cassell (Gerry); Frank Wilson (Jock); John Howard (Jeff).
Production Company: South Australian Film Corporation.
Running Time: 90 minutes.

STORY

Jeff Howard, a young champion footballer, is signed by Collingwood Football Club after holding out for more money. The difference is made up personally by club president Ted Parker. Jeff's presence is resented by the other footballers. At the same time, machiavellian machinations are taking place in the boardroom, where the club's administrator, Gerry, is conniving with vice-president Jock to oust Ted. In addition, the committee is planning to dispense with coach Laurie. Jeff's poor start to the season brings him into conflict with Laurie, who clashes with Ted. Ted is ousted after a trumped-up scandal; Laurie learns of the plans to get rid of him. Jeff determines to prove his status as a champion. To confound the committee, and especially Jock, the team members throw themselves into a desperate bid to get to and win the grand final—which they do.

COMMENT

Coming so soon after the popular and critical success of *Breaker Morant* (although principal cinematography was complete before *Breaker Morant* was released), *The Club* was bound to be seen as something of a potboiler for Beresford. In a sense, it is little more than a rendering of what is essentially a stage play into the medium of the cinema. Bruce Beresford once again displays his exceptional grasp of the demands of cinema as he succeeds in translating what is little more than a series of dialogue sequences (interspersed with brief scenes of football action) into something more like a film than a play. It must be admitted that at times this skill does falter, and Beresford is forced to use nearly every possible "setup" in the filmmaker's repertoire to add interest and variety to the ever-succeeding scenes of dialogue. That he has managed to do so is further tribute to his skills as a director.

The Club represents the fourth David Williamson play translated by him for the screen. Two, *Stork* (1971) and *The Removalists* (1975), are fairly disappointing; three, *Don's Party, The Club,* and *Travelling North,* are very good, with *Don's Party* bordering upon brilliance. *The Club* maintains Williamson's insightful examinations of Australian males (there are virtually no women at all in the film), particularly in groups— en masse they do not present a very attractive picture. *The Club* also reveals Williamson's ongoing love-hate relationship with the Australian male. His comedy, which is extremely funny, brings his characters close to caricature but never quite goes quite that far: even the most ridiculous or villainous of his characters do have some redeeming human characteristics.

The Club is well served by its cast—perhaps none better than Graham Kennedy (a popular local TV show host), who manages to combine to perfection the ludicrousness and almost pathetic devotion to the club that the character of Ted Parker requires. The others are just as good, and it is not inappropriate to mention that most of the footballers are just that, real-life footballers.

The Club is an examination of power (perhaps linking it slightly with *Breaker Morant*)—of duplicity in attaining and retaining that power. It is slightly nostalgic inasmuch as it examines an Australian Rules Football Club (an enormously popular semiprofessional game in the southern states) at a time when the game and its administration are passing out of the hands of those who are involved (as players or administrators) because they love the game (and the club) and into the hands of wealthy dilettantes and professional administrators. This undertone of regretted change places *The Club* in line with the nostalgic preoccupations in mainstream Australian cinema and reveals links with some of Williamson's other cinematic writing, particularly *Gallipoli*.

Overall, *The Club* is a highly amusing, highly entertaining piece of cinema. The emphasis on the game of Australian football itself is not overwhelming—which is just as well since it is not universally played in Australia and is totally unknown overseas. Enough actual games are shown to demonstrate football's exciting qualities and to break up the otherwise claustrophobic dialogue scenes. It is instructive to compare *The Club*'s attitude toward football to that of *Warming Up,* which utilizes football as a metonym for mindless machismo. *The Club* is rather more subtle or perhaps more ambivalent. While Jeff at one stage denounces the "macho bullshit" of football, and both players and administrators reveal the limited outlook and insensitivity of the "typical" Australian male, the film nonetheless firmly positions its audience to sympathize strongly with the players and coach and to share the winning orientation of the team. In this respect it shares a well-known formula with a long history of sporting films from many different cultures (up to and including the 1989 American film *Major League*).

But, perhaps most importantly, *The Club* is one of the few Australian films that both are contemporaneous in time and location and reveal a real insight into and understanding of the Australian character. This is not to say that the power struggle that provides the narrative structure is unknown in other countries (these themes appear in *The Natural*

[USA, 1984], as well as the aforementioned *The Major League*) or indeed other institutions than sporting clubs (boardrooms and bureaucracies); but the specific manner of the struggle and the particular nature of the personalities involved are irredeemably Australian.

The Coca-Cola Kid | 1985

Director: Dusan Makavejev.

Producer: David Roe.

Screenplay: Frank Moorhouse.

Director of Photography: Dean Semler.

Editor: John Scott.

Production Designer: Graham (Grace) Walker.

Music: William Motzing.

Sound: Mark Lewis.

Cast: Eric Roberts (Becker); Greta Scacchi (Terri); Bill Kerr (T. George); Chris Haywood (Kim); Max Gillies (Frank); Paul Chubb (Fred); Rebecca Smart (DMZ); Tim Finn (Philip).

Production Company: Grand Bay Films.

Running Time: 94 minutes.

STORY

Becker, whiz-kid American troubleshooter for the Coca-Cola Company, newly arrived in Australia, quickly discovers an area where no Coca-Cola whatever is sold. Traveling to Anderson Valley, Becker learns that T. George McDowell has run his own drink factory since the 1920s and has kept out all other drink companies. Becker plans to take over the stubborn McDowell and also searches for the "authentic" Australian sound for promotional purposes. He resists the sexual approaches of his secretary Terri (not knowing she is McDowell's daughter) and the entreaties of a revolutionary waiter convinced that Becker is with the CIA. Becker infiltrates Coca-Cola into Anderson Valley, causing McDowell to destroy his own factory. Shocked, Becker leaves Coca-Cola to move in with Terri and her daughter DMZ.

COMMENT

A number of the important films of the New Australian Cinema were adapted from recognized and well-known (in Australia) literary sources. Even so, there has not been a very strong degree of cross-fertilization between Australian literature and cinema. The only noted

The Coca-Cola Kid. Cinema Enterprises.

Australian authors who have written screenplays are the Nobel Prize winner Patrick White (*The Night the Prowler*), Thomas Keneally (*Silver City*), and Frank Moorhouse, who adapted his own material for *The Coca-Cola Kid* and wrote the screenplay for *Between Wars* (1974) and *The Ever-lasting Secret Family* (1988).

The Coca-Cola Kid is also a unique production in another way. A number of very early films of the New Australian Cinema were directed by foreign directors: *Walkabout* (Nicholas Roeg, British), *Wake in Fright* (Ted Kotcheff, Canadian), *Ned Kelly* (Tony Richardson, British, 1970). Nonetheless, the overwhelming tendency of the New Australian Cinema has been profoundly nationalistic. Not all directors of these films have been Australian born, but few have been imported to direct any specific project, and fewer still have brought international reputations. Dusan Makavejev is the exception. There seems little doubt that some of the conspicuous appearances of obvious Australian cultural symbols (kangaroos, didgeridoos, "Waltzing Matilda") in *The Coca-Cola Kid* are a direct consequence of the director's unfamiliarity with Australia or the effect of its novelty. *The Coca-Cola Kid* does not achieve quite the mirror of amazement that Roeg's *Walkabout* reflects, but its narrative is structured around a two-way clash of cultures, one internal to Australia and one external.

The Coca-Cola Kid is one of a relatively small number of significant Australian films that demonstrate an awareness of the world beyond the geographic and cultural borders of Australia; others include *The Year of Living Dangerously, Far East* (1982), even *Gallipoli*—the last, with *Breaker Morant,* demonstrating the dangers of that outside world. *The Coca-Cola Kid* does so without going outside those geographic borders. Like *Newsfront,* it brings the outside in. But even within its structure, the film points to a "true" Australia with Anderson Valley as its metaphor. It is Australia in mythic microcosm—remote, rugged yet beautiful, basically independent and self-sufficient, old-fashioned and (by American Standards) out-of-date, and, again by American standards, ripe for economic plundering. *The Coca-Cola Kid* posits a conflict between two cultures, Australian and American, presented in economic terms.

The film may not be anti-American in the usual sense but the implication is certainly that the Australian way of life (represented here by a rugged individualism and patriarchal but benevolent authoritarianism existing in a quintessential bush setting) is destroyed by America (in the guise of the Coca-Cola Company, which is constantly presented throughout the film as the equivalent, the liquid representation, of the American way of life). While the film does permit Australians themselves a role in the destruction, they are thoroughly identified with the city—business executives in glass skyscrapers, American in architectural inspiration. The powerful cultural polarity of bush/city is demonstrated yet again, this time in a film of more sensitivity, more sophistication, than is the norm for the New Australian Cinema. Cultural myths are buried deep in *The Coca-Cola Kid,* but the resonances are felt continually.

If films like *Gallipoli* and *Breaker Morant* (as prime examples) are concerned with excising from Australian cultural mythology any suggestion of a dependent relationship with England, then other films have suggested that familial relationships are being forged with the United States. *The Man from Snowy River, The Coca-Cola Kid,* and, to a lesser extent, *Undercover* are in the forefront of this movement. The Americanization of Australia that was hinted at (without enthusiasm but with a recognition of historical inevitability) in *Newsfront* is presented as problematic (as to what form it should take) in *The Man from Snowy River* and as a virtual fait accompli in *The Coca-Cola Kid*. Becker's conscience, awakened by his contact with Australia and its culture, may be pricked by what he has done; but in the larger sense, what is done is done. Anderson Valley, the last bastion of Australian economic independence, has been taken by storm. Becker himself may have been Australianized (though it is significant that his freedom is attained by American dollars, ironically supplied by an Australian revolutionary group), but Australia itself has been further Americanized. (A reaction against this Americanization may be detected in *Dead Calm* [1989], through the positing of the psychotic killer who threatens a nice Australian couple as American—for no good narrative reason.)

Crocodile Dundee 1986

Director: Peter Faiman.
Producer: John Cornell.
Screenplay: Paul Hogan, Ken Shadie.
Director of Photography: Russell Boyd.
Editor: David Stiven.
Production Designer: Graham Walker.
Music: Peter Best.
Sound: Gary Wilkins.

Cast: Paul Hogan ("Crocodile" Dundee);
Linda Kozlowski (Sue); John Meillon
(Wally); Mark Blum (Richard); David
Gulpilil (Neville).
Production Company: Rimfire
Productions.
Running Time: 102 minutes.

STORY

Sue Charlton, a reporter for the American magazine *Newsday*, travels to the Australian outback to do a story on Michael J. "Crocodile" Dundee, who, it is claimed, was savaged by a crocodile but managed to drag himself through hundreds of miles of bush to safety. After enduring some rough pub hospitality Sue goes off with Mick Dundee into the bush to retrace his steps. She is attracted to the laconic and unsophisticated Mick, especially after he saves her from a crocodile, and invites him back to New York. Mick's first experiences of a big city cause him a few problems; his bushman skills see him through. When Sue's boyfriend Richard publicly announces their engagement, Mick decides to go walkabout—to see America. Sue realizes that she loves Mick, and they are reconciled in a crowded subway station.

COMMENT

Crocodile Dundee is the most successful film of the New Australian Cinema and probably the most successful Australian film ever. An answer to the question "why?" can be only partly related to the film's quality; although it is a better-than-competent piece of cinema with a tighter, better-constructed script than many others, it is still at best only a good, workmanlike film. No doubt within Australia, and to a lesser extent outside Australia, part of the appeal (thanks to a series of commercials) is the appearance in the film of Paul Hogan. The main answer is to be found in two related aspects of the film. First, it is arguably the most Australian film of the New Australian Cinema—a bold claim given that two-thirds of its action takes place in Manhattan and that it is up against some stiff opposition for that title, especially from *Gallipoli*. Second, *Crocodile Dundee* wins audiences over by its very unpretentiousness. It is a simple film, almost naive, certainly unsophisticated in narrative, theme, and characterization. It is, in a very real sense of the word, charming.

As with many films, the Australianness of *Crocodile Dundee* is located firmly in two aspects of its filmic construction: landscape and character. The film continues the aestheticization of the Australian landscape familiar from the earliest productions of the film revival, which persists in the most recent. The outback section of the film, the first third of the narrative, while important for setting the character of Mick Dundee, is more significantly concerned with displaying the exotic beauty of the ancient landscape. As is so often the case, the landscape becomes another character in the narrative, but here it is neutral, even benign (crocodile attacks notwithstanding). Nonetheless, the Australian landscape retains its capacity to engage and occasionally even to startle its viewers. Its function is to provide an explanation for the characters located within it and the dramas in which they find themselves.

Mick Dundee is characterized in the film in two ways, which a familiarity with Australian cinema might lead one to suppose to be at first

mutually contradictory. The order of the construction of his characterization is important. On first meeting him, Mick is very much an ocker
within the prevailing Australian definition. He will retain those ocker
characteristics when he goes to New York. But they are quickly overlaid
by the more positive cultural attributes of the bushman. Mick Dundee
is the amalgam of both Archy (the bushman) and Frank (the lar-
rikin/ocker) in *Gallipoli*. In no other film, not even *Newsfront*, has there
been such a complete rendering of the character of the mythically
typical Australian. Despite Mick's bushman status, in *Crocodile Dundee*
we see the apotheosis of the ocker. No longer is he a figure who carries
a certain stigma of cultural embarrassment; by showing that the bushman and the ocker are not simply opposite sides of the same coin but
can actually be the same side, *Crocodile Dundee* reconciles two important
cultural perceptions of Australian identity—and implicitly recognizes
that the "pure" bushman image is an anachronistic one. By absorbing
the ocker, or being absorbed by him, the bushman is made culturally
contemporary. Mick Dundee's overseas journey parallels that taken
some fourteen years earlier by the quintessential (until Mick Dundee)
ocker, Barry McKenzie (in *The Adventures of Barry McKenzie*); but it also
differs in key aspects. The most significant difference is that Mick goes
to the United States; the gradual eclipse of the importance of England
in Australian cultural perceptions that many films have documented is
completed by *Crocodile Dundee*.

The most significant similarity is in the essential innocence, the
naiveté of Mick and Barry. Whereas Barry McKenzie is innocent to the
point of being almost moronic, Mick Dundee is much more a holy
innocent. The film rides, and rides successfully, a very fine line between
allowing Mick to appear dim and suggesting he is not quite as naive
as he appears. But it is inescapable that Mick Dundee and Barry
McKenzie share many narrative incidents in their Candide-style journey through essentially alien cultures. It is a lack of worldliness that
figures both these characters and at the same time gives them heroic
status in terms of Australian's perceptions of themselves.

After a number of years of loss of direction by the New Australian
Cinema, *Crocodile Dundee* proved that Australian film was on the right
track all the time with the nationalistic films of the late 1970s.

Dawn! 1979

Director: Ken Hannam.

Producer: Joy Cavill.

Screenplay: Joy Cavill.

Director of Photography: Russell Boyd.

Editor: Max Lemon.

Art Director: Ross Major.

Music: Michael Carlos.

Sound: Ken Hammond.

Cast: Bronwyn Mackay-Payne (Dawn); Tom Richards (Harry); John Diedrich (Gary); Bunny Brooke (Mother); Ron Haddrick (Father); Gabrielle Hartley (Kate); Kevin Wilson (Bippy).

Production Company: Aquataurus Film Productions.

Running Time: 115 minutes.

STORY

Dawn Fraser, working-class brat, is taken on by swimming coach Harry Gallagher and soon reveals her championship potential. She wins a gold medal at the 1956 Olympics in Melbourne. By the Rome Olympics in 1960, Dawn's rebelliousness is getting her into trouble with the Amateur Swimming Union, although she is one of Australia's most popular sports stars. Despite family tragedies, Dawn wins a third gold medal at the 1964 Tokyo Olympics, but is caught while trying to steal a flag from the Imperial Palace gardens. Dawn's marriage breaks up after her daughter is born. Her rebelliousness leads to her being banned from swimming competitively for ten years, effectively finishing her swimming career. After a series of love affairs, Dawn finds herself coaching back in the working-class milieu of Balmain.

COMMENT

Despite an Australian cultural obsession with sport, there are very few films of the New Australian Cinema that find subject matter in sport or in sportsmen/women. When one of the few films that does so is as bad as *Dawn!* this absence may be considered hardly surprising. *Dawn!* and *Phar Lap* (some four years later) are, at the level of basic story structure, remarkably similar. Both are variations of the Ugly Duckling/Cinderella tale. Both deal with that mythological perennial: the "little Aussie battler" (the battler in question is in fact physically quite big—"little" here refers to the relative social power of the figure). It seems not unreasonable to suggest that the only difference between the two films (other than the fact that the protagonist of one is human, of the other equine) is the competence and craftsmanship with which a basically conventionalized and formulaic narrative is handled. *Phar Lap* is well handled, competently made in nearly all aspects; *Dawn!* by nearly any standards (even permitting a certain charity toward the New Australian Cinema because it was new) seldom rises above the banal.

If it was not for the fact that *Dawn!* tells the story of one of Australia's most colorful sporting heroines—an individual whose very life exemplified (at least according to this film and popular reports of the time) the very myth of the rugged individualistic Australian battler—male or female—this film might best be avoided.

Because Dawn Fraser's life *did* indeed appear to offer a real-life demonstration of the validity of the Australian mythos—the determinedly independent individual who battles and succeeds for a time against the entrenched forces of the ruling classes (personified here, as in *Phar Lap,* as the committee governing the particular sport)—*Dawn!* cannot simply be ignored.

The conception of the life of Dawn Fraser as the subject for a feature film seems, of itself, an attractive one, although it raises the intriguing question of the possibility that soap opera (from which this film's narrative structure is undoubtedly derived) is in fact often an accurate reflection of real life. The raw material of Dawn Fraser's personal history certainly resembles a soap opera, especially in view of the fact that the material is assembled without any real sense of social context (other than a passing and far from subtle reference to Dawn's working-class family in the film).

It is instructive to note that the production (but not the release) of *Dawn!* coincided almost exactly with *Newsfront* and to note the lessons of the latter film in both a narrative and a technical sense. *Newsfront* demonstrates brilliantly how archival footage, reconstruction, and normal shooting may be integrated in such a way that "actuality" and "fiction" become virtually indistinguishable, with the significance of each enhancing the other. Ken Hannam has not chosen to use such an integration (other than the credit sequence and a few very fleeting moments) in *Dawn!* The audience has no real sense of Dawn Fraser as an actual sportswoman (save for a few "bottom of the pool" shots here and there).

More damagingly when compared with *Newsfront, Dawn!* has little or no social context; there is no broader sense of an Australia existing beyond the pub mateship of Balmain. Dawn's achievements and her disappointments seem isolated and of little relevance in a social sense. *Phar Lap,* historically more remote and without a human protagonist as such, managed this rather better. This lack of social context might not have mattered a great deal if it could be argued that Dawn Fraser (the character in the film, that is) was constructed as a timeless myth-hero. But again the film fudges the focus: Dawn is not sufficiently developed as a fictional character in her own right or as a representative Australian hero. The strands of both are there, but they are not woven, separately or together, into a convincing, coherent tapestry.

As with *Phar Lap,* these problems may result from the need to be faithful to the actual biography of a historical individual, which in turn creates tensions in the narrative that are, especially in the case of *Dawn!,* unresolved. The result is a film that is neither a consistent fictional narrative (cause and effect, the backbone of narrative structure, is lacking) nor a documentary (or docudrama). *Dawn!* might have had something to say, not only on the nature of the Australian myth-hero (with the interesting twist that the hero was female), but also on questions of feminism, and so aligned itself with films like *The Getting of Wisdom, My Brilliant Career,* or *Puberty Blues.* Its cinematic inadequacies mitigate against any such sustained analysis.

Death of a Soldier | 1987

Director: Philippe Mora.
Producer: David Hannay, William Nagle.
Screenplay: William Nagle.
Director of Photography: Louis Irving.
Editor: John Scott.
Art Direction: Geoff Richardson.
Music: Allan Zavod.

Cast: James Coburn (Dannenberg); Bill Hunter (Adams); Reb Brown (Leonski); Maurice Fields (Martin); Max Fairchild (Fricks).
Production Company: William Nagle/David Hannay Production.
Running Time: 105 minutes.

STORY

Melbourne, 1942: the uneasy relationship between the Australian inhabitants and the thousands of American servicemen awaiting action in the Pacific is threatened by a series of brutal murders of local women for which an American soldier may be responsible. Major Dannenberg of the American Military Police is under orders from the U.S. Army hierarchy to try to hold the lid on a potentially dangerous situation. The American top brass are determined to make an example when the killer is caught, and the Australian government agrees to allow military rather than civil jurisdiction to prevail. Local detectives Adams and Martin are equally determined to carry out their own investigation. Eventually Private Edward Leonski is arrested, tried by military court-martial, and executed, despite evidence (refused admission) that he is suffering from a clinically recognized mental disorder.

COMMENT

Comparison of *Death of a Soldier* and *Breaker Morant* is almost inevitable. Both narratives deal with scapegoats of political expediency. But what is at stake in *Breaker Morant* and not in *Death of a Soldier* is the idea that one nation is victimizing members of another. Whatever *Breaker Morant*'s dramatic power, its ideological power derives from a simple opposition: Australia/England. *Death of a Soldier* attempts a similar opposition, this time Australia/America, but because the prosecuted and the prosecutors are all American, the dramatic emphasis afforded this structural opposition by the conventions of the cinematic courtroom drama is missing. The opposition must be activated in other ways.

It is a blatant statement of the obvious to note that Australian cinema is profoundly introspective. This, however, becomes a crucial insight when examining certain significant absences, particularly the absence of awareness of other cultures that are, or may be presumed to be, important influences. The virtual absence of America and Americans is intriguing because at times Australia has been compared historically and culturally with America and also because American popular culture (especially film, television, and music) has tended to dominate in cinemas and on the airwaves. Historically, Australia has depended upon an actual (during World War II) and a presumed (since 1945) American military presence for its security. Despite claims to the contrary, Australia did not jettison cultural dependence upon England in order to replace it with conscious cultural dependence on America— the evidence of *Crocodile Dundee* notwithstanding.

Death of a Solider demonstrates this degree of unconsciously fostered cultural blindness. The narrative, other than the location and the fact that the victims are Australian, need not have taken much note of Australia at all. The major players in the drama—based on well-documented facts—are all American. The significance of the incidents is more relevant to America and American history—except for the question of whether a foreign country has the right to try to execute one of its nationals for crimes carried out in Australia against Australian nationals. This turns out to be a crucial question around which the relationship of Australia to America might usefully have been explored. Is Australia, despite all its attempts to ignore politico-economic reality, actually in a subordinate/subservient relationship to the United States? The film raises the question—it could hardly ignore it—but then tries to avoid it.

The presence of the two Australian policemen as a sort of mini–Greek chorus serves not only to outline the theme of injustice and expediency—which links *Death of a Soldier* very strongly with *Breaker Morant*—but also to provide, by deliberate contrast, a representation of Australian perceptions, attitudes, indeed philosophies and thus to activate the thesis/antithesis: Australia/America. It also suggests thereby the manner in which Australian culture is "superior," or at least more appropriate in these circumstances than American culture. This is also a reflection both of the traditional xenophobia and of the Australian inferiority complex (appropriately called by one Australian critic the "cultural cringe"). Australia's need consistently to reinforce a sense of self-worth is confirmed by the moral superiority of the doughty, down-to-earth Australian cops. The film fails to register any irony here, given the general cultural attitude toward the police. Few other Australian voices are permitted to be heard.

Since *Death of a Soldier* is concerned with relating a historical miscarriage of justice, Major Dannenberg is given the full set of liberal attitudes through which the nature of this miscarriage can be understood: he is concerned with fundamental principles of justice that are being ignored for short-term expediency. Even so, Dannenberg's legalistic "humanity" is in contrast with the more earthy, instinctive fellow-feeling of the Australian cops.

Given the lack of a unified cultural attitude to America, it is difficult to say just what interest Australian audiences might have in what is a matter of American legal history. The presence of the Australian cops as the audience's proxy does raise some issues of the cultural rela-

tion/dependence of Australia on America—they are, after all, seen to
be powerless to affect the course of injustice—but such issues are left
unresolved, which in itself reflects the feeling that Australia does not
really want to examine these issues for fear of what the answers might
be.

The Devil's Playground 1976

Director: Fred Schepisi.
Producer: Fred Schepisi.
Screenplay: Fred Schepisi.
Director of Photography: Ian Baker.
Editor: Brian Kavanagh.
Art Direction: Trevor Ling.
Music: Bruce Smeaton.
Sound: Don Connolly.

Cast: Simon Burke (Tom); Nick Tate
(Victor); Arthur Dignam (Francine);
Charles McCallum (Sebastian);
Jonathan Hardy (Arnold); John
Diedrich (Fitz); Gerda Nicholson (Mrs.
Allen).
Production Company: The Film House.
Running Time: 107 minutes.

STORY

Tom Allen, a student at a Catholic seminary/boarding school run by an
order of brothers, begins to question life in the enclosed and oppressive structure of the school. Many of the brothers also have moments of
uncertainty, and some find release in the few journeys permitted to the
outside world. In an institution dedicated to declaring the body "un-
clean" and the "devil's playground," the awakening sexuality of the
adolescent boys causes more problems than usual. Some of the boys
form a secret fanatical organization that is really more concerned with
sadomasochistic sexual practices. The society is discovered when its
leader is drowned attempting to prove his ability to transcend physical
extremes. Tom's disenchantment finally leads him to run away from
the school.

COMMENT

The Devil's Playground is a highly personal film and its worth is a reflection of director Fred Schepisi's intimacy with the subject matter. While
it is overall too quiet a film, too semiautobiographical to rank with
other films that have been accorded enduring status, it is both a typical

product of the New Australian Cinema and something of a curiosity—given the relative unimportance of religion and religious institutions in the dominant cultural mythology of Australia. Australian heroes are usually in conflict with more diffuse circumstances—the environment, social conventions, and society in general rather than its organizations. Arguably, the seminary in *The Devil's Playground* is outside the social norm—whereas schools in the other New Australian Cinema productions are part of the social structure. This point is made by the film on a number of occasions, although the lack of consistent representations of "normal" society to which the seminary stands in contrast mitigates against such a polarity being one of the major themes. *The Devil's Playground* is also atypical in the way in which it is personal and introspective.

The Devil's Playground does, however, seem more in keeping with the general tenor of the New Australian Cinema in a number of other ways. On one hand, it can be grouped with productions loosely categorized as "growing up" films, in which the central character is an adolescent who commences but does not necessarily complete a narrative journey from childhood toward maturity. The central idea occurs in such films as *The Getting of Wisdom, My Brilliant Career, The Irishman, The Mango Tree, Puberty Blues,* and others.

The theme of growing up is nearly always associated with the theme of innocence, and the journey to maturity nearly always invokes some sense of its loss. The loss of innocence is seldom complete, so the gaining of maturity is seldom complete either. Innocence is a dominant cultural perception of Australia, individually and nationally. It is often disguised as openness, lack of sophistication, a type of unworldliness. Innocence is a theme of *The Devil's Playground,* but loss of innocence is not. Tom does not lose innocence in or through his decision to leave the seminary—although it is not difficult to register that the film assumes he will through prolonged contact with the world outside. What Tom sheds is ignorance or the artificial fostering of a false innocence that the seminary encourages.

Like so many of the early productions of the New Australian Cinema, *The Devil's Playground* is nostalgic about the past. Although not set as far back as some of the more celebrated Australian films, it nonetheless celebrates a past that is seen, although not without ambiguity, as reassuring, comforting, and, above all, innocent.

While Schepisi is clearly exorcising some personal devils through the

seminary experiences of Tom, he is a long way removed from con-
demning the institution and its practices. The brothers are, on the
whole, presented with understanding, sympathy, and not a little affection. More importantly, the occasional intrusion of outside society
presents brief glimpses of an even more nostalgic nature. Tom and his
family represent a sentimentalized view of an innocence as profound
as but more acceptable than that of the seminary.

It may seem to be going too far to argue for *The Devil's Playground* as a
metaphor for Australia were it not for the example of *Newsfront* and the
cultural concern for the myth of innocence in so many Australian films.
The temporal setting of *The Devil's Playground* is important. As *Newsfront* has pointed out, the immediate postwar period until the mid-
1950s was an important transition for Australian society—a period in
which it lost its isolation (its innocence) and was dragged (willingly or
otherwise) into the real world. Many films of the New Australian
Cinema are concerned with attempting to rediscover that lost innocence, perhaps even to reactivate it. *The Devil's Playground* is not one of
those; it is not a eulogy for the past, but neither is it an interrogation of
it. It tends to say, in a much more limited, much more personal way
than *Newsfront,* "this is where we came from."

It is the element of intimate involvement with the central subject
matter that separates *The Devil's Playground* from other school films
(e.g., *The Getting of Wisdom*). That intimacy has been transferred to the
film in a way that makes *The Devil's Playground* a thoroughly engaging
film, an enjoyable experience, and an impressive feature film debut for
Fred Schepisi.

Dimboola 1979

Director: John Duigan.
Producer: John Weiley.
Screenplay: Jack Hibberd.
Director of Photography: Tom Cowan.
Editor: Tony Paterson.
Art Director: Larry Eastwood.
Music: George Dreyfus.
Sound: Lloyd Carrick.

Cast: Max Gillies (Vivian); Bruce Spence
(Morrie); Natalie Bate (Maureen); Bill
Garner (Dangles); Irene Hewitt
(Florence).
Production Company: Pram Factory
Pictures.
Running Time: 89 minutes.

STORY

English journalist Vivian Worcester-Jones arrives in the small country town of Dimboola just as it is preparing for a grand social event: the wedding of Morrie McAdam and Maureen Delaney. The wedding is threatened, however, by two events. Morrie's mother reveals that Morrie's father may actually be Maureen's disreputable Uncle Bayonet. And when Maureen receives a photograph (taken by Morrie's "best mate," Dangles) of Morrie in a compromising position with a stripper at a party, she calls the wedding off. The town musters to the rescue, a reconciliation is effected, and the wedding takes place. The truth of Morrie's parentage is established, and the bride and groom leave for the honeymoon. Most of the rest of the townspeople manage to pair off as well. Vivian is convinced he has only touched the surface of Australian life.

COMMENT

Dimboola is a film that did not fare well with the critics (with rare exceptions) upon its initial release. It is possible that by 1979, with the international success of "art(istic)" films like *Picnic at Hanging Rock,* the New Australian Cinema was adjudged to be becoming respectable and *Dimboola* reminded audiences and critics of its crude beginnings (e.g., *The Adventures of Barry McKenzie, Alvin Purple*). A rampant celebration of all that is irreverent, vulgar, and crude in Australian culture—an affectionate demonstration, free of obvious satirical intent, of Australia at its most lowbrow on the wide screen—may have touched the sensitive cultural-cringe nerve that lies not far below the surface of most commentators on the Australian arts.

Dimboola looks very much like a cross between *Barry McKenzie* and *Don's Party.* The film is populated by Barry's "relatives," or with the country cousins of the guests at *Don's Party.* Arguably there are too many of them; *Barry McKenzie* restricted the Australian characters to only a few, and *Don's Party* had a limited guest list. In *Dimboola* there are a whole town and outlying districts full of them. But what really differentiates this film from the other two films (and most of the ocker comedies) is the total absence of malice on the part of the filmmakers. There is no sense in which it could be said that its characters and

Dimboola. National Film and Sound Archive/John Weiley.

caricatures are offered as objects of satire or ridicule. (This is true, too, of the one non-Australian character, the "pommie," Vivian Worcester-Jones.) *Dimboola* is closer to *The Odd Angry Shot:* "Australians being Australians" (i.e., ockers) are presented as they are and not as targets for middle-class "cultivated" disdain—ockers as clowns certainly but not as fools. At the same time, they do not have the heroic status of *Crocodile Dundee.*

Dimboola offers perhaps the only affectionate portrait of small-town life in the New Australian Cinema (*Warming Up* comes close as does *Dusty* in a more limited way). The rarity of positive views of the country town is significant in the Australian cultural context—although, with the exception of some Hollywood westerns, small country towns do not fare well in American and English cinema generally. This seems to be because country towns have been bequeathed the cultural disadvantages of the cities in Australian mythology with few of the advantages. *Dimboola* runs against the grain of the prevailing cultural (and cinematic) perception. This may be another reason why it fared so badly: it disrupts too many prejudices.

Dimboola has other things going for it, however. In terms of comedy films, it stands out because it offers comedy in depth. It is not content with offering a single comic narrative device that has to suffice for the whole film or with limiting its view. In this it is close to the maniacal inventiveness of *Barry McKenzie* but less dependent upon one single unifying character. While Vivian Worcester-Jones serves as a link throughout the rather episodic construction of the narrative, he is not the central character. As the title suggests, the town itself is the central character rather than any of its individual denizens. Peripheral action is just as important as the slender narrative thread of Morrie and Maureen's wedding (will they?/won't they?).

There is a tension in *Dimboola* in the subtext that threatens to disrupt its integrity. This was variously reported as arising from differences between the writer (Jack Hibberd, from whose own well-known play the film was adapted) and the director (John Duigan). Hibberd apparently wanted something completely anarchic, Duigan something softer, more affectionately observed. There are moments, too, when the comedy has an air of desperation. This is particularly true of the few scenes with Bayonet and Mutton. The inclusion of songs seems rather arbitrary and random but not disruptive; indeed, they add a curious piquancy to the action.

It is not surprising that John Duigan found himself in a somewhat uneasy position with his material. His first film (*Mouth to Mouth*) and his later films (*Winter of Our Dreams, One Night Stand, The Year My Voice Broke* [1987]) have revealed him to be a director of considerable sensitivity, far happier with films that are not formulaic or bound by generic conventions. It is not a surprise that the genre film *Far East* (1982) should be Duigan's least satisfactory film.

A sense of humor is one thing, a sense of comedy is another. It has been occasionally argued that Australians make poor professional comedians because the culture encourages every Australian to be a comic. So, by extension, few Australian directors have proved themselves adept at making comedies. *Dimboola* is not the failure that many critics said it was. It is nowhere as embarrassing as some films made before or since that masquerade as comedies. Indeed, it has much to recommend it.

Don's Party 1976

Director: Bruce Beresford.

Producer: Phillip Adams.

Screenplay: David Williamson.

Director of Photography: Don McAlpine.

Editor: Bill Anderson.

Sound: Desmond Bone.

Cast: John Hargreaves (Don); Ray
    Barrett (Mal); Jeanie Drynan (Kath);
    Pat Bishop (Jenny); Graham Kennedy

(Mack); Harold Hopkins (Cooley);
Graeme Blundell (Simon); Veronica
Lang (Jody); Clare Binney (Susan);
Candy Raymond (Kerry); Kit Taylor
(Evan).

Production Company: Double Head
    Productions.

Running Time: 91 minutes.

STORY

On election night, 1969, Don Henderson throws a party for some friends, most of whom are confident of a Labor party victory at the polls (after twenty years). Various friends arrive: his old mentor from the university, Mal, and his wife Jenny; a conservative couple, Simon and Jody; Mack (who announces he has left his wife); the incorrigible womanizer Cooley and his most recent girlfriend Susan; and Evan and his artistic wife Kerry. It gradually becomes apparent that Labor is losing the election. The men get drunker, various sexual assignations are attempted, most unsuccessfully, and barely disguised hostilities flare before the party settles down into alcohol-induced reminiscences. In the morning, the election has been lost, and Don is left to clear up the debris from the night before.

COMMENT

The first *Barry McKenzie* film gave early notice of Bruce Beresford as a director of note through the sheer confidence—one might say impertinence—of its handling. But *Don's Party* demonstrated for the first time the extent of Beresford's brilliance as a *metteur en scène,* a brilliance that was to flourish in his subsequent films and to be revealed most fully with *Breaker Morant* four years later. The "content" of *Don's Party* is due to David Williamson (who adapted his own successful play). But to take the inevitably static nature of the play (extremely well known at that time) and replace the theatrical tempo with a wholly cinematic tempo is the work of a director who understands his medium.

There is no doubt that *Don's Party* was even more embarrassing than *The Adventures of Barry McKenzie*. Its revelation was of Australians (and Australian society in microcosm) for what they may be: uncouth, aggressive, insecure, hostile, and devoid of the ability to sustain meaningful relationships between men and women and even more importantly (given the cultural significance of the mateship ethos) between men and men. All this was pretty hard to take—that is, hard for the critics who attacked the film on a number of grounds that now look quite spurious. Australian audiences, however, loved it. It struck a chord, and the chord was (as with *Barry McKenzie*) ockerism. Here were Australians as they "really are" rather than hiding their philistinism behind a patina of etiquette borrowed from other cultures.

Don's Party may have been a little ahead of its time in predicting the growing sense of national pride, the burgeoning sense of not merely accepting Australian culture for what it is but actually celebrating it. There is no doubt that Australian films from the mid-1970s were in the vanguard of the national revival and contributed to it positively and significantly.

In the 1980s, few Australians would be prepared to say of the ockers (male or female) in *Don's Party* "that is not how we are" (even though such an image entirely ignores the multiethnic structure of contemporary Australian society). In 1976, it was still something of a shock (despite *Barry McKenzie*) to discover that ockers were not simply working-class figures or clowns in narratives, but that ockerism was well entrenched in the middle-class suburbs. At the time, and this is part of the purpose of *Don's Party,* representations of ordinary Australians as ockers could, and did, make Australians cringe with embarrassment. The wholesale adoption of the ocker as the dominant and desired icon of the Australian still had some time to go before its flowering could take place with *Crocodile Dundee.*

It is ironic that this cultural acceptance of the ocker should have come through *Don's Party* (and, to a lesser extent, *Barry McKenzie* and more serious films), which was intended as a satire on the inadequacies of Australian culture to permit the development of satisfactory and satisfying relationships between men and women and as a critique of the fact that the mateship ethos, rather than promoting a sense of bonding and community, actually disguised a system of hostility, envy, jealousy, and aggression toward others designated as mates.

Despite its unrelenting comedy, *Don's Party* has a serious purpose: it is, like a number of Australian narratives, an examination of failure, of ambition unfulfilled and avoided. It is, bluntly, a film about the failure of the Australian male. The defeat of the Labor party despite early promise (and the gradual revelation of this fact) is an exact parallel to the failure of nearly everyone at Don's party, but especially of Don himself: brilliant student, would-be novelist "reduced" to an ordinary suburban schoolteacher. There are few tales of successful men in the Australian cinema; there are many tales of failure and defeat. This is a recurring leitmotif in much Australian literature as well and is firmly entrenched in Australian cultural perceptions.

Don's Party is an important film not only because of its undoubted quality as a piece of cinema but also because it is so preeminently a film that came from within, and thus comments so devastatingly upon, Australian culture. It is a film that serious critics dismiss at their peril. But it is also a film that can delight the audience through its audacious humor, its frankness, and its verve.

Dusty 1983

Director: John Richardson.
Producer: Gil Brealey.
Screenplay: Sonia Borg.
Director of Photography: Alex McPhee.
Editor: David Grieg.
Production Designer: Robbie Perkins.
Music: Frank Strangio.
Sound: John Phillips.

Cast: Bill Kerr (Tom); Noel Trevarthen (Harry); Carol Burns (Clara); Nick Holland (Jack); John Stanton (Jordan); Kate Edwards (Mrs. Muspratt); Dan Lynch (Ron).
Production Company: Dusty Productions/Kestral Films.
Running Time: 88 minutes.

STORY

Tom Lincoln, farmhand to Harry Morrison, buys a kelpie pup, not realizing that its mother was a dingo. The farmers in the district have hired a professional dingo hunter, Railey Jordan. Tom gives the pup, Dusty, to Jack, Morrison's elder son, promising to train him while Jack is away at college. Dusty develops into a first-class sheep dog and Jack realizes that he properly belongs to Tom. Dusty's wild nature reveals itself, and he starts to kill sheep. Reluctantly, Tom agrees that Dusty must be shot but cannot do it. Morrison wounds the dog, who runs off. Tom quits and he and Dusty live in the bush in cattle country where there are no sheep to tempt Dusty. Tom is taken ill and dies. Jack lets Dusty go to roam free with other dingoes.

COMMENT

On the face of it, a simple story of a man and his dog must appear to be another children's film along the lines of, say, *Storm Boy*. But *Dusty* is not merely (or even) a children's film, in the usual sense of the term.

Dusty is an unpretentious film to the extent that its observational, uncommitted approach may seem bland. Dramatic, even emotional moments are underplayed. The drama related to the "ownership" of Dusty—to the extent that he is owned by anyone—is hardly apparent. Yet this dramatic situation is part of a larger one, the father/son relationship between Tom and Jack. This is hinted at; and a certain element of Harry's jealousy of Tom and Jack's closeness is vaguely suggested. In the end, Jack "inherits" Dusty after Tom's death and, in direct defiance of his father, lets him go free. But these and other possible dramatic situations are not given any narrative importance. It must also be recognized that to raise the level of human drama in the narrative would deflect attention from the narrative's actual center, Dusty.

Dusty is not important simply because of his interactions with humans but because he contains within him the two basic conflicting forces that structure the film's very theme: the conflict between nature (or natural instinct) and culture (or the taming of nature). Dusty is, on one hand, a wild creature who is descended from animals that once roamed the country without fear or restriction, with the right to feel it was "their land." On the other hand, he is trained to use his abilities in special ways—he is "socialized" and is expected to deny his wild side. Dusty's situation is paralleled in two ways within the construction of the narrative. Tom Lincoln is the human equivalent of Dusty. He is also "a wild creature": a bushman who has been tamed (by accepting permanent paid employment) but who retains his instinctive feeling for the bush and the freedom it offers. He is not part of the society that has been created by and through the taming of the wilderness: at the bush dance (a celebration of community in a manner reminiscent of John

Ford), Tom is shown to be an outsider who has no part or place in this ritual of social confirmation. In a much more abstract way, the very farming activities of Morrison (and his neighbors) also reflect this theme of taming the wild and the impossibility of totally doing so. The incursions of dingoes demonstrate that the wild is always there.

This opposition of wild/tame (or nature/culture) is not demonstrated as a site of irreconcilable conflict. Indeed, the film is concerned with the place of things, people, and animals in a larger scheme that permits a measure of uneasy compatibility. Dusty is a transitional figure in this opposition, as, oddly enough, is the dingo hunter, Jordan, who articulates on several occasions the dingo's point of view. His position is ironic: he understands the dingo, but he destroys it at the behest of the farmer. The farmers themselves form the other side of the equation. Although treated with considerable sympathy, Morrison is seen to be clearly motivated by nothing more than his desire to use the land to his advantage. He and his wife are representatives of the pioneering stock of which Australian myth is so proud in the abstract but so scathing in actual presentation, who are more interested in bending the land to their will (their heroic cultural role) than in understanding its wild side and accommodating it.

What remains interesting and perhaps unique about *Dusty* is that it avoids drawing this opposition in simple terms of black and white or heavily favoring one perception over the other. Although one of the first, and most notable, social realism films of the New Australian Cinema was *Sunday Too Far Away,* this approach has tended to be reserved for contemporary films dealing with conditions of social existence in the cities. Farming itself, as an activity and a way of life, has been largely ignored in the New Australian Cinema. In focusing on rural existence as a way of life, as a social organization carefully observed, *Dusty* is a rare exception.

Dusty is very much an observational film, and it profits enormously by avoiding overdramatization, indeed by avoiding overcharacterization. Its success (and its weakness) is in the very way in which it has been cinematically constructed. Its observational style, its disinclination to heighten its drama or overemphasize character, and its somewhat disjointed, elliptical editing style serve to avoid oversimplification of its themes or insistence that one side of its structural opposition nature/ culture is more important than the other. *Dusty* does serve as a convincing counter to the excesses of films that place nature and people in irreconcilable conflict in the bush or suggest that existence in the bush ultimately has an inescapable brutalizing effect on men (and women).

Eliza Fraser 1976

Director: Tim Burstall.

Producer: Tim Burstall.

Screenplay: David Williamson.

Director of Photography: Robin Copping.

Editor: Edward McQueen-Mason.

Art Director: Leslie Binns.

Music: Bruce Smeaton.

Sound: Desmond Bone.

Cast: Susannah York (Eliza); Trevor Howard (Fyans); Noel Ferrier (Fraser); John Waters (Bracefell); John Castle (McBride); Martin Harris (Graham).

Production Company: Hexagon.

Running Time: 122 minutes.

STORY

Eliza, the attractive wife of Captain James Fraser, is the object of not unwelcome attention from Captain Rory McBride, traveling with them on Fraser's ship. Fraser stops at the convict settlement of Moreton Bay to offload McBride. David Bracefell, a convict, finds himself in Eliza's bed and she helps him escape. Fraser's ship is wrecked and they become prisoners of an aboriginal tribe with whom Bracefell is now living. A rescue party from Moreton Bay sets out. Bracefell is betrayed into surrendering the Frasers. Eliza helps Bracefell escape again. Fraser is killed when a plan by Fyans to rid himself of McBride goes astray. Eliza and McBride run a sideshow in which she gives an exaggerated account of her adventure. Bracefell turns up, having made a new life in New Zealand, and Eliza leaves with him.

COMMENT

At first glance, *Eliza Fraser* may seem little different from the many historical reconstruction films that were the mainstay (and the most successful productions) of the 1975–1982 stage of the New Australian Cinema. The period it reconstructs is, admittedly, a little unusual—the early colonial period as opposed to the time around the turn of the century favored by, say, *Picnic at Hanging Rock* or *My Brilliant Career*.

The convict period of Australia's colonial past has not been much touched upon in the New Australian Cinema. Curiously, it has proved to be a fertile period for television drama.

Eliza Fraser is different as a period reconstruction film not so much because of its location in time but because unlike other period reconstructions it does not display any particular regard for historical accuracy. That is to say, the period provides color and location but not much actuality (and as such stands in remarkable contrast to writer David Williamson's later screenplay for *Gallipoli*). Generally speaking, Australian films have made a virtue of historical veracity, allowing their narratives in turn to be shaped by that history. *Eliza Fraser,* while not flaunting history (except inasmuch as there was a real Eliza Fraser whose actual history intersects the cinematic narrative bearing her name at only a few points), is more concerned with telling a story.

It is unfortunate, then, that the way the film does tell that story is so unsatisfactory. In endeavoring to touch all narrative bases, the film tends to sprawl unnecessarily. This is not helped by the film's inability to be sure just what it is (a flaw of other Burstall/Williamson collaborations, such as *Petersen* and *Duet for Four* [1982]). It ranges from broad bedroom farce to epic adventure. Its comic tone, too, is decidedly uneven: it is difficult, for example, to find anything funny in the shipwrecked crew resorting to murder and cannibalism. Sympathies are aroused only to be undermined by reducing the figures who arouse such sympathy (especially Captain Fraser) to mere clowns. Even Eliza herself, who manages to retain a certain Victorian matronly poise (except when in the proximity of Bracefell), resorts at times to clownishness for comic effect.

Eliza Fraser is not without interest from an Australian perspective at least. The film demonstrates on a number of occasions the failure of authority; Australian cultural attitudes to authority, part of the myth of egalitarianism, are firmly entrenched in the subsurface of the narrative. There are three captains in the story, all variously figures of ridicule and ineffectual figures of authority. Captain Fraser is pompous, incompetent, and totally ineffectual. Captain Fyans is raddled, drunken, corrupt, and self-seeking. Captain McBride, the least likely of this highly unlikely trio to have achieved such a position, is a coward and a debaucher—although not totally irredeemable through a certain larrikin style.

The most successful characters, therefore, are Eliza and David Bracefell, a woman and a convict, socially the least powerful. They have better capacities for simple survival and for ultimate triumph over odds and opposition both natural and social. It is no accident that Bracefell (although rather naive for someone who has been a sailor and a convict) is the most heroic of all the characters: he is most at home in the bush—which in Australian terms is what creates heroes.

Eliza Fraser also offers at least some images of aborigines in something like their "natural" setting—that is, largely unaffected by white inroads into their culture. They are treated with surprising sympathy by the narrative, the humor of the contrast between white and black being very much at the expense of the whites. But they provide little more than colorful background to the adventures of Eliza. They are neither the savages nor the cannibals Fraser thinks they are; when the chief does not carry out his intention to marry Eliza after learning that Fraser is not her father (as he thought) but her husband, they are shown to have better moral standards and greater capacity for restraint than the whites. (His desire to marry her is perhaps the only time the film is overtly racist, in the assumption that black men are obsessed with sexual relations with white women.)

Despite the fact that *Eliza Fraser* is perhaps less interested than other films of the New Australian Cinema in a reverence for historical accuracy and is a breath of fresh air for that, it fails to convince either as epic adventure or as comedy.

Evil Angels (USA: *A Cry in the Dark*) 1989

Director: Fred Schepisi.
Producer: Verity Lambert.
Screenplay: Robert Caswell, Fred Schepisi.
Director of Photography: Ian Baker.
Editor: Jill Bilcock.
Production Designer: Wendy Dickson, George Liddle.
Music: Bruce Smeaton.
Sound: Gary Wilkins.

Cast: Meryl Streep (Lindy); Sam Neill (Michael); Maurie Fields (Barrett); Charles Tingwell (Muirhead); Bruce Myles (Barker); Nick Tate (Charlwood).
Production Company: Cannon Entertainment/Golan Globus in association with Cinema Verity.
Running Time: 121 minutes.

STORY

Nine-week-old Azaria, daughter of Seventh-Day Adventist pastor Michael Chamberlain and his wife Lindy, disappears while they are on holiday at Uluru. Lindy claims a dingo has taken the child from their tent. A search fails to find the baby, but bloodstained baby clothes are found. There is intense media interest. A finding that the child was taken by a dingo fails to satisfy the police, the press, or public opinion. With expert opinion denying the dingo theory, Lindy is arrested for murder. The trial, followed by all of Australia through the media, results in the now pregnant Lindy being convicted. Michael and his family never give up the fight to prove Lindy's innocence. Some years later, new evidence comes to light. Lindy is released.

COMMENT

Evil Angels commences with a declaration that the story is true, but this is not a documentary even within terms of reconstruction or reenactment: it is fiction even if it claims scrupulous adherence to the truth. In terms of the film it does not matter what happened to Azaria Chamberlain; it is the way in which the film, unconsciously, aligns itself with a mythology of the Australian bush that was rehearsed from the earliest beginnings of the New Australian Cinema (and originated in the Australian psyche much before that) that fascinates. Given that *Evil Angels* is based on the real-life events of the tragedy of the Chamberlain family, it may seem cruel or tasteless to draw comparisons with the fictitious scenario of *Picnic at Hanging Rock,* but the film invites comparison without meaning to and in so doing confirms the potency of Australian mythology.

Briefly stated the points of comparison are the inexplicable disappearance of a female or group of females in the Australian bush; association with a natural landmark of considerable mystical or spiritual potency; the fact that those who disappeared were never found; and considerable public disbelief in postulated explanations. Whereas *Picnic at Hanging Rock* relies heavily upon the mythic potential of the bush to swallow up humans, *Evil Angels,* tied down by its reliance upon well-recorded events, must examine the ways in which Australia— represented by the law, by the media, and by anonymous representatives of the public—tried to find a logical (nonmythic) explanation. Even so, the film cannot avoid showing a scene in which aboriginal Australians express no need to look for rational explanations. Here an opposition of European Australia and "real" Australia is fleetingly raised, the point being the futility of trying to explain the power of Australia (the land, the landscape, the ecology) within terms borrowed from an alien culture, the law and logic of Enlightenment Europe.

In a curious way, the late New Australian Cinema reverted to its beginnings—not in the sense of copies or remakes but in ways in which late films reflected upon and confirmed the early emphases of the New Australian Cinema. *Crocodile Dundee* revived the ocker comedy of the earliest years; *Shame* rewrote *Wake in Fright* in terms of 1980s feminism; *Evil Angels* found the real-life equivalent of *Picnic at Hanging Rock*. Each of these films, in its own terms a long way removed from the self-consciously nationalistic films of the first decade of the New Australian Cinema, found (perhaps without really trying) its basic substance in the basic ideology of Australian identity.

For this reason *Evil Angels* is oddly ambiguous in its attempt to suggest that Lindy Chamberlain was the victim of the media, of the legal system, of public opinion, and possibly of political expediency. The film is fairly certain that she *was* the victim of these things; it is uncertain *how* she was the victim of them. *Evil Angels* is constructed cinematically of a number of threads: the main one is the Chamberlain family itself; second, the uncaring, biased, and sensation-seeking response of the journalistic media; third, the police investigation; fourth, the reaction of "ordinary" Australians; fifth, political self-interest; and sixth, the land itself. While the dominant narrative thread is that of Lindy and Michael Chamberlain, the reasons for that narrative even existing are located in the other five threads. Together they do not, however, form a fully coherent narrative structure. The film as a whole has a problem: while the various threads are obvious, the pattern they form is not. The film seems anxious to tell the Chamberlains' story from within while emphasizing a whole cultural and social context. That the Chamberlains were victims is clear enough; but of what and how (let alone why) is less coherently argued.

While confirming the power of the myth of the bush, *Evil Angels* undercuts the myth that the power of the bush may be matched by egalitarianism. It suggests, or points to, the failure of cultural con-

sensus that Australia as a whole (and the New Australian Cinema) had
been attempting to foster throughout the 1970s and 1980s. While the
film can point to the irony of Lindy Chamberlain being a public "sacri-
ficial victim" because (in part) it was postulated she had sacrificed her
own daughter, it cannot (or does not) explain why the Australian public
would even wish to create such a victim. The potency of the images of
Australian cultural identity is too great to allow them to be pulled
apart. Schepisi tried, bravely, to do so with *The Chant of Jimmie Blacksmith* ten years before. Critical and public response objected to his
doing so then. At a time when it might have been possible to renew the
attack successfully, Schepisi avoids joining battle. An interrogation of
what the Lindy Chamberlain case *meant* to Australia is sadly lacking.

Fast Talking 1984

Director: Ken Cameron.
Producer: Ross Matthews.
Screenplay: Ken Cameron.
Director of Photography: David Gribble.
Editor: David Huggett.
Production Designer: Neil Angwin.
Music: Sharon Calcraft.
Sound: Tim Lloyd.

Cast: Rod Zuanic (Steve); Toni Allaylis
(Vicki); Chris Truswell (The Moose);
Gail Sweeney (Narelle); Dave Godden
(Warren); Peter Hehir (Ralph); Steve
Bisley (Redback).
Production Company: Oldata
Productions.
Running Time: 95 minutes.

STORY

Steve, a street-wise school kid, lives with his unemployed drunken
father and small-time drug pusher brother in an outer industrial suburb of Sydney. He is considered to be a no-hoper by the school staff,
with whom he is in constant trouble. Steve meets Redback, a motorcycle mechanic and one-time racer who, recognizing in Steve the image
of his former self, gets him involved in reconstructing a bike for himself. In order to finance the work on the bike, Steve supplements his
pushing of "soft" drugs at school with a few other petty crimes, but he
refuses to become involved in delivering hard drugs for his brother.
Eventually his misdemeanors lead to his expulsion; narrowly avoiding

capture by the police after stealing the vice-principal's car, he makes a break for freedom on his bike.

COMMENT

Rebellion against authority, or at least a refusal to accept authority, is one of the cornerstones of the Australian mythic identity. It is hardly surprising, then, that a great many films have narratives structured around this theme and that they frequently have protagonists who are defined by their attitude toward authority. But despite the importance that "manly independence" is given in the cultural mythology of Australia, many filmic narratives are, at best, ambivalent about authority.

Seldom is authority, especially social authority, totally rejected in the New Australian Cinema. It may be questioned; that is the healthy Australian attitude. It may be sometimes shown to be administered by fools and incompetents; that is, after all, what is expected of institutions. In narratives of the latter type authority is more likely to be questioned, even fought against and sometimes defeated (for example in *Annie's Coming Out*), but seldom is it shown to be totally irrelevant.

This is, however, the case with *Fast Talking*. The curiously charismatic hero Steve (curious in that he is a weasel-faced, smart alecky, subcriminal punk) demonstrates in his unchanging response to the authority of the school, family, police, or society in general that these various forms of oppressive authority are totally irrelevant, except inasmuch as they demand constant vigilance to avoid being crushed by their agents. Steve takes this antiauthoritarian stance of the Australian character to its almost logical conclusion. If it was not for the fact that he has no real power himself to change anything, he might be described as truly anarchist. But while he clearly does not regard these various forms of authority as having any weight in his personal philosophy, he is equally powerless to avoid them or to do much to escape the consequences of his flouting of their laws and rules.

In the extremity of Steve's response to his limited world and his even more limited future, *Fast Talking* is unusual. Other films of the New Australian Cinema have followed somewhat similar narrative structures but have invariably allowed space for negotiation between the protagonist and the particular form of authority. In *Street Hero,* Vinnie's rebellion against the oppressive nature of the school is defused by finding a way in which his energies can be channeled into (socially) acceptable responses. In *Moving Out,* Nino's incipient rebellion (which is more adolescent confusion than revolt) is also channeled by a sympathetic teacher. *Puberty Blues* allows its two main protagonists not so much rebellion against school authority (or family authority) as against the authority of peer group norms (which are shown to be stultifying in any case).

Again, *Fast Talking* contrasts with these other high school films in its very presentation of the conduct of the school itself. In these other films, the school and particularly the teachers are all presented in exaggerated or stereotyped ways. In *Fast Talking* both the school and its teachers (while frequently figures of deserved ridicule) are extremely accurate—excruciatingly accurate at times. In fact, despite a rather romantic edge to the narrative, *Fast Talking* is figured by an extraordinary sense of accuracy in its *mise-en-scène*—something it shares with *Moving Out* and *Puberty Blues.* Doubtless, the accuracy is due to writer/director Ken Cameron's own background as a teacher—demonstrated in his earlier short feature, *Temperament Unsuited* (1971).

Fast Talking has too many strands. All involve Steve but are not otherwise integrated. The dominant thread is of course the school and Steve's relation to it, but there is also the subplot with Redback and the motorbike, a subplot with a trainee-teacher, Steve's family life (drunken father, absent mother who appears once fleetingly, criminal brother), and so on. So much is raised in terms of subplots that in the end the integrity of the film rests solely upon the character of the narrative's hero (or perhaps antihero). Steve is without doubt one of the few unromanticized (or nearly completely unromantic) larrikins in the New Australian Cinema. Steve has all the larrikin qualities. He is also resolutely antisocial (a quality of the historical larrikin usually overlooked in the myth) even though the film redeems him somewhat through his concern for his dog, his refusal to push drugs for his older brother, and the fact that he is, in spite of everything, an attractive character: he is after all quite intelligent, funny, and even sensitive.

Although the film does not show it, it implies that society will catch Steve and exact its retribution for his larrikin ways. So Steve is like most heroes of Australian narratives: involved in circumstances beyond his control and inevitably defeated by those circumstances no matter how strongly he tries to avoid this. *Fast Talking* is, however, intriguing to the extent that it is one of the very few really subversive texts of the New Australian Cinema.

Fatty Finn 1981

Director: Maurice Murphy.
Producer: Brian Rosen.
Screenplay: Bob Ellis, Chris McGill.
Director of Photography: John Seale.
Editor: Robert Gibson.
Art Director: Lissa Coote.
Music: Grahame Bond, Rory Donohue.
Sound: Tim Lloyd.

Cast: Ben Oxenbould (Fatty); Bert Newton (Mr. Finn); Noni Hazelhurst (Mrs. Finn); Gerard Kennedy (Tiger); Greg Kelly (Bruiser); Lorraine Bayly (Maggie); Henri Szeps (Mr. Zilch).
Production Company: Children's Film Foundation.
Running Time: 90 minutes.

STORY

Hubert "Fatty" Finn has his heart set on earning enough money to buy a secondhand crystal set in time to hear Bradman " 'spiflicate the poms" in the forthcoming test series. The intervention of his impecunious father or his longtime rival "Bruiser" Kelly or even just plain bad luck means that Fatty is always losing the money he has just gained. Although he alienates the members of his own gang and is berated by his mother for failing to buy her a box of chocolates for Mother's Day (Mr. Finn has borrowed all Fatty's savings), Fatty remains cheerful. With the judicious use of a female goat, Fatty manages to distract the favorite and win the annual goat race. At home, his father has confessed the truth, and all is forgiven. Fatty gets his longed-for crystal set.

COMMENT

Fatty Finn is concerned not so much with creating a narrative set in a historical or mythical past as with drawing its narrative from one of the cultural artifacts of the past, taking as its source and its overall structuring mechanism the characters and the plots of a famous Australian newspaper comic strip of the same name. Thus the nostalgia of the New Australian Cinema turned in upon itself, seeking expression not through representation of a regretfully lost past (although that is extant in the subtext of *Fatty Finn*) but through the re-creation of one of the very elements of that past: the comic strip "Fatty Finn," which was ahistorical in the first instance.

It is further worth noting that a film based upon the same comic strip was made during Australia's earlier cinematic "golden age": *The Kid Stakes* (1927). So this 1981 version looked back not merely to an earlier Australia but also to earlier films. There have been few examples in the New Australian Cinema of remakes of early silent films (or sound films for that matter) except perhaps *The Lighthorsemen,* a remake of *The Forty Thousand Horsemen* (1941), and *Robbery under Arms* (1985), of which there were several earlier versions.

Fatty Finn moves away from the obsessive concern with detailed and accurate period reconstruction that both enhances and hinders other period films. Its *mise-en-scène* is that of the comic strip rather than that of the family album (an emphasis carried even further in what must be viewed as its companion piece, *Ginger Meggs*). If accuracy of reconstruction can be said to exist anywhere in *Fatty Finn*, it is in the way character and location are made to look as if they had stepped out of the pages of the newspaper comic strip—even though the film is in color. Thus, although the film is basically shot on location for a greater part of its narrative, there is no contradiction between "real" environment and comic-book characters.

Part of this lack of contradiction is due to the script, which makes few concessions to the fact that *Fatty Finn* is *only* a children's film. That is not to say that the film goes over the heads of children or that it is in some way misconceived. It is indeed one of those rarities, a film for children that may be enjoyed at an adult level. The humor of *Fatty Finn* is knowing, tongue-in-cheek, and at times even cruel. This is no doubt due to the influence of Bob Ellis as scriptwriter, who has consistently shown himself to be one of the most capable as well as one of the wittiest screenwriters of the New Australia Cinema. Although *Fatty Finn* continues the theme of innocence that is fundamental to so many films of the New Australian Cinema (especially the period films), the innocence is not the innocence of the naïf (cf. *The Adventures of Barry McKenzie*) but of the larrikin: street-wise (to use 1980s terminology) but not corrupted.

Fatty himself is without doubt the embryonic Australian urban hero—the character variously described at different times (and for different reasons) as the larrikin or the ocker. He combines the Australian mythical traits of the battler with the street-wise attributes of the larrikin. He is certainly not above a little ingenious cheating at the frog-hopping contest or indeed at the goat races. And he displays the proper attitude to the English with his desire to own a crystal set in order to hear Australia beat the English at cricket. It is not hard to see Fatty as the younger version of Frank Dunne in *Gallipoli;* he has the same mixture of intelligence, cheek, and charm; although a seemingly arbitrary fate frequently takes a hand to interfere with his plans, Fatty (like Frank) is equally capable of not only surviving but bouncing back.

Fatty Finn is told with pace and humor and, although basically episodic, it is held together by a central thread (Fatty's attempts to get the money to buy a crystal set) and by consistent characterization. It is helped enormously by the role of Fatty being taken by Ben Oxenbould and by the supporting children (some of whom turn up again in *Doctors and Nurses* [1981] and *Ginger Meggs*)—and by the fact that the writers have kept the focus on the children and resisted the temptation to introduce (and stereotype) adult figures beyond those immediately necessary, a mixture that works less well with two later films that invite immediate comparison, *Doctors and Nurses* and *Ginger Meggs.*

Unfailing good humor that is frequently tongue-in-cheek and also cognizant of the social conditions of the time in which the story is set—which in turn balances rather than contradicts the fantasy/comic strip *mise-en-scène*—adds to the appeal of the film. *Fatty Finn* is more socially conscious than *Ginger Meggs*—not so much in terms of reconstruction but in sensitivity to the social realities of the time. These remain, however, as threads in the tapestry from which the narrative is woven rather than as the pattern that determines its shape.

The F. J. Holden 1977

Director: Michael Thornhill.

Producer: Michael Thornhill.

Screenplay: Terry Larsen.

Director of Photography: David Gribble.

Editor: Max Lemon.

Art Director: Monte Fieguth.

Music: Jim Manzie.

Sound: Don Connolly.

Cast: Paul Couzens (Kevin); Eva Dickinson (Anne); Carl Stever (Bob); Graham Rouse (Sergeant); Gary Waddell (Deadlegs).

Production Company: FJ Films.

Running Time: 101 minutes.

STORY

Kevin lives and works in the western suburbs of Sydney. His life revolves around his car (an F. J. Holden he is restoring), drinking with his
mates, and casual sex. Kevin meets Anne at a pub. Despite the fact that
Bob, Kevin's best mate, makes love to Anne first (in the back seat of the
F. J.), it is Kevin that Anne is attracted to. The pair see more of each
other, and Anne comes to Kevin's parents' place for dinner. Kevin's
casual attitude toward sex and his constant drinking in the company of
Bob lead to an argument, and the couple split up. Kevin gets drunk
and tries to speak to Anne at a party. He is thrown out but before
leaving hurls a garden gnome through the front door. After drinking
the rest of the night away with Bob, Kevin arrives home to find the
police waiting for him.

COMMENT

The F. J. Holden car occupies a potent place in the popular culture of
Australia. The first model of a range of cars made exclusively in Australia by General Motors after World War II, it was the (only) Australian
car well into the fifties and is looked upon with considerable sentiment
not only by many who once owned one (frequently as their first car) but
also by the subculture of young car enthusiasts. It was, for a time, a
potent symbol of egalitarianism: it only existed (like the Ford Model T)
as one basic vehicle and thus was driven by all classes before the advent
of different models (for different incomes).

When it was first released, *The F. J. Holden* garnered some extremely
positive critical reviews and was even compared with mid-European
realist films of the preceding decade or so. Now these reviews seem
overly rhapsodic about a film that, while perhaps having the virtue of
showing Australia and Australians in a way much closer to the actual
than to the mythical conditions of their existence, nonetheless seems
frequently to make too much art of too little reality.

A few films point out that life in the suburbs of Australian cities is (or
may be) as dreadful as in the bush, but for totally different reasons. The
inner city has the narrative value of chaos, of tension, of change, even if
these inner cities are far from pretty (as films like *Mouth to Mouth* and
Hard Knocks reveal). But the suburbs, as films as seemingly different as

The F. J. Holden. National Film and Sound Archive/Michael Thornhill.

The F. J. Holden and *Stanley* show, are simply dreadful in their life-draining ordinary dullness. *The F. J. Holden* more than any other of the few films that locate themselves in the suburbs reflects and represents that enervating dullness in all its lackluster awfulness. It is hard to think of a recent film that states so clearly the hopelessness of those working and middle-class Australians trapped in the existential void of boxlike homes, mown lawns, and garden gnomes.

A realist approach is perhaps the only one that could be taken to a subject such as that of *The F. J. Holden.* Drama, in any narrative functional sense, is lacking in this setting—so drama must arise as if from real life, from the minutiae of accurate observation of the everyday. *The F. J. Holden* has a powerful ability convincingly to bring home the stultifying monotony of the lifestyle. More particularly, it displays the seeming hopelessness for adolescents in these environments.

Adolescents are the focus of the film, of course, but the adults are shown to be already "lost." The story, such as it is, of Kevin and Anne is in its way as tragic as any version of Romeo and Juliet, although the "star-crossed lovers" are not doomed by incompatible family loyalties but by a combination of environment and, in the specific matter of the actual break, friendship loyalties—mateship—between Kevin and Bob. But even if the possibility of a happy ending had been contemplated, the film makes only too clear in its sequences of the couple's respective families what the future would hold.

The film cannot totally avoid the charge that it too views its subject matter through middle-class tinted (tainted?) glasses. Too often the film suggests a condescending and slightly disdainful approach to its own material. The film wavers between documentary or neorealist observation and patronizing mockery—the latter almost distastefully so in the presentation of Kevin's family. Ironically, this is partly the consequence of the success of the realism of the film overall. At other times, however, the film slips its neorealist leash and seems to make movements in the direction of adolescent comedy along the lines of *Puberty Blues*. These attempts at comedy are neither sustained nor successful; although they at least serve to suggest that life in the suburbs is not all doom-and-gloom (and again it is important to recognize that this is the external view of the film rather than the felt life of the characters). But these touches of comedy tend further to disturb the balance of the film.

Along with *Puberty Blues, The F. J. Holden* reveals attitudes toward sex that are casual, unfeeling, almost animalistic. *Puberty Blues,* while hardly finding these sexual relations between the adolescents admirable, does manage to make them amusing at the same time. In *The F. J. Holden* they are chilling and far from romantic. This may be the film's most significant contribution to the New Australian Cinema. Unsatisfactory as a film in the final analysis, it does attack romance in two ways: first, clearly it finds little that is romantic in life in the suburbs; second, it perhaps underlines by contrast the frequent overromanticization inherent in many films of the New Australian Cinema.

The Fringe Dwellers 1986

Director: Bruce Beresford.

Producer: Sue Milliken.

Screenplay: Bruce Beresford, Rhoisin
   Beresford; from the novel by

Nene Gare.

Director of Photography: Don McAlpine.

Editor: Tim Wellburn.

Production Design: Herbert Pinter.

Music: George Dreyfus.

Sound: Max Bowring.

Cast: Kristina Nehm (Trilby); Justine
   Saunders (Mollie); Kylie Belling
   (Noonah); Bob Maza (Joe); Ernie

Dingo (Phil); Malcolm Silva (Charlie).

Production Company: Fringe Dwellers
   Productions/Ozfilm.

Running Time: 98 minutes.

STORY

The Comeaway family live, with other aboriginal families, in the shanty town on the edge of Curgon. Trilby, the adolescent daughter, is determined her family should "better themselves" and with older sister Noonah, who is training as a nurse, persuades her parents, Joe and Mollie, to move to a Housing Commission house in town. To Trilby's chagrin, other relations move in as well, and then Joe gambles away the rent money. The family returns to the fringes. Trilby becomes pregnant by Phil, a local aboriginal stockman, but refuses to marry him. Her newborn child dies as a result of a possible accident, and Trilby packs her bags, heading for Sydney and what she hopes will be a better future.

COMMENT

Australian culture, despite the monolithic image of its dominant myths of identity, and despite the overwhelming evidence of the New Australian Cinema to the contrary, is a vital (but not volatile) mixture of many dislocated cultures. One of the many cultures that is dislocated, although not by geographic distance, is the aboriginal culture. It is, more than immigrant (sub)cultures, "other." Its "otherness" is, however, special for historical reasons: aboriginal culture has been dislocated by being culturally overwhelmed. The argument that immigrants have chosen to come to Australia and ought at least to be aware of and identify to some extent with the dominant culture cannot apply (despite arguments for assimilation) to aboriginals.

Thus, Australian cinema has largely ignored representations of aboriginals. They have appeared as central figures within their own narratives in only five films: *The Fringe Dwellers, Manganinnie, The Chant of Jimmie Blacksmith, The Wrong Side of the Road* (1981), and *Short Changed* (1986). The aboriginal as "other" informs these films differently, but it is dominant only in *The Chant of Jimmie Blacksmith* and *Short Changed*.

The Fringe Dwellers is noteworthy, and controversial, because of the manner in which it virtually ignores the cultural (and political) possibilities of "otherness." Racism is not more than marginally on the agenda of *The Fringe Dwellers*. The low-key discrimination of the white townspeople is rendered more as a matter of bad manners and bad taste than as deeply entrenched racism, a question of subcultural or class difference and outlook rather than implacable and irrational hatred on the basis of race.

The Fringe Dwellers is a social comedy not a cultural one. As such it represents a stream more noticeable in Australian literature than in Australian cinema: the family-based narrative that finds both comedy and tragedy (or at least melodrama) in the doings of a poor, lower-class family. In structuring its narrative and its themes in this way, the film "normalizes" aboriginals. That is to say, it suggests they are not substantially different from *all* Australians. The men, especially Joe and his brother Charlie, are really ockers in almost every sense: fond of beer and gambling, shy of work, easygoing and feckless, but ultimately harmless. A certain amount of the comedy does arise from representations of aboriginals that run the risk of touching upon stereotypes gleaned from dominant white views, particularly in the emphasis on sharing everything but especially accommodation with a seemingly limitless family circle. The charge of misrepresentation or resort to stereotyping is avoided by the manner in which the film successfully "deculturizes" the Comeaways' actions, in which, for example, gathering a fluctuating collection of friends and relatives is seen as simply gregariousness or mateship.

The Fringe Dwellers also brings aboriginality unproblematically into cultural centrality in an extratextual way. It is, in many respects, another film based upon the recurring theme of growing up in Australia. The central figure, Trilby, is like Laura in *The Getting of Wisdom* or Sybylla in *My Brilliant Career,* an adolescent Australian girl struggling to avoid becoming entrapped by social and/or economic pressures that would seem to be conspiring to limit her in terms of possibilities and individuality. Unusually, *The Fringe Dwellers* is a film that deals not only with growing up but also with coming-of-age. These two are by no means synonymous. Australian culture is, metaphorically, seemingly stuck in perpetual adolescence—despite apparent and usually self-deluding moments of maturity. Thus growing up in Australia does not carry with it, *ipso facto,* a sense of gaining maturity. In *The Fringe Dwellers,* however, there is a sense in which Trilby does mature; it takes both the reverse in the family fortunes and her pregnancy and the subsequent death of her child to bring about Trilby's first definite move toward a coming-of-age. This leads her to recognize (like Laura in *The Getting of Wisdom*) that she must escape or at least distance herself from those who would endeavor, consciously or unconsciously, to raise a prison wall of rules, conventions, and accepted social norms. The film ends without triumph or failure but with the seeds of a possible (if obscure) future for Trilby.

The Fringe Dwellers met with some strong opposition from politically active aboriginals upon its release, but it was approved by others. Arguments were raised about its faithfulness to the "reality" of the lived experience of aboriginals and of representations of their culture: film narrative was confused (as it too often is) with some notion of documentary veracity. The film is a view of aboriginal existence; it is not the only view. What makes it interesting is the manner in which it ignores rather than promotes aboriginal "otherness."

Gallipoli 1981

Director: Peter Weir.
Producer: Patricia Lovell.
Screenplay: David Williamson.
Director of Photography: Russell Boyd.
Editor: Bill Anderson.
Design Consultant: Wendy Weir.
Music: Brian May.
Sound: Don Connolly.

Cast: Mel Gibson (Frank); Mark Lee (Archy); Bill Hunter (Barton); Robert Grubb (Billy); David Argue (Snowy); Tim McKenzie (Barney); Harold Hopkins (Les); Bill Kerr (Uncle).
Production Company: Associated R & R Films.
Running Time 105 minutes.

STORY

May, 1915: eighteen-year-old Archy Hamilton determines to join the army while attending a country athletic meeting. Thwarted in his first attempt to join the Light Horse regiment, he falls in with Frank Dunne, a fellow athlete. They journey to Perth, where Archy is successful in his second attempt to join up. Frank is rejected and joins the infantry. They are reunited in Egypt and persuade Archy's CO to allow Frank to transfer to the Light Horse. The Light Horsemen are sent to Gallipoli and used in an attack on the Turkish trenches. They are mown down charging the reinforced Turkish positions. Frank tries in vain to bring a message to halt the attack but is too late to prevent the last wave from going over the top. Archy is killed running as if in a 100-yard dash across no-man's-land.

COMMENT

Gallipoli is at once an ambitious and an obvious film to be made in Australia. It deals with one of the most firmly entrenched cultural legends, in which the myth of national identity is so precisely adumbrated as to retain a cultural potency that is undiminished even some seventy years after the historical events that gave rise to the legend.

Gallipoli, produced at the very beginning of the 1980s, is also an obvious choice for the Australian cinema. The rebirth of feature film production coincided with, and perhaps even foreshadowed, a cultural revival in Australia. It is no coincidence that a fair percentage of the films of this rebirth explored Australia in terms of historical reconstructions that examined how Australians became what they are. Thus, these films, and *Gallipoli* is perhaps the epitome, combine a rediscovery of a national identity lost or threatened with loss with a celebration of that national identity as already understood through the cultural myths.

While *Gallipoli* is explicable as an example of a limited but familiar Hollywood formula, the "buddy" film, for Australian audiences it has far greater resonances. *Gallipoli* tells in almost pure form one of the dominant organizing myths of Australian national identity. Its historical accuracy is apparent through writer David Williamson's use of the published documentation of Anzac historian Bill Gammage. The mythical accuracy is determined by the film's central thematic cores of mateship, competition, and innocence explored through the construction of the film's two main characters, Archy Hamilton and Frank Dunne.

Archy and Frank are both Australian stereotypes—indeed almost archetypes. Archy is the bushman, the "pure" Australian, this purity being further emphasized in a spiritual sense by his fair beauty and his worldly innocence. Frank is the urban Australian (thereby mythically less pure), the larrikin, wise in minor ways (forging birth certificates, riding in freight trains, gambling) but as innocent as Archy of the realities and duplicities of the world outside Australia. In these two beautiful young men, the film has brought together the mythical representatives of Australian identity, bush and city, bushman and larrikin, for a shared experience that thus becomes a shared experience for Australia in general.

Gallipoli re-creates the bushman/pioneer image before it turns its narrative attention to the specifics of the Anzac legend. In so doing it follows, in a narrative form, the historical/cultural genesis of the myth of national identity itself. But in addition to its utilization of the bushman image in the depiction of one of its two major characters (and one of the minor characters as well), this film also utilizes the image of the ocker for its other main characters (and for several of the minor characters). *Gallipoli*'s narrative (which is strictly linear chronologically) can be segmented into three broad sections, each of which deals with or presents one of the mythic images of Australians: the first third of the film's running time is concerned with the bushman image; the middle third allows the ocker to dominate; the final third concerns itself with the presentation of the Anzac legend itself. *Gallipoli* shows more clearly than perhaps any other film just how the forging of the Anzac legend's mythic dimensions was indeed a melting together of all the mythic qualities of the other legends—including the larrikin/ocker image.

That the Anzac legend creates a socially all-encompassing myth is evidenced by the manner in which *Gallipoli* brings together all social classes. The workers and the landowners—the representatives of the extremes of social strata—are revealed to share a common image: Australia's egalitarian myth. Archy and Frank, despite social differences, run against each other, jump a train together, and finally go to war together. Further, these disparate social groups are revealed to have common goals: the war and, particularly for the narrative thrust in the first instance, joining up.

But the film is unable to desert the proposition that the "true" Australian is the bushman. It is through the two characters of Archy (bush) and Frank (city) that the fundamental Australian cultural opposition is most clearly delineated. Both, because of their essential innocence, are admirable. But Archy is the purer of the two; he makes the "ultimate sacrifice." His death is the death of the mythically true Australians. Present-day Australians are, so to speak, the descendants of Frank Dunne. For this reason the New Australian Cinema, consciously or unconsciously, needs to educate contemporary audiences in regard to what Australia and Australianness *ought to be*. One of the undoubted masterworks of recent Australian cinema, *Gallipoli* is a film that never fails to move audiences both in Australia and overseas.

The Getting of Wisdom 1977

Director: Bruce Beresford.

Producer: Phillip Adams.

Screenplay: Eleanor Witcombe.

Director of Photography: Don McAlpine.

Editor: William Anderson.

Art Director: Richard Kent.

Music: Franz Schubert, Sigismund Thalberg, Arthur Sullivan.

Sound: Desmond Bone.

Cast: Susannah Fowle (Laura); Barry Humphries (Rev. Strachey); John Waters (Rev. Shepherd); Sheila Helpmann (Mrs. Gurley); Patricia Kennedy (Miss Chapman); Hilary Ryan (Evelyn); Kim Deacon (Lilith).

Production Company: Southern Cross Films.

Running Time: 100 minutes.

STORY

Laura Tweedle Rambotham, the daughter of a country postmistress, is sent to Melbourne to an exclusive Ladies' College. Her imagination and forthrightness bring her into conflict with the snobby girls and the school's code of conduct. Laura curbs her natural enthusiasm and intelligence in order to be accepted by the others. In order to increase her standing, Laura invents a romance with the new minister, Reverend Shepherd. When the truth is revealed, she is ostracized by the other girls. Laura is befriended by Evelyn, an older girl from a wealthy family, and becomes emotionally attached to her—to the detriment of her studies. In the end, Laura does manage to pass her exams and wins a music scholarship to Leipzig.

COMMENT

Although the precredit sequences suggest that *The Getting of Wisdom* is another pretty period piece set in the Australian bush, the action

The Getting of Wisdom. National Film and Sound Archive/Phillip Adams.

quickly moves to the claustrophobic atmosphere of the Presbyterian Ladies' College in suburban Melbourne. Of course, the film is still a period piece (and, thanks to the combined skills of the art director and the director of cinematography, a pretty one) but the *reconstruction* of period does not seem all that important while the *sense* of period does. *The Getting of Wisdom* may not have started the trend of elaborate and nostalgic period films in Australia, but it certainly did nothing to stem the tide and is, in any case, better than most.

The theme of growing up (the getting of wisdom) is one that seemed to have a particular attraction for Australian filmmakers in the second half of the 1970s. At least half a dozen major films took this theme as their central narrative device. This exploration of the theme—nearly always in a period setting—culminated in *Gallipoli,* in which the metaphoric equation between the coming to maturity of the characters of the fiction and the coming to maturity of Australia as a nation and as a culture was finally and conclusively demonstrated. It is perhaps to be expected that this idea of growing up should appeal to those involved in a film industry that was doing just that itself. But it is also perhaps

typical of director Bruce Beresford that, whereas most of these comparable films are highly romantic (cf. *My Brilliant Career*), *The Getting of
Wisdom* is much harder, more comic, and more sardonic.

There is a very real sense in which, while Laura gets wisdom, learning to play by the rules even if she uses the rules for her own advantage,
she also retains sufficient wisdom to recognize the futility and frustration the rules will impose. But this does not mean Laura has gained
maturity or lost her innocence. The final scene of the film has Laura in
total defiance of all the rules of the college removing her gloves,
throwing away her hat, and running gleefully through the park, thus
confirming an innocence, a childlike response to the world, that is
culturally very Australian. Australians don't want to, or don't, see the
wisdom of coming-of-age—it smacks of the "foolishness" of the Old
World and is not part of the New World they inhabit and have helped to
form. Here a curiosity needs to be noted. *If* the film is simply another
nostalgic period piece that offers a favorable (even smug) view of
Australia disguised as (personal) history, then a real question is raised
regarding Laura's "escape" to Europe (the scholarship in Leipzig).
Thus the final scene as Laura runs, unfettered at last, through the park
may be understood as running away not simply from the school but
from Australia—or at least away from urban Australia, with its adoption of European manners that is not matched with an adoption of
European Culture. Since the overall thrust of the film's themes is
toward a freeing of Laura's spirit, there is an ambiguity in the way the
film suggests what might be culturally Australian in that freeing.

Perhaps undeservedly, *The Getting of Wisdom* (which was produced
between the two) is compared with *Picnic at Hanging Rock* (also set in
the repressive atmosphere of a Victorian boarding school) and *My
Brilliant Career* (which also deals with the gaining of wisdom and self-
knowledge by a country girl). These other films are better known,
possibly because they use the Australian landscape rather more, possibly because they are more romantic than this occasionally cynical,
occasionally satirical film. It also may be that the timing of the release
of *The Getting of Wisdom* was not quite right.

The feminism of *My Brilliant Career,* coming two years later and
being noticeably more strident than in *The Getting of Wisdom,* may have
helped its acceptance. The feminist possibilities of *The Getting of Wisdom*
are ambivalent. Although the despicable Reverend Shepherd is shown

to be a male chauvinist of the most tyrannical kind, much of the oppression of Laura, mainly carried out by women anyway, is not because she is female but because she is too much the nonconforming free spirit. After all, what she wants is simply the "birth right" of all Australians—a fair go. The film does not suggest that she is denied a fair go in any direct way by a patriarchal social system. Such an interpretation must take a whole system of extratextual factors for granted. This offers a direct comparison with *My Brilliant Career*. There are other similarities in the two narratives. Both deal with the awakening of an Australian girl to a life beyond that conventionally defined for women. Laura seems, however, to be challenging life on rather more levels than Sybylla in *My Brilliant Career*. This makes her history more interesting, but, because of her age, less conventionally romantic.

Ginger Meggs 1983

Director: Jonathan Dawson.
Producer: John Sexton.
Screenplay: Michael Latimer.
Director of Photography: John Seale.
Editor: Phillip Howe.
Production Designer: Larry Eastwood.
Music: John Stuart, Kim Thraves.
Sound: Tim Lloyd.
Cast: Gary MacDonald (Mr. Meggs);
Coral Kelly (Mrs. Meggs); Paul Daniel
(Ginger Meggs); Drew Forsythe
(Tiger); Daniel Cumeford (Eddie);
Shelley Armsworth (Min); Scott
Grayland (Alex).
Production Company: John Sexton
Productions.
Running Time: 95 minutes.

STORY

Ginger Meggs vows to give up fighting in order to win the hand of Min. The vow proves hard to keep: under extreme provocation, he knocks down his archrival, Eddie Coogan. Disguised as a girl, Ginger gatecrashes a birthday party he has been banned from. Eddie sees through Ginger's disguise and a wild, cream-cake-throwing fight ensues. In disgrace, Ginger decides to run away from home. He is befriended by Alex, a young circus performer. Ginger returns home; after rescuing Min from a runaway horse, he is forgiven and accompanies her to the circus. Ginger discovers that the trapeze artists are responsible for a series of burglaries. He retrieves the stolen diamonds, helps in the capture of the crooks, and with the reward money buys his missing pet monkey back from the animal trainer.

COMMENT

Ginger Meggs represents the third part of what might loosely be termed the "Kids' Comic Book Trilogy": *Fatty Finn, Doctors and Nurses* (1981), and *Ginger Meggs. Doctors and Nurses,* strictly speaking, is not adapted from a comic strip; but it shares both the basic structures and some of the creative personnel of the other two. *Ginger Meggs* and *Fatty Finn* do not have the literal role reversals of *Doctors and Nurses* (children play adults in the latter), but there is no doubt that for the most part the children—especially the eponymous heroes of the former two films— are more mature, wiser, in short, more adult than the adults.

Ginger Meggs is based, like *Fatty Finn,* on a long-running syndicated newspaper comic strip by the same artist, Syd Nicholls. Its geographic location is less easily determined than *Fatty Finn*'s Sydney locale. Where *Fatty Finn* indicates (by use of a clever matte shot of the as-yet-incomplete Sydney Harbor Bridge) where its story takes place, *Ginger Meggs* is less precise: a suburban environment, or perhaps rural, or perhaps a mixture of the two. It is something of a never-never land that manages to exist as a fantasy location that is devoid of the actualities of real locations. It really does not matter all that much, although it is tempting to see the lack of an equivalent character to the semicriminal S. P. bookie, Tiger Murphy, of *Fatty Finn* as indicative of the absence of the "rapacious city" and the location of the action in the more "wholesome" atmosphere of the small rural town. The villains are more those of childhood fantasy: the nasty Captain Hook—the borrowing of title (and appearance) from Peter Pan must surely be significant. There is a "Tiger" in *Ginger Meggs:* Tiger Kelly (the use of Irish surnames for unlikable, criminal, or larrikin characters is intriguing), but Kelly is not much more than an ineffectual bully/clown rather than a member of the criminal or nearly criminal classes like his nicknamesake in *Fatty Finn.*

This less than certain social setting is a further indication of the lesser social consciousness of *Ginger Meggs.* It may, however, be due to the comic-strip inspiration itself, which also seemed more remote from the social realities of *Fatty Finn*. Again, the later historical location of the story—presumably the late 1940s although the sense of period is inconsistent—may mean the social/economic conditions of postwar Australia were less likely to be such an inescapably determining factor in the narrative itself than in *Fatty Finn*, set in the 1930s.

This overall lack of context—historical, geographic, and social— tends to isolate *Ginger Meggs* as little more than the cinematic equivalent of a comic strip. But lack of context also serves to make the film more nostalgic than *Fatty Finn* by presenting a picture of innocence untrammeled by social reality.

Ginger himself is an essentially Australian character. The celebrated larrikin element is present in him (as it was in the character of Fatty Finn); he is not above fighting and cheating a little to achieve his ends. Although an ocker in the making, Ginger (again like Fatty) seems to have too much interest in the company of the opposite sex fully to meet the more chauvinist definition of the adult model. The outlines of a future ocker are definitely there, and this in itself demonstrates the depths at which the cultural image of the Australian male is imbedded in the national mythos—that a fictional child who comes to the screen via newspaper comics should nonetheless be structured by a set of conditions seemingly drawn from "real" life.

There has been a greater attempt to orient *Ginger Meggs* to a child audience than in either *Fatty Finn* or *Doctors and Nurses*. There are fewer attempts to include dialogue that is witty or joking at an adult level or requires an adult knowingness. The story itself as well as the episodic incidents that support the central structure are more directly appealing to children. The characters, too, through faithfulness to the comic strip originals (especially the amazing physical accuracy of Mr. Meggs), are not adult concepts of children (or adult concepts of children's concepts of adults) but children's concepts of children.

The comparison of *Ginger Meggs* to *Peter Pan* is a more accurate comparison than one that sees this film as another in the genre of growing up in Australia. Its characters remain fixed in comic-book never-never land. The nostalgia is not only, or even so much, for a lost golden age of Australia, as for the lost age of childhood—a nostalgia that is culturally universal.

Goodbye Paradise 1983

Director: Carl Schultz.

Producer: Jane Scott.

Screenplay: Bob Ellis, Denny Lawrence.

Director of Photography: John Seale.

Editor: Richard Francis Bruce.

Production Designer: George Liddle.

Music: Peter Best.

Sound: Syd Butterworth.

Cast: Ray Barrett (Stacy); Robyn Nevin

(Kate); Janet Scrivener (Cathy); Lex
Marinos (Con); John Clayton (Todd);
Don Pascoe (McCredie); Paul Chubb
(Curly); Robert (Tex) Morton
(Godfrey).

Production Company: Petersham
Pictures.

Running Time: 110 minutes.

STORY

Michael Stacy, dismissed deputy police commissioner, is offered $4,000 by his boyhood friend Senator McCredie to find the senator's daughter Cathy. Stacy's investigation leads him to stumble upon a right-wing conspiracy to conduct an army coup in order to force the secession of the Gold Coast from Australia. Stacy's snooping causes him to be considered a sufficient threat to be beaten up; when this does not stop him, a bomb is planted in his car that kills his girlfriend Kate. McCredie dies under mysterious circumstances. Stacy locates Cathy at New Eden, a quasi-religious center run by Todd, an old buddy of Stacy's from army days. The coup is foiled by the intervention of army intelligence and the Australian Security Intelligence Organisation (ASIO). Promising to keep quiet, Stacy returns to his beachside boardinghouse room.

COMMENT

The New Australian Cinema has often wandered into genre movies, sometimes almost accidentally but occasionally deliberately. Seldom has it ventured into a genre production with such confidence, such nonchalance, and such success as in *Goodbye Paradise*.

The private eye picture would seem to be the particular province of Hollywood (despite occasional sorties into the field by French cinema). While *Goodbye Paradise* is not strictly a private eye film (Stacy is not a private investigator), it utilizes the conventions of the genre thor-

oughly and without self-consciousness—for the most part. The makers
have very astutely found in Australia's Surfers Paradise on the Queensland Coast an antipodean equivalent of Raymond Chandler's Los An-
geles and "Bay City," complete with "mean streets," neon-lit bars, dingy
hotels, and corruption that permeates all levels of society. In the tradition of the Hollywood private eye film, it makes full use of the location
and its multiple levels of existence as a suitable stage on which to play
out the multilayered story of search and discovery that is the essential
narrative structure of the genre.

Despite the fantastic and narratively absurd ending, what is fascinating about *Goodbye Paradise* is the manner in which it prefigures the
exposure of a depth of corruption and deceit within the police force,
underworld, and political arena in Queensland that a royal commission
some two years later would bring to light. What looked at the time like
an interesting and unexpected sojourn in the area of a well-established
Hollywood genre with hindsight looks like an exercise in something
akin to neorealism.

Goodbye Paradise uses the conventions and, more importantly, uses
them with conviction to create a film narrative that is not an imitation
(pale or full-blown) of Hollywood prototypes but essentially (even
quintessentially) Australian. But the mix—Hollywood convention,
Australian nuance—is so finely tuned that a non-Australian audience,
while missing many local references, will be none the poorer. The film
does not rely upon local knowledge to be understood or, importantly,
to be enjoyed. At one level, *Goodbye Paradise* does suggest that there is
still truth within the mythic conception of the rapacious city—and the
rural-idyll sequences do for a short while offer (as the name suggests)
an Edenesque bush contrasted to the nasty city. Since the underlying
tone of the films of this genre is cynicism, Eden is shown to be more
false than the city, which at least knows itself to be corrupt.

The convention of the private eye genre that insists that corruption is
ubiquitous throughout all levels of society is at odds with Australian
perceptions of the mythical importance of cultural identity to innocence. *Goodbye Paradise* is somewhat at odds with most of the New Australian Cinema. To what extent the conventions are (as with *Attack Force
Z*) stronger than naturalized perceptions of Australianness is a matter
of critical debate. But *Goodbye Paradise* is not totally alone in a more

cynical (while not openly iconoclastic) view of Australian society: *Heatwave*, for example, and *Stir*, in a different way, present similar attitudes.

The film's narrative loses both its own direction and its genre formula consistency with its overbright and overblown scenes of ludicrous destruction at its climax. Seemingly, even the film's makers found they could not take seriously the sequence of mass destruction in New Eden when the coup is ruthlessly put down: they overlaid the soundtrack with the version of the *1812 Overture*, which was used by the Australian army in its recruiting advertising.

This lapse (both visual and aural) is a pity: *Goodbye Paradise* has all the hallmarks of one of the best genre films of the New Australian Cinema—and is perhaps one of the best films altogether. Its integrity as a unified narrative, structured by the conventions of the genre and enlivened by its own originality, is betrayed by the obvious and self-reflexive jokiness of the ending. Other than for this rather curious and radical reversal in narrative tone, *Goodbye Paradise* probably has one of the best scripts of Australian Cinema of the past decade. Many Australian films have been criticized, and rightly so, for the inadequacies and weaknesses of their scripts. *Goodbye Paradise* refutes any such criticism as a generalization: its extremely literate script provides humor, tension, mystery, and a suitable sense of the enigmatic throughout.

As it stands, *Goodbye Paradise* serves as an object lesson in filmmaking whereby a good script, good acting, and good directing can combine to make a film that is memorable not merely because it touches upon some sensitive or celebrated aspect of Australian culture and society, but because it is, in and of itself, an excellent film.

Hard Knocks | 1980

Director: Don McLennan.

Producer: Hilton Bonner, Don McLennan.

Screenplay: Don McLennan, Hilton Bonner.

Director of Photography: Zbigniew Friedrich.

Editor: Zbigniew Friedrich.

Sound: Lloyd Carrick.

Cast: Tracey Mann (Sam); John Arnold (Munch); Bill Hunter (Brady); Max Cullen (Newman); Penelope Stewart (Raelene); Kristy Grant (Debbie).

Production Company: Ukiyo Films.

Running Time: 85 minutes.

STORY

Sam (Samantha) is caught by the police soon after snatching a purse from an old lady and is sent to a detention center. After release, she is soon back into a life of crime, graduating to housebreaking and armed robbery. Caught again, she spends more time at the detention center. With the help of sympathetic social workers, Sam decides to go straight on her release and is encouraged to pursue a career in modeling. After moving out of the house she shares with her feckless father into a flat of her own, Sam begins to get some work as a model. But she soon discovers that continued employment depends upon supplying sexual favors. She continues to be harassed by the police, and her flat is vandalized, although it is not clear whether the perpetrators are the police themselves or a disgruntled former friend from the detention center.

COMMENT

The outback films (usually historical/period pieces) of the New Australian Cinema are located, both in narrative and in characterization, in the *heart* of Australian culture—at least mythically. The city films, on the other hand, are more frequently than not located, in narrative and characterization, on the *fringes* of Australian culture—but within the actuality of Australian society.

The protagonists of these inner city films are more often than not social outcasts or those who live on the fringes of acceptable society. They are delinquents, the unemployed, immigrants, or petty criminals. Yet many of the films offer an alternative but still valid view of the myth of the "little Aussie battler." They are engaged in a struggle: sometimes simply to survive but more often both to survive and to give a little meaning to their lives.

Hard Knocks is very much in this line. On first viewing, it resembles something of a cross between *Mouth to Mouth* and a contemporary *Caddie*. But in fact, despite some resemblances in story material and/or setting to these two films, *Hard Knocks* is quite different from both. It resolutely avoids the period romanticization of *Caddie* and, while having something of the tough realist structure of *Mouth to Mouth*, is far more fractured in its narrative and more elliptical in its editing style. It is indeed a film that does not sacrifice cinematic aesthetics for realist observation.

The manner in which the film switches between time periods in its course has the effect of making the narrative seem more "real" in that it tends to become snatches from an observed life rather than a narrative with dramatic and chronological flow. This leads to a certain loss of characterization even of the main character, Sam, with the consequence that external forces (of which only the unsympathetic police are sufficiently developed) take on more importance than internal ones in any understanding of the film.

The style of *Hard Knocks* was a bold departure for the New Australian Cinema—which had shown a tendency to prefer to follow the conventions of the traditional Hollywood film. It is curious how the style seems to be so suited to the subject matter when it is realized that comparable films (e.g., *The F. J. Holden* or *Mouth to Mouth*) are much more straightforward, more neorealist, in their style. In its way, *Hard Knocks* is more adventuresome than the films of Paul Cox or Stephen Wallace, both of whom are considered to be bold challengers of conventions with their individual approaches to their films.

Once again, it is difficult to ignore the fact that, as in so many city films of the New Australian Cinema, the central character is a woman (*Caddie, Heatwave, The Killing of Angel Street,* etc.) who functions better than most of the men around—is indeed stronger than most of the men. This raises again the potent cultural polarity of bush and city in the Australian mythos whereby the city is seen as being rapacious, corrupt, and life-denying. Thus, no man can be "of the city" and still a hero in Australian mythological terms (unless he is an ocker/clown hero). A city hero must be, almost by default, a woman. But more than this, even if men are heroes in the appropriate setting of the bush, they are defeated heroes in the final analysis. Women—heroes of the city— are frequently triumphant. This is not strictly true in *Hard Knocks*, given its ambiguous ending, but Sam's narrative journey has nonetheless been one of continued progress despite the hard knocks she has received along the way. In this she ranks with other heroines of the narratives of the New Australian Cinema.

There is no doubt that *Hard Knocks* does not paint a pretty picture of aspects of contemporary society—although its focus is very narrow and its structure tends to mitigate against Sam's environment and circumstances being registered as metonymic for contemporary Australian society in general. What is surprisingly attractive about the film is the apparently passionless manner in which it constructs and observes its characters. Even the two detectives are not painted any blacker than they ought to be. More importantly, there is a lack of the condescension that marred *The F. J. Holden,* or the amused disdain that permitted comedy to be made of "real life" in *Puberty Blues.* In this sense *Hard Knocks* is less bourgeois than either of these films, reflecting the greater confidence in their basic material of the makers of this film. There is a bitterness at the core of *Hard Knocks* that is not in the films it has been compared with. The fair go syndrome seems not to be functioning here. There is a nihilist underpinning that exceeds the more normal if curiously optimistic fatalism/stoicism of Australian culture.

Heatwave 1982

Director: Phillip Noyce.

Producer: Hilary Linstead.

Screenplay: Marc Rosenberg, Phillip Noyce.

Director of Photography: Vincent Monton.

Editor: John Scott.

Production Designer: Ross Major.

Music: Cameron Allan.

Sound: Lloyd Carrick.

Cast: Judy Davis (Kate); Richard Moir (Stephen); Chris Hayward (Houseman); Bill Hunter (Duncan); John Gregg (Lawson); Anna Jemison (Victoria); Carole Skinner (Mary); Dennis Miller (Mick).

Production Company: *Heatwave* Films.

Running Time: 93 minutes.

STORY

Sydney roasts in a heatwave. Architect Stephen West finds himself unwillingly drawn into the battle that is raging between developer Peter Houseman and the residents of old housing that has to be demolished to make way for his futuristic redevelopment. The fight is headed by Mary Ford; but after her mysterious disappearance, the leading role is taken by anarchist Kate Dean. Houses are burnt and blown up, and threats are made against Kate. The union that has put work bans on the project is defeated by the employers. Houseman's solicitor is murdered, and Houseman's financial empire collapses. The project is taken

Heatwave. National Film and Sound Archive/Hilary Linstead.

over by the mysterious Selco Nominees, run by a local criminal boss who is shot dead at a New Year's party by his junkie mistress. The heatwave breaks and torrential rain falls.

COMMENT

Heatwave is the second film to use as the core of its narrative the controversy and corruption surrounding the redevelopment of the inner city area of Sydney. The other, *The Killing of Angel Street,* was released a few months prior to *Heatwave.* Both films are based to an extent on fact: the actuality of redevelopment battles in Sydney in the 1970s, including the "disappearance" of a key figure in those battles and the manner in which key unions placed "green bans" on the work sites. Somewhat like *Goodbye Paradise,* these two films seem to be based upon unofficial or street knowledge of corruption and chicanery in both high and low places. However, the "factuality" is regional: Australians who live in Sydney may be more *au fait* with the background of the stories, those in other parts of the country and outside it less so. The films still succeed as films, of course.

Other than these basic plot premises, the two films are as unlike as chalk and cheese. Where *The Killing of Angel Street* spells out its narrative in strict terms of black and white/good and evil, *Heatwave* consists of constantly shifting shades of gray. It has a far more complex narrative that uses all sides of the conflict to provide dramatic interest and to suggest that motives and actions are more confused and more intricate than the simplicity of *The Killing of Angel Street* would suggest.

This complexity of plot is reflected in a more consciously aesthetic approach to the film overall. The cinematography and the montage are more at the service of the narrative in *Heatwave*. The *mise-en-scène* has something of the feel of *film noir* (a feeling coincidentally intensified by the release at the same time of the American film *Body Heat* [USA, 1981], which also makes much of the literal presentation of heat as a "character"). This *noir* ambience is not consistent throughout, but the sense of the heat is. As in *film noir*, there is an aura of futility about the actions taken by the protagonists: there is (or will be) no final victory (as in *The Killing of Angel Street*)—in the end there are only losers.

Heatwave does not have the same social axe to grind as *The Killing of Angel Street*. There is a sense in which the film is no more concerned about the plight of the dispossessed than it is about the condition of the financiers. It does not even offer an emotional involvement with Stephen, who appears both obsessed (with his design) and compassionless. Kate is a more empathetic figure, but again her motives are not made fully explicit. Aspects of the character of Kate Dean are located within the usual mythic dimensions of the Aussie battler (e.g., *Caddie* et al.). But the existence of community-based action to overcome the odds is only partly suggested (it is stronger in *The Killing of Angel Street*). The possibility of a people-based narrative is lost by narrative focus on an individual and individuated protagonist, and by the revelation that criminals are involved—the problem being, in other words, a legal and not a social one. Australian cinema is not strong on political themes at this level. In *Heatwave* the concern is with the plot, the twists, turns, and surprises of the narrative; the telling of the story is more important than what the story tells. For this reason, the interactions between characters within the story and the bringing together of particular individuals are sometimes rather forced and can only be justified by making the telling more important than what is being told. This telling is, admittedly, very well done; on this level, *Heatwave* is a more exciting and more involving film than *The Killing of Angel Street*.

It is also a less culturally specific film. While both derive inspiration for their narratives from certain historical realities related to the re-development of inner Sydney, the characters of *The Killing of Angel Street,* and in a sense their attitudes too, strike one as being more Australian than those of *Heatwave. Heatwave,* while it makes no attempt to disguise its national origins—characters speak with Australian ac-cents and so on—also makes no attempt to celebrate it. It is a good example of an internationalized film of the 10BA period.

Director Phillip Noyce has shown himself capable of fascinating tales in *Newsfront*—although the earlier film is quite different from this one—and most recently in *Dead Calm* (1989). *Heatwave* lacks the politi-cal commitment of *Newsfront* and even that, in a different sense, of *The Killing of Angel Street.* It is a thriller, and as such works well.

Hoodwink 1981

Director: Claude Whatham.

Producer: Errol Sullivan, Pom Oliver.

Screenplay: Ken Quinnell.

Director of Photography: Dean Semler.

Editor: Nicholas Beauman.

Production Designer: Ross Major.

Music: Cameron Allan.

Sound: Gary Wilkins.

Cast: John Hargreaves (Martin); Judy Davis (Sarah); Dennis Miller (Ralph); Max Cullen (Buster); Wendy Hughes (Lucy).

Production Company: CB Films.

Running Time: 90 minutes.

STORY

Charismatic crook Martin Stang is arrested by the police while enjoying time with his mistress Lucy. He manages to escape but is betrayed by a dancer he picks up in a bar and is returned to prison. He hits upon the subterfuge of pretending to have gone blind. At first, the authorities refuse to believe that Martin is blind, but his acting becomes so con-vincing that he is sent to a minimum security prison. Here he meets and falls in love with Sarah, wife of the prison chaplain, Ralph. Martin's love for Sarah prevents him from carrying out his plan to escape when on day release in her care. Eventually, the impossibility of the relation-

Hoodwink. National Film and Sound Archive/C. B. Films.

ship between Martin and Sarah drives them apart, and Martin makes good his escape with the help of Sarah and her husband.

COMMENT

The very structure of *Hoodwink* reflects uncertainty on the part of the makers. A number of narrative possibilities are explored but never fully exploited. Uncertainty about how to deal with the material affects its presentation; concern with a realistic *mise-en-scène* seems at odds with a story that demands a tone of fantasy (or at least more heightened fictionality) to match the central character and his history. The comic tone of the film suffers from the contrasting visual environment. It must be admitted that this is not totally to the film's detriment; it makes of Martin Stang a much more "true" Australian character (an ocker— and thus a character to whom a certain element of comedy attaches mythically). But it does make it difficult for an audience to know quite how to respond to the film as a whole or specifically to Martin Stang as its hero.

Stang would at first seem to be a "lovable rogue"—rogues in the Australian cultural context having more than a touch of the larrikin about them. He is a criminal, but he has winning ways: cheeky, spontaneous, and, of course, attractive to women. Much of the early part of the film is structured around the picaresque adventures of this modern Ned Kelly—and great play is made of his ability to outwit the police. There is, however, a darker edge to the Long Bay jail sequences that, while never actually suggesting the dehumanizing conditions of prison in the manner of the violently realistic *Stir,* are nonetheless grimly unfunny. There is nothing amusing in the nurse who, mistakenly thinking that earlier Stang was planning a breakout with prison hospital staff as hostages and yet believing Stang to be blind, throws his medicine on the floor. (The lack of logic of this action is overlooked for the sake of the nastiness of the scene.)

The intrusion of the romantic love interest with Sarah also unbalances the film. It also seems out of place in the characterization of Stang. He is defined at first through his casual, selfish attitude toward women; despite a briefly displayed affection for his family, it is difficult to accept that he should so easily and uncynically fall in love. Sarah's explanation of the lack of physicality in her marriage to permit her attraction to Stang is equally implausible and arbitrary—especially as an excuse for her so easily to abandon her religious principles. There is considerable difficulty in accepting this relationship despite earlier efforts in the film to demonstrate Stang's irresistible charms. The rather perfunctory and chauvinistic characterization of Sarah is not helped by being played by Judy Davis, who is noted for playing strong women in *My Brilliant Career, Winter of Our Dreams,* and *High Tide* (1987). (There is a curious link between Sarah and the character of Miss Quested played by Davis in David Lean's British film *A Passage to India* [1984].)

Hoodwink does, in its diminishment of women, truly if unconsciously reflect a significant aspect of dominant Australian cultural perceptions. Stang is very much a cultural stereotype, and the fact that he is a criminal in no way disturbs his acceptability to an Australian audience: criminality does not diminish, but may enhance, cultural identification. Stang with considerable initiative, panache, impertinence, and humor makes monkeys out of agents of authority, notably policemen and warders, and the audience is encouraged to applaud him for it. Stang is a larrikin, and one of the few satisfactory portrayals of this mythic creature in the New Australian Cinema. Unusually for a hero of an Australian narrative, this particular hero is triumphant—his final victory is not even a limited one but is total; and unlike *Fast Talking*, in the case of his juvenile equivalent Steve Carson, the film does not even imply possibility of capture for Stang.

Rather than condemn *Hoodwink* for its weaknesses, it is fairer to see it as one of the films of the early 1980s that reflected the continued energy and commitment of the New Australian Cinema. It is also a film that indicates industry uncertainty about where it should (or could) be headed after the success of the films of the late 1970s. *Hoodwink* deserves praise for at least attempting to escape from the box-office formulas of historical/mythic narratives. It draws its inspiration from Australian cultural perceptions (despite a British director) and is undoubtedly Australian in "feel" to that extent.

In Search of Anna 1979

Director: Esben Storm.

Producer: Esben Storm.

Screenplay: Esben Storm.

Director of Photography: Michael Edols.

Editor: Dusan Werner.

Art Director: Sally Campbell.

Music: John Martyn, Allan Stivell.

Sound: Laurie Fitzgerald.

Cast: Richard Moir (Tony); Judy Morris (Sam); Chris Haywood (Jerry); Bill Hunter (Peter).

Production Company: Storm Productions.

Running Time: 91 minutes.

STORY

After serving six years for his part in an armed robbery, Tony returns to his Melbourne home in a working-class suburb. The spot where he buried the money from the robbery has been built over by high-rise flats. Jerry, who was involved in the robbery but informed on Tony, beats Tony up to find out where the money is. After threatening to kill Jerry but in the end leaving him alive but shaken, Tony starts a trip to Sydney to locate his girlfriend Anna. Abandoning Jerry's car, Tony gets a lift in an old Buick with Sam, a beautiful and enigmatic woman. They slowly drive to Sydney, getting to know each other on the way. Tony learns that Anna has moved to Queensland and stays a few days with

In Search of Anna. National Film and Sound Archive/Carol Jerrems.

Sam and her lover Peter. Sam goes with Tony to Queensland. They locate the house Anna is living in, but Tony no longer feels the need to see her.

COMMENT

The narrative construction of *In Search of Anna* is nonchronological, a fractured narrative punctuated by sequences that serve less as flashbacks to memories than as another narrative that needs to be understood in order to understand the central narrative. In this the film is not particularly unusual in cinematic terms, although it is rather unusual in the Australian context.

   In Search of Anna's departure from mainstream Australian cinema is, however, more apparent than real. It is in the technique, the aesthetic construction of the narrative (mainly through editing), that the film is different from the conventional Australian film of the period. In other ways, it shows a greater continuity with the perceptions of Australia that inform, shape, and underlie so many films. Most particularly, *In Search of Anna* is built upon that perpetual cultural opposition of bush and city that occurs in so many cinematic narratives (and, of course, in literature, theater, painting, and so on).

The highly mannered style of construction of *In Search of Anna*'s narrative may tend to disguise this opposition, but overall the movement of the narrative and the journey toward personal awareness and fulfillment of the two principal travelers, Tony and Sam, is away from the city (culturally *negative*) and toward the bush (culturally *positive*).

Tony is making the journey away from the particular social conditions of his area of Melbourne. It is quite strongly implied that this milieu is partly responsible for Tony becoming a criminal. It is clear that the "prison" of suburban Melbourne has driven Tony's mother to suicide and has virtually reduced his father to a monotonously vegetative existence whereby any capacity for emotional contact with his wife and Tony has been sucked out of him. Tony himself refers to this life as a prison on a number of occasions.

Sam is escaping a totally different social setting. She lives in affluent comfort in Sydney. *In Search of Anna* is at pains, therefore, to suggest that it is not simply social situation or relative economic status that provides Tony with his drive to escape, to find a meaning and a freedom denied him. Sam, too, for all her material well-being, is equally in need of self-discovery. This release and this freedom are found, significantly, in the bush—not the outback perhaps but definitely the bush of southern Queensland. In one of the few times when *In Search of Anna* actually slips into an expressionistic metaphorical mode (despite its montage, it is basically constructed from a realist aesthetic), the film has Tony literally "confront himself" in a bush setting—in a fit of cathartic release, he smashes a window with his fist.

The bush's mythological place in Australian culture is again confirmed through the antinomy of bush/city, attributing to the bush the power to liberate what the city has entrapped. But in addition to the general cultural perception of the bush, *In Search of Anna* places the opposition in subculturally specific terms. The journey that Tony and Sam make to Queensland has particular resonances for those who live in the southeast corner of Australia, particularly in Melbourne but also in Sydney. Queensland has taken on something of the equivalent mythic status of the West in American culture: it is a promised land, a place of both escape and opportunity. (*Travelling North* utilizes this same image of Queensland.)

In Search of Anna avoids obvious stereotyping in its characterization:

Tony is not another screen ocker. His character is a little difficult to come to terms with. He is at times rather simple (uncomplicated, not dimwitted)—especially when seen in Melbourne and through his voice-over narrated letters to Anna; at other times, in his capacity for self-awareness and in his relationship with Sam, he is articulate and sensitive. The punctuated structure of the narrative helps avoid any obvious difficulties in accepting this ambiguity in Tony's characterization.

Sam is not as finely (or complexly) drawn, and the development of her character as a liberated woman sometimes runs the risk of cliché. By taking these two characters together, *In Search of Anna* is interesting in its presentation of a relationship between a man and a woman on approximately equal terms. It also allows the woman an autonomy that is not simply forced upon her by circumstances largely beyond her control (as in, say, *Caddie* or *Cathy's Child*) but is the product of both her own choice and social conditions (as in *Monkey Grip*). In essence *In Search of Anna* does not represent, thematically at least, a radical departure from mainstream Australian cinema. It does, however, represent a refreshingly different cinematic approach.

The Irishman 1978

Director: Donald Crombie.
Producer: Anthony Buckley.
Screenplay: Donald Crombie.
Director of Photography: Peter James.
Editor: Tim Wellburn.
Art Director: Graham Walker.
Music: Charles Marawood.
Sound: Gary Wilkins.

Cast: Michael Craig (Paddy); Simon Burke (Michael); Robyn Nevin (Jenny); Lou Brown (Will); Tony Barry (Dalgliesh); Gerard Kennedy (Chad); Bryan Brown (Haywood).
Production Company: Forest Home Films.
Running Time: 110 minutes

STORY

Michael Doolan lives in awe of his father Paddy, a teamster who hauls goods from the coast to the remote inland town where they live. He looks forward to Paddy's return—as does Jenny, Paddy's long-suffering wife. Paddy's homecoming renews the conflict with his oldest son, Will. Will finds work, to his father's disgust, with Eric Haywood, a local

The Irishman. National Film and Sound Archive/Anthony Buckley.

carter who uses a motor truck. A fight with Will over Paddy's drunken treatment of Jenny results in Paddy leaving home. Michael gets a job with the dour local farmer Dalgliesh, but takes the opportunity of a muster to the coast to look for Paddy. He finds him at a logging camp still working with the team. Paddy is killed in an accident. A more grownup Michael returns to the Dalgliesh farm.

COMMENT

The Irishman is profoundly nostalgic for the simple, lost lifestyle of the pioneers—who made the country "what it is today" while at the same time (the essential corollary in the Australian context) being made by the land itself. This nostalgia is partly narrative. The life of the central figures in the drama, the Doolan family, is harsh, poor, and at the whim of economic and environmental conditions. Yet they are, despite internal tensions, a caring, feeling family bound together by lack of material wealth rather than riven by it. The film also reflects a time when a man could be his own boss, or a boy could knock off work to go fishing, or all classes could be brought together by the simple rural ritual of the country race meeting.

The other part of *The Irishman*'s nostalgia is created and sustained by the *mise-en-scène*—by the cinematography and calculated aesthetic use of the Australian landscape, the quality of the light in the bush, and the meticulous period reconstruction—at once familiar, friendly, and strange. *The Irishman* is one of the leading exponents in Australian cinema (with *Burke and Wills* and *Crocodile Dundee*) of this artistic use of the visual possibilities of landscape and light (although the use of environment is even more rigorously and calculatedly structured into *Picnic at Hanging Rock*'s very meaning). In short, *The Irishman* is a beautiful film to look at; even the rather dingy houses of the far-from-prosperous pioneers are made to look pretty through the cinematography.

The Irishman also demonstrates its affinities with other Australian films through its two main thematic concerns. The loss or destruction of a lifestyle is narratively described through the figure of Paddy Doolan (the Irishman of the title). Along with the (literal) destruction of Paddy Doolan is the destruction of a whole way of life represented by the tiny town he lives in and the changes that are wrought upon it as the narrative unfolds. Like so many Australian heroes, Paddy Doolan is independent, resourceful, capable, and distrustful of change and authority. And like so many Australian heroes, he is finally defeated because these attributes are not, of themselves, sufficient to resist the changes.

On one hand, *The Irishman* suggests a negative view of progress, of change, of the inevitable movement of Australian society into the mainstream of twentieth-century Western culture. On the other hand, and in apparent contradiction, *The Irishman* celebrates growing up and offers a positive view of a movement toward maturity through the character of Michael, Paddy's son. The film might even be said to have two narrative streams—one centered upon Paddy, the other on Michael. But this second theme—displayed as usual through the learning experiences of an adolescent who comes to a fuller realization of his/her own power, place in society, and consciousness through the situations and actions of the narrative—is strangely muted, or at least ambiguous.

In other films of the genre, the adolescent protagonist is usually in rebellion against adult authority or at least actively seeking his/her own way in contradiction to the conventions in some manner. In *The Irishman* the revolt against patriarchal authority is actually located in the less central character of the older brother, Will: Michael never loses a childish hero-worship of his father.

This hero-worship of his father is one aspect of Michael's search for an adequate father figure throughout the narrative. The search is literal at one point when Michael seeks his father in the logging camp, but Michael's relations with the enigmatic drover Chad and the gruff Dalgliesh are clearly constructed along father/son lines—especially as the (underdeveloped) character of Dalgliesh suggest an active intention on his part to "adopt" Michael. Michael's growing up is, unlike that of other comparable protagonists (with the exception of Jamie in *The Mango Tree*), not a growing away; by placing him at the conclusion with the surrogate father, Dalgliesh, and in a rural setting (both of which he is pleased with), the film reconfirms a basic nostalgic stance toward a mythic innocence encapsulated as history. It is equally important that Michael's character has not undergone more than minimal development. In essence he seems little different from what he was at the beginning of the film—save for the presumed effect of the passage of time.

The Irishman suffers from comparison with other films of the same thematic preoccupation; but it does add further fuel to the arguments that claim the existence of a "growing up" genre of films in the New Australian Cinema.

Kangaroo 1986

Director: Tim Burstall.

Producer: Ross Dimsey.

Screenplay: Evan Jones, based on a novel by D. H. Lawrence.

Director of Photography: Dan Burstall.

Editor: Edward McQueen-Mason.

Production Design: Tracy Watt.

Music: Nathan Waks.

Sound: Paul Clark.

Cast: Colin Friels (Somers); Judy Davis (Harriet); John Walton (Callcott); Julie Nihill (Vicki); Hugh Keays-Byrne (Kangaroo); Peter Cummins (Struthers); Peter Hehir (Jaz).

Production Company: Naked Country Productions.

Running Time: 110 minutes.

STORY

After suffering persecution in Britain during the Great War, and dissatisfied with European culture in general, writer Richard Somers arrives in Sydney with his wife Harriet in 1922. Although claiming to be unimpressed with the dullness of suburban Australia, Somers finds himself drawn via his neighbor, war hero Jack Callcott, toward the protofascist leader "Kangaroo." At the same time, the union movement tries to interest Somers in writing for them. Somers procrastinates, unable to commit himself to either cause. Following a bloody riot, initiated with police connivance by Kangaroo and his private army, Somers refuses to tell the dying Kangaroo that he loves him. Callcott rebuffs Somers, and Somers and Harriet leave Australia.

COMMENT

Kangaroo is adapted from a novel by D. H. Lawrence generally accepted as being very strongly informed by his actual experiences and observations while on a short visit to Australia in 1922. The possibility that Richard Somers is D. H. Lawrence is rather peculiarly confused by the epilogue, a brief written coda that is in keeping with what has almost become a convention in the New Australian Cinema, to the effect that "D. H. Lawrence left Australia . . ." This information is extremely odd, given that no character by the name of D. H. Lawrence appears in the narrative of *Kangaroo*. The film's makers seem unsure whether they are making a version of *Kangaroo* (the novel) or a bio-pic that might have been called *D. H. Lawrence in Australia*. This confusion carries through the structure of the narrative, which does not engage the dramatic possibilities of a specifically imagined Australian history but remains more or less with Somers/Lawrence and his reactions to the occasional bits of history that he observes or is a peripheral participant in.

Nonetheless, *Kangaroo* is interesting because it provides a view of mateship in which the concept and the practice step down from their mythical pedestal and become a lived ideology. To this extent, *Kangaroo*, which in its novel form was more a prediction of a possible Australian future (which did not eventuate), provides an insight into a period of Australian history in which the dominant cultural hegemony was faced with the real possibility of rupture. This theme, challenge to community cohesion, is refracted through the presence of an observer rather than mirrored by what he is observing. The theme of threat to social cohesion is a consistent one in Australian television miniseries productions of the 1980s but is generally absent from the cinema, which finds its historical settings in times of consensus and not disruption. The possibility of social disintegration is graphically presented on several occasions in *Kangaroo;* it is the very background to the whole social situation that Somers observes and sometimes participates in. The narrative structure keeps it, unfortunately, in the background.

Mateship becomes a divisive rather than a unifying concept in *Kangaroo.* It is mateship as much as anything else that motivates Jack Callcott, provides Kangaroo with his powers as a leader (even though his concept seems rather more than tinged with homoeroticism—and megalomania), and fascinates Somers. But the film does not endorse this view of mateship; neither does it go so far as to take a convincingly iconoclastic view of it.

Unusually, even perversely, given the opportunities for integrating the landscape into the drama (a convention of the New Australian Cinema), *Kangaroo* almost ignores the landscape. Given that the film is an outsider's view of Australia (or at least the novel is), it is peculiar that no real attempt is made to present a visualization of that "alien" (and alienated) view. It is ironic that for once use of the bush in an ontological fashion might have been appropriate. It is even more odd given Lawrence's own response to the bush, which informs much of the novel.

There is, overall, an insufficient sense as to where the social conflict in the narrative has arisen. Because of the film's insistence on Richard and Harriet Somers as the central characters, the background to the political and social conditions in Australia can only be sketched in through exposition by others more intimately involved. The Somerses' comments on the disappointing dreariness of Australian suburban civilization—"Is this all men can do with a new country?"—provide little more than what is in any case a deeply felt cultural dissatisfaction with the uniformity of Australian cities, then and now. Because of the centrality of Somers and the inevitability that the audience identifies with him in particular, the possibility of the film rejecting the old European culture Somers represents (and affects to despise) is considerably reduced. Indeed, while Somers rejects European culture—the reason he travels to Australia—he also finally rejects Australian culture as well. This does, in the final analysis, provide an intriguing underpinning to *Kangaroo*. For, despite the brazen trumpeting of the merits, mythical or real, of Australianness in much of the New Australian Cinema (and elsewhere), there remains a seldom-expressed feeling that white culture has not managed an adequate response to the possibilities of Australia. *Kangaroo*, in a confused and ambivalent way, seems to raise this cultural bogeyman. But having done so, it does not quite know what to do with it. The film lacks a character of sufficient attraction whose views, attitudes, or philosophies might provide a focus of thematic identification.

The Killing of Angel Street 1981

Director: Donald Crombie.
Producer: Anthony Buckley.
Screenplay: Michael Craig, Cecil Holmes, Evan Jones.
Director of Photography: Peter James.
Editor: Tim Wellburn.
Production Designer: David Copping.
Music: Brian May.
Sound: John Phillips.

Cast: Elizabeth Alexander (Jessica); John Hargreaves (Jeff); Reg Lye (Riley); Alexander Archdale (B. C.); David Downer (Alan); Caz Lederman (Nancy); Norman Kaye (Mander).
Production Company: Forest Home Films.
Running Time: 100 minutes.

STORY

Jessica Simmons arrives home in Sydney after several years overseas to find her father B. C. actively involved in a campaign to save the homes of Angel Street from developers. Initially unsympathetic, Jessica becomes fully involved with the struggle to thwart the developers after B. C.'s mysterious death—which the residents of Angel Street are sure was murder. As Jessica becomes more active in the fight and develops a relationship with Jeff, a communist union leader, threats are made against her, her brother, and others in the street. When Jessica arranges to appear to tell her story on a current affairs television show, she is menaced again and Jeff is murdered. Shaken, Jessica goes on TV to expose the activities of the developers and the police. The demolition is stopped.

COMMENT

It is perhaps inevitable that *The Killing of Angel Street* should be compared with *Heatwave,* which it preceded by a few months. Both films are based upon publicly acknowledged facts surrounding certain inner city developments in Sydney in the late 1970s, particularly the involvement of criminal organizations, the corruption of various government officials, and the disappearance of an important antidevelopment campaigner.

The Killing of Angel Street is less consciously a work of cinema aesthetics than the *film noir*–inspired *Heatwave.* Stylistically, it is little more than a good tele-movie: a suspenseful story well told. If the film contains few surprises, it does, however, manage to embrace a considerable number of truly exciting moments—and if the opposing sides are a little too black and white (all the residents of Angel Street are lovable, attractive, sympathetic; all the villains, slimy, threatening, corrupt, and thoroughly nasty), a degree of suspense and shock is still maintained throughout.

The Killing of Angel Street had a mixed reception on first screening, being called "melodrama" and "soap opera" by its detractors and "astonishing" and "courageous" by its supporters. It is difficult to deny that the film frequently sacrifices social comment for drama and that its characterization is crude, if entertaining. In the end, the film does "cop out": all the nastiness (of which there has been no small amount) is laid at the feet of organized crime, attempting to launder money into legitimate enterprises. The chairman of the board of developers is shown to be a well-meaning fathead; the police are absolved by omission; and the suggestion that the Justice Department was intimately involved is headed off by simply suggesting that the government will cover up with a rigged enquiry to save face.

There is, however, an element of truth in the background to the story of *The Killing of Angel Street*—and this raises a possibility that the filmmakers did not wish to become the targets of either the criminals involved or the government by suggesting too strongly just what was really going on. Of course, the film is fiction and not, presumably, intended to be docudrama by any measure.

The cheerfulness at the end of the film as the demolition equipment is withdrawn and the "people" celebrate with a jazz band and beer rather oddly overlooks the fact that two people (at least) with whom Jessica had close emotional ties have been murdered. The director, Donald Crombie, is perhaps too interested in making an entertaining film (which this is, to be sure) to maintain a feeling of credibility based in "reality" or to pursue some of the social implications of his narrative.

Nonetheless, it is interesting to see an Australian film in which the "people" as a group or a community (especially one with an urban setting) are perhaps as important in the drama as are significant individuals and one that makes a strong, if muted, case for collective action. It is a pity, therefore, that the implications of Jessica's shock at finding that the social institutions that are there to protect the individual are the very things that individuals have to be protected from are not followed up.

Even so, *The Killing of Angel Street* is one of a number of city films that have strong female protagonists—or protagonists who become strong by being forced onto their own resources. Jessica is less a "natural" crusader than Kate in *Heatwave* and, unlike nearly all the heroines of such films (*Caddie, Cathy's Child, Hard Knocks,* etc.), is middle class. In showing the gradual awakening to social consciousness of a "typical" member of the bourgeoisie, at least, *The Killing of Angel Street* is political. Like *Heatwave* and *Goodbye Paradise,* it comes as close as any film to suggesting something is rotten in Australian society at the political and business levels. Revelations in the media, the courtrooms, and commissions of enquiry in various places in the years since *The Killing of Angel Street* was made have indicated that there is a high level of corruption and chicanery in both private and public sectors. But few films of the New Australian Cinema, and certainly not *The Killing of Angel Street,* are interested in going any further than suggesting in a very fictionalized manner the possibility of conspiracies and corruption. The image of Australia as a society free of the rottenness and corruption "typical" of Europe and North America is not seriously disturbed by this film.

The Killing of Angel Street is a well-written thriller. Its direction may be little more than workmanlike and its social conscience sacrificed to the demands of drama and suspense, but it remains an enjoyable film.

Kitty and the Bagman 1982

Director: Donald Crombie.
Producer: Anthony Buckley.
Screenplay: John Burnley, Philip Cornford.
Director of Photography: Dean Semler.
Editor: Tim Wellburn.
Production Design: Owen Williams.
Music: Brian May.
Sound: John Phillips.
Cast: Liddy Clark (Kitty); John Stanton (The Bagman); Val Lehman (Lil); Gerald Maguire (Cyril); Colette Mann (Doris); Paul Chubb (Slugger); Danny Adcock (Thomas); David Bradshaw (O'Rourke); Reg Evans (Chicka); Anthony Hawkins (Mornington).
Production Company: Forest Home Films.
Running Time: 93 minutes.

STORY

Kitty O'Rourke arrives in Australia from England as a war bride in 1919 to find her "officer-hero" husband is in fact an ex-corporal wanted by the police. A detective, the "Bagman," puts Kitty in charge of a nightclub—a deliberate ploy to provide a balance of power with Big Lil, the powerful local madam. When O'Rourke gets out of jail, Lil encourages him to take over Kitty's operation, but he is killed trying to murder Kitty. The shadowy powers that control gambling and prostitution ensure that Kitty is brought into line. Lil discovers that Kitty's partner Cyril is planning a train robbery and beats him to it. The Bagman helps Kitty recover the proceeds. Lil retaliates, but finally she and Kitty make a truce based on natural respect.

COMMENT

Director Donald Crombie's almost unchallenged position as Australia's only consistent director of "women's pictures" (*Caddie, Cathy's Child, The Killing of Angel Street*) continued with his production of *Kitty and the Bagman*. *The Irishman* stands out as the rare Crombie film that does not have a female protagonist.

Kitty and the Bagman. National Film and Sound Archive/Anthony Buckley.

Kitty and the Bagman, however, shows much stronger links with Crombie's earlier work than simply having a woman as the central narrative character. The film has more than a superficial resemblance to *Caddie.* It could almost be an alternative version of the story: what might have happened had Caddie herself not followed the "straight and narrow" but drifted into (or chosen to move into) the criminal underworld and/or prostitution. *Kitty and the Bagman*'s narrative is set a few years earlier than *Caddie,* but the circumstances of the eponymous heroines of the two films are remarkably similar. Each finds herself forced to rely upon scarcely realized personal strengths when betrayed by her husband. Each is forced into an alien environment and left to find her own resources in order to survive. Each works (for varying periods) in a pub. Each makes her own way by a combination of sheer guts, perseverance, and learning from experience to a point (at which the narrative abruptly concludes) where each achieves relative autonomy.

In both cases, this autonomy is indeed relative. For neither heroine makes her way without the help of men. Each has a protector who provides much in the way of support. The Bagman is central to the manner in which Kitty is able to work her way to her powerful position at the film's conclusion. Caddie is less dependent upon any *one* man but is dependent upon different men at particular points. Both women are also used by men (in addition to their husbands) at various times.

The similarities between *Kitty and the Bagman* and *Caddie* do not extend to Crombie's approach to his material. Arguably, he has deliberately changed his style and particularly his *mise-en-scène* in order to attempt to create a contrast to *Caddie* (and his other films as well). *Kitty and the Bagman* has a far more heightened visual approach, heavily stylized in set, lighting, and costumes. The predominantly *film noir* lighting and sets in most of the film are occasionally oddly out of place with other sets that look rather like those of a Hollywood musical. The *film noir* feel to some of the narrative and some of the relations between characters (especially between Kitty and the Bagman) contrasts rather jarringly with the parts of the film that are high comedy. Finally, on this point of unevenness of treatment, the obvious references to *Cabaret* (USA, 1972) in the nightclub scenes are unbelievable. Melbourne as a site of Weimar Republic–style decadence just refuses to ring true.

Kitty and the Bagman is, then, a film about (yet another) little Aussie battler (forgetting for the moment that Kitty is ostensibly a "pom"— i.e., English). The difficulty is that Kitty's tenacity, toughness, and resourcefulness are rather more implied than demonstrated. The film sacrifices this particular aspect for action and comedy. The narrative does not offer any fully worked out alternative to this diffused theme.

Some attempt is made to create narrative complexity by suggesting further depths of corruption beneath the surface of the story of Kitty (and Lil): the brothel, illegal gambling dens, and grog places are presumably "licensed" by more reputable and more powerful members of society. These implications are not carried through, and the film retains the cultural image of Australia as perhaps a bit naughty but basically innocent. (In this aspect, the film shows some continuities with *The Killing of Angel Street* as well.)

Permitted less narrative space but more intriguing is the possibility of a social/cultural positioning of Kitty and Big Lil. The Bagman makes a short speech about Lil being "one of the people" and "having the loyalty of the people," and the almost palatial home that Kitty acquires is contrasted with Lil's more modest terrace house. Lil is first seen distributing sweets to the kids in the street. This theme evaporates somewhere and may have only been suggested by historical knowledge of the actual characters upon whom the story was (rather loosely) based.

Kitty and the Bagman avoids the obsession with historical veracity that plagues many period productions of the New Australian Cinema. In its apparent deliberate failure to take historical representation seriously enough, it resembles *Eliza Fraser:* history provides background but does not totally determine narrative.

Kostas 1979

Director: Paul Cox.

Producer: Bernard Eddy.

Screenplay: Linda Aronson.

Director of Photography: Vittorio
Bernini.

Editor: John Scott.

Art Director: Alan Stubenrauch.

Music: Mikis Theodorakis.

Sound: Lloyd Carrick.

Cast: Takis Emmanuel (Kostas); Wendy
Hughes (Carol); Tony Llewellyn-Jones
(Tony); Kris McQuade (Jenny); Chris
Haywood (Martin).

Production Company: Kostas Film
Productions.

Running Time: 93 minutes.

STORY

Kostas Andropolous, a Greek immigrant living in Melbourne, is attracted to Carol, an Australian woman he sees at the airport and later carries in his taxi. Summoning his courage, Kostas calls at Carol's house and talks her into going out with him. A tentative romance develops and blossoms despite misgivings by friends on both sides. Kostas returns to his former profession as a journalist working for a local Greek-language newspaper. Cultural differences begin to intrude into the relationship; after Kostas gets into a fight with an obnoxious guest at Carol's dinner party, she ends the affair. Being informed that his mother has died, Kostas leaves to return to Greece. Carol is reconciled with him at the airport before he catches his plane.

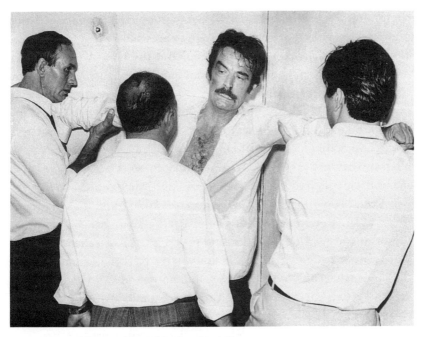

Kostas. National Film and Sound Archive/Paul Cox.

COMMENT

At a time when the New Australian Cinema had become firmly established with local and international successes, particularly with films that showed considerable polish in their production values, *Kostas* looked like a throwback to the tentative learning-by-doing films of the early part of the 1970s. Part of this lack of polish is simply a reflection of the budget. Also, this was only the second fictional feature film by director Paul Cox. Perhaps overriding these considerations is the approach of the director himself. Although it was not obvious at the time, *Kostas* was a pointer to a very important talent in the Australian cinema that was going to make itself felt in the 1980s.

Taken by itself, *Kostas* has similarities to a number of social realism films of the 1970s, beginning with *Sunday Too Far Away,* continuing with *The F. J. Holden, Cathy's Child,* and *Mouth to Mouth,* and extending into the 1980s. At one level, then, *Kostas* seems to be a serious attempt to examine, or at least reflect, the lives and conditions of immigrants in contemporary Australia. Given the demographic importance of immigration, especially since the mid-1940s, this would seem to be an obvious source of narratives and themes. But the New Australian Cinema's main concern has been to explore and propagate the dominant cultural myths of Australia and to ignore social reality in favor of mythic reality. There are, therefore, only a few films that address this topic or take characters or actions from the facts of postwar immigration to Australia: *Silver City, Moving Out, Cathy's Child,* and one or two others. Not unnaturally, then, *Kostas* (like these other films) has as a major thematic preoccupation the concept of alienation.

It would be wrong, however, to see the exploration of alienation in *Kostas* as situated totally within the problem of cultural clash between the protagonist's Greek origins and his adopted Australian social setting. This is certainly part of the film's narrative structure: clearly, the difficulties that threaten to end the affair between Kostas and Carol are largely spelled out in terms of cultural incompatibility—but not totally.

The theme of alienation is not simply or totally cultural. Kostas is alienated in other ways. His desire to live alone (he consistently refuses to move in with his cousin and her husband), the distance (clearly of his own making) from other members of the Greek community, his own admission of his inability to feel at home in Greece as well as in Australia—all these add up to a personal alienation that transcends simply being an outsider in a foreign culture. In this way *Kostas* is linked with later films by Paul Cox: *Lonely Hearts, Man of Flowers,* and *My First Wife.* Alienation is at the center of all these films. Their protagonists are, to degrees that border on the profound, alienated from society, from normality. Each is making some effort to overcome that alienation. The films are explorations of those efforts, centering their narrative structures around impossible or difficult relationships and thereby exploring both the alienation and the efforts to overcome it. The impossible relationship in *Kostas* is between a Greek man and a middle-class Australian woman; the impossibility is both cultural and a consequence of Kostas's own psychological makeup.

While other Australian films place their narratives of relationships in environments that frequently threaten to or actually do overpower the relationships themselves, Cox's films allow the relationships to subsume the environment. Thus, despite the emphasis on things Greek in *Kostas*—both location in Melbourne and home movies of Greece—the film is not truly concerned with the question of the clash of cultures or of the existence of subcultures within the overall culture of Australia. These aspects provide a dramatic framework for the narrative and a metaphorical reflection of the actual conditions of Kostas's alienation. As Cox goes on to reveal in later films, he is interested in people in a deeper sense while at the same time avoiding oversimple or expedient psychological "insight." Cox recognizes that people are complex and that their motives and motivation may be hidden and inaccessible— what drives Kostas into seeking a relationshp with Carol is barely hinted at. Flashbacks provide only a little insight into why he is what he is. In this construction (or rather, this presentation as a given) of character, Kostas is comparable (even interchangeable) with Peter in *Lonely Hearts* and related to Charles in *Man of Flowers*. But it is true at the same time that alienation and/or uncertainty about identity are the opposite side of the coin from the brash self-assertiveness often displayed in the period/historical films and the ocker comedies of the New Australian Cinema.

The Last of the Knucklemen 1979

Director: Tim Burstall.
Producer: Tim Burstall.
Screenplay: Tim Burstall.
Director of Photography: Dan Burstall.
Editor: Edward McQueen-Mason.
Art Director: Leslie Binns.
Music: Bruce Smeaton.
Sound: John Phillips.
Cast: Gerard Kennedy (Tarzan); Michael
Preston (Pansy); Michael Duffield (Methuselah); Peter Hehir (Tom); Michael Caton (Monk); Stewart Faichney (Tassie); Steve Rackman (Carl).
Production Company: Hexagon Productions Pty Ltd.
Running Time: 93 minutes.

STORY

Two new arrivals, the ex-teacher Monk and the enigmatic Tom, join a bored group of laborers on a remote wildcat mining venture. The workforce is kept in line by Tarzan, "the last of the knucklemen." The work is hard and the living conditions primitive, with boredom relieved by gambling and occasional visits to the nearby town. Pansy, the most rebellious of the laborers, unsuccessfully endeavors to set up a fight between Tarzan and Carl, a huge German miner from another site. Pansy and Carl drunkenly goad Tarzan and Tom. Tom, however, reveals his skills as a karate fighter and beats Carl. This reveals him to be the "karate bank robber" sought by the police. Tarzan proceeds to give Pansy the fight he has been looking for—without a wager.

COMMENT

It would be tempting to treat *The Last of the Knucklemen* as a rather run-of-the-mill film, an inferior Howard Hawksian men-in-groups drama, if it were not for the fact that the narrative virtually re-creates in a contemporary setting the narrative conditions of *Sunday Too Far Away*. The characters of *The Last of the Knucklemen* are wildcat miners, not shearers (and thus arguably less a skilled elite), but the setting is the same: the remote outback, far from "civilization," with only other members of the crew for almost perpetual company and only work, drinking and gambling, and sleep to fill the twenty-four hours of the day. But *The Last of the Knucklemen* is not simply a contemporary rendering of the *Sunday Too Far Away* narrative (albeit with rather more story than the earlier film): it sheds a very different light upon the concept of mateship, the cornerstone of the Australian cultural mythos.

Whereas *Sunday Too Far Away* presents a grittily realistic view of mateship, and *Gallipoli* presents a highly romanticized view, *The Last of the Knucklemen* presents an iconoclastic view. Pansy (an admittedly obnoxious character), about to win the life savings of Methuselah at a game of poker, makes a short speech in answer to Tarzan's claim that "friends" don't play for such stakes, which concludes, "Yeah, we live together, we eat together, and we crap together. So what?" Despite the fact that the film has begun with an act apparently demonstrating the solidarity of mateship, nobody challenges Pansy's view of their relationship, not even Tarzan. This indictment of the concept of mateship goes straight to the heart of what in the Australian legend is claimed to be the very conditions that created mateship and ensured its continuance: the sharing of a common set of harsh material living/working conditions. It implies that mateship is a matter of choice rather than circumstance (an idea that *Gallipoli* may hint at but does not emphasize). It also gives voice to the hostility and aggression demonstrated in *Don's Party*.

While it is certainly true that the words "mates" and "mateship" do not arise in the sequence ("friends" is used instead, the connotation of which is arguably quite different in the Australian context, mates being more culturally powerful) and that the denouncement of mateship is made by the least sympathetic character in the whole narrative (the audience is encouraged to dislike him from the outset and looks forward to his comeuppance throughout), these two factors only partly soften the interrogation of mateship that the film offers. Indeed the very existence of "knucklemen" suggests that mateship is at best a fragile concept—although Tarzan is employed to impose external order on the group rather than internal order within it.

On balance, and with the exception of this interrogation of mateship, *The Last of the Knucklemen* is not an especially interesting film. With only rare exceptions, it makes no real use of the near-desert landscape in which it is situated—despite the possibilities of linking the barren environment thematically with the barren lives of its characters. Burstall "denies" the landscape in *Kangaroo* as well; yet both these films cried out for a thematic linking of landscape and dramatic conflict.

For the most part, *The Last of the Knucklemen* resembles an ocker comedy, although without the satirical intent and execution of *Barry MacKenzie* or *Don's Party*. In this it is rather close to *The Odd Angry Shot*—it shows "Australians being Australians"—but it lacks the richly humorous dialogue of *The Odd Angry Shot* (or even *Sunday Too Far Away*). There are shallow attempts to raise the characters slightly above stereotyped ocker images, but these seldom lead anywhere and are left hanging as reminders that these men do not exist in an outback limbo but possess some sort of background histories.

Unlike *Sunday Too Far Away*, *The Last of the Knucklemen* does not find this group of men unreservedly admirable; for all its realism, *Sunday Too Far Away* is still rather romantic in its view of the shearers. This makes *The Last of the Knucklemen* much more an examination of the internal tensions in male grouping, but it then tends to weaken this examination by its trivial plot and its tendency to place the two main characters, Tarzan and Pansy, into black and white polar moral positions. What might have been seen as a sparring for leadership position is obscured by the unrelievedly vicious opportunism of Pansy. He does not share Tarzan's philosophy—therefore he is not Tarzan's rival.

The centrality of Tarzan in the narrative and his character's function as a "boss" (or boss surrogate) employed to (literally) beat the workmen into submission if necessary ultimately lead to an equivocal view of mateship and its corollary, negative attitudes toward authority.

The Last Wave | 1977

Director: Peter Weir.

Producer: Hal McElroy, Jim McElroy.

Screenplay: Peter Weir, Tony Morphett, Petru Popescu.

Director of Photography: Russell Boyd.

Editor: Max Lemon.

Production Designer: Goran Warff.

Music: Charles Wain.

Sound: Don Connolly.

Cast: Richard Chamberlain (David); Olivia Hamnett (Annie); Gulpilil (Chris); Nandjiwarra Amagula (Charlie); Frederick Parslow (Reverend Burton).

Production Company: Ayer Productions.

Running Time: 106 minutes.

STORY

Corporate lawyer David Burton is called upon to defend a group of aboriginals charged with the manslaughter of another aboriginal in the backstreets of Sydney. David's uneasiness about the case takes a strange turn when he recognizes one of the defendants, Chris, as a figure from a recurring dream. His obsession with the case causes problems with his wife and family. David is convinced that the killing was tribal retribution and nearly gets Chris to admit as much. At night, as David's house is torn apart by an inexplicable storm, Chris comes to David and takes him to a hidden sacred site below the city sewers. Paintings and artifacts indicate an apocalyptic tidal wave predicted to destroy Sydney. Crawling out of a storm water drain onto the beach, David experiences a vision of a gigantic wave.

COMMENT

An analysis of *The Last Wave,* with its emphasis on the ineffable and the spiritual, suggests a continuing thread throughout all of Weir's pre-

The Last Wave. National Film and Sound Archive/Hal McElroy.

American films and therefore demands an examination of the connections among them. The most telling comparison, however, is with the film with which it is most closely linked: *Picnic at Hanging Rock* was narratively dependent upon a mystery that was not merely insoluble, but also essentially inexplicable. *The Last Wave* offers mystery and offers explanation; but the resolution of its narrative enigma is ultimately unsatisfactory.

Picnic at Hanging Rock couched its mystery in terms that could be accepted only by reference to the myths underlying the text. Thus its only narrative course of action was to deny resolution to its enigmas. *The Last Wave* posits narrative enigmas that depend upon the narrative for context and thus for their solution. But beneath the narrative enigmas lies the same sense of the inexplicable carried over from *Picnic at Hanging Rock,* which creates a tension that narrative resolution cannot of itself satisfactorily resolve.

The central narrative enigma surrounds the nature and form of the aboriginal secrets defended by the five men on trial. For the time that these secrets remain narrative unknowns, the film maintains its suspense and its interest at a high level; and as long as the nature of these secrets is only partly hinted at, the film works at a satisfactory level of dramatic tension. But as more is revealed (i.e., made rational or explicable to a white audience) the secrets seem less tenable as an explanation for the very mystery the film itself generates.

This is partly because the narrative posits two strands of dramatic tension that, while complementary to an extent, are also partly contradictory. First, there is the mystery surrounding the death of one of the aboriginals and the corollary of why the others will not say what happened (the audience knows that it was a ritual death by magic); second, there is the mystery surrounding David Burton himself: what do his dreams mean and what is the connection with the aboriginal secrets?

These two narrative strands are presented through a cinematic style, a *mise-en-scène*, that consistently suggests that strange, elemental, and even supernatural forces are controlling and guiding the destiny of the individuals, particularly David Burton. The achievement of the film cinematically does not seem to be matched by the disappointing narrative denouement. But, interestingly enough, that very denouement brings *The Last Wave* back into *Picnic at Hanging Rock* territory: the knowledge that David Burton gains does not provide him with power— he is as helpless (or even more so) in the light of what he knows at the end of his search as he was at the beginning.

The Last Wave is one of only a few films of the New Australian Cinema to comment on the place and position of the aboriginal in Australian society. At times a trifle less than subtle, the film does demonstrate white Australia facing the alien (aboriginal) culture in its midst—a culture that is hidden and ignored but exists despite the overwhelming hegemony of white culture. While the film is obviously sensitive to the aboriginals, it does run risks when it uses their presence or their actions as dramatic threats to other characters—even if the threat is perceived by the characters rather than "real." The film uses certain incidents between whites and aborigines to create dramatic tension. In these moments the film comes close to suggesting that the aboriginals are a threat to whites (a threat that *The Chant of Jimmie Blacksmith* shows to be real, if justifiable in that particular instance), in strange contradiction to its otherwise clear intention.

Given the deeply embedded racism of Australia's cultural mythology, it is interesting (and perhaps inevitable) that the protagonist of *The Last Wave* should be non-Australian, an American (or at least played by Richard Chamberlain with a distinctly American accent). Burton is thus an individual who is outside Australian culture—just. His status as an alien is important to the narrative, but does it also permit him to be outside the white Australian's historically fostered blindness to and prejudice toward the aboriginal?

The Last Wave makes the point a number of times that "we [white culture] have lost our dreams." As David Burton goes on to say, "They come back and we don't know what they mean." It is arguable that much of the direction of the New Australian Cinema has been to rediscover Australia's forgotten dreams, to present them anew.

The Lighthorsemen 1987

Director: Simon Wincer.

Producer: Ian Jones, Simon Wincer.

Screenplay: Ian Jones.

Director of Photography: Dean Semler.

Editor: Adrian Carr.

Production Design: Bernard Hides.

Music: Mario Millo.

Sound: Lloyd Carrick.

Cast: Peter Phelps (Dave); Gary Sweet (Frank); John Walton (Tas); Tim McKenzie (Chiller); Jon Blake (Scotty); Sigrid Thornton (Anne); Tony Bonner (Bourchier); Bill Kerr (Chauvel).

Production Company: Picture Show/RKO Pictures.

Running Time: 131 minutes.

STORY

Palestine, 1917: mates Tas, Chiller, and Scotty, troopers in the Australian Lighthorse, are dismayed when another of their section, Frank, dies of wounds. His replacement Dave is resented at first. Although he wins approval by courageously saving their horses while under attack from the air, in action Dave cannot bring himself to kill. After nearly losing his own life, he reluctantly transfers to the Mounted Field Ambulance. The British High Command, tired of the two-year stalemate in the desert war, decides on an attack on Beersheba. The attack goes badly. Faced with a real danger of running out of water, the Lighthorsemen rush the Turkish defenses in a magnificent and death-

defying charge. The defenses are breached and Beersheba taken. Tas
is killed and Chiller and Dave wounded.

COMMENT

The Lighthorsemen is based on a well-documented incident of World War
I, which provided the substance of a previous famous Australian film,
The Forty Thousand Horsemen (1941). *The Lighthorsemen* is not a remake,
although there are similarities in addition to the climactic charge at
Beersheba, especially the narrative focus on a trio of mates and a
romantic subplot for a major character—although the latter is a trifle
more plausible in this later version. Indeed, plausibility and historical
and military accuracy are high on the agenda of *The Lighthorsemen*—so
much so that the filmmakers seem uncertain at times whether they are
telling a story or recounting a history.

    The Lighthorsemen has many of the hallmarks of being *Gallipoli II,* so it
is unsurprising that it focuses much attention on the matter of mateship. The initial four "musketeers" are mates in much the same manner
as Snowy, Barney, Billy, and Frank in *Gallipoli*. They all knew each
other before joining up, having worked together back in Australia. But
very little information is given about their backgrounds; unlike the
situation in *Gallipoli,* we meet these four as soldiers and know them as
nothing else except for passing comments. The outsider who will
replace one of them, Dave, is given an Australian and family context—
little enough, it is true, but sufficient to strengthen his status as an
(inside) outsider. For not only is Dave brought in to replace the dead
Frank, but it is strongly implied that he is a different type of Australian
altogether—and that difference is not simply historical (he joined after
due thought and not with an idealistic view that the war was a bit of a
lark that would be over in six months) but also, and importantly,
cultural: Dave is from the city (or near enough, an outer suburb of
Melbourne). The others are, by implication, from the bush and so are
"genuine" Australians.

    The cultural delineation of Dave, especially in contrast to the others,
works in two somewhat ambiguous ways. First, by his actions—he can
ride, shoot, and generally show all the skills appropriate to a Lighthorsemen—he shows that he (and, by implication, urban Australians)
shares in the mythic centrality of the bushmen. Second, since for the

drama of the attenuated plot Dave is revealed to be "incomplete"—
while courageous, he cannot bring himself to kill—it is important
that his background suffices to provide a cultural explanation for this
"flaw." A true bushman has no problems with killing: the myth of the
bush often carries with it the strong suggestion that one of its effects is
to brutalize those who live in it.

The character of Dave, central to the story because the others are
given little dramatic space to develop, invites comparison with both the
central characters of *Gallipoli*, Archy Hamilton and Frank Dunne. Like
Archy, Dave is something of a romantic idealist, although not as starry-
eyed. He is, nonetheless, an innocent in most ways even if not quite as
"pure" as Archy. The major difference between the two is that Archy is
a bushman. Like Frank, then, Dave is an urban Australian though no
larrikin and, importantly, seems to lack a particular aspect that while
not making him a coward differentiates him from the others. Like
Frank, Dave redeems himself at the very end by an act of considerable
bravery and near sacrifice.

Mateship is taken for granted in *The Lighthorsemen* and is demonstrated rather more in its absence—the reaction to Dave taking Frank's
place. The affection that is built up—making Dave rather like D'Artag-
nan in *The Three Musketeers*—is partly a result of his meeting certain
mythic criteria (prowess and initially courage under fire) but is partly a
result of Tas becoming a surrogate father or big brother to Dave (who
has lost his own brother earlier in the war). The story does not give the
mates the same opportunities as the four mates in *Gallipoli*, and this
also ensures that there is no taint of ockerism about them.

While recognizing the historical fact that the Australian Lighthorsemen were under English command, *The Lighthorsemen* does not take a
clearly anti-English stance. It is quite affectionate to some "poms,"
especially when they have the good taste to cheer the Lighthorse for
their courage and recognize them as soldiers and not some undisciplined "rabble." Unlike *Gallipoli*, this film does not blame the deaths of
these Australians on the English. More than this, but arising from it,
the film is not underpinned by the sort of melancholy fatalism that, for
all its humor, informed *Gallipoli*. *The Lighthorsemen* does not create
perfect (Australian) heroes in order to martyr them. Although rather
more concerned with the broader historical picture, this film resembles
The Odd Angry Shot as much as it does *Gallipoli*. But more than either, it

takes the parameters of Australianness for granted and not in need of detailed exposition.

Little Boy Lost 1979

Director: Terry Bourke.

Producer: Alan Spires.

Screenplay: Terry Bourke.

Director of Photography: Ray Henman.

Editor: Doris Haller.

Art Director: Bruce Barber, Jai Hyland.

Music: Bob Young.

Sound: Phil Judd, Ron Green.

Cast: John Hargreaves (Jacko); Nathan Dawes (Stephen); Tony Barry (O'Day); Lorna Leslie (Dorrie); Julie Dawson (Ruth); James Elliott (Harry); Don Crosby (Cyril); Les Foxcroft (Grumpy).

Production Company: Summitt (International) Films.

Running Time: 92 minutes.

STORY

While in the bush with his father Jacko, four-year-old Stephen Walls becomes separated and lost. An initial search party organized by Constable O'Day fails to find him when he is frightened off by the group's drunken crashing and shouting. The following morning, hundreds of people turn up to comb the area. The local police are unable to cope with the task of organizing the search in a systematic way. Despite the presence of an aboriginal tracker, Stephen continues to avoid the searchers. As several days pass, it becomes clear that the police will not find Stephen without the aid of the local bushmen. O'Day passes control of the search to them. On the fourth day, Stephen is found and carried home by the rejoicing crowd.

COMMENT

Little Boy Lost is one of those minor films of the New Australian Cinema that is interesting less for itself than because certain aspects of its narrative structure and theme are solidly based in the cultural mythology of Australia. The film does not seem to be too confident about what it wants to say, let alone how it should say it. It has a tangled mess of random subplots, seldom motivated and even less frequently resolved.

The film is ostensibly based upon the actual events that surrounded the disappearance and eventual location after four days of a small boy in rugged bush country in the New England area of New South Wales. While this is no doubt the major narrative strand, it is oddly ignored, muted, or undervalued in terms of overall importance. The real narrative trajectory of *Little Boy Lost* is not toward finding the boy (which can be taken for granted even if the facts of the case are not known to the audience) but toward the moment when the bushmen take over the organization of the search and then find the boy.

The bushmen are given an almost mystical status from the outset of the film, somewhat akin to that of the aboriginal tracker, with two narratively significant exceptions: the aboriginal is actually seen to be functioning in a quasi-mystical way and also, importantly, he is frequently ignored by the others. The bushmen are not actually defined or indeed fully differentiated (physically or by the *mise-en-scène*) from the others in the search—they are just referred to as a special group, "the bushmen," throughout. In Australian cultural terms the mere title "bushman" gives the individual so designated a mythical status that separates him from mere city-folk, town-dwellers, or even farmers. His is a quasi-magical communion with the bush.

The conflict in *Little Boy Lost* is not man (or child in this case) against the bush, despite the film's spurious attempts to give the bush a metaphorical menace in the shape of an eagle that watches and at one point, it is suggested, actually attacks Stephen. (In even less convincing counterbalance to the malevolent eagle there is a lamentable attempt to introduce some cute fauna in the shape of a wallaby Stephen talks to.) The conflict of the narrative centers around the denial of the bushmen's rightful role in finding the boy. The dramatic buildup, after the initial loss of Stephen, is toward the moment when the bushmen take over the search, assuming their rightful function. Unfortunately, the film has not managed to make it clear what was wrong with the organization of the search in the first place, so it cannot make it clear in what way the bushmen's organization is superior to the previous way the search was conducted. In fact, it hardly seems different at all—except, of course, that it is successful. This has the effect of either increasing the mysticism surrounding the bushmen or simply relying upon mythic perceptions that accept it as natural that the bushmen would of course find Stephen.

While enhancing the image of the bushman (more implicitly than explicitly), *Little Boy Lost* offers some rather ambivalent attitudes toward other entrenched cultural myths. The idea of mateship and community spirit is emphasized by the manner in which so many people gather to assist with the search, with scenes of women making sandwiches, husbands turning up at the search center, and so on. Yet this palpable demonstration of collectivity is undercut by the manner in which the first searchers have to be dragged reluctantly out of the pub (by shutting off the beer supply), their drunkenness, and their lack of interest and general incompetence. Indeed, as suggested by Stephen's actions in running away from the crashing, shouting band of searchers, he finds the bush more hospitable and inviting than the company of these men. It is ironic, then, that it is the very people looking for him who cause Stephen to remain lost. *Little Boy Lost*, like so many films of the New Australian Cinema, finds pioneer/small-town folk less than admirable generally and is only too pleased to suggest, if not demonstrate, a qualitative difference between them and the true bushmen.

Overall, despite its rather disjointed construction, frequently awkward and superficial dialogue, and uncertainty of direction, *Little Boy Lost* manages to present a rather full range of Australian cultural attitudes toward authority, mateship, aboriginals (the native tracker is greeted with barely disguised racism by Stephen's mother), and religion (the local clergyman is not merely useless, but distinctly unpleasant). All these attitudes are paraded without a great deal of subtlety but nonetheless seldom without ambiguity. This ambiguity does not become as it might have the structuring device of the film; as a consequence, *Little Boy Lost* is left rather formless—not documentary but not satisfactory narrative fiction either.

Lonely Hearts | 1982

Director: Paul Cox.
Producer: John B. Murray.
Screenplay: John Clarke, Paul Cox.
Director of Photography: Yuri Sokol.
Editor: Tim Lewis.
Production Designer: Neil Angwin.
Music: Norman Kaye.
Sound: Ken Hammond.

Cast: Norman Kaye (Peter); Wendy
   Hughes (Patricia); Jon Finlayson
   (George); Julia Blake (Pamela);
   Jonathan Hardy (Bruce).
Production Company: Adams Packer
   Film Productions.
Running Time: 95 minutes.

Lonely Hearts. National Film and Sound Archive/Paul Cox.

STORY

Middle-aged Peter Thompson makes use of the services of an introduction agency to meet Patricia, a shy and somewhat dowdy bank clerk.
Their relationship grows slowly and tentatively: Patricia has no sexual
experience and is attempting to break away from her oppressive parents. Peter talks Patricia into taking part in an amateur production of a
Strindberg play, and gradually she begins to find the outside world less
frightening. The relationship is threatened, however, when Patricia
finds herself unable to face full sexual commitment to Peter. She tries
to end the relationship. After being arrested for shoplifting, Peter goes
into further depression. He and Patricia are brought back together by
the energetic if self-interested actions of George, the play's director.

COMMENT

Lonely Hearts, coming some three years after Paul Cox's previous feature film, *Kostas,* continues the themes that the earlier film explored (as
did the even earlier *Inside Looking Out* [1977]—a revealing title). It does
so with greater confidence in the handling of the material and more

importantly with characters who are not only more credible and more attractive but better developed. This does not simply imply greater insight into the characters being offered to the audience. To an extent this is true, but it is also untrue: for example, Patricia's relationship with her parents is shown, but the explanation thus provided is too simplistic in explaining why she is the way she is (somewhat like the background provided for Kostas in that film). On the other hand, Peter's character is more complex (although he is not necessarily a more complex personality psychologically) because his character is built up piecemeal without oversimple exposition or the suggestion of a single cause for his "condition." Cox has more confidence with his material in *Lonely Hearts* and is more willing to provide complex surfaces to explore his themes.

This confidence is exemplified by Cox's willingness to allow a comic tone in *Lonely Hearts,* which was co-written by John Clarke, a well-known Australian humorist. This makes *Lonely Hearts* a more engaging film than *Kostas.* The comedy, however, has something of an unsettling effect at particular points in the narrative.

The comedy is broad, almost farcical at times, which plays against the essentially realistic milieu of the film as a whole. In this realism (or more accurately, naturalism) mixed with comedy *Lonely Hearts* is rather different from Cox's next film, *Man of Flowers,* in which the very structure of the film is less rigidly "realistic" but the humor is more muted and rather more cerebral.

Alienation is again the dominant theme of *Lonely Hearts,* once again explored through a structure that constructs a seemingly impossible relationship that reflects the efforts of two individuals to overcome their sense of alienation. In *Lonely Hearts,* however, the impossibility of the relationship does not rely upon such direct causes as in *Kostas* (i.e., cultural background and perceptions), although Cox still hedges his bets by providing Patricia at least with clear conditions resulting in her inability to make emotional commitment: her oppressive and interfering parents. Peter's condition and the causes for it are implied rather than stated with such directness; this makes his character more satisfactory both in narrative terms and in terms of audience response. Peter's alienation is presumably a product of his previous sublimation of his self in order to look after both his mother and his institutionalized father. But there are no clear reasons given why Peter has become alienated from "normal" society—or why he now decides to try to overcome that sense of separation through developing a heterosexual relationship. Patricia's alienation is in fact more profound than Peter's and is a product of a totally cosseted existence with her parents.

It is the seeming impossibility of the relationship that is the key structural point in *Lonely Hearts*. The chance of Peter and Patricia's relationship being fulfilled, let alone consummated, seems for a while even less likely than the chance for Kostas and Carol; yet the fact that the former are together at the end seems more satisfying. Of the two, Patricia is the least developed both in the dramaturgical sense of characterization and also in the narrative sense of social awareness. The film is kinder to her: she is not often the butt of humor. Peter is rather more often made fun of; his character, however, is better able to handle it. Most of the comedy exists in peripheral characters: George (the play's director), Bruce (Peter's brother-in-law), and so on. The degree of comedy in *Lonely Hearts* represents a departure for Paul Cox: his earlier films are decidedly unfunny. The comedy in *Lonely Hearts* modifies the narrative, softening the quite genuine emotional content and removing Peter and Patricia a little from full audience sympathy. The comedy in Cox's next film, *Man of Flowers,* is much more fully integrated into its subject.

Lonely Hearts, despite winning the Australian Film Award for Best Film in 1982, is something of an interim film between *Kostas* and *Man of Flowers.* But the award is richly deserved. The crudeness of *Kostas* is not present in *Lonely Hearts.* It is a very polished piece of filmmaking— some of the polish being due to the depiction of the two central characters by Norman Kaye and Wendy Hughes, both members of what could be described as Paul Cox's ensemble. *Lonely Hearts* is a thoroughly believable film that combines wit and insight, sensitivity and a sense of humor.

Mad Dog Morgan 1976

Director: Philippe Mora.
Producer: Jeremy Thomas.
Screenplay: Philippe Mora.
Director of Photography: Mike Molloy.

Editor: John Scott.
Art Direction: Bob Hilditch.
Music: Patrick Flynn.
Sound: Ken Hammond.

Cast: Dennis Hopper (Morgan); David Gulpilil (Billy); Frank Thring (Cobham); Jack Thompson (Manwaring); Bill Hunter (Smith); John Hargreaves (Baylis); Michael Pate (Winch).

Production Company: Mad Dog Pty Ltd.

Running Time: 104 minutes.

STORY

Dan Morgan, released after spending six brutal years of a prison sentence for highway robbery, is shot when stealing a horse. After he is nursed back to health by part-aboriginal Billy, the two start careers as bushrangers, leading the police of New South Wales a merry dance. Morgan's reputation grows as his exploits become more and more public. Morgan determines to return to Victoria to have his revenge upon those who earlier imprisoned him. The enormous police hunt set up gradually closes in. Billy is caught and tortured. Morgan, sick and tired, is surrounded at a homestead and, despite police orders, is shot and killed. The callous authorities have his body desecrated in the name of "science."

COMMENT

Bushrangers occupy a special place within Australian mythology. They exist in specific narratives, historical or fanciful, rather than in a more general set of cultural perceptions. Practically all stories of bushrangers, real or fictional, follow a particular structure: they nearly always become outlaws by being forced into it by the "establishment." Usually poor and working-class, they are eventually forced to seek revenge for the wrongs done them; bushranging, which at first is a lark, becomes earnest when, usually unwillingly, they are forced to kill for survival. Although supported by the "ordinary" people, they are eventually betrayed and hunted down. Dan Morgan's history (at least as told in *Mad Dog Morgan*) is no different.

The reason why bushrangers should not have provided material for the New Australian Cinema other than this film is difficult to ascertain. It may be that the bushranger legend is too inflexible, too structured, and thus too familiar. It may be that while, like the convict, he represents an appropriately Australian attitude toward authority, displaying independence and, more than the convict, the ability not merely to survive but to be at one with the Australian bush, he goes too far in stepping outside the law. The bushranger is the cultural intermediary between the convict and the larrikin, one of the steps taken by the Australian male (in abstract) on the way to becoming the ocker. The bushranger may be too typical, too mythical, his history so much a repository of Australian mythical attributes and cultural perceptions that filmmakers have avoided him because he is too obvious, too stereotyped, his legend too easily a narrative cliché.

Mad Dog Morgan, while attempting to avoid a simple narrative trajectory and to add some psychological complexity to Dan Morgan, is guilty of a great deal of cliché, not so much with Morgan himself (although his actual story follows almost exactly the legend as summarized above) but certainly with the brutal representatives of authority and especially with the police. The film does accurately reflect the deep-seated Australian attitude toward authority and particularly the police, but it is too obvious. Even Morgan's part-aboriginal partner Billy does not transcend cliché (even for a rare appearance of an aboriginal in the New Australian Cinema): the film is too much at pains fully to equate Billy in both a natural and a mystical sense with the bush. The parallels in situation between Morgan and Billy as social outcasts is rather forced as well.

Fortunately, *Mad Dog Morgan* takes for granted a certain familiarity with the bushranger legend. It does not feel any necessity to re-create every aspect of the legend in order to explain what is going on. The result is, nonetheless, an episodic patchwork quilt of a narrative structure that has something of the feeling of what a bushranger's "public progress" may have been—appearing, committing some outrage, and disappearing again.

This, however, forces a great deal—after the opening expository scenes—upon the portrayal of Morgan by American actor Dennis Hopper. Hopper's powerful and eccentric performance gives considerable insight into how and why Morgan came to be called "Mad Dog"; ironically, in so doing he moves Morgan away from cultural centrality as the "underdog/battler" in Australian mythological terms and into a specific position as an "aberration." (He is considered to be so by the authorities, who speculate on whether or not Morgan is fully human.)

There is certainly a complexity, although unevenly presented, to *Mad Dog Morgan.* Part of this complexity is the less than flattering demonstration of Australia's brutal, inhuman past. The film demonstrates in its opening sequences (in Peckinpah-inspired bloodshed) the full extent of Australian racism—massacres of Chinese on the goldfields—and throughout emphasizes ingrained class structure. The similarities in these aspects, and indeed in overall narrative shape, with *The Chant of Jimmie Blacksmith* are obvious: society has driven a basically innocent man to criminality and murder and has in fact provided the lessons by which Morgan and Jimmie learn to behave in the way they ultimately do. Both narratives are based on fact, so the similarities in structure may indeed say something about Australia's social history. As with Jimmie, it is difficult until the very end to feel any particular sympathy with Morgan. While Australian cultural perceptions do value the underdog, there is a strong sense that even the underdog must conform to certain conventions, certain perceptions in order to be(come) an Australian hero. Morgan does not do this.

Mad Max 1979

Director: George Miller.

Producer: Byron Kennedy.

Screenplay: James McCausland, George Miller.

Director of Photography: David Eggby.

Editor: Tony Patterson, Cliff Hayes.

Art Direction: John Dowding.

Music: Brian May.

Sound: Gary Wilkins.

Cast: Mel Gibson (Max); Joanne Samuel (Jessie); Hugh Keays-Byrne (Toecutter); Steve Bisley (Goose); Tim Burns (Johnny Boy); Robert Ward (MacAffee); Vincent Gil (Nightrider).

Production Company: Mad Max Pty Ltd.

Running Time: 90 minutes.

STORY

Sometime in the future: Max is employed as an "interceptor" by Main Force Patrol, whose job is to keep the roads safe. After the failure of other Main Force pursuers to stop a bikie who has escaped from custody in a powerful car, Max takes over and drives the escapee to his (accidental) death. Max and his close friend Steve the Goose are called to the scene of a bikie-gang rampage and manage to capture one of the members—who is later released on a technicality. Max wishes to leave the force but agrees, at the insistence of his chief MacAffee, to go on leave. While Max and his family are vacationing, Max's wife and baby boy are killed by the same motorbike gang. Max returns, takes a powerful car, and goes off to seek revenge. Despite being ambushed and injured, Max manages to locate and wipe out the whole gang.

COMMENT

Mad Max and its successors are probably the best-known Australian films (except for *Crocodile Dundee*) within and especially outside Australia since the revival of film production began in the early 1970s. This is partly because *Mad Max* is one of the few Australian films that actually takes on the competition (i.e., Hollywood) at its own game and wins. By using a formula well known to Hollywood—or rather a combination of formulas—George Miller has directed a film as good as, and frequently a lot better than, many comparable Hollywood productions. (This success indeed spawned more than a few Hollywood copies of the *Mad Max* films.) *Mad Max* combines the well-known revenge story (from many a western and more recently from urban films like *Death Wish* [USA, 1974]) with elements of road movies (signaled by their concern with fast cars and spectacular crashes).

Mad Max succeeds through its visual treatment. The first ten minutes contain some of the most exciting driving sequences—complete with obligatory destruction—that have been managed for any film. It is not simply that a few cars, caravans, and even telephone boxes are demolished or that a few lives are (fictionally) put in danger—it is the way in which these scenes are photographed and constructed on the editing deck that is impressive. The remainder of the film displays the same meticulous attention to cinematic construction placed entirely at the disposal of narrative, telling a story in the most exciting, most engaging way possible.

It may be possible to see *Mad Max* extending the theme, perhaps epitomized by the Clint Eastwood *Dirty Harry* films, that there is little difference save an inherent sense of right and wrong between those with a badge and those without. There is no doubt that the audience is positioned to see Max's revenge as wholly justified. The difficulty with pursuing this thematic line is that the film itself provides few props to support it. There is little or no sense of a wider society that the Toecutter threatens or that Max protects. Max's chief may claim society needs heroes (and Max is of the mold), but the existence of that society can only be imputed. Its few representatives are mainly innocent bystanders. (And Max's status as a mythic hero has to wait to be conferred in the second film of the cycle.) It is also true that Australia has no real image of the future—other than the *On the Beach*-inspired scenario in which Australia might be literally the last place on earth in the aftermath of a nuclear war in the two sequels to *Mad Max*. It is tempting to suggest that Australia's lack of an imaginable future is due to the underlying cultural uncertainty as to whether Australians ought to be here at all. The *Mad Max* films easily dispense with all but the most meager society of postapocalypse survivors. But do the *Mad Max* films really take place in Australia?

Australian society, being basically a twentieth-century culture, is as obsessed with the motor car as American society; while it may not share (or display) the same confused mixture of love and hate in its attitude to the car, it certainly shares many of the iconic perceptions: power, strength, freedom, and so on. Concepts of revenge, let alone its successful execution, can hardly be claimed to be closely associated with exclusively Australian attitudes either. Indeed, the fact that Max is a successful, if damaged, hero places him at odds with many of the heroes of Australian narratives (cinematic or literary).

There is little, then, that can be drawn from *Mad Max* that is uniquely Australian. Even the landscape in the first of the *Mad Max* films is not especially iconically identified with the Australian (cinematic) landscape. Most of the action could have taken place in any American midwestern prairie state. It may very well be this lack of overt or celebrated Australianness that makes *Mad Max* (or the *Mad Max* films altogether) so outstanding in the Australian context. They may represent one of the very few occasions when attempts to make "cultureless" or international films in Australia have actually succeeded.

Mad Max was made with a very perceptive eye on, and acute understanding of, the commercial possibilities of a particular type of filmmaking. The fact that it succeeds where not a few other Australian films with similar ambitions have failed is proof that it is the quality of the production (script, direction, etc.) that counts more than the content. "It ain't what you do, it's the way that you do it" would seem to be the lesson for other Australian filmmakers who have set their sights on making films that deny any Australian cultural specificity.

Mad Max: Beyond Thunderdome 1985

Director: George Miller, George Ogilvie.
Producer: George Miller.
Screenplay: Terry Hayes, George Miller.
Director of Photography: Dean Semler.
Editor: Richard Francis-Bruce.
Production Designer: Graham (Grace) Walker.
Music: Maurice Jarre.
Sound: Robert Savage.
Cast: Mel Gibson (Mad Max); Bruce Spence (Jedediah); Tina Turner (Aunty Entity); Frank Thring (The Collector); Angry Anderson (Iron Bar); Frank Grubb (Pigkiller); Angelo Rossitto (The Master); Helen Buday (Savannah); Mark Spain (Skyfish).
Production Company: Kennedy Miller Productions.
Running Time: 107 minutes.

STORY

Max accepts despotic ruler Aunty Entity's offer to return Max's stolen property if he can defeat the Blaster in Thunderdome. Max defeats Blaster but cannot kill him when he is revealed to be no more than an overgrown child. For breaking the deal Max is tied to a horse that is driven out into the desert. He is rescued by a girl from a tribe of children, the survivors of a plane that crashed escaping from a nuclear holocaust. Learning that Max is not the "captain" they are waiting for, some of the tribe leave their sanctuary and head out into the desert. Max goes after them. They make it to Bartertown but are forced to flee, pursued by Aunty Entity. The children escape by plane after Max distracts the pursuers. Max is left alone in the desert.

COMMENT

It is impossible to ignore the most obvious commercial success story of the New Australian Cinema: the *Mad Max* trilogy. There is little about any of them that can be said to be culturally specific to their Australian origins. This is even more true of the third film, *Mad Max: Beyond Thunderdome*. Yet writer/director/producer George Miller does not attempt to disguise the fact that the film is made in Australia: most of the actors speak with obvious Australian accents. There are some allusions to Australia: the city to which the "lost children" return is clearly Sydney—the war/time-ravaged remnants of the Sydney Harbor Bridge and the Opera House figure prominently. Not that this is important—overseas audiences will not suffer from not recognizing the postholocaust city as Sydney. Other locations are less obviously Australian. It is, however, to George Miller's credit that he has not attempted to avoid Australian accents, even Australian idiomatic speech, for the sake of an international market.

The heroic status of Max himself has moved further away from cultural specificity with each succeeding film. There is no possibility of promulgating a thesis that Max is an Australian hero in *Mad Max: Beyond Thunderdome*. His heroic status is cross-cultural; he is a myth-hero in the manner described by Joseph Campbell in *The Hero with a Thousand Faces* (Miller admits that he was influenced by the work). The narrative of *Mad Max: Beyond Thunderdome* even removes the parallels with the hero of both Hollywood and spaghetti westerns noted in *Mad Max II*.

What works for all three films when taken as a trilogy is that each offers a narrative that is not dependent upon the others. Although all three films together tend to offer a mythic structure that enhances Max's total heroic status, each story is different—so much so that any attempt to make them continuous in some way would create logical absurdities. Each story has its own integrity. But it must also be recognized that the character of Max is a constant and that his function in each drama is at least partly dependent upon his function in the others. Nonetheless, Miller has deliberately ignored the possibilities of either his character or his audience demonstrating an awareness of an actual (but fictional) history of his main character garnered from his previous incarnations.

Mad Max: Beyond Thunderdome is (like *Mad Max II*) both more of the same and also sufficiently innovative to avoid being charged with being a remake. Some of the ideas in *Mad Max: Beyond Thunderdome* can be traced to the earlier films. The Feral Child of *Mad Max II* becomes a whole tribe of lost children in *Mad Max: Beyond Thunderdome*. The leather-clad warriors of *Mad Max II* (descendants of the bikies in *Mad Max*) become Aunty Entity's armed guards. *Mad Max: Beyond Thunderdome* and *Mad Max II* have very similar conclusions: the story of Max is shown to be an oral folk legend told by and to the descendants of those he saved from chaos.

Intriguingly, *Mad Max: Beyond Thunderdome* offers a reversal of the position of *Mad Max II,* in which Max, like the essential western hero, saves the struggling community from the forces of barbarity and savagery in order that it might have an opportunity to grow, prosper, and perhaps provide a better future. In *Mad Max: Beyond Thunderdome,* Bartertown might arguably be what the embryonic community saved by Max could have evolved into if the rosy promise of the end of *Mad Max II* proved to be illusory. In *Mad Max: Beyond Thunderdome* Max is instrumental in bringing about the near destruction of Bartertown (not unlike the Clint Eastwood western *High Plains Drifter* [USA, 1973]). That he does not succeed is justified inasmuch as Bartertown is not totally evil. In fact, given the imputed state of the world, it is not such a terrible place.

If the narrative of *Mad Max: Beyond Thunderdome* fails anywhere, it is in its failure fully to juxtapose the natural and innocent existence of the lost children with the oppressive (capitalistic-inspired?) corruption of Bartertown. The film is perhaps too concerned with giving value for money in terms of action, special effects, and elaborate futuristic sets to examine the consequences of not spelling out this central structural opposition. Thus the film tends to look like two films (or two ideas) perforce stuck together rather than one integrated narrative. As with so many of the fantasy films originating from Hollywood, cinematic spectacle has been permitted to get in the way of narrative rationality. In the light of *Mad Max: Beyond Thunderdome*'s very real attribute as a well-constructed piece of cinema, this may seem a minor objection, but it may also point to a trend that can be fatal (to the series) if undetected by the filmmakers themselves (cf. George Lucas's *Star Wars* series). The producers' (Kennedy-Miller) greater interest since making this film in producing miniseries for the television market mitigates against the possibility that there will be more *Mad Max* films.

Mad Max II (USA: *The Road Warrior*) 1982

Director: George Miller.

Producer: Byron Kennedy.

Screenplay: Terry Hayes, George Miller.

Director of Photography: Dean Semler.

Editor: Michael Chirgwin, David Stiven,

Tim Wellburn.

Art Direction: Graham Walker.

Music: Brian May.

Sound: Lloyd Carrick.

Cast: Mel Gibson (Max); Bruce Spence

(Gyro Captain); Mike Preston (Pappagallo); Vernon Wells (Wez); Kjell Nilsson (Humungus); Emil Minty (Feral Child); Max Phipps (Toadie).

Production Company: Kennedy Miller Entertainment.
Running Time: 94 minutes.

STORY

The world has been devastated by a global conflict. The Wastelands are prowled by scavenging hordes of barbarian warriors. Max roams the wastes looking for fuel. The pilot of a gyro copter leads him to a small group of beleaguered people who are pumping and refining oil while fighting off the barbarians led by the giant Lord Humungus. In return for providing a truck capable of hauling their precious fuel through the desert to an unknown "paradise" in the north, they agree to provide Max with fuel for his car. Max returns with a truck; when his own car is destroyed, he offers to drive the truck in the breakout. After a deadly pursuit, the truck crashes, revealing that it is loaded with sand—another vehicle has escaped with the fuel while the barbarians were busy chasing Max.

COMMENT

Sequels to successful films are almost unknown in the New Australian Cinema. There was a sequel to *The Adventures of Barry McKenzie* and also to *Alvin Purple*, but the failure of the lackluster second versions of these two films may have discouraged production of sequels—until *Crocodile Dundee*, of course. (There was also a sequel to *The Man from Snowy River*.) The *Mad Max* cycle is unique among Australian productions: there has been not one sequel but two. (It is arguable that *Alvin Purple* has a second sequel, a film called *Melvin, Son of Alvin* [1986], of which the less said the better.)

Unlike its few Australian companions and many of the Hollywood sequels, *Mad Max II* is a film that is easily as good as if not better than the first. Each succeeding *Mad Max* film has shown a greater degree of originality in the narrative. This is not to say that certain aspects of the formula have not been retained: the fascination with high-powered vehicles as instruments of destruction in both *Mad Max* and *Mad Max II* and the presence of bizarre warrior/barbarians (the descendants of the bikies in *Mad Max*) in *Mad Max II* and *Mad Max: Beyond Thunderdome*. Overall, these films have displayed a capacity for reviving and refreshing convention and cliché that places them apart from the tired old same-again sequels of so many Hollywood productions.

Mad Max II is even more like a western in its narrative structure (and also in its location) than its predecessor. But where *Mad Max* was like a western of the late 1950s (especially in its concern with the motif of revenge), *Mad Max II* is more like a spaghetti western. This is particularly so in its cinematic emphasis on the physical appearance of characters rather than their actions and in its creation of villains who are not only evil without any need for psychological explanation but are also personified to some extent rather than abstract. The villains in *Mad Max II* make those of the first film seem little more than Boy Scouts being a trifle naughty. *Mad Max II* also demonstrates the paring away to reveal the essential conventions of the genre that typified the spaghetti western. There is more story than in *Mad Max,* but incidentals are deleted so that there is greater focus on what is essential to the narrative. The spaghetti western has been described as being the "opera of violence" and the description is equally apt to *Mad Max II*—as in opera, the violence belongs to another plane of reality.

The heroic status of Max is enhanced in *Mad Max II.* In the previous film, Max was only an ordinary man driven by extraordinary events (the killing of his family) to enact a revenge that took him beyond normality—thus the "Mad." That ordinariness is further peeled away in *Mad Max II* (not the least by deliberately removing the "prettiness" of actor Mel Gibson by makeup). Max's heroic status is demonstrated from the outset (for the audience), although the "good" people he must help need longer to see it—as they always do in this narrative formula. Max comes closer to being a full-fledged mythic hero in *Mad Max II;* but it is interesting to note that, if the journey of the myth-hero as outlined by Joseph Campbell in *The Hero with a Thousand Faces* is applied to Max's own journey, then all three films are needed to complete all the functions of the myth-hero.

The mythical status of Max is further underlined by the distance that the narrative itself has moved away from "reality," that is, away from any connection with social conditions as they are today. The narrative has moved into a realm more closely identified with that of legend and fable: an uncertain time zone and a location removed from the familiar trappings of twentieth-century existence. Without moving into a hypothesized outer space (as with *Star Wars* [USA, 1977]) *Mad Max II* has, nonetheless, moved into the realm of fables. And in the process, Max has acquired further legendary status. He is thus not the hero "for our times" (as might conceivably be argued through the comparisons between Max and, say, the Harry Callaghan personifications of the *Dirty Harry* films of Clint Eastwood) but is closer to a universal hero, the warrior of myths and legends. Yet no single creation of a myth-hero can be totally removed from the time, the place, and the culture of his creation. Although each reappearance of Mad Max would seem to remove him further from contemporary reality, it must still be recognized that he is a contemporary 1980s hero related to Dirty Harry or Rambo, not created out of a social/cultural void.

The Man from Snowy River 1982

Director: George Miller.

Producer: Geoff Burrowes.

Screenplay: John Dixon, Fred (Cul) Cullen.

Director of Photography: Keith Wagstaff.

Editor: Adrian Carr.

Production Designer: Les Binns.

Music: Bruce Rowland.

Sound: Gary Wilkins.

Cast: Kirk Douglas (Harrison, Spur); Jack Thompson (Clancy); Tom Burlinson (Jim); Sigrid Thornton (Jessica); Lorraine Bayly (Rosemary); Chris Haywood (Curly); Tony Bonner (Kane).

Production Company: Edgley International, Cambridge Films.

Running Time: 100 minutes.

STORY

After the accidental death of his father, Jim Craig must leave the "high country" and prove himself before claiming his inheritance. Jim gets a job with the rich landowner Harrison. He is attracted to Jessica, Harrison's spirited daughter; at her instigation, and in her father's absence, he breaks in Harrison's prize thoroughbred colt. Following an argument with her father, Jessica becomes lost in the mountains and is rescued by Jim. Dismissed when Harrison learns of his love for Jessica, Jim is returning to the high country when he learns that the colt has escaped and joined a wild mob—and that he is blamed. Reluctantly, he joins all the horsemen from the district in the hunt: he is the only one able to pursue the horses through the mountain country and to return with the whole mob.

COMMENT

Like *Gallipoli*, *The Man from Snowy River* takes as its subject one of the most firmly entrenched of Australian legends, although it derives from a literary rather than a historical inspiration. "The Man from Snowy River" is a poem known to nearly all Australians from their school days. The poem itself (by A. B. "Banjo" Patterson, one of Australia's most popular nationalist poets) only provided the film with its basic inspiration, the final fifteen minutes of the film's story, and four of the main characters: the anonymous "man from Snowy River"; Clancy "of the Overflow"; Harrison, the squatter; and the "colt from Old Regret."

In the film, the narrative is fleshed out with a name for "the man," Jim Craig, and with motives for his actions in recapturing the colt where no other could (or dared to): to prove his right to live in the high country; to win Harrison's daughter; and to clear his name. Of these plot devices, only the first is implicit in the poem: the demonstration of the heroic qualities of the bushman. The film's narrative requires the man to prove his status as a bushman; the poem assumes it by the very fact of "the man" coming from the "Snowy River"—which is both a geographical and a mythical location (i.e., where "true" Australians come from).

In expanding one of the most popular Australian poems, the filmmakers have created a narrative that takes on an almost archetypal narrative-legend form, a claim that can best be supported by pointing out the parallels between *The Man from Snowy River* and the story of Sir Gareth from the Holy Grail legends. Like Gareth, Jim Craig must prove himself before his right to a title (the Man from Snowy River) can be accepted, through a series of tasks. The final task is single-handedly capturing the herd of wild horses that includes the famous colt from "Old Regret." In so doing, he will win the respect of his elders and peers and the hand of the fair maiden. Like Gareth, he must go into exile: leave the high country and go to the "flats" to prove himself. The parallels are omnipresent. Lancelot takes the form of Clancy of the Overflow. There is even a Merlin in the form of the "wise old hermit,"

Spur. Jessica, Harrison's daughter, has her equivalent in the Lady Lyonesse, who has to be rescued by Gareth as Jessica is rescued by Jim. It can even be argued that the chase to capture the wild brumbies is like the quest for the Holy Grail. (The leader of the wild horses is given a mystical, supernatural quality throughout.) Interesting as this close parallel between two legend-narratives may be, what it really boils down to is a familiar formula that occurs in many narratives, be they folktales, legends, or fictional films. But the makers of *The Man from Snowy River* have run the risk of presenting cliché, and it is a risk that has not been circumvented. Politely, it may be argued that the film uses well-worn formulas; less politely, the film has been compared with television soap operas. It falls somewhere in between, and the action scenes and use of landscape go some way toward redeeming the lack of subtlety in the storyline.

The comparisons with the formulas of medieval legends notwithstanding, *The Man from Snowy River* has still imparted an Australian flavor to each of the narrative conventions. In a comparable way, it is a fable for its time as the Arthurian Grail legends were fables for their time. Unlike *Gallipoli*, *The Man from Snowy River* does not enhance its (legendary) source but "reduces" it to the level of formulaic romance. Mythical Australian elements are still present, especially when the narrative is closest to the poem and when it uses the landscape in its mythical connotations: the environment that creates (and maintains) Australia's culture-heroes.

The Man from Snowy River shows a wholehearted embracing of the most persistent Australian myth of self-identity, especially in its assertion that the untamable bush is central to understanding what Australia means—or nearly untamable bush: Jim (being of that special breed, the "true" Australians) can tame it in part.

In passing it should be noted that *The Man from Snowy River II* (1988) virtually repeats the story of this film, although it does give more narrative importance to the class conflict between the wealthy landowners and the pioneer bushmen that is raised but not emphasized in the first version. An intriguing contrast between the two is the absence of mateship in the first and its presence in the second. In both, Jim's universal myth-hero status transcends his status as an Australian cultural hero.

Manganinnie | 980

Director: John Honey.	Sound: John Schiefelbein.
Producer: Gilda Baracchi.	Cast: Mawuyul Yanthalaway
Screenplay: Ken Kelso.	(Manganinnie); Anna Ralph (Joanna);
Director of Photography: Gary Hansen.	Phillip Hinton (Edward).
Editor: Mike Woolveridge.	Production Company: Tasmanian Film
Production Designer: Neil Angwin.	Corporation.
Music: Peter Sculthorpe.	Running Time: 90 minutes.

STORY

Manganinnie, the "red fire woman," is left alone in the Tasmanian bush after her husband is killed and her tribe scattered by white soldiers and settlers. Wandering, avoiding being seen by whites, she sees Joanna, the small redheaded daughter of a white settler. The two meet and go into the bush. Manganinnie searches for her tribe, teaching Joanna aboriginal myths and survival techniques. Near the sea Joanna drops the firestick, and Manganinnie is left without the spiritual protection of fire. Attempting to steal fire from some trappers, she is captured. Joanna helps her escape and steals flint to rekindle the fire. Manganinnie despairs of finding her tribe, returns Joanna to her family, and dies. Joanna kindles Manganinnie's funeral pyre and sings her spirit to the Dreamtime.

COMMENT

Where aborigines make a rare appearance in Australian film, their characters and functions are usually constructed around some element of mysticism associated with the environment, with the bush. This is an expected cultural perception that is not unique to Australia: the "savage" is usually considered to be closer to the natural world; narratives that involve this perception frequently carry the implication that "advancement" has resulted in "civilized" society losing contact with its natural origins. It is not surprising that the prevailing cultural perceptions of the aborigines should grant them mystical communion with the Australian landscape: white Australian cultural perception of the bush itself is a mixture of wonderment, awe, and fear.

Manganinnie pursues this theme of equating the aboriginals with a mystic but natural communion with the bush, and its corollary that whites have lost contact (to their detriment) with the natural world. It takes a child to comprehend the mysterious and wonderful spell that Manganinnie offers. This contrast of "understandings" of the world (and the universe) is emphasized by the juxtaposed versions of creation myths—Judeo-Christian and aboriginal—offered in the film. The aboriginal Dreamtime and the Bible are both offered to Joanna, and she is able to turn her back on the sterile myths of her father's Bible readings, embracing the life-enhancing myths of Manganinnie's storytelling.

While the history of the deliberate genocide carried out by the whites in Tasmania against the aborigines is well known, the film seems to offer no particular comment upon this, merely using it as the narrative situation that leads to Manganinnie meeting Joanna. This may be partly because the film was intended for an audience that would include children; and it may be partly because the main emphasis of its narrative was to be upon this unlikely relationship of aboriginal woman and white child. This relationship, central to the core of the film, is, however, based more upon mystery than upon any comprehensible attraction. The mystery is never really solved—the parameters of the mystery are never fully spelled out.

Like *Walkabout*—with which, despite a different aesthetic approach, it has very strong affinities—*Manganinnie* photographs the Australian landscape and places figures in it to represent the aborigines' mystic communion with the land, which is culturally reflected by their Dreamtime stories and their designation of places as sacred sites. Certainly, the Tasmanian landscapes are photogenic and quite different from those that are more familiar from films shot on the mainland (as is demonstrated in the only other film shot in Tasmania's wilderness, *The Tale of Ruby Rose* [1988]), but the images lack the capacity to shock or amaze that *Walkabout's* imagery has.

Like the two white children in *Walkabout,* Joanna travels through the Australian bush, seeing it for the first time and being introduced to and taught about its mysteries by a "supernatural" helper. Unlike the white children in *Walkabout,* Joanna is able to learn from her aboriginal guide; white enculturation has not blinded her yet. The implication of

Manganinnie is that what Joanna learns is significant; the difficulty is that the film is too detached to spell these things out.

Manganinnie is affected by an undercurrent of death, the certainty that Manganinnie will die, and with her a whole culture, way of life, and way of understanding. Like Joanna's singing away of her spirit at the conclusion, the whole film is a eulogy for the lost contact with nature that the destruction of the aborigines represents, not only for aborigines but for uncomprehending whites as well. The recurring image of fire that dominates the whole film (as it dominates Manganinnie's existence) is one of both purification and destruction. But it also represents the ultimate union of the aboriginal with nature: Manganinnie, sister to the moon, is made one with the universe—as her Dreamtime story of the coming of fire to earth from the stars confirms. *Manganinnie* is, however, as much about white mythic perceptions of the "savage" as it is about aboriginal myths.

As an attempt to present aboriginal culture *Manganinnie* still deserves much praise. It is, in this regard, much more convincing than *The Last Wave*, which wanders off into a mysticism that seems to have little to do with aborigines, or *Walkabout*, which seems too awestruck to be able to organize its thoughts. *Manganinnie* is, as a cinematic experience, an oddly remote one. As such it may be a true demonstration of the gulf that exists and perhaps cannot be bridged between the two cultures, which nevertheless recognize the experience of Australia as their ontological essences.

The Mango Tree 1977

Director: Kevin Dobson.
Producer: Michael Pate.
Screenplay: Michael Pate.
Director of Photography: Brian Probyn.
Editor: John Scott.
Art Direction: Leslie Binns.
Music: Marc Wilkinson.
Sound: Barry Brown.
Cast: Geraldine Fitzgerald (Mrs. Carr); Christopher Pate (Jamie); Robert Helpmann (Professor); Gerard Kennedy (Preacher); Carol Burns (Maudie); Diane Craig (Miss Pringle); Tony Bonner (Hinkler).
Production Company: Pisces Productions.
Running Time: 102 minutes.

STORY

Jamie Carr, in his last years at school, lives with his grandmother in a remote Queensland town at the end of World War I, in which he has lost his father. The "Professor," a drunken remittance man, becomes ill near the Carr home and is cared for by Mrs. Carr. In another part of town, the fanatical "Preacher" Jones takes charge of his niece Maudie when her mother goes mad. But his obsession with permissive behavior leads to his own madness, and after killing the town's policeman, he is shot down by a returned soldier. Jamie has his first sexual experience with Miss Pringle, his French teacher. He also takes a flight with Captain Hinkler, a flyer who served with his father. The town is struck by an influenza epidemic in which the Professor dies. After the death of his grandmother, Jamie leaves.

COMMENT

Inevitably, *The Mango Tree* is assigned to the category of "growing up in Australia" films, which seem to be an obsession of the Australian cinema. It predates the more famous examples of this genre and cannot therefore be accused of simply following a trend. In shape and appearance it is very much in keeping with the tendency of Australian cinema to make period subjects, located in the bush, utilizing the photogenic variety of the Australian outback and offering a nostalgic narrative based upon an individual growing up in circumstances that are shaped (or selected) from within the dominant strands of Australian cultural mythology.

The Mango Tree is different from the other films of this genre (*The Getting of Wisdom, My Brilliant Career, The Irishman, Puberty Blues*, etc.) in that, unlike the protagonists of these other films, Jamie Carr is very much in the thrall of others and is certainly not in rebellion against what these others represent or against oppression and the conformity they would force upon him. Jamie grows into, rather than out of or away from, as he grows up.

It is interesting to note that the male protagonists of "growing up" films are seldom in open or direct defiance of social convention and that they learn or mature through participation and observation—

The Mango Tree. National Film and Sound Archive/Pisces Productions.

particularly the latter in Jamie's case. Female protagonists, on the other hand, are almost inevitably in conflict with social conventions, with the restrictions and demands that society and the adult culture would place upon them.

Although the story is situated in 1917/1918, *The Mango Tree* is taken from a novel of much more recent origin. Placing the story at the end of World War I is clearly deliberate: it gains from the unspoken implication of the national coming-of-age resulting from Australia's involvement in that war. Mostly, however, the film gains from its period reconstruction the recurring element of nostalgia that permeated nearly all the Australian films of the 1970s; it presents simpler, purer times when attitudes toward moral questions were supposedly clearer and more easily arrived at, and, importantly, when Australia was an isolated community (like the town in *The Mango Tree*) capable of making its own destiny—or at least on the threshold of doing so (as urged to do in Mrs. Carr's patriotic speech).

The film wears its nationalism on its sleeve like many of its contemporary Australian productions, even embarrassingly so when it permits the matriarchal Mrs. Carr to make a speech about Australia for Australians—followed by an even stronger speech along the same lines by the newly converted "displaced" Englishman, the Professor. Like much in *The Mango Tree*, this incident seems arbitrarily placed—nothing in the previous narrative (save the part where Mrs. Carr "converts" the Professor) seems to suggest that a lack of concern or interest in being Australian has been a defining characteristic of the town.

The Mango Tree, while a traditional member of the genre in the ways mentioned above, is rather different in its presentation of a strong and positive matriarchal figure. While *My Brilliant Career* three years later does present a family ruled by a matriarch, in that film the grandmother is clearly the chief figure of the social domination that the heroine opposes. In *The Mango Tree*, Mrs. Carr not only seems to rule the town—her dominance of Jamie, albeit loving, is both total and unopposed. She is, within narrow parameters, the nonconforming spirit. This has the effect of shifting the narrative focus from Jamie to Mrs. Carr; even though the film starts and finishes with Jamie (repeated scenes of his leaving by train), the events of the narrative at times seem only incidentally related to him. Jamie remains throughout (except for his relationship with Miss Pringle) an observer rather than a participant, but the effects of his observation are seldom demonstrated. Even his decision to leave town after his grandmother's death seems to be at the instruction of (the now absent) Miss Pringle rather than as a result of any decisions of his own.

The only true sense in which the film actively allows Jamie narrative development (other than the simple passage of time and the accumulation of witnessed incident) is in his gradual sexual awakening and sexual fulfillment in his relationship with Miss Pringle. Sexual maturity is not closely linked with the theme of loss of (or threat to) innocence, which is the constant subtext of the "growing up" films of the New Australian Cinema. (I would not argue, however, that sexuality is absent from those films, but that it is at least submerged.) This allows *The Mango Tree* a certain distance from other films of this genre; but of all these films, it is the least interesting, a direct consequence of its lack of conflict.

Man of Flowers 1984

Director: Paul Cox.
Producer: Jane Ballantyne, Paul Cox.
Screenplay: Bob Ellis, Paul Cox.
Director of Photography: Yuri Sokol.
Editor: Tim Lewis.
Production Designer: Asher Bilu.
Music: Excerpts from Donizetti's *Lucia di Lammermoor*.
Sound: Lloyd Carrick.

Cast: Norman Kaye (Charles); Alyson Best (Lisa); Chris Haywood (David); Sarah Walker (Jane); Julia Blake (art teacher); Werner Herzog (father); Hilary Kelly (mother).
Production Company: Flowers International.
Running Time: 91 minutes.

STORY

Charles Bremer lives alone in a big house inherited from his mother. He indulges his taste for flowers, filling his house and garden with them. His emotional contact with others does not extend much beyond his voyeurism as Lisa, an artists' model, strips for him. Charles endeavors to exorcise his childhood memories of a repressive father and his obsessive attraction to female beauty through letters to his dead mother. Lisa's relationship with an egotistical failed painter, David, collapses, but Charles is unable to offer an alternative relationship. He does, however, decide to help Lisa. Charles arranges David's death and then has the corpse bronzed and presented to the city. Alone at the end, Charles nonetheless has learned to look out rather than in: to stare out to sea as Lisa used to do.

COMMENT

There is greater organic unity in and between the films of Paul Cox than in the (frequently more numerous) productions of other Australian directors. It is possible to trace a sense of development of ideas and approach, a refining of themes, in his works from *Inside Looking Out* (1977) to *Man of Flowers* and beyond to *My First Wife* and later films. This does not mean that his films are all the same or that they are only minor variations on a theme. Each of his films can and does stand on its own, but it is difficult to discuss any one of them without referring to the others. It is almost like tracing the creative trajectory of a filmmaker through his productions.

Man of Flowers is such a natural consequence of *Lonely Hearts* that it seems like an inescapably logical sequel. This feeling is enhanced by the presence of Norman Kaye in the central role of a seemingly socially paralyzed protagonist. Charles Bremer seems the extension of the psychological possibilities of Peter Thompson (and of Patricia) in *Lonely Hearts*. His search for meaningful relationships with others is much more doomed than Peter's because his initial points of contact and departure with "normal" society seem so much more remote. His alienation begins in childhood, whereas Peter's is a given and also seems to be temporary, the result of finite circumstances and not of deep-seated and irreversible psychological causes. Charles is permanently alienated; his actions are directed toward coming to terms with this isolation and separation rather than ending them.

Alienation, particularly personal/sexual but social as well, has been a constant Cox theme since *Inside Looking Out,* but none of his previous films had so plumbed the depths of profound alienation. Other films have held out the hope, indeed the reality, of a personal relationship that will defeat or at least modify this sense of alienation. No such relationship is possible in *Man of Flowers.* The relationship between Charles and Lisa cannot extend beyond voyeurism. The structure of impossible relationships from earlier Cox films is doubled in *Man of Flowers.* Lisa is at the center of a double helix: the relationship between Lisa and Charles is impossible because of his emotional sterility; the relationship between Lisa and David is impossible because of David's emotional parasitism.

While Charles may learn from his encounter with Lisa and others, he does not learn to integrate but to cope with alienation. Indeed, unlike *Kostas* and *Lonely Hearts,* this film does not show integration through close personal contact with another as a necessarily desirable outcome, even a need, let alone an answer for Charles. Although his loneliness is at times so acute as to cause him to weep, the film prefers to explore alienation by denying him integration.

That this approach does not make Charles pitiable is the consequence of the film's structure as unexpected black comedy. This is the result of the writing by Bob Ellis, who in other films (*Newsfront, Fatty Finn, Goodbye Paradise,* etc.) has shown a sense of existential absurdity and blackness unique in Australian cinema (at least before *Bliss* [1985]).

Man of Flowers differs from earlier Cox films in the very deliberate aestheticism of its images. The *mise-en-scène* borders on expressionist and is certainly in contrast to the documentary or neorealist styles of *Kostas* and *Lonely Hearts*. In keeping with its gothic theme, *Man of Flowers* is more consciously aesthetic than other Cox films.

The question still remains as to how Australian these films are. While it may be said that *Kostas* was firmly rooted in the social reality of immigrants in Australia, later Cox films seem deliberately to deny such precise social location. While alienation, in some sense of the term, lies at the very heart of Australian cultural mythology—Australians are after all aliens in an alien land—alienation as a theme is rare in the New Australian Cinema. Where it does appear, it is frequently in films by "outsiders"; *Walkabout, Wake in Fright*. But these two examples are both bush-located. Urban alienation is normally presented as social aliena-tion in terms of being an "outcast": delinquent (*Fast Talking, Hard Knocks*), unemployed (*Mouth to Mouth*), or black (*The Last Wave, The City's Edge*).

Cox's films are concerned with personal, psychological alienation and as such seem rather more European in temperament than most Australian productions. (The closest film of recent Australian cinema is John Duigan's *Winter of Our Dreams*.) Nonetheless, Cox's films stand out as so much gold in the midst of a great deal of dross in the New Australian Cinema in the early 1980s—and of them all, *Man of Flowers* stands out most.

Maybe This Time | 1980

Director: Chris McGill.
Producer: Brian Kavanagh.
Screenplay: Anne Brooksbank, Bob Ellis.
Director of Photography: Russell Boyd.
Editor: Wayne le Clos.
Production Designer: Chris Webster.
Sound: Lloyd Carrick.
Cast: Judy Morris (Fran); Bill Hunter
(Stephen); Mike Preston (Paddy); Jill
Perryman (mother); Ken Shorter
(Alan); Leonard Teale (Minister);
Michelle Fawdon (Margo).
Production Company: Cherrywood Film
Productions.
Running Time: 100 minutes.

STORY

Fran, a research assistant at a university, is concerned that she is growing older without finding emotional stability. Her affair with Stephen
ends after his wife discovers them together. A trip home to the country
results in a liaison with Alan, an old flame, but his limited view of life
and a disastrous weekend away together convince Fran that she has no
future with him. A liaison with Paddy, the university lecturer she works
with, promises fresh excitement; but Paddy's honest refusal to enter
into total emotional commitment leaves Fran just as unfulfilled as ever.
She decides to meet a school friend in Greece with whom she has been
in long and intimate correspondence. Despite learning of her friend's
death just before she boards the airplane, Fran decides to leave Australia anyway.

COMMENT

It is difficult to determine what the filmmakers had in mind by simply
watching *Maybe This Time*. With hindsight and cognizance of later films
with which writer Bob Ellis was involved (*Fatty Finn*, *Goodbye Paradise*,
and especially the film he also directed, *Unfinished Business* [1985]) it is
possible to assume that what was intended was a social/sexual comedy.
The film itself offers only fleeting moments when this possibility seems
actually to have borne fruit and to have produced scenes that are
genuinely funny. It might be possible to interpret the film as a female
answer to *Alvin Purple* except that it is too intelligent although just as
raunchy. There is a strange mixture of theatricality and almost documentary realism, but the mixture does not seem to be integrated. The
cinematography throughout is simply functional; it does not seem to
operate in any way consciously to add to the meaning of individual
scenes or to the overall meaning of the film itself. The film may be
deliberately neorealist in this regard or it may simply have no discernible aesthetic style.

Maybe This Time may be a post–women's lib view of women's role and
function in Australian society; but if so, the film is so personal, so
focused on the central character of Fran that it is hard to grant it metaphoric or metonymic attributes. Indeed, many of the other women
characters come very close to caricature (especially Fran's mother and

her next door neighbor). There is a sense of development by Fran, but her awareness of the way in which she is used by men is counterbalanced by two factors. First, there is a real sense in which she uses men as well to meet her own needs. Second, the men are treated (by the narrative) with considerable sympathy and understanding throughout. They seem, like nearly everyone else in the film, extremely reasonable—although of course functioning strictly from the standpoint of their own needs. This reasonableness about the male characters suggests that *Maybe This Time* did not have any satirical intent; the essential element of ridicule is missing.

Fran does not match up, in narrative stature, to the other heroines of the New Australian Cinema (e.g., Sybylla in *My Brilliant Career,* Laura in *The Getting of Wisdom,* Jessica in *The Killing of Angel Street,* etc.) because she does not seem to be challenging the social and cultural status quo. *Maybe This Time* does not challenge the masculine ethos of Australian culture—or if it does, it certainly does not do it any damage. The men are selfish, of course, and too totally immersed in their dominant male roles to allow Fran emotional autonomy, but Fran's actions (belying her letters to her absent friend) do not suggest that she fully seeks it. It is true that few Australian films have actually taken a discernibly feminist viewpoint—not even *My Brilliant Career,* generally considered to be a feminist text. The female protagonists have tended to be "victims" of oppression first, little Aussie battlers (against that oppression) second, and women only in the third place. Fran, her narrative situation, and the themes the film offers at the conjunction of character and situation are at least a little informed by feminist debate, but *Maybe This Time* is not a feminist film.

It is interesting to note that the resolution of the problem Fran faces (that she does not fit because of her inability to accept either the traditional role her reactionary mother would wish or the liberated woman role that her lovers would place her in) is to leave Australia "for good." This, in actuality, is a solution often sought by quite a few Australians. The importance given to this resolution—it is not simply a convenient way of ending the film—is the closest that *Maybe This Time* really gets to a direct comment (or a noncliché one) on contemporary Australian society.

The film does contain references to political events in Australia, especially the curious events of 1975 (the dismissal of the elected government by the governor-general), but these do not provide insight into character or exist as subjects in their own right. Social circumstances also appear almost irrelevant, which again seems aesthetically at odds with the neorealist approach.

Maybe This Time may be a narrative that charts one woman's growth to consciousness, but it is a trifle too obvious at times and at other times wanders off into quasi-poetic obscurity (especially in the voice-over narration of Fran's letters). It may be that the makers, in attempting a cerebral social/sexual comedy, have been a little too sophisticated, too clever by half. By avoiding the pitfalls of dualism, they have concocted a film that is too reasonable and ultimately, therefore, simply bland.

Monkey Grip 1982

Director: Ken Cameron.
Producer: Patricia Lovell.
Screenplay: Ken Cameron, Helen Garner.
Director of Photography: David Gribble.
Editor: David Huggett.
Production Designer: Clark Munro.
Music: Bruce Smeaton.
Sound: Mark Lewis.

Cast: Noni Hazlehurst (Nora); Colin Friels (Javo); Alice Garner (Gracie); Lisa Peers (Rita); Harold Hopkins (Willie); Candy Raymond (Lillian); Tim Burns (Martin).
Production Company: Pavilion Films.
Running Time: 101 minutes.

STORY

Nora lives with her ten-year-old daughter Gracie in the Melbourne suburb of Carlton. She meets Javo, a friend of her current lover Martin, and begins a stormy relationship, complicated by Javo's addiction to drugs. Nora's life revolves around her work as an occasional journalist for a small magazine, her daughter, and a small group of friends. Nora writes some songs for a rock band. She resists becoming involved with one of the musicians, trying to make the relationship with Javo work, but Javo's drug habit intensifies. When Javo takes up with Lillian, an actress, Nora resigns herself to the end of the relationship. She writes a short story based on the three-way relationship between Lillian, Javo, and herself.

COMMENT

Social realism has tended to mean (and not only in Australian cinema) films that have found their material in an observational approach to stories involving the lower socioeconomic stratum of society or the subcultures on the fringes of society. This definition is true of Australian films like *Mouth to Mouth, Hard Knocks,* and *The F. J. Holden.* What helps make *Monkey Grip* significant is that it does not find social reality on the fringes of society with the (from a bourgeois point of view) economically or culturally disadvantaged but finds its subject matter within the center of Australian society. While it may be argued that the population of *Monkey Grip* represents a subgroup (and all societies are made up of subgroups of one sort or another), the people observed in *Monkey Grip* are not the underprivileged. They are educated, articulate, and in most respects middle-class. They live in a world of art, music, theater and film, and literature. While perhaps not members of the intelligentsia, they are (both narratively and in the actuality from which these fictional characters derive) light years away from the ockerism of the outer suburbs and equally removed from the inner city disadvantaged (of, say, *Mouth to Mouth*). *Monkey Grip* does not have the appeal to the liberal conscience of *Mouth to Mouth* or the patriarchal moral condescension of *The F. J. Holden.*

Monkey Grip is not an easy film because it does not contain a conventional narrative. There is only the faintest suggestion in its episodic construction of a cause-and-effect linking, although there is a sense of chronological movement. In this regard, there is a sense of closure: the film begins one summer at the swimming pool and ends the following summer at the same pool. The film does have the central thread of Nora's impossible relationship with Javo and is at least partly held together by a spare but telling voice-over (in the past tense) by Nora.

The overall appearance of *Monkey Grip,* in absence of an apparent narrative trajectory, is one of acute observation. But the film does not resemble a documentary. It is, instead, the translation of closely observed reality to a fictional construction—not reconstruction but fiction imbued with startling veracity. No small part of this verisimilitude is due to the extraordinary performance by Noni Hazlehurst in the role of Nora. There is also amazing accuracy in the re-creation of speech patterns in the dialogue, which is not simply idiomatic or (as with *Palm Beach*) obviously improvised. This is one of the few scripts of the New Australian Cinema where the dialogue has both dramatic and narrative purpose while seeming to be without either.

Despite the fact that it has been adapted from a novel, *Monkey Grip* seems a complete work of cinema. It is not a cinematic spectacle (like *The Man from Snowy River,* for example), but it is a film that suggests that it could only exist as a film. It is "about" almost nothing. There is none of the moral indignation so often associated with social realism. There is neither criticism nor praise for the conditions of existence or for the actions of the characters. It is being at once fictional creation and observation that makes *Monkey Grip* so remarkable—and the fact that it does it so well.

It is impossible to discuss *Monkey Grip* and to praise it for its freshness, its originality, without also acknowledging that it is another production of the New Australian Cinema that posits a strong female protagonist in an urban location and thereby suggesting an inevitable (but perhaps not negative) comparison with films like *Caddie, Cathy's Child,* and *The Killing of Angel Street.* In *Monkey Grip,* as in these other films, the woman (and women in general) is let down by a man (or men), but is clearly stronger, more capable, in short, more able to survive in the city than men. *Monkey Grip* does not, like these other films, overdramatize (for narrative purposes) the fight for survival and the conflict of a woman making her own way in society. On one hand, it would seem that Nora does not have any particular battles in this sense except that of her own making in her *amour fou* with Javo. But it must also be recognized that the men in the film, especially Javo, are less strong than the women, less capable of survival (as witnessed by Javo's frequent recourse to drugs). The environmental and social conditions of this film may not have the drama of the other films, but the implications are much the same. *Monkey Grip* is not a feminist text so much as a film informed by feminism. It is also one of the most accomplished films of the second decade of the New Australian Cinema, and one of the best Australian films overall.

Mouth to Mouth 1978

Director: John Duigan.
Producer: John Duigan, Jon Sainken.
Screenplay: John Duigan.
Director of Photography: Tom Cowan.
Editor: Tony Paterson.
Art Direction: Tracy Ward.
Music: Roy Ritchie.
Sound: Lloyd Carrick.

Cast: Kim Krejus (Carrie); Sonia Peat
(Jeanie); Ian Gilmour (Tim); Serge
Frazzetto (Sergio); Michael Carmen
(Tony).
Production Company: Vega Film
Productions.
Running time: 96 minutes.

STORY

Carrie and Jeanie, close friends, escape together from a detention center for adolescents and find temporary jobs in Melbourne. They meet Sergio and Tim, two boys from the country who have come to Melbourne to look for work. After a night out Carrie and Jeanie invite the boys back to the derelict warehouse they live in. Tim and Sergio move in. Jeanie and Sergio are happy together, but Carrie still longs for her old boyfriend, Tony. After their job finishes, Carrie and Jeanie help support themselves by shoplifting while Tim and Sergio contribute their dole money. To get the money to open a stall at a market, the girls work as escorts; Jeanie doesn't like it but Carrie enjoys the money she earns. After Tony savagely beats an old man who shares the warehouse, the police visit the warehouse and Jeanie is put back in the institution.

COMMENT

Very few Australian films manage a balance between narrative and observation that permits each to inform the other. *Mouth to Mouth* is such a film. And few films of the New Australian Cinema have questioned so completely the image of Australia as the "lucky country" or revealed the social realities that lie beneath the cultural image. The disadvantages or deprivations faced by the quartet of young people in *Mouth to Mouth* are not cultural (as is patronizingly suggested of the adolescents at the center of *The F. J. Holden*) but social and, more importantly, economic. Although escapees from an institution, Carrie and Jeanie are not "bad kids." They are not (as yet anyway) involved in drugs or in any real criminal activities (although it is possible that if society continues to fail them shoplifting might lead to further criminal behavior). The two boys, Sergio and Tim, are not social offenders in any way—other than being unemployed.

These four and their story represent a side of society usually ignored by the New Australian Cinema in its search for representations of the Australian "dream," with its implied concern to present the country as one unified culture sharing the same perceptions and aspirations. The realities of social existence have provided considerably less inspiration than nostalgic perceptions of Australia's past. It is perhaps because of those very realities that filmmakers have turned to the past.

None of this detracts from the very real achievements of *Mouth to Mouth*. Indeed, it made both critics and public sit up and take notice when it was first released. It challenged the nostalgic and romantic view of Australia that was prevailing in film production at the time. It also represented a form of personal filmmaking that had been largely lost since the early days of the New Australian Cinema as a consequence of rising budgets, greater commercial confidence, and an eye on overseas markets. There was in the very structure of the film a discernible sense in which the director (as well as the actors) was personally committed not only to the production but to the subject. (John Duigan has remained very much within this sphere of personal filmmaking, as evidenced by *One Night Stand* and *The Year My Voice Broke* [1987].)

One of the most frequent terms used in discussions of *Mouth to Mouth* is "honest"—a suggestion, therefore, that the prevailing romantic images of Australia being purveyed at the time were failing really to convince their audiences. The social reality did not agree with the mythic images of an imagined past. Refreshingly honest as the film may have been, it cannot be said that it started a trend for neorealist views of the underbelly of Australian existence. Very few of the films of the New Australian Cinema that followed in the new few years were social realism; the production of period romance and genre films continued unabated (and produced some of the very best films). This is not to suggest that the New Australian Cinema totally recoiled from social realism. John Duigan's later film *Winter of Our Dreams* showed that he, at least, could still find much to say through this aesthetic. (He also mixes realism and nostalgia in *The Year My Voice Broke*.) It is true that these films do not concentrate exclusively, or even especially, on social conditions but on relationships that are affected by social conditions. It is difficult to escape the conclusion, however, that Australian filmmakers (and by inference their public) are less than keen on finding material in contemporary Australian society, let alone interrogating its realities.

Although somewhat schematic in its "pairing off," *Mouth to Mouth* is a film that, for once, manages to deal with the concept of sexuality without coyness or recourse to ocker-inspired perceptions. Sexuality is seen as a bonding between these young people, particularly between Sergio and Jeanie. It is what transcends the conditions and deprivations of their existence. The film examines social alienation at many levels, but not sexual alienation, and personal alienation only through Carrie.

Mouth to Mouth is not totally iconoclastic. It shares with many films the concept that the city is the arena in which women are most at home, most successful, and most capable of adapting. It is, after all, Carrie and Jeanie who introduce the two boys to the realities of surviving in an urban environment. It is not insignificant that the boys are from the country and less able to survive in the city than the two girls. The fact that a film like this, given its apparent refusal to operate within accepted cultural perceptions, should subscribe without reluctance to the perception that the city is the appropriate place for women suggests that cultural perceptions cannot simply be set in opposition to social reality and that the two exist symbiotically.

Moving Out | 1983

Director: Michael Pattinson.

Producer: Jane Ballantyne, Michael Pattinson.

Screenplay: Jan Sardi.

Director of Photography: Vincent Monton.

Editor: Robert Martin.

Production Designer: Neil Angwin.

Music: Umberto Tozzi, Danny Beckermann.

Sound: Geoff White.

Cast: Vince Colosimo (Gino); Kate Jason (Mrs. Condello); Peter Sardi (Lino); Sylvie Fonti (Mrs. Simonelli); Luciano Catenacci (Simonelli); Brian James (Aitken); Ivar Kants (Clarke).

Production Company: Pattinson-Ballantyne Productions.

Running Time: 91 minutes.

STORY

Gino, the adolescent son of Italian immigrant parents, is caught on a tightrope between two worlds: the traditional Italian culture of his parents and the Australian working-class milieu of the inner Melbourne suburb in which they live. Gino's parents wish to move to an outer suburb, the first rung up the social ladder for immigrant families. Gino sees this as a loss of Australian friends and a retention of the family's essentially Italian lifestyle. He is also in conflict with his teachers at school, which he considers irrelevant. A brief relationship with an Australian girl ends when they are caught, with several others, breaking into a house. With the completion of term, and the finality of the move from the old home, Gino accepts his future a little more happily.

COMMENT

Moving Out does not really have a plot as such; its narrative construction is that of the documentary: episodic, seemingly constructed of glimpses of an ongoing reality, and held together only by the continual presence of Gino. Indeed, the very style of the film is, for the most part, documentary—or, to use another filmic term, neorealist. (It is perhaps no coincidence that neorealism is associated with the Italian cinema and *Moving Out* is centrally concerned with an Italian family.) While the structure of the narrative is documentary and many of the scenes, especially those of Gino at home, have the "raw" feeling of actuality shooting (possibly enhanced by the inexperience of some of the actors), there are, nonetheless, quite a few scenes in which the realism of the film is lost through stereotyping or through a pursuit of comedy. Despite the film's sympathy for the immigrant families who are its focus, they are not infrequently presented as crude ethnic stereotypes—and nowhere is this more apparent than with the arrival of Gino's relatives at the airport.

Moving Out was praised at the time of its release for its accurate and sensitive portrayal of the social conditions of immigrants in Australia. There is no doubt that it seems more interested in representation (rather than dramatization) than other films with similar themes (e.g., *Kostas* or *Cathy's Child*). But it does, in keeping with most narrative

Moving Out. Jane Ballantyne.

fictions, provide a narrative core by focusing on a central character. In so doing, the film runs considerable risks: it places Gino in too many positions of conflict and alienation. To explore the question of assimilation into mainstream Australian culture, it puts Gino in conflict with his parents. As he says at one point, "You come out here a wog. You stay one, or you don't. It's as simple as that." He is in conflict with his teachers and (by extension) the school system in general. Also, Gino is experiencing the usual adolescent alienation and identity crisis (*Moving Out* is, again, not the only film to concern itself with this crisis: *Fighting Back* [1982], *Fast Talking,* and *Puberty Blues* among others have explored the same territory).

   Moving Out is another "growing up in Australia" film—different from the others that share this thematic preoccupation in that Gino grows up in an identifiably subcultural community rather than within a culturally central community like, say, the protagonists of *The Mango*

Tree or *My Brilliant Career*. But, like those films of this genre that have a male protagonist, Gino grows into rather than away from the prevailing social situation—at least, the rather rapidly arrived at conclusion suggests that this is so. The conclusion—the family does move, Gino goes along with them quite happily—is, however, less a resolution than an imposed ending. The major thrust of the narrative has been Gino's refusal to move on the grounds (partly) that it is a further retrograde step in maintaining the family as Italian first and Australian perhaps barely at all. His acceptance of the move seems to suggest he has grown out of his juvenile petulance, but also that wanting to "be Australian" is childishly petulant as well.

Growing up, then, is an issue for both adults and children in *Moving Out* only if it is accepted that assimilation is an equivalent of growing up or maturing within the broader, dominant Australian culture. In this regard, this film is a seemingly *subversive* text to the extent that Gino's family does not grow up. But failure or refusal to grow up is a hidden but omnipresent aspect of Australian culture in the broadest sense. That Gino accepts the move is a measure of maturity on his part but a step back (or away) from the Australianization that has separated him from his parents. All this means that *Moving Out* is actually quite an interesting and meaningful examination of an aspect of the "real" Australia that cinema frequently ignores: the multicultural nature of contemporary society.

There is no doubting the honesty of *Moving Out*. Nor can much argument be made with the realist style of the film—the casting is for realism and not glamour, and the capture of working-class and immigrant speech patterns is startling (because of its rarity in Australian cinema). But Gino's overall passivity in the face of constant conflict is faintly disturbing. Perhaps this is because actor Vince Colosimo (whose first role this was) cannot sufficiently register the internalization of the essential conflicts of his social, cultural, and adolescent condition. Or it may be that histrionic outbursts of rebellion or objection would undermine the determinedly realist approach of the film. The resulting suggestion that Gino has come to terms with his situation—his dual cultural identity, the move to the new home—is, however, without narrative motivation and begins to look like a traditional happy ending rather than the natural (or plausible) conclusion of what has gone before.

My Brilliant Career 1979

Director: Gillian Armstrong.
Producer: Margaret Fink.
Screenplay: Eleanor Witcombe.
Director of Photography: Don McAlpine.
Editor: Nick Beauman.
Art Director: Luciana Arrighi.
Music: Nathan Waks.
Sound: Don Connolly.

Cast: Judy Davis (Sybylla), Sam Neill
(Harry); Wendy Hughes (Helen);
Aileen Brittain (Mrs. Bossier); Robert
Grubb (Frank); Julia Blake (Mother);
Peter Whitford (Julius).
Production Company: Margaret Fink
Films.
Running Time: 100 minutes.

STORY

Sybylla finds life on a drought-affected "selection" stifling. She is delighted at an invitation to stay with her maternal grandmother, Mrs. Bossier, on the prosperous Caddagat station. Taken in hand by her "widowed" Aunt Helen, Sybylla gains confidence in herself. She spurns the condescending attentions of English jackeroo Frank Hawdon and expresses her determination never to marry. Although attracted to Harry Beecham, a local squatter, Sybylla refuses his proposal of marriage. After a brief and miserable period as a governess to the slovenly McSwat family, Sybylla returns to the drudgery of the farm. She refuses Harry's renewed proposal and, as a new day dawns, optimistically posts the manuscript of an autobiographical book she has written to a publisher in Edinburgh.

COMMENT

My Brilliant Career insists on being placed within the category of "growing up in Australia" films—of which there are (perhaps too) many in the New Australian Cinema. But this film is not simply the inheritor of a narrative formula that gradually accumulated increasing cultural significance. It is also a film that touches upon some central concerns of Australian social perceptions. That said, it needs to be acknowledged that *My Brilliant Career* teeters dangerously close to being little more than a stunningly beautiful film that gives visual pleasure but not much intellectual substance. Rather like an old-fashioned chocolate box, the packaging is beautiful to behold but inside there is only sugary sweetness that gives an instant response but dissipates quickly. But the film is deceptive in this; there is more going on than first meets the eye.

Of course, there is the obvious feminist theme running throughout, which, while occasionally strident, lacks a contemporary (late 1970s) gloss; it is very much the protofeminism of the story's original author, the late-Victorian author Miles Franklin. This feminism is enhanced by the dominant creative presence of women in the production in the roles of director, producer, and writer. The feminism personified in the rebellious character of Sybylla is, however, defused (or at least modified) by two considerations: one intratextual, the other extra-textual.

In the first instance, Sybylla's refusal to consider suppressing her own personality and talents (the latter being more self-professed than demonstrable) in the conventional subordinate social role of wife and mother can be read (and is occasionally inferred to be read) as the rejection of dulling conformity by a young, confident, and naturally rebellious adolescent spirit. It is not just because she is female that Sybylla wishes to shape her own destiny, although the fact that she is female does add a further dimension of drama and conflict to her determination. In this regard, Sybylla finds a counterpart in Laura in *The Getting of Wisdom*. (It is no accident that both these films were made from novels written about the same time by women.) Both Laura's and Sybylla's rebellion is that of an intelligent and willful spirit refusing to be straitjacketed by social convention—and Laura's in particular is hardly touched by any sense of sexist oppression.

It should also not be overlooked that most of the attempts at oppression of Sybylla are, in fact, made by women: her mother, her grandmother, Aunt Helen, even—in a kindly way—Aunt Gussie. (Of course, the argument may be made that these women are also victims of patriarchy and "know not what they do.") Men actually are either immaterial in a direct sense (Sybylla's father, Frank Hawdon), encouraging (Uncle Julius), or, in the case of Harry Beecham, would genuinely seem to offer Sybylla a measure of freedom her female relatives would deny her. For these reasons it is difficult to maintain the view that *My Brilliant Career* is simply or strictly a feminist tract.

In the second instance, then, it can be argued that in her refusal to submit to social convention and her objections to parental authority, Sybylla is reflecting the mythic values of Australian independence of the individual. This mythic ethos of independence and the rejection of arbitrary authority (social, cultural, or otherwise) is usually the preserve of the Australian male. Australia's cultural mythology does permit women such a role, however, even if it is limited in terms of the amount of freedom Sybylla thirsts for. Sybylla's battle for independence takes place in the bush, which enables her to share some of the mantle of the pioneer woman.

My Brilliant Career's greatest achievement is as one of a number of truly significant films that "tell Australians what we are" by "showing us what we were." While it is possible to argue that the film overromanticizes (both aesthetically through *mise-en-scène* and narratively), it is one of the few films that takes a serious (as opposed to sardonic and comically contemptuous) view of the pioneers. Its concern is not, of course, to do that (*We of the Never Never* does so much more directly). While the film finds it difficult to consider the grubby McSwat family subjects for serious contemplation (with the exception of the sequence about reading the wallpaper), it does, nonetheless, narratively unite the squatters (at Caddagat and Five Bob Downs) with the "cockies" (Sybylla's own family). For its own purposes, *My Brilliant Career* allows the prosperity of the family at Caddagat and the poverty of the family at Possum Gully to be exaggerated; but the sense of triumph and achievement against odds that the film's conclusion provides derives from, and add to, the myths of the bush and the pioneers as positive factors in the making of Australian culture.

My First Wife 1984

Director: Paul Cox.
Producer: Jane Ballantyne, Paul Cox.
Screenplay: Paul Cox, Bob Ellis.
Director of Photography: Yuri Sokol.
Editor: Tim Lewis.
Production Designer: Asher Bilu.
Music: Christoph Willibald Gluck, Joseph Haydn, Carl Orff, Ann Boyd, Renée Geyer, Franz Sussmayr.
Sound: Ken Hammond.

Cast: John Hargreaves (John); Wendy Hughes (Helen); Lucy Angwin (Lucy); David Cameron (Tom); Charles (Bud) Tingwell (Helen's father); Betty Lucas (Helen's mother); Robin Lovejoy (John's father); Lucy Uralov (John's mother).
Production Company: Dofine.
Running Time: 100 minutes.

STORY

John, a serious musician and radio announcer, has his smug naiveté shattered when Helen, his wife of ten years, tells him that she is having an affair and wants to leave him. At first, John is unable to take it in. He visits his dying father, an immigrant from Russia, in the hospital. His emotional turmoil turns to anger when he visits Helen at her parents' home, and he later attempts suicide. Helen returns to John and takes him home from the hospital, but refuses to make love. She continues to see her lover. John kidnaps his daughter Lucy from his parents-in-law but later returns her. A reconciliation is implied as John, Helen, and Lucy leave together after his father's funeral.

COMMENT

My First Wife represents something of a continuation of themes and concerns explored in Paul Cox's previous two films (*Lonely Hearts* and *Man of Flowers*) and at the same time a return to both a style of filmmaking and themes that predate these two. It explores, as do nearly all of Cox's feature films, personal relationships that seem doomed, with an intensity that is far more likely to be compared with Ingmar Bergman than with any contemporary Australian director. These explorations are nearly always of emotional and sexual relationships under considerable pressure. The central relationship that supplies the narrative and is the subject of scrutiny in *My First Wife* is more direct and more "normal" than is usual in a Paul Cox film. It is, as always, the relationship between a man and a woman, but in this case a relationship in danger of disintegration.

Because it is concerned with a relationship that is seemingly ending rather than tentatively trying to form, *My First Wife* is a return to concerns that Cox had expressed in his 1977 *Inside Looking Out*. Both these films, separated by seven years, are about marriages coming apart, about alienation not through separation but through and despite proximity. Alienation in *My First Wife* is only partly social—John is of Russian immigrant background, with attitudes and perceptions culturally different from those of Helen's middle-class Australian background. The alienation in *My First Wife* is more profoundly personal than in earlier Cox films and more deeply felt and violently reacted to because it is so unexpectedly and devastatingly revealed.

My First Wife is also a return for Cox to a style, an aesthetic of filmmaking, that had slipped away in his films from the mid-1970s onward. It is an experimental, artistic, European style that fractures narrative rather than presenting it in the linear, cinematic realistic aesthetic of *Kostas* and the other films. *My First Wife* is the sort of film that Cox made before he became commercially respectable with *Lonely Hearts*. It contains expressionistic or atmospheric sequences that are largely inexplicable in narrative terms: images of trains and images of trees taken from a moving train window. Other images seem irrelevant even in any thematic way: Asian peasants planting rice, for example. And Cox continues his aesthetic habit of using Super 8 "home movie" footage for flashback and memory sequences. But except for aesthetic continuity, it is extremely difficult precisely to locate the meaning of these scenes and these images.

The apparent schematic structuring of three contrasting marriages—John and Helen, John's parents, Helen's parents—seems to suggest seeing the film as an examination in contrasting marriage relationships. But the film tends to characterize both sets of parents, and their marriages, in terms that approximate caricature rather than serious observation (with regard to Helen's parents at least, this is one of the very few places where *My First Wife* even hints at the comedy that informed *Lonely Hearts* and *Man of Flowers*).

My First Wife resists easy dissection of its structure. It is a film about "nothing" more than John and Helen at a point when their ten-year-old marriage is breaking up. There is no real sense of why it is breaking up—or, rather, the reason for the breakup is so mundane as to seem unlikely. Yet this may well be part of Cox's purpose: the ludicrous ordinariness of the way the breakup is brought into the open serves as an extreme contrast to the violent personal emotions unleashed. But it is impossible to ignore the connection the film constantly makes between sex and death. Here the parallels between the various marriages is most evident, particularly between John and Helen's marriage and that of John's parents. (John's dying father tells him that his own marriage went through a similar crisis many years previously.) Both marriages are also breaking up: one by separation by choice of the partners (or one of them at least), the other by forced separation by death. Death is never far from the surface of *My First Wife*—physical death and emotional death.

My First Wife is not a film of action (in the sense that actions have the narrative function of exploring the themes). In this, the comparison with the films of Ingmar Bergman is even more pronounced. It is unusual, therefore, for an Australian film—particularly a commercial one—to have such a deliberately "arty" feel to it, to eschew narrative (not that it is plotless), and to construct itself of images that are so clearly intended as aesthetic contrasts: reality contrasted to expression. *My First Wife* serves, however, to reconfirm Paul Cox's status as a genuine Australian *auteur*.

Newsfront 1978

Director: Phillip Noyce.
Producer: David Elfick.
Screenplay: Phillip Noyce, Bob Ellis.
Director of Photography: Vincent Monton.
Editor: John Scott.
Art Direction: Larry Eastwood.
Music: William Motzing.
Sound: Tim Lloyd.

Cast: Bill Hunter (Len); Chris Haywood (Chris); Wendy Hughes (Amy); Gerard Kennedy (Frank); John Ewart (Charlie); Angela Punch (Fay); Don Crosby (A. G.); John Dease (Ken).
Production Company: Palm Beach Pictures.
Running Time: 111 minutes.

STORY

Len Maguire, head cameraman for Cinetone News, films postwar migrants arriving in Australia and engages in friendly rivalry with cameramen working for the competition, Newsco (headed by his brother Frank). Len's marriage to a devout Catholic, Amy, goes wrong when work keeps him away from home. The domestic crisis worsens due to the Menzies government's referendum to outlaw the communist party—an issue that splits Australia on political and religious grounds. Len moves out and lives with Fay, previously Frank's mistress. Television threatens the newsreel business. A final lease on life comes with the Melbourne Olympics in 1956. The hostilities between Russian and

Hungarian water polo players are filmed by Len, but on principle he refuses to sell footage to Frank for use as anticommunist propaganda.

COMMENT

Newsfront is as profoundly nostalgic as *Gallipoli,* although it is much more politically conscious. This is not to say that this film is more ideological—the fractured complexity of its narrative structure when compared with *Gallipoli*'s linearly direct narrative movement complicates its ideological stance. Like *Gallipoli, Newsfront* presents an atavistic approach to its mythic material; it is a film about innocence. Whereas in *Gallipoli* innocence is uncomplicated, natural, part of the myth, in *Newsfront* innocence is constantly challenged; it has to battle to be maintained, but it is a futile rearguard action and in the end is no longer mythically tenable. *Gallipoli* is about the destruction of innocents; *Newsfront* is about the end of innocence. It is nostalgic because it does not suggest anything of comparable mythic power—maturity, wisdom, worldliness—to replace the lost innocence. The film implies that the end of innocence is the end of that which is uniquely Australian (represented by the "real" Australian personified in Len Maguire). *Gallipoli* and *Breaker Morant* revealed Australians coming to terms with the outside world by going into that outside world. *Newsfront* begins and ends with the outside world coming into Australia and shows Australia's myths as too fragile to withstand the impact.

Newsfront's nostalgia is not of the rose-tinted variety. It does not postulate a golden age when life was necessarily more simple and straightforward. It is occasionally iconoclastic; it skeptically queries the truth of some of Australia's myths of cultural identity. It does, nonetheless, create a central character of heroic proportions, perhaps more heroic than any other protagonist in Australian films. His heroism is the final stand of the "true" Australian character as formed by unique conditions before that character succumbed to the suffocating effect of undeniable suburbanization and to the impossibility of maintaining an essentially Australian character isolated from the cultural and material inroads of the rest of the world.

Newsfront has a narrative trajectory that in itself demonstrates the movement from a state of innocence to a state of, if not full maturity, at least worldly wisdom. It does so by taking a large canvas, a narrative of

Newsfront. National Film and Sound Archive/David Elfick.

some eight years in "real" duration. This whole trajectory is, moreover, demonstrated by the opening precredit sequence of old newsreel footage that begins with views of innocence, moves through a veritable collage of Australian images, and concludes with images of death and destruction—although the last image of this opening sequence returns to the innocent beginning in order to commence the narrative both historically (just after World War II) and in terms of the state of innocence that is the starting point of the narrative.

The themes these images suggest will be reiterated within the narrative that follows, and the trajectory of that narrative will be the same as the trajectory traced in these opening actuality shots. Through the character of Len Maguire, the film constructs the same journey from a state of innocence to the (implied) destruction of that innocence. The film does not in fact permit Len Maguire's heroic status to be compromised: the film finishes before Len can actually be forced into final confrontation with his loss of innocence. Indeed, the film ends as Len makes a final, and apparently futile, stand in rejection of the corruption or compromise that follows the loss of innocence. The implications, however, are clear—and for this reason, *Newsfront* must be considered (despite the moments of skepticism it may provide) an exercise in nostalgia.

Len Maguire carries with him the central cultural image of Australian identity. *Newsfront* is not a fictional drama about an individual's loss of innocence; if it were, it would take on aspects of classic tragedy: a man brought down by his own flawed nature. The film is equally (or perhaps predominantly) about Australia's loss of cultural and social innocence. It states quite clearly that this innocence is lost forever and finds in the arrival of broadcast television the most potent moment of this loss and the impossibility of its return.

Whereas *Gallipoli* may reiterate the myth that Australia became a nation in 1915, *Newsfront* argues cogently that Australia's status as a unique national culture was lost in 1956, the year of the Olympic games in Melbourne and the coming of television. *Newsfront*'s nostalgia is not so much regret over the passing of Australian cultural innocence in general as it is regret over the loss of this mythic creature, the dinkum Aussie.

It is also one of the finest films of the New Australian Cinema. It is intelligent and thoughtful and carries its Australianness not as banner or marketing device but as the most natural thing in the world.

The Night the Prowler 1978

Director: Jim Sharman.

Producer: Anthony Buckley.

Screenplay: Patrick White.

Director of Photography: David Sanderson.

Editor: Sara Bennett.

Production Designer: Luciana Arrighi.

Music: Cameron Allan.

Sound: Don Connolly.

Cast: Ruth Cracknell (Doris); John Frawley (Humphrey); Kerry Walker (Felicity); John Derum (John); Terry Camilleri (prowler).

Production Company: Chariot Films.

Running Time: 90 minutes.

STORY

The suburban placidity and comfort of Humphrey and Doris Bannister's home is shattered when their daughter Felicity claims to have been raped by a prowler. Felicity refuses to be examined. Doris seems more personally affected than Felicity, who breaks off her long engagement with John, a career diplomat. Her lifestyle changes. Doris expresses an inability to understand the changes taking place in Felicity but sees them as her own personal traumas. Felicity takes to roaming the streets late at night dressed in leather and carrying the knife she claims to have been threatened with. Vandalizing a house, Felicity recalls the night of the "rape" and reveals it was not a rape at all—or if it was, it was she who did the raping. Felicity comforts a dying old man in a wrecked house and is freed from her past through finding compassion.

COMMENT

There can be no doubt that Australia is a bourgeois society and that the New Australian Cinema has, for the most part, confirmed this through the majority of its productions and supported it by implication when not directly asserting it. Even the potentially subversive perception of the ocker tended not to offer more than a passing critique of the

dominant bourgeois culture or to suggest that the Australian bourgeois consists of ockers anyway.

As there have been very few films that have questioned the very
"factual" basis of Australian dominant myths (*Wake in Fright* is a rare
example of such an extended critique), so there have been very few
films that have actually questioned the reality of middle-class existence
in Australia. Certainly, occasional films have suggested that life in the
suburbs can be, and is, pretty dreary. Usually these films refer to
working-class suburbia. But it is difficult to find another production of
the New Australian Cinema that offers (at least for a little more than
half its length) such a sustained, insightful, and indeed vicious attack
on middle-class Australia.

The Night the Prowler is a black comedy of Australian suburbia. In this
it is not unique. But no other films have managed quite the same
degree of blackness. Although the film begins with more comedy than
darkness, the bitter edge of the film's humor comes to dominate. Doris
Bannister may not be far removed from Edna Everage (from the *Barry
McKenzie* films) but there is, in her characterization, a hard edge of
reality that the grandly and exquisitely caricatured Edna Everage does
not possess. There is, amid the comedy, an accuracy in representation
of both the characters and, more importantly, the materiality of these
characters' existence. The furniture, the fittings, the decor—indeed
the very house the Bannisters live in—have been chosen because they
represent an exaggeration of the "norm" but also precisely because
they are the norm. The drama and the construction of the film cinematically serve to isolate and emphasize these things, making them
seem more ghastly—or rather revealing them to possess inherent
ghastliness.

The Night the Prowler does not offer any implication that the Bannisters cannot be held to be totally culpable in the matter of their condition, perceptions, and reactions to circumstances. Nor does it provide a
sense of what has made the Bannisters and their bourgeois circle of
friends and acquaintances what they are; it does not suggest that external conditions may have contributed to this materialistic nightmare.

The Night the Prowler is not, however, simply an attack on Australian
middle-class existence. Indeed, that theme tends to fade somewhat as
the narrative progresses. As the narrative turns inward to focus more

fully on Felicity herself and not on Felicity as an image held by others (particularly her mother), so the film's thematic concerns seem to change. The narrative becomes a search, a quest, by Felicity for her own identity—although it is still made clear that her "loss of identity" is the consequence of her smothered, oppressed middle-class upbringing. It is perhaps not a little ironic, then, given the apparently iconoclastic purpose of the writer and director, that in so creating Felicity's dramatic journey to selfhood they should touch upon a recurring theme of the New Australian Cinema.

The desire for independence, for autonomy, for responsibility for one's own actions occurs and recurs as a leitmotif throughout the Australian cinema of the period. There are a number of other films that have central protagonists who are young (and sometimes not so young) women realizing their strengths, their abilities, and their individuality and taking faltering but never failing steps toward exercising these. (These include films as diverse as *Puberty Blues*, *Caddie*, *Cathy's Child*, *My Brilliant Career*, *The Getting of Wisdom*, and *Maybe This Time*.)

The Night the Prowler is not, then, quite so far removed from the mainstream of Australian cinema as it may appear to be. In production terms, it certainly shows a willingness to try to integrate form and content a little more obviously than might be the case in the generally conservative aesthetic of the New Australian Cinema. It has a distinctly theatrical feel. This may be due to the influence of White's literary and theatrical writing or to Sharman's greater experience of theatrical production, but it is also to some extent clearly deliberate. It is more noticeable in the early parts of the film when the black comedy dominates, and distinctly less noticeable when the filmic narrative moves away from comedy. This makes *The Night the Prowler* an uneven work, but still a powerful if unsustained indictment of the Australian bourgeoisie.

The Odd Angry Shot 1979

Director: Tom Jeffrey.

Producer: Sue Milliken, Tom Jeffrey.

Screenplay: Tom Jeffrey.

Director of Photography: Don McAlpine.

Editor: Brian Kavanagh.

Art Director: Bernard Hides.

Music: Michael Carlos.

Sound: Don Connolly.

Cast: Graham Kennedy (Harry); John
Jarratt (Bill); John Hargreaves (Bung);
Bryan Brown (Rogers); Graeme
Blundell (Dawson); Richard Moir

(medic); Ian Gilmore (Scott).
Production Company: Samson Films.
Running Time: 90 minutes.

STORY

Bill, a member of the Australian elite SAS regiment, is given a twenty-
first birthday party at home before his unit leaves to join the task force
in Vietnam. There the members of his patrol group, led by older
Corporal Harry, find themselves in a round of jungle patrols in which
the weather is as much an enemy as the Viet Cong. One member of the
group, Scott, is killed; another, Rogers, loses both feet when he steps on
a mine. As the tour of duty continues, the endless rhythm of danger in
the jungle and boredom is relieved only by a drunken party with some
American artillery men (which ends in a riot) and by recreation leave in
Vung Tau. After fighting off a determined Viet Cong push (during
which Bung is killed), Harry and Bill end their tour of duty and return
to Australia.

COMMENT

Perhaps involvement in the Vietnam conflict has not weighed as heavily upon the Australian social conscience as it has in the United States.
Or perhaps the limited nature of Australia's involvement, when combined with the cultural expectation of defeat (very much part of the
Australian sense of identity), has meant that there has not been a need
to explore the whole issue of Vietnam. Certainly, there have been very
few films that have seen fit to make even passing mention of Vietnam.
(It is perhaps worth noting that there have been two substantial Australian television miniseries made in the 1980s that deal with aspects of
the involvement in Vietnam.)

The image of the Australian as soldier in this film is of the Anzac
legend as it stands, suitably culturally relevant, in the 1980s. Given the
order in which *The Odd Angry Shot, Breaker Morant,* and *Gallipoli* were
made—1979, 1980, 1981, respectively—it is almost as if *The Odd Angry
Shot* commenced a search: "This is what we are like now," it seemed to
say, "but how did we get here?" Each of these films, by giving the

The Odd Angry Shot. National Film and Sound Archive/Samson Productions.

parameters and structure of the legend so fully, operates as a cultural explanation as to why the Australians in the film (and, by partial extension, Australians in general) are the way they are. The legendary structure is less obvious in *The Odd Angry Shot,* but this, quite simply, is because there is no need to present the legend as such. Its cultural naturality is given: the film needs only to show Australia and Australians as they "are" and doing what Australians "do."

There is no cultural division of the Australians in *The Odd Angry Shot,* no neat presentation of types as in *Gallipoli* or *Breaker Morant* with the concomitant suggestion that there is only one who is the "true" Australian. In this film all the characters, both major and minor, are equally Australian. It would be possible to discuss the film as an ocker comedy were it not for the important fact that it deals with Australians in uniform and, despite an occasionally ambiguous attitude, tends to see them as slightly different from Australians out of uniform—but not sufficiently different to deny them cultural status as Australians. Quite the contrary, as the legend insists, Australians become more Australian as soldiers: Australia did not really become Australia until Australians proved themselves as soldiers. And then, as the ocker image has demonstrated, all Australians (not just bushmen, pioneers, and Anzacs) became Australians when they became ockers (if they are not automatically ockers *because* they are Australian). The mythic circle has turned in on itself with *The Odd Angry Shot:* instead of Australians becoming soldiers (as in *Gallipoli* and the Anzac legend), here soldiers become ockers.

The Odd Angry Shot is concerned with the group as a group, not with individuals who might occasionally be part of a group. The men in the group are all soldiers, members of an elite army group, the Special Air Service. More than this, they are all members of a small unit with this particular regiment, Patrol Group 22. And loyalty (or rather, in this Australian context, mateship) is defined by loyalty to the group and not especially to the regiment, to the army, or to Australia. The narrative is constructed around incidents involving this group; it can be hardly said to have a story as such but is a series of chronologically narrated events linked by the participants and the overall narrative situation of the war in Vietnam. *The Odd Angry Shot* does recognize the historical fact of Australia's involvement in that conflict, but it is no more a film about Vietnam than *Breaker Morant* is about the Boer War. It is a film that examines one of the essential aspects of the cultural myths of Australian identity: mateship.

Taking the form of the conventional war film or, more accurately, of the war comedy (as perhaps typified by *M*A*S*H* [USA, 1970]), the filmmakers have created a genre film that provides both characterizations and humor that are specifically Australian. But, unlike *M*A*S*H*, *The Odd Angry Shot* is not black comedy. It separates the comic sections of its narrative from its serious sequences of men at war. This does not mean that some of the action scenes do not contain humor, but that they are not essentially comic.

The Odd Angry Shot often borders upon being embarrassing in the same way as *The Adventures of Barry McKenzie:* the demonstration of "Australians being Australians" tends to emphasize crudeness, vulgarity, and gaucherie that transcend naiveté. It is, however, a very funny film. Its philosophy is that of the common lot of the (Australian) fighting man; Vietnam provides a location but not the subject of historical or social examination.

One Night Stand 1984

Director: John Duigan.

Producer: Richard Mason.

Screenplay: John Duigan.

Director of Photography: Tom Cowan.

Editor: John Scott.

Production Designer: Ross Major.

Music: William Motzing.

Sound: Peter Barker.

Cast: Tyler Coppin (Sam); Cassandra
Delaney (Sharon); Jay Hackett
(Brendan); Saskia Post (Eva).

Production Company: Astra Film
Productions.

Running Time: 94 minutes.

STORY

Sydney, New Year's Eve: four young people—Sharon and Eva, two friends from school days; Brendan, a drifter from a broken home; and Sam, a deserter from the United States Navy—find themselves trapped in the Sydney Opera House as World War III breaks out. As the night wears on and tiny bits of news of nuclear destruction in Europe and North America seep through, the four try to maintain normality in the face of incomprehension. They increasingly turn to each other, and even the seemingly hopelessly "macho" Brendan—at first a target for the girls' ridicule—reveals depths of sensitivity beneath his uncouth exterior. Finally, as these initially fragile relationships begin to turn to mutual dependence, they are ordered to take shelter in the underground railway. Outside, nuclear bombs strike Sydney.

COMMENT

One Night Stand caused mixed reactions on its release, and it must be admitted that it encourages mixed reactions. It is an odd film to find coming from Edgley International (the distributor of the film), which has shown itself to be much more interested in producing epic films that are calculated to touch on the cultural myths of Australia in a rather direct sense (*The Man from Snowy River, Phar Lap,* and *Burke and*

Wills). *One Night Stand* not only lacks the epic sweep of these other ventures but is also a film of social comment—which can hardly be said of the others.

Director John Duigan had shown with his previous films that he is one of perhaps too few Australian directors with a social conscience, especially in *Mouth to Mouth* and *Winter of Our Dreams*. He publicly stated that *One Night Stand* was to be seen as an antinuclear statement that emphasized the impossibility of ordinary people applying the rules of normal existence to the incomprehensibility of nuclear annihilation. In this, he is perhaps too successful. The central foursome's total ignorance of the drama of the consequences and effects of nuclear war is too complete—especially difficult to accept given that Sam, the American, has jumped ship because he was aware of the impending holocaust.

There are formal links between *One Night Stand* and Duigan's earlier films. As with *Mouth to Mouth*, the narrative revolves around a quartet of adolescents, lost in a world not of their own making and without any real understanding of it, thrown together by dint of circumstance, and trying to make sense of (in this case) the fatally nonsensical. But Duigan's approach has moved from neorealism in *Mouth to Mouth* to surrealism in *One Night Stand:* the disjointed structure of the film denies narrative structure and at times suggests a play within a play that is further interrupted by odd moments of surrealistic absurdity.

There is a curious aggression at the base of the developing relationships, particularly between Sharon and Brendan. This is partly because Brendan is little more than an apprentice ocker with a crude approach to sex, and partly because Sharon is clearly more intelligent, more socially competent than he is. Their relationship is, however, the one that develops most and is in fact consummated. Sam and Eva, both in fact "outsiders" (he an American, she from a Czechoslovakian immigrant family), while softer, more vulnerable, are less capable of commitment. Sam seems to be suffering from the same emotional sterility as Rob in *Winter of Our Dreams*.

It is difficult to determine whether the muted quality of *One Night Stand* is intended or not. The comedy ranges from straightforward humor to tinges of black comedy but does not settle for either. The disruption of such narrative as exists by flashbacks and (in the turmoil of the flight to the underground station) intercutting with Fritz Lang's

Metropolis (Germany, 1926) puzzles rather than enlightens. Those sections of the film that take place outside the Sydney Opera House—a sort of prologue and epilogue—seem unconvincing, even crass.

Nonetheless, the sequences within the Opera House, where the "reality" of the outside world (or the horror of it) is permitted to ebb and flow but never to disappear, maintain a palpable degree of tension. The fantastic incongruity of the architecture of the Sydney Opera House provides an inescapably logical setting for the end of the world—particularly in Australia, where architecture is noted for its functionality rather than its aesthetics, and the ruling philosophy is "she'll be right." The future, except for the science-fiction futurist heroics of *Mad Max,* has held little interest for Australian culture in general or for the Australian cinema in particular.

The past is more attractive and interesting. Given a certain nihilism, or at least fatalism, at the core of the white experience of Australia, it is perhaps not surprising that any future is not really of much interest. *One Night Stand,* like *Mouth to Mouth,* seems to posit a lack of hope for the next generation of Australian adults. In the play on meaning that the title evokes (a fleeting, noncommitted sexual liaison), the film raises the implication that white or European culture's affair with Australia is a one night stand, and perhaps also humanity's relationship with the world as well.

One Night Stand may be one of the most intelligent and considered of recent Australian films—or it may be a flawed work of social conscience. But it does not seem to be a protest. The Australian brand of fatalism has penetrated to the narrative core of the film.

Oz 1976

Director: Chris Ofven.
Producer: Chris Ofven, Lyne Helms.
Screenplay: Chris Ofven.
Director of Photography: Dan Burstall.
Editor: Les Luxford.
Art Director: Robbie Perkins.
Music: Ross Wilson.
Sound: Danny Dyson.

Cast: Joy Dunstan (Dorothy); Bruce Spence (Surfie); Michael Carmen (Mechanic); Gary Waddell (Bikie); Graham Matters (Wizard); Robin Ramsay (Good Fairy).
Production Company: Count Features.
Running Time: 90 minutes.

STORY

Dorothy is knocked unconscious when the van she is riding in with members of the band who played at a dance in her small town has an accident. She wakes to find herself in a remote and empty country town. In an incongruous boutique called the Good Fairy she is given a pair of red shoes as a reward for killing the local hood (which she denies) and is urged to get to the city to see the last appearance of rock star the Wizard. Dorothy sets out, pursued by the truckie brother of the dead hood. She meets a Surfie (afraid of the sharks), a Mechanic (who doesn't care for anyone else), and a cowardly Bikie. Together they gatecrash the Wizard's final concert party, but he turns out to be the creation of publicity and very ordinary. Dorothy wakes up back at the accident to discover the others leaning over her anxiously.

COMMENT

To remake *The Wizard of Oz* (USA, 1939) in 1970s Australia is curiously appropriate, if only because Australia is known colloquially as Oz. But *Oz* is not really a remake; it is a reinterpretation of the famous film. It takes the narrative structure, several characters, and many of the incidents of the original, but it makes them essentially Australian. It is not simply a matter of grafting an Australian location and a few accents onto preexisting material—no matter how archetypal that material may be. At the same time, this film does not lose touch with its illustrious inspiration. A great deal of the charm and vitality that *Oz* engenders is in the way it both retains parameters of the original and changes them.

The strong elements of fantasy engendered and maintained by the studio-constructed *mise-en-scène* of *The Wizard of Oz* are totally lacking in *Oz*. Although engaged in a fantasy, the *mise-en-scène* is inescapably realistic. The film was shot entirely on location and has more footage of Australian country roads than *Mad Max*. *Oz* is also comparable with *Easy Rider* (USA, 1969): the movement of characters through the landscape accompanied by rock music forms a large part of its narrative structure. *Oz* is a grittily realistic, almost documentary, presentation of the geographic and material conditions of existence in rural Australia —thus reconfirming the dual interpretations of the film's title and of its recurrent song on the soundtrack, "Living in the Land of Oz." Indeed, it does not seem unreasonable to suggest that the film does just that: it faithfully reproduces living in the land of Oz—if in limited perspective.

Oz is not a musical like its original—it is a rock movie. In keeping with the conventions of that genre, most of its musical numbers are performed on the soundtrack rather than on film (except for the one number in the Wizard's performance). But as in musicals, the songs comment upon action, character, and situation in some way; all of the characters Dorothy meets along the way have their own songs related to their own specific images and/or needs. By not having the songs performed on film as such, the fantasy elements are played down and the road movie elements are extended.

The characters Dorothy meets, who help her on her way and are also helped by her, are nearly all representatives of particular Australian subcultures. But these characters—Surfie, Mechanic, Bikie—turn from and go well beyond simple stereotypes to become affectionately observed Australian types who are, nonetheless, not constructed myth-ically—or not totally anyway. While the film is romantic, except for the rather cynical ending, it is clearly not nostalgic. In this it differs from *The Wizard of Oz*—the Australian Dorothy expresses no great desire to get back to whatever the equivalent of Kansas might be. Indeed, she wants to get well away from her uncle's pig farm and the limited existence it represents. The characters are not paragons of Australian mythic virtues, but neither are they simple caricatures of members of specific subcultures.

Oz is also ambivalent in its attitude toward the Australian cultural dichotomy of bush and city. While cinematically it would seem to celebrate (without eulogizing) the Australian landscape, it nevertheless does suggest a sterility at the center of rural life and a lack of contact between people. While its movement is from bush to city in search of magical answers, it shows (like its original) that magical answers are not forthcoming, that a goal is not achieved in arriving but in the jour-ney—but (unlike its original) it does not teach Dorothy that "there's no place like home." There is a strong sense in which Dorothy's (imagined) journey has been futile. The city is shown to be (as Australian mythic perceptions would confirm) decadent, corrupt, rapacious, and unfeel-ing. If it were not for the overall lightness of touch, the element of fantasy, and the comic construction, *Oz* might almost be depressing in the emptiness it reveals at the heart of Australian existence.

Oz should perhaps be ranked with other youth films of the New Australian Cinema, although it does not share the overwhelming concern with growing up that is a constant thematic concern in those films. Nonetheless, in a limited way, it does present an "awakening" for a young female protagonist and might therefore be reasonably compared with *Puberty Blues* and *The Getting of Wisdom* to that extent at least. The fact that *Oz* adheres to the conventions of the rock movie, however, ensures a considerable distance from these other films and indeed almost accords it unique status. *Oz* is unpretentious but entertaining.

Palm Beach 1979

Director: Albie Thoms.

Producer: Albie Thoms.

Screenplay: Albie Thoms.

Director of Photography: Oscar Scherl.

Editor: Albie Thoms.

Music: Terry Hannigan.

Sound: Michael Moore.

Cast: Bryan Brown (Paul); Julie McGregor (Kate); John Flaus (Larry Kent); Nat Young (Ned); Ken Brown (Nick).

Production Company: Albie Thoms Productions.

Running Time: 88 minutes.

STORY

Three people, each engaged in an individual search, travel to Sydney's beach suburb of Palm Beach. Nick a surfer, looks for LSD with his friend Ned, who must locate a supply in order to inform the police and get off a drug charge; Paul, in an unhappy relationship and unemployed, looks for a job; and Larry Kent, a private detective, looks for a runaway teenager. These searchers mingle without ever actually meeting although Nick's search for drugs also leads, inadvertently, to locating the missing girl. Kent gives up his search. Paul, driven to desperation, attempts to rob a supermarket but shoots a policeman and is eventually caught.

COMMENT

Palm Beach draws attention to the other side of the New Australian Cinema, to that area of film production variously called "experimental," "alternative," "fringe," or any of another half-dozen titles that serve to distinguish the films, their production, and their aesthetics from mainstream commercial cinema. *Palm Beach*'s director, Albie Thoms, stands outside commercial cinema by inclination and declaration.

Historically it can be claimed that filmmakers working in the experimental cinema were partly responsible for the climate of interest and encouragement that finally led to the rebirth of native filmmaking in Australia. But cross-fertilization between these two film cultures is rather hard to discern. *Palm Beach* represents at least one occasion when the two forms of production came together. (The films of Paul Cox also represent a meeting of these different aesthetics but with a greater sense of commercial appeal within the arthouse cinema context.)

Palm Beach is rather less experimental than many other alternative productions (including other films by Albie Thoms) and has been compared (not without justification) to films by Andy Warhol. While it operates from a different aesthetic practice (or industrial practice), it is not inaccessible. It has an interest in narrative even if the manner of structuring the narrative challenges dominant practice. The film draws its narrative structure directly from its material rather than imposing the structure upon it. The material of the film is, in fact, explained in its title—although this creates a problem. *Palm Beach* has particular resonance for Australians living in Sydney and rather less for those who do not: for instance, the importance of being from south of Sydney Harbor rather than north, a cultural division that is specific to Sydney. *Palm Beach* is thus a film that examines a subculture but does so in the terms of that subculture itself—it is not an anthropologist's view. Australian cinema always examines Australia in its own terms. *Palm Beach* is comparable to *The F. J. Holden* in its focus on a specific subculture.

Palm Beach examines the beach (or surf) subculture with the additional resonances of Palm Beach itself. A substantial subculture is centered upon the beach (a term that encompasses not only the strip of sand next to the sea but suburbs in particular geographic locations, and uses of the sea, especially surfing). This subculture extends beyond surfing (although this is a major defining characteristic) to include attitudes toward drugs, work, and sex. And, as *Palm Beach* shows, the subculture itself has fringes. Despite the importance of the beach and surf (both within this subculture and within the broader context of

Australian society in general), there have been only a few films that have spent any time at the beach and even fewer that actually draw upon, let alone seriously examine, the beach subculture. (*Puberty Blues* comes close, but is not specifically about beach subculture.)

Palm Beach structures itself upon the mythology of this surf subculture as thoroughly as other Australian films structure themselves upon the dominant cultural mythology. But at the same time it suggests a subculture under attack by the dominant culture through "assimilation" and gradual erosion. This theme is expounded basically through the persistent soundtrack of commercial radio through nearly all sequences. This particular use of the soundtrack is one of the aesthetics of the alternative cinema, as are the improvised nature of the dialogues, the use of a hand-held camera, minimal editing within scenes, avoidance of close-ups for dramatic emphasis, and the further use of sound in carrying dialogue from one scene over into another. All these have an inhibiting effect on the film. They work to prevent any one narrative from gaining prominence. And they inhibit the usual sense of identification through characterization. The result is a documentary feel to the film, a sense that the examination of the subculture is "real." But *Palm Beach* is constructed and, in the final analysis, the filmmaker's detachment is more assumed than actual.

An extraordinary sense of veracity is created in *Palm Beach,* mainly through the agency of allowing actors (or nonactors in some cases) to improvise their own dialogues. But reality is not simply present in the surface of things. Much of the reality of any culture lies in its perceptions of itself and its relation to the world, in its mythology and its culturally structured way of organizing experience. More fictional (commercially mainstream) films of the New Australian Cinema are just as capable of showing Australians "as they are." On the other hand, few other productions have been so successful in showing a specific subculture within Australian society.

Petersen 1974

Director: Tim Burstall.
Producer: Tim Burstall.
Screenplay: David Williamson.

Director of Photography: Robin
    Copping.
Editor: David Bilcock.

Art Direction: Bill Hutchinson.   David Phillips (Heinz); John Ewart
Music: Peter Best.   (Peter); Sandy McGregor (Marge);
Sound: Ken Hammond.   Helen Morse (Jane).
Cast: Jack Thompson (Petersen); Jacki   Production Company: Hexagon.
    Weaver (Susie); Wendy Hughes   Running Time: 107 minutes.
    (Trish); Arthur Dignam (Charles);

STORY

Tony Petersen gives up his electrician business to study arts at the
university. Although married with two children, he has an affair with
his English lecturer, Trish. Petersen takes part in public sexual display
to protest against discrimination against women. When all others are
helpless, he routs a gang of bikies who gatecrash a birthday party.
Visiting an old friend, Peter, in the country, Petersen refuses to become
his partner and spoils the friendship by making love to Peter's wife
Marge. He and Trish spend an idyllic weekend at a beach cottage;
Trish says she wants his baby, but changes her mind and accepts a job at
Oxford. Petersen fails his exams and, feeling betrayed by Trish and by
the system in general, gets drunk and beaten up by the police. He
returns to work as an electrician.

COMMENT

Petersen was bound to be seen as another sex romp/ocker film in something of the same mold as the *Alvin Purple* films (and to a lesser extent
the *Barry McKenzie* films), and much of the film provides support for
just such a categorization. In 1974 the ocker qualities of the eponymous hero of the film were bound to cause critical difficulties: the ocker
had not achieved any sort of artistic acceptance, and his cultural position was still far from confirmed. Paul Hogan had yet to make his mark
on Australian popular culture. Ironically, it is at least partly due to the
examination of ockerism by writer David Williamson—not so much in
this film but in later films, especially *Don's Party*—that the ocker moved
from a comic stereotype to acceptance as a culturally (and mythically)
accurate definition of the Australian male.

It must be added that *Petersen* is not a good film. It is unfair to expect
Burstall to carry the full responsibility. Williamson must carry some as

well. The very structure of the narrative itself leads almost to the feeling that the writer held the cinema in some sort of contempt. It seems an unavoidable conclusion that Williamson inserted scenes and actions that were not in keeping with the overall tenor of the film, or indeed even integrated closely with the actual story, but were written in merely to provide "what movies always have in them." The spurious scene with the bikies gatecrashing a party is the prime example. It is as if Williamson saw no need for the sort of subtleties demanded by writing for the theater (with which he was and is more familiar). The inclusion of such gratuitous scenes makes the emotional balance of the film swing wildly from clichéd cinematic romance to serious drama to farcical comedy, disrupting consistency of characterization and even seriously interfering with any sense of narrative direction and purpose.

The makers of the film seem uncertain what to do with the character of Petersen, having "created" him by putting him in a situation first (working-class hero in middle-class academia) and attempting to work backward from there. The idea of putting a "typical" Australian (tradesman/sportsman/family man/fighter) into a university situation where his virtues would inevitably lead him into conflict with highbrow culture (there is a strong streak of anti-intellectualism in Australian culture) must have seemed to be an excellent opportunity to demolish ivory-tower academia and to discover the virtues of the "true" Australian. Unfortunately, it seems that the makers had no real idea of what the "true" Australian was. This may well be a reflection of the cultural flux of the time the film was made; six years later, with *Gallipoli*, Williamson demonstrated no such confusion.

What makes *Petersen* an interesting film is that it does, for all its imperfections, offer a very real attempt at a new reading of the ocker. Comparisons with Alvin Purple (Petersen is more cerebral, less Candide-like) and Barry McKenzie (Petersen is, if nothing else, infinitely more sexually successful) are perhaps inevitable. What *Petersen* in fact presents is the ocker with a human face (albeit one pummeled by the police at the end). Petersen is more normal than almost any other representation of ockers in Australian film—not as exaggerated as those in *The Odd Angry Shot* and well removed from the essentially moronic Barry McKenzie. The flaws and inconsistencies in character construction overwhelm the possibilities for a genuine representation of a "real" ocker (as opposed to his fictional form) and make it difficult to accept *Petersen* as providing a mirror image of the real Australian male.

Romance does not suit the ocker. The mythical Australian male is romantic in the image of the "noble savage" rather than in the sophisticated post-Renaissance man of Western civilization. *Petersen* cannot quite make up its mind which of these two images to subscribe to. This does have the benefit of suggesting that the cultural perception of the Australian male is more complex than it sometimes seems (or is ofttimes assumed) to be—a useful corrective to the more prolific one-dimensional portrayals in the New Australian Cinema generally.

Later screenplays by Williamson (especially those adapted from his plays, but notably *Gallipoli*) show that he has managed to expand and consolidate his construction of the ocker, and to provide more convincingly the missing dimension that too easily, in other hands, leaves him a comic stereotype.

Phar Lap 1983

Director: Simon Wincer.

Producer: John Sexton.

Screenplay: David Williamson.

Director of Photography: Russell Boyd.

Editor: Tony Paterson.

Production Designer: Larry Eastwood.

Music: Bruce Rowland.

Sound: Gary Wilkins.

Cast: Towering Inferno (Phar Lap); Tom Burlinson (Tommy); Martin Vaughan (Telford); Ron Leibman (Davis); Vincent Ball (McKinnon); Judy Morris (Bea); Celia de Burgh (Vi); Georgina Carr (Emma).

Production Company: John Sexton Productions–Michael Edgley International.

Running Time: 118 minutes.

STORY

The beloved Australian racehorse Phar Lap dies in the United States in 1932. The news shocks Australia. Flashback to 1928: a colt from New Zealand does not live up to his impressive bloodline. Owner Dave Davis tells trainer Harry Telford to sell the horse. Telford pleads to be allowed to lease the horse, given the name Phar Lap. The horse and strapper Tommy Woodcock form a mutually affectionate relationship. Phar Lap begins a winning streak, captures the imagination of the

Australian public, and earns the ire of the conservative Australian Jockey Club. Phar Lap wins the 1930 Melbourne Cup despite a tremendous weight handicap. Davis takes the horse to Mexico, where he wins the richest race ever held. Shortly afterward, Phar Lap dies in strange circumstances.

COMMENT

Given the importance that is placed upon sport and sporting achievement in Australian culture, it is surprising that there are so few films of the New Australian Cinema that take sport as their central narrative structure: *Dawn!* (with not a few parallels to *Phar Lap*); *The Club* (which is not really about sport but about power); *The Coolangatta Gold* (1984) (which is not about surf-racing but about Oedipal conflict). Sport is a cultural obsession of Australians about which the New Australian Cinema has little to say.

Yet as *Phar Lap* and *Dawn!* reveal (and this is supported by many Hollywood sports films), the sports film formula usually requires a protagonist who is both heroic and tragic (often a real historical figure). It has been noted by many observers that Australian culture is devoid of real-life heroes; Australians do not, by and large, revere their politicians; statesmen (if there have been any) do not receive cultural accolades; neither do generals. The arts receive occasional and usually grudging recognition. Australia's only real folk heroes are Ned Kelly (a bushranger), Donald Bradman (a cricketer), and Phar Lap.

This lack of real-life heroes cannot be accounted for simply by recourse to the explanation of the Australian tendency to "cut down the tall poppies," or by claims that the egalitarian nature of the cultural mythos celebrates conformity and community (through mateship). It may be more accurate to say that, given the ever-changing structure of Australian society (a state of cultural flux for some two hundred years), individual heroes do not have a long cultural life, although the mythic structuring of the (abstract) Australian hero remains constant.

The real Phar Lap was a hero for his time (or rather was *made* into a hero for his time): the late 1920s and early 1930s—the depth of the depression. The film is a little uncertain about whether to re-create the conditions of the period that made Phar Lap a hero and thus present him as a hero-in-context or whether to make him a contemporary hero for the 1980s. It does something of both: period costume, vintage cars, and historical locations essentially place *Phar Lap* in the past; the structure of the narrative makes Phar Lap a contemporary hero. Neither view dominates. Not enough is made of the period (other than ostensibly accurate visual reproduction) really to place *Phar Lap* in a precise social context. Writer David Williamson's interest (as this and his other films have shown) is in people and their relations with each other rather than in their environment and social circumstances. This accounts for the almost classical tragedy of Phar Lap as hero of his own drama: his death is the consequence of his "tragic flaw," his spirit that drives him to run to win.

Comparison with the *Rocky* movies (USA, 1976 and on) is inevitable—and with other rags-to-riches, unknown-to-champion sports stories before and since. Phar Lap's trainer, Harry Telford, is the equivalent of all the crusty and curmudgeonly old boxing managers (as in *Rocky*) or cynical coaches (as in *The Natural* [USA, 1984]). Tommy Woodcock's relationship with Emma is conventional cinematic romance; McKinnon and the Australian Jockey Club committee are conventional institutional villains. Except that the hero is not human (and thus more story accumulates around the human characters who surround the hero), *Phar Lap* confirms rather than denies filmic conventionality.

It is unclear to what extent history (as it is assumed to be) and commercial considerations have determined the conventional nature of *Phar Lap*'s narrative. The film is certainly an atypical piece of work for David Williamson, but it may be that the combination of his skill and the legendary position held by the real Phar Lap in Australian cultural consciousness helps to raise the film out of what could easily have been the cinematic and dramatic doldrums. *Phar Lap* wisely avoids the emotionalism and sensationalism the story could have allowed.

In so doing, the film may have demonstrated that Phar Lap is not a hero for our times but a timeless hero: the character Phar Lap meets many of the conventional and cultural demands for a hero but the film *Phar Lap* lacks the cultural specificity to make him an Australian hero for and of the 1980s. Within the Australian context it is not possible to divorce Phar Lap the actual horse, Phar Lap the legend, and Phar Lap the character within the narrative fictional film. Such a distinction may be easier for non-Australian audiences.

Picnic at Hanging Rock 1975

Director: Peter Weir.

Producer: Jim McElroy and Hal McElroy.

Screenplay: Cliff Green.

Director of Photography: Russell Boyd.

Editor: Max Lemon.

Art Direction: David Copping.

Music: Bruce Smeaton.

Sound: Don Connolly.

Cast: Rachel Roberts (Mrs. Appleyard);

Dominic Guard (Michael); Vivean Gray (Miss McCraw); Anne Lambert (Miranda); John Jarratt (Albert); Margaret Nelson (Sara); Jane Vallis (Marion); Karen Robson (Irma); Christine Schuler (Edith).

Production Company: Picnic Productions.

Running Time: 115 minutes.

STORY

St. Valentine's Day, 1900: girls from Mrs. Appleyard's College of Young Ladies take a picnic excursion to a local geographic site, Hanging Rock. One girl, Sara, is prevented from going by Mrs. Appleyard. At the Rock, four girls, Miranda, Irma, Marion, and Edith, go off to explore; with the exception of Irma, all disappear. A teacher, Miss McCraw, is also missing. All search efforts prove fruitless. Michael Fitzhubert, haunted by the memory of Miranda, commences his own search. With the help of his uncle's groom Albert, Michael finds Irma on the Rock. Gossip and speculation cause students to be withdrawn from the school. Sara, who was in love with Miranda, kills herself after being told she will be sent back to an orphanage. The mystery is never solved.

COMMENT

Much was (and still is) made of the lack of resolution to the central narrative enigma of *Picnic at Hanging Rock:* the mystery of the disappearance of the girls and Miss McCraw (and of Michael's and Irma's experiences on the Rock) is never explained. But, in the Australian context, there really is no necessity for an explanation. The bush has held, since the earliest times of European settlement, a dread fascination. It has become the overriding natural element credited with creating Australians as a race apart from others. There is also a hidden side to the cultural perception of the bush: a place of primeval terror, implacably hostile to human existence. This attitude is sometimes given

metaphoric form in the Australian cinema (*Razorback,* for instance).
But this fear of the outback is usually resistant to precise articulation.
That is why *Picnic at Hanging Rock* is so successful. It does not attempt
to locate the supernatural malevolence of the bush in comprehensible
fears: animals (as in *Razorback* or *The Long Weekend* [1977]), brutalized
men (as in *Wake in Fright*), or even the ecological conditions themselves
(as in *Walkabout*). The bush is simply the bush, a place where beautiful
young girls and down-to-earth mathematics teachers vanish without
trace. The how and why are not merely inexplicable; they don't *have* to
be explained.

Yet this conception of the "terror" of the bush needs to be tempered
with the recognition that *Picnic at Hanging Rock* does not suggest that
anything awful has happened to the girls who disappeared. They
appear to go to their fate with calm assurance, even eager acceptance.
Certainly, Edith is driven to hysteria when the other girls "enter" the
Rock; but it is the effect on others—Mrs. Appleyard, Sara, Michael—
that is most devastating. The malevolence of the bush is not so much in
itself but as a result of the incompatibility between the bush and human
beings.

Picnic at Hanging Rock also captures superbly the ambiguity of the
bush: on one hand, the terror that lurks within it; on the other, its
incomparable beauty. Although many films of the New Australian
Cinema make startlingly effective use of the undeniable cinematic
qualities of the Australian landscape (in many respects unlike landscape anywhere else in the world), few have done so more successfully
than this film. The haunting, supernatural quality of the landscape is
captured cinematically in a way that continues to stun audiences.

Picnic at Hanging Rock is consciously constructed with an eye toward
pictorial composition. Many sequences commence with action in fro-
zen tableau as if in a painting, and this highly structured *mise-en-scène* is
integrated with a deliberately hesitant approach to dialogue (especially
by the use of silence) and with an editing style that utilizes long dis-
solves and a rhythm that frequently holds shots and scenes slightly
beyond their "natural" moment.

The structuring principle behind all the compositions is the "look":
the look of characters within the narrative, especially of the girls toward each other in the opening sequences—and again specifically
toward Irma when she returns to the college after her rescue. Characters within the film are always looking, sometimes at each other but not

infrequently seemingly at nothing at all. It is ironic that, with all the looking, no one "sees" what happens to the girls. The audience is positioned by looking as well: the composition of the images is constantly constructed not simply (or even) to "see" the actions but so that the audience looks at the object of the camera's gaze. The camera often looks at the Rock, so there is the inescapable feeling that the Rock looks at the participants in the drama it has precipitated.

The feeling of the Australian bush as a living entity is nowhere as completely and brilliantly created as in this film. The entire aesthetic construction of the film is integrated into its themes, its content, its meaning: its aesthetics may almost be said to be its meaning. What is unusual in this pictorialization of the bush is its concomitant construction as a site of sensuality. There is something vaguely sexual about the manner in which the girls "embrace" the Rock, go (in)to it like a lover. But there is an undertone of repressed sexuality to the whole film, which surfaces only occasionally: the question of whether Irma has been sexually assaulted and, of course, the hothouse of barely suppressed sexuality in the college itself. And it should not be overlooked that the events take place on St. Valentine's Day. As with Peter Weir's next film, *The Last Wave,* it is by no means clear what all this means—if anything. The menace of the bush in *Picnic at Hanging Rock* is as much sexual as anything else.

The Picture Show Man 1977

Director: John Power.
Producer: Joan Long.
Screenplay: Joan Long.
Director of Photography: Geoff Burton.
Editor: Nick Beauman.
Art Director: David Copping.
Music: Peter Best.
Sound: Ken Hammond.

Cast: John Meillon (Pop Pym); John Ewart (Freddie); Harold Hopkins (Larry); Rod Taylor (Palmer); Sally Conabere (Lucy); Garry McDonald (Lou).
Production Company: Limelight Productions.
Running Time: 98 minutes.

STORY

The mid-1920s: Maurice (Pop) Pym, with his son Larry and pianist Lou, travels the remote outback towns of Queensland with a moving

The Picture Show Man. Limelight Productions Pty Ltd.

picture show. Pop's parsimony causes Lou to take up with the rival Palmer's Pictures. His place is taken by the dapper Freddie. When Larry meets Lucy, a squatter's daughter, at a country race meeting, he insists on running an open-air cinema in one of the towns Pym has on his itinerary. Pop's footsteps are constantly dogged by Palmer, and violence is only narrowly avoided on several occasions. With the coming of sound, Pym's Pictures looks set for financial collapse until Freddie provides some capital from his accumulated winnings on the horses. Larry makes the break from Pop and goes off with Lucy. Pop and Freddie go back on the road.

COMMENT

It is probably unfair (or prejudicial) to say that *The Picture Show Man* disappoints, but it does. After viewing the film, it is difficult to avoid the feeling that there was so much potential but so little realization. The content, the period, the action all seem to have been rich with promise, but in the final analysis that promise has failed to materialize. The film drifts past the viewer as if it were no more than a slow-moving series of cameos held together by the only really consistent character, Pop Pym. A constant comment heard during the 1970s within the film production industry in Australia was that scripts were seldom reworked sufficiently before shooting began, and this may very well point to the problem of *The Picture Show Man:* it has not really been formed on the page before being transformed onto celluloid.

Putting it onto celluloid has been successful, however, in the way so many films of the New Australian Cinema have been successful: the cinematography. Once again, the Australian landscape, its scenery and especially its light, has found its way onto the screen wonderfully. *The Picture Show Man* is one of many Australian films that deserve praise for their photographic qualities. The quality of the cinematography, however, serves only to emphasize the paucity of story, character, and theme.

It is in narrative structure rather than cinematic presentation that the film falls down. Of course, the nature of a traveling picture show exhibitor's life is bound to mean a series of encounters with various characters in different locales, but *The Picture Show Man* introduces its characters into the plot a trifle too randomly or by relying on what might be called "Dickensian" coincidence: a character (or two) will suddenly appear in the plot fortuitously.

Concurrently, there is perhaps a little too much concern with the minutiae of the conditions of the traveling picture show operation. This obsession with the documentary accuracy of the conditions, practice, and machinery of silent picture exhibition in Australia would seem to be the result of producer/writer Joan Long's experience with documentaries with the Commonwealth Film Unit (now Film Australia) and, more particularly, her work in constructing a compilation documentary on the history of early Australian cinema, *The Pictures That Moved* (1969). Yet the film is oddly reticent on things such as where Pop gets his films or how he exchanges them (if he does).

Like so many Australian films in the second half of the 1970s, *The Picture Show Man* is profoundly nostalgic, yearning for simpler times and simpler places. Urban Australia might not have existed for all the reference to it in this film (possibly explaining why there is no reference to how Pop gets the prints that he screens). Pop Pym is a representation of the mythical pioneer, taking hardship, environment, and climate in his stride in the great outback. But the country folk and townspeople who might be expected to enhance this pioneer image are, in fact, barely represented at all except as rustic, bucolic, and none-too-intelligent faces at the picture shows.

The Picture Show Man is a comedy, well served by John Meillon and John Ewart as Pop and Freddie. But an obvious affection for these pioneers has interfered with comic invention; while the Australian idiom is occasionally accurately observed, it is seldom permitted sufficient play to broaden into comedy. Of passing and yet intriguing interest is the character of Palmer, the rival picture show man. Although played by expatriate Australian Rod Taylor, he is clearly an American and thus more than simply a rival who provides an opportunity to display Pop's irascibility while at the same time adding conflict to the otherwise minimal drama. Palmer's nationality may reflect historical fact: American interests brought about the decline of Australian film in the interwar period, which producer Joan Long would know from her work on compilation documentaries. It also reflects a culturally stereotyped attitude toward Americans in terms of their presumedly sharper business acumen and chicanery, as seen in *Undercover* and *The Coca-Cola Kid*. Palmer is thus pushy, brash, and always up-to-date, a contrast with the more conservative and more skeptical and thus more Australian Pym.

The Picture Show Man does speak of a hidden history that deserves to be known and appreciated. That it does not make enough of that history is the reason the film is disappointing rather than simply mildly diverting. Together with *Newsfront*, it is a rare film that registers any sense of awareness of Australian cinema history—it could have done more with that knowledge.

The Plumber 1979

Director: Peter Weir.
Producer: Matt Carroll.
Screenplay: Peter Weir.
Director of Photography: David

Sanderson.
Editor: Gerald Turney-Smith.
Art Direction: Wendy Weir, Herbert
  Pinter.

Music: Rory O'Donohue.

Sound: Ken Hammond.

Cast: Judy Morris (Jill); Ivar Kants (Max); Robert Coleby (Brian); Candy

Raymond (Meg).

Production Company: South Australian Film Corporation.

Running Time: 76 minutes.

STORY

Brian and Jill Cowper, recently returned from fieldwork in New Guinea, live in university accommodations in Adelaide. Brian does research at the university; Jill is writing her thesis in anthropology. Their domestic serenity is disturbed by the arrival of the enigmatic and slightly sinister Max, who claims to be the resident plumber. Although Jill claims there is nothing wrong with the plumbing, Max insists there is and commences to demolish the bathroom bit by bit. In addition to his destructive plumbing work, Max's odd and vaguely threatening behavior disturbs Jill, but Brian, busy trying to impress a visiting delegation in order to get a position in Geneva, pays little attention. Failing to get rid of Max through the "proper channels," and feeling even more threatened, Jill takes the battle to him. She hides a valuable watch in Max's van and watches as he is arrested.

COMMENT

The Plumber continues Peter Weir's two trademarks: his interrogation of Australian myths and his interest in the possibility of unexplained menace intruding into everyday existence. The interrogation is seldom vicious—rather a gentle questioning, sometimes hidden by black comedy (*The Cars That Ate Paris*) or by sensuality (*Picnic at Hanging Rock*). Weir does not challenge cultural assumptions head-on in his films— and *Gallipoli* reconfirms in precise detail the most potent narrative cultural legend of Australia. His questioning is oblique and informs the narrative structure of his films rather than providing the essential drama. Even so, the narrative tension of *The Plumber* is partly located in the concept of class hostility, which challenges the myth of Australia as an egalitarian society.

The Plumber is different from these other Peter Weir films in that it has a protagonist who fights back, identifies the menace, and defeats it. In Australian cultural terms, it is no accident that the protagonist who thus wins is female. Jill looks at first as if she is another protagonist unable to deal with a force that exudes a more fundamental malevolence. But despite the fact that, in the characters of Max and Jill, *The Plumber* sets up a clash of cultures somewhat akin to that of *The Last Wave*, both of these characters are products of the same culture. They may represent different subcultures—bourgeois and working-class—but plumbers and academics exist in the same cultural framework, unlike the white and aboriginal dichotomy that informs *The Last Wave*.

This view persists despite the film's sometimes ingenuous attempts to equate Max with the witch doctor of Jill's New Guinea experience (and, more generally, through editing the soundtrack with the supposedly more primitive culture of Jill's anthropological dissertation). Clearly, the audience is expected to see a parallel between Max's invasion of the Cowpers' flat and Jill's anecdote of the witch doctor's invasion of her tent in New Guinea. And both are defeated by Jill's actions in driving out the invader.

Thus Jill (unlike the audience if it makes these connections) may not be able to articulate the menace that Max represents but she can recognize that the menace does exist, despite (or perhaps because of) the impotence of her husband to deal with it, and is able to find the resources within herself to defeat the menace—or at least to defeat its agent this time around.

Weir's Australian films are structured around a narrative threat that is diffuse and difficult to define precisely; the narratives tend, nonetheless, to provide some form of arena for the menace and to allow opposition to it or a search for an explanation. Thus, for example, *The Last Wave* has the narrative situation of culture conflict although the central menace that threatens the diegetic world of the film is beyond the parameters of this conflict. So, too, *The Plumber* contextualizes the menace in what ultimately becomes a battle for survival along class lines, with victory finally in the hands of the bourgeoisie—the battle is fought on their ground with their tools (which are as diverse as grammar and the police). It is significant, then, that Peter Weir's last film before making *Gallipoli* should show the triumph of bourgeois culture over the elemental forces represented by Max/witch doctor. In this *The Plumber* is a long way from *Picnic at Hanging Rock* but is a logical stepping-stone to the myth-enhancing, culture-confirming, narrative legend of *Gallipoli*.

In shape and form, *The Plumber* is not as profound as Weir's earlier films. In fact, in comparison with films both before and since, it appears quite lightweight. This is no doubt partly due to its intended release on television and partly to the restricted situation of its narrative (which only occasionally moves outside the campus flat), the limited number of characters, and a domestic narrative that seems to have few ramifications beyond its immediate setting (unlike the apocalyptic visions of Armageddon that shatter the familial domesticity of *The Last Wave*). But *The Plumber*, for all its apparent modesty, is a more complex narrative than either *Picnic at Hanging Rock* or *The Last Wave*, offering a sense of resolution that is in keeping with its structure. It is Peter Weir's most complete film before *Gallipoli*—even if it is less likely to be noticed than *Picnic at Hanging Rock* and *The Last Wave*. Enigmatic as some of its narrative structure may be (who in reality is Max? what does he want?), it is "complete." Menace appears, is identified (if not precisely categorized), and is challenged and defeated. The narrative resolution that evaded Weir (or was avoided by him) in *Picnic at Hanging Rock* and *The Last Wave* is strongly in place in *The Plumber* and later films.

Puberty Blues | 1982

Director: Bruce Beresford.
Producer: Joan Long, Margaret Kelly.
Screenplay: Margaret Kelly.
Director of Photography: Don McAlpine.
Editor: Bill Anderson.
Art Director: David Copping.
Music: Les Gock, Tim Finn.
Sound: Gary Wilkins.

Cast: Nell Schofield (Debbie); Jad Capelja (Sue); Geoff Rhoe (Garry); Tony Hughes (Danny); Sandy Paul (Tracy); Leanda Brett (Cheryl); Jay Hackett (Bruce); Ned Lander (Strach).
Production Company: Limelight Productions.
Running Time: 90 minutes.

STORY

Debbie Knight and Sue Vickers, two school friends from a predominantly middle-class Sydney beach suburb, are accepted into an elite "surfies" group. Initial joy at being members of this group palls as their days are spent watching the boys surfing and their nights spent as mere sex objects for the boys. After being dropped by her first boy-friend, Debbie takes up with the more sympathetic Garry; but when it seems that she may be pregnant, Garry ignores his responsibilities and slips

Puberty Blues. Limelight Productions Pty Ltd.

into drug-induced inertia. Following Garry's death from an overdose, the mind-dulling routine of the group proves too much for Debbie and Sue. They buy a surfboard and, despite the jeers and taunts of both the boys and other girls, prove adept at surfing. They look forward to a more independent existence.

COMMENT

Puberty Blues was director Bruce Beresford's ninth film in as many years, his last before going to the United States to direct *Tender Mercies* (USA, 1983), and provided further confirmation of his status as the most prolific, most varied, and perhaps most successful of recent Australian directors. While it remains difficult to identify strong thematic preoccupations or a sense of continuing personal or intellectual commitment in his series of films, it is difficult to deny that Beresford is one of the most accomplished and most cinematic of Australia's directors.

Puberty Blues seems a slight subject, one that would appear to suggest little need for deep analysis—an approach that is reinforced by the comic way in which its narrative is structured and presented and by the frequent reliance upon comedy where another film (or other filmmakers) might have been tempted to offer seriousness. In some ways, Puberty Blues resembles a number of high school/adolescent peer group films that were popular Hollywood products around the time of its release. But its origins are not the commercial cinema but a previously published novella/biography by two Sydney schoolgirls.

Comic as it may be, its demonstration of the stultifying effects of a particular adolescent subculture centered upon surfing is powerful and not a little disturbing. Although the "adult world" does intrude into this narrative—through parents and school—the film makes no real attempt to suggest a wider social setting for the creation and maintenance of the denial of individuality that this particular subgroup emphasizes. The most that can be claimed in this regard is that the film suggests the awfulness of the male-dominated Australian culture and hints at the mind-dulling condition of living in "lotus-land." But it also offers hope in the emancipation of Debbie and Sue, although it may be less the product of embryonic feminism than simply of the gradual maturity of two reasonably intelligent girls.

As with a number of Australian films that place their action within an urban environment, women are shown to be more capable, more intelligent, and more alive than men (Beresford's earlier The Getting of Wisdom and later The Fringe Dwellers demonstrate this in totally different contexts). This enhances the great cultural dichotomy of Australia—the outback/the city—and perhaps demonstrates that the city is no place for a man. Certainly the teenage males in Puberty Blues are a rather unappealing lot, apprentice male chauvinist ockers all. But the two heroines redeem this otherwise bleak society with hope for the future, and the humor of the film's treatment redeems the narrative as well.

Puberty Blues is one of a number of "growing up in Australia" films, a genre of the New Australian Cinema: My Brilliant Career, The Getting of Wisdom, The Irishman, The Mango Tree, The Devil's Playground, Street Hero, Fast Talking. Like the last two, Puberty Blues takes place in a contemporary setting; like the first two, it has as its protagonists teenage girls. Within this genre it is interesting to note that those with male protagonists generally deal with the manner in which they grow to maturity *within* the system; those that have female protagonists construct this process of growth through opposition to and rebellion against the system. As *Puberty Blues* shows, the rites of passage for girls in the teenage subculture of Crunulla are designed to entrap girls in passive or submissive social (and sexual) roles. Most of the "growing up" films, then, offer examinations of cultural perceptions either by confirming them (if the protagonist is male) or by interrogating them (if the protagonist is female). *Puberty Blues* (more than *The Getting of Wisdom* and *My Brilliant Career*) represents the contemporary cultural clash of the male-dominated Australian ethos with feminism. The film's "theater" is perhaps limited to a specific subculture, but it is possible to argue that the ramifications of its themes have wider social implications.

This is especially true when it is realized that *Puberty Blues*, unlike *The Getting of Wisdom* and *My Brilliant Career*, shows quite unequivocally that Debbie and Sue are breaking out of an oppressive regime that is male-dominated. It is true that other females are as much or more the agents of that domination, but it is significant that *Puberty Blues*, unlike the other films, makes it clear that they are agents of a patriarchal if adolescent social system.

Although the unfailing good humor of *Puberty Blues* softens the blows, the film nonetheless joins the growing group of films that find the Australian suburbs more or less charmless. The ordinariness of Australian existence holds no attractions, it seems, for its filmmakers.

Razorback | 1984

Director: Russell Mulcahy.
Producer: Hal McElroy.
Screenplay: Everett de Roche.
Director of Photography: Dean Semler.
Editor: Bill Anderson.
Production Designer: Bryce Walmsley.
Music: Iva Davies.
Sound: Tim Lloyd.
Cast: Gregory Harrison (Carl); Arkie
Whiteley (Sarah); Bill Kerr (Jake); Chris Haywood (Benny); David Argue (Dicko); Judy Morris (Beth); John Ewart (Barman); John Howard (Cameraman).
Production Company: McElroy and McElroy.
Running Time: 95 minutes.

Razorback. National Film and Sound Archive/McElroy & McElroy.

STORY

Jake Cullen, a professional kangaroo shooter, has his home destroyed and his baby grandson carried off by a giant boar, a razorback. Beth Winters, an American journalist, comes to the same outback town of Gamulla to expose the kangaroo slaughter. She runs foul of the psychotic Baker brothers, Benny and Dicko. The razorback frightens them off and kills Beth. When her husband Carl arrives in Gamulla to investigate, the Baker brothers take him kangaroo shooting at night and leave him in the bush. Carl staggers to Sarah Cameron's isolated farmhouse. After being attacked by Dicko, Jake is left to be killed by the razorback. Carl hunts down Benny and goes to a pet food factory to find Dicko. The razorback is already there and kills Dicko. Carl manages to trick the razorback into falling into the meat-slicing machinery.

COMMENT

Razorback is a reminiscent film. The basic plot line is highly reminiscent of *Jaws* (USA, 1975). The kangaroo hunt the ghastly and psychopathic Baker brothers take Carl on is reminiscent of similar sequences in *Wake in Fright*. The Baker brothers' truck, a cross between a meat wagon and an armored car, is reminiscent of the surreal vehicles in *The Cars That Ate Paris* and *Mad Max*. Despite the similarities, *Razorback* is not simply a dry-land *Jaws*: it is not the similarities that count but the differences. And the key difference is the actual cinematic treatment of the narrative, the very way in which the elements of cinema have been utilized to frame and enhance and absorb the story material. These differences are significant because of what they reveal.

Put simply, *Jaws* was constructed in what is called cinematic narrative realism; the approach, the style of presentation, was in keeping with the dominant cinematic practice of photographic realism (no matter how bizarre the subject matter). *Razorback* is a long way from realism in its cinematography. It has become a truism that Australian movies since 1970 have been pictorially excellent—especially those located in the outback. This pictorial excellence, which has usually (but not always) greatly enhanced the thematic concerns of the films, has nearly always been "naturalistic," the landscape as it is being felt to carry sufficient impact by itself through those very photogenic properties and, occasionally, its alien shapes and colors. Russell Mulcahy, noted for his work in music videos, has deliberately avoided realism or, more accurately, heightened the realism and, with cinematographer Dean Semler, has created a cinematic nightmare that is as startling as it is unexpected in the Australian cinema.

Razorback is a cinematic nightmare not simply because of its story material, but because of the photography, the selection of locations, the sets, and the way in which the characters are written and portrayed. Other than being a visual treat and having an exciting story well told, *Razorback* is a source of fascination for its implications about a key aspect of Australian culture: the idea of the outback, the bush, the great interior of Australia, as a place of terror. This idea has run like a hidden thread throughout the entirety of the colonial and postcolonial experience of Australia, surfacing only occasionally but tellingly.

To take only cinematic examples, it is easy to point out how this hidden terror lurking in the heart of the bush is made manifest in *Picnic at Hanging Rock, Wake in Fright, The Cars That Ate Paris*, and *The Long Weekend* (1979). In all these films, the bush is not a benign place of great and innocent beauty and equally not a site of struggle to conquer nature and carve out a new society. Instead, it is a place of hidden, random, and inexplicable terrors. The experience of the bush in this perception is one of dehumanization and brutalization if one is permitted to continue to live in it at all—and *Razorback* suggests that is by no means a certainty. The pig in *Razorback* is only part of the nightmare, a metaphor in any case for less readily identifiable horrors. As in *Wake in Fright*, the very people who populate, no matter how sparsely, this awful place are part of the horror as well. As a result of the environment they live in, they have become as brutal, as frightening, as dehumanized as the very landscape itself.

Through the highly stylized approach taken by Mulcahy, *Razorback* eloquently captures this intriguing and frequently denied perception of the bush. If *Jaws* merely tells audiences what they already know—that the sea is full of lurking menace—*Razorback* also tells audiences what they already know but frequently pretend is not so in their tales of mighty bushmen like *The Man from Snowy River*—that the interior of Australia is also full of lurking menace. *Razorback* confirms in a thoroughly cinematic fashion what Australians at least already feared. But the nightmare lingers.

The American presence in *Razorback* is somewhat odd. At the pragmatic, commercial level it may have been felt that the use of Gregory Harrison in the cast would make the film more marketable in the United States. Of course, an American is even more an outsider in the bush than an urban Australian. Yet Carl's effectiveness (he alone defeats the razorback) makes him similar to Becker in *The Coca-Cola Kid* and Max in *Undercover*. There are times, it seems, that American ingenuity is indispensable in the face of Australian stoic acceptance.

Rebel | 1985

Director: Michael Jenkins.

Producer: Phillip Emanuel.

Screenplay: Michael Jenkins, Bob Herbert; based on the play *No Names . . . No Packdrill* by Bob Herbert.

Director of Photography: Peter James.

Editor: Michael Honey.

Production Design: Brian Thomson.

Music: Ray Cook, Peter Best.

Sound: Mark Lewis.

Cast: Matt Dillon (Rebel); Debbie Byrne (Kathy); Bryan Brown (Tiger); Bill Hunter (Browning); Julie Nihill (Joycie).

Production Company: Phillip Emanuel/Village Roadshow Corp.

Running Time: 98 minutes.

STORY

Sydney during World War II: Kathy McLeod, a singer at the Air Raid Club (a nightclub for American servicemen) meets Rebel, a marine who, after being wounded on Guadalcanal, has deserted while on recuperation leave. Kathy, married to an Australian soldier fighting in New Guinea, tries to resist Rebel's advances. They fall in love, although the relationship is constantly threatened by Kathy's need to be loyal to her absent husband. Rebel is haunted by nightmares of being wounded by and killing a Japanese soldier. He tries to leave Australia with the assistance of black marketeer Tiger Kelly, but the American military police and Australian police are closing in. Caught, Rebel escapes but gives up his chance of freedom to return to Kathy and is arrested at the Air Raid Club.

COMMENT

As a film that takes no interest in the predominantly naturalistic conventions of Australian cinema and has no panoramic views of landscape and no painstakingly authentic period reconstruction (despite being set during World War II), *Rebel* stands almost alone (except for a few sci-fi movies like *Mad Max: Beyond Thunderdome* and *The Time Guardian* [1987]). It is tempting to claim that *Rebel* is more consciously aesthetic than is usual in the New Australian Cinema, but the naturalistic/impressionistic conventions of most Australian films (especially those with bush settings) are also consciously, even self-consciously, achieved. *Rebel* has some similarities to sections of *Razorback* (although *Razorback* deliberately moves into video expressionism, *Rebel* is more theater-inspired) and to the coffeehouse scenes in *Street Hero* (which had the same production designer). Also instructive in terms of this deliberate avoiding of period reconstruction is a comparison with *Death of a Soldier,* a film with a similar narrative setting—American servicemen in Australia during World War II—that pursues the usual aesthetic approach of verisimilitude in *mise-en-scène.*

But *Rebel* and *Death of a Soldier* are fundamentally different films: *Death of a Soldier* is based on fact and approaches docudrama format; *Rebel* is a musical, not so much in the conventional Hollywood sense (as *Starstruck* is) but seemingly inspired by *Cabaret* (USA, 1972). The numbers in *Rebel* serve the same narrative function as those in *Cabaret:* they comment upon the drama rather than propel the narrative. Sometimes the songs are in ironic counterpoint to the action or to the characters; sometimes they foreshadow developments. There is an anachronism in musical style that serves as an indicator of a certain unevenness about the film as a whole. The aestheticization of period does not succeed in overpowering the historical actuality of the story and setting—although this may be in part a measure of the power of the predominance of the period film in the New Australian Cinema. The drama, a melodrama of intimate personal relations, is somewhat ill at ease with the over-the-top performance of the musical numbers and especially with the neon-cluttered decor and overrich color saturation throughout.

Since accuracy of location is deliberately eschewed, *Rebel* stamps its Australianness in several ways upon what is after all a universal dramatic theme. One is through the minor characters. The larrikin black marketeer Tiger Kelly (not to be confused with the same-named character in *Ginger Meggs*), played almost inevitably by Bryan Brown, provides the Australian identity, the base from which the other characters strike away. His laconic, sardonic Australianness emphasizes the alien otherness of Matt Dillon's Rebel, the contrast between American and Australian behavior and speech being nowhere as clearly delineated in any other relationship in the film—even in the dominant relationship of Kathy and Rebel. This difference in attitude and outlook finds a parallel in the brief scenes of American and Australian police. The Australian detective Browning (again almost inevitably played by Bill Hunter) in his greater capacity for empathizing with the underdog and objecting to (if not rejecting) officious authority strikes a particularly Australian note against the more harshly American (or Americanized) MPs.

Nonetheless, *Rebel* is not stridently nationalistic. It makes no real use of historical attitudes toward Americans at the period of the story or of present-day attitudes. The differences between Rebel and Kathy are only partly informed by cultural differences; only a little dramatic tension derives from the fact that Kathy's Australian husband is fighting in the Pacific while Rebel, the American marine, is resting/hiding in Sydney. Kathy's resistance to Rebel's advances seems simply related to his brash personality. Rather than resenting Rebel's presence (a

historically accurate reaction), many of the Australian characters seem
to take his side, to see him as the underdog, a sort of honorary "Aussie
battler." The psychological justification for Rebel's desertion, conventionally enhanced by his romance with Kathy, is less convincing than
his fight, futile as it is, against authority. For this reason he is more to
Detective Browning than simply a criminal to be hunted down: his
crime is being against authority rather than felonious.

Kathy's character is less strongly delineated; as is often the case in
Australian movies, she is not an initiator of action, although she does
manifest some of the "guts" of the other urban heroines of the New
Australian Cinema. She has elements of the liberated woman, although
this is placed within the historical situation of World War II and her
independence is thus provisional.

The Settlement 1983

Director: Howard Rubie.
Producer: Robert Bruning.
Screenplay: Ted Roberts.
Director of Photography: Ernest Clark.
Editor: Henry Dangar.
Art Director: John Watson.
Music: Sven Libaek.
Sound: Max Bowring.

Cast: Bill Kerr (Kearney); John Jarratt
    (Martin); Lorna Leslie (Joycie); Tony
    Barry (sergeant); Alan Cassell (Lohan);
    Kate Wild (Mrs. Crow); Elaine Cusick
    (Mrs. Lohan).
Production Company: Robert Bruning
    Productions.
Running Time: 95 minutes.

STORY

Kearney and Martin are latter-day "swaggies," making their way
around rural areas of Queensland in the mid-1950s. They move into
an abandoned shack on the outskirts of the tiny community of Cedar
Creek at the time of a shearers' strike. Martin befriends a barmaid,
Joycie. After Joycie stays all night to help nurse the ill Kearney, she is
sacked by the pub owner. This seeming *menage à trois* attracts the
indignation of the sexually repressed, hysterical wife of the police
sergeant. The women of the community confront Joycie. The policeman's wife goes berserk and burns the shack down. Recognizing the
impossibility of living together as a threesome, Joycie, Martin, and
Kearney split up but almost immediately come back together.

The Settlement. National Film and Sound Archive/Robert Bruning Productions Pty Ltd.

COMMENT

The Settlement is set in the bush and in the past at the time of the shearers' strike (which also occurs at the end of *Sunday Too Far Away*). The film thus evokes all the cultural perceptions of the bush, the type (or stereotype) of characters who are likely to be located in this setting, and the type of dramatic situations and conflicts likely to occur there. It also evokes the nostalgia that has become part and parcel of the New Australian Cinema. It offers no interrogations of Australian cultural perceptions—it reconfirms them.

First and foremost, *The Settlement* is concerned with mateship in its "pure" form, simple, direct, and unquestioned. Kearney and Martin are mates. There is no need for any explanation as to how they became mates, and none is offered. But if neither of these men articulates their relationship beyond the usual laconic "He's m' mate," then Joycie (unusually for a woman in this situation) is the mouthpiece for mateship. She stipulates as a condition of her staying with the two men that she will leave at the first sign of jealousy from either of them. She recognizes that the relationship between the two men is more important than, transcends, any relationship between a man and a woman. At the end of the film, when it becomes clear that, as a threesome, they will continue to meet incomprehension and intolerance, it is Joycie who insists upon going alone (or staying alone while Martin and Kearney leave). It is unfortunate that for narrative purposes, and for the sake of a humorous and happy ending, the film allows Martin and Kearney to appear to agree to separate with ease (although with the culturally appropriate lack of articulated sentiment).

The Settlement is quite clearly a believer in male bonding; the other "pairs" who receive narrative attention, the police sergeant and his wife and the publican and his wife, are delineated by failures of compatibility at both sexual and friendship levels.

The Settlement continues the Australian love/hate perception of small country towns, an ambiguous cultural attitude compounded by the fact that rural communities are quite clearly much closer to the bush and must therefore absorb some of its favorable mythic attributes, yet are also proto-cities and therefore also share some of the mythic negatives of urban existence.

Although Cedar Creek is observed with some affection in *The Settlement,* by and large its image is negative. It is shown to be life-denying in contrast with the life-enhancing attitudes, existence, and indeed philosophy of Kearney and Martin. It is a source of both ignorance and intolerance (and perhaps envy).

Despite an occasionally demonstrated touch of fine comic observation, the people of Cedar Creek are little more than stereotypes and consist of a parade of nasty, narrow-minded, but otherwise hardly differentiated individuals who exist to make life difficult for Kearney, Martin, and Joycie. The conservatism of rural Australia touched upon in the film runs the gamut from religion-inspired "wowserism" through sexism to simple dislike of strangers. There is little or no attempt to provide any individual psychological explanation for the attitudes of the townspeople (or the few who are given individual narrative development). Like the people of Bundanyabba in *Wake in Fright,* the inhabitants of Cedar Creek are the way they are because of where they are. The attempt to draw parallels between the sexual repression of the community as a whole and that of the sergeant's wife seems narratively necessary but psychologically unconvincing.

By placing its story in the past, *The Settlement* manages to evoke nostalgia without running the risk of that nostalgia being seen to be in contradiction to contemporary Australian society. The film is concerned with the illustration of simple Australian virtues: mateship, cheerfulness in adversity, "proper" disrespect for authority, egalitarianism (Kearney and Martin are joined by the striking shearers when attacked by the local "cockies"), ability to survive, and so on. It is not so much a film about these things (as *Gallipoli* clearly is) as a film that is totally structured by them—not merely taking them for granted but adopting them completely. It is, in short, an excellent example of the way in which cultural perceptions are "naturalized" and become the commonsense understandings of the way things are. This is a modest film no doubt, but one with a certain charm, and one that demonstrates how the lessons of the mid-1970s have resulted in polished essays (although of no particular brilliance) in the 1980s.

Shame 1987

Director: Steve Jodrell.

Producer: Damien Parer and Paul D. Barron.

Screenplay: Beverly Blankenship, Michael Brindley.

Director of Photography: Joseph Pickering.

Editor: Kerry Regan.

Production Designer: Phil Peters.

Music: Mario Millo.

Cast: Deborra-Lee Furness (Asta); Tony Barry (Tim); Simone Buchanan (Lizzie); Peter Aanensen (Cuddy); Gillian Jones (Tina); Margaret Ford (Norma); David Franklin (Danny).

Production Company: Barron Films and UAA Films.

Running Time: 94 minutes.

STORY

Asta Cadell, a city lawyer, stops in the small country town of Ginborak while she waits for parts for her motorcycle. She stays with Tim Curtis, the local mechanic, and is disturbed by the town's conspiracy of silence about the rape of Tim's daughter Lizzie by six young men. It seems this is not the first such rape. Asta's ability to look after herself gains her the respect of some of the women and the resentment of the men. Her reputation attacked by the mothers of the boys involved, Lizzie presses charges. A drunken mob attacks the Curtis home, beats up Tim, and abducts Norma, his mother. Lizzie and Asta escape on the motorbike. Norma is rescued by the women, but Lizzie, waiting at the police station, is abducted by two young men. Fighting back, she falls from the moving car and is killed. All the women unite in their determination to see that things are changed in the future.

COMMENT

Without denigrating the real merits of *Shame,* it is feasible to suggest that it is *Wake in Fright* revisited. Standing at the opposite ends of the period that can legitimately be called the New Australian Cinema, these films suggest something rotten at the core of Australian culture and, by extension, Australian mythology as well. What is rotten is, loosely put, masculine culture: the grouping of men and the particular form of oppression that follows. In *Shame* the oppression is sexual rather than social as in *Wake in Fright,* and it is directed at women rather than at men. *Wake in Fright,* subscribing to the perception of the Australian environment as harsh and brutalizing, questioned the function of the "sacred" concept of mateship (between men) as an appropriate response to surviving in that environment. *Shame* is not so blatantly iconoclastic. Mateship is on the agenda; it is not, however, male mateship but female mateship, a concept that in the context of Australian culture would have been difficult to postulate let alone accept in the first decade of the New Australian Cinema.

It is ironic, then, that while *Shame,* sensitive to the social changes wrought by feminism in the 1970s and 1980s and a document of that very feminism in action, should pose a context for a female mateship that is easily comparable to the conditions that gave rise to male mateship in the first place. The mateship slowly engendered throughout the film is created by the conditions of brutality and deprivation (social rather than environmental, but still physical) that are the dominant features of the women's existence. What this suggests is that the myth of mateship is still a powerful determinant of cultural perceptions of how social relations *ought* to be managed, even in the late 1980s. The distinct difference is that the gender emphasis has shifted: women are mates now.

The result of this shift is more completely to place men and women into a social structure based on conflict and confrontation. *Wake in*

Fright placed men against men; women were irrelevant. In *Shame,* men still form intractable groups centered on the pub and held together by the magnet of masculinity, beer, and oppression of women. This latter goes beyond chauvinism or sexism to suggest something more fundamental. If anything this is a weakness in the film's structure: the motivations for the men's attitude and actions toward women are not validated. The men are so isolated in their single-sex group that it is barely registered that many of these men are married. The ready acceptance that gang rape is simply "lads acting like nature intended" and that women "get what they deserve" is offered as a taken-for-granted attitude.

The mateship, the bonding that develops among all the women of the town, is rationalized dramatically and thematically. The way in which masculine power has functioned by divide and rule added to physical strength (and subverting authority in the form of the local cop) is demonstrated by the way in which the mothers of the sons involved in the rape rationalize their sons' actions as being a natural response to sexual incitement by the women assaulted. The film is, however, uncertain as to whether these women are simply unable to see what is going on or do not wish to recognize the truth. In a way, it does not matter: in the end, faced with the martyrdom of Lizzie, the women declare themselves, united, to be "far from bloody satisfied."

The use of an isolated community is a convenient narrative device: it limits the possibility of easily available intrusion of external factors and the opportunity for "escape." (Even so, it is far from clear why any of the women who have been attacked in the past stay in Ginborak.) On the other hand, the small town can be a useful metaphor for Australian society: Australia in microcosm (while at the same time saying "this is not *us*"). Even so, it is still clear that small towns have a particular set of cultural perceptions attached to them that place them between the bush and the city, sharing some of the mythic dimensions of both, but also being the focus of negative aspects of both (the dehumanizing effects of society, the narrow-mindedness of isolation). In *Shame,* however, the city is represented, as is so often the case in Australian films, by a strong woman. Asta's strength is a result of having lived/survived in the city: she can *be* strong but not have *grown* strong in Ginborak. (There is an undeveloped suggestion that her individuality and independence are also threatened by the city.) From the outset and throughout, Ginborak is given nothing to recommend it. The ease with which Australian filmmakers can postulate small towns as places in which "normal" humanity can easily be subverted and inverted without having to explain why is indicative of a deeply rooted cultural perception. *Shame*, like *We of the Never Never*, takes the strong city woman into the bush, but still clothes her in the mythic perceptions of Australianness.

Silver City 1984

Director: Sophia Turkiewicz.

Producer: Joan Long.

Screenplay: Sophia Turkiewicz, Thomas Keneally.

Director of Photography: John Seale.

Editor: Don Saunders.

Art Director: Igor Nay.

Music: William Motzing.

Sound: Mark Lewis.

Cast: Gosia Dobrowolska (Nina); Ivar Kants (Julian); Anna Jemison (Anna); Steve Bisley (Viktor); Debra Lawrence (Helena); Ewa Bok (Mrs. Bronowska); Joel Cohen (Daniel); Tim McKenzie (Roy); Halina Abramowicz (Ella).

Production Company: Limelight Productions.

Running Time: 100 minutes.

STORY

Nina is one of a large number of Poles who immigrate to Australia immediately after World War II. She is placed in an immigration hostel (nicknamed Silver City) in the country. Here she meets Julian, a married man who has immigrated with his wife, child, and mother-in-law, and slips into a romantic relationship with him. They set up house in a 1950s housing-shortage converted shed. In the long term, Julian cannot desert his family; after failing his law exams, he drifts back to his family and out of Nina's life. They meet more than twelve years later on a train. Julian has become a clerk, while Nina has gone on to become a schoolteacher. Their discussion of the past is the frame in which the story is told.

COMMENT

Silver City was not the first Australian film since 1970 to take as its central theme the conditions of immigrants to postwar Australia. *Kostas, A*

Silver City. Limelight Productions Pty Ltd.

Promised Woman (1975), *Cathy's Child,* and *Moving Out* all have narratives constructed around this basic premise. *Silver City* differs from these comparable films in two main ways. First, it is a period film, set in the late 1940s. (In passing, it should be noted that its reconstruction of period is convincing and avoids excess—something that cannot be said of other period films in recent Australian cinema.) Second, and perhaps more important, *Silver City* is distinctly more anti-Australian than any of those other films, although it is true that these films have in general shown "established" Australians in a not-too-favorable light.

The tendency in all these immigrant narratives to stereotype Australians or at least to make them a butt of humor becomes an obsession in *Silver City.* No doubt Australians were rather unsympathetic and occasionally hostile to postwar (and subsequent) immigrants. In *Silver City* there is hardly an Australian who is not ludicrous, corrupt, nasty, a potential rapist, or a barely disguised fascist. Even vaguely sympathetic characters are treated with ridicule. In demonstrating the racism of the

Australians, the film demonstrates its own racism. This is perhaps understandable given the extent to which multiculturalism is ignored in Australian cinema—and, in the broader context, ignored in the dominant culture. Although much political lip service is given to the idea of multiculturalism, beneath the official surface there is a consistent cultural perception that newcomers ought to assimilate. This is arguably part of the Australian inferiority complex (the "cultural cringe") being exorcised by insisting "they" should become just like "us." *Silver City* in passing disturbs this taken-for-granted view.

The makers of *Silver City* may not have set out to make a film that was anti-Australian, but that is what they have made. It is perhaps the lateness of the film in the history of the New Australian Cinema that permits it to "get away with" an anti-Australian stance (which is, of course, a counter to the dominant cultural perceptions of what Australia and Australianness are). The history of the New Australian Cinema in the period 1976–1981 has been figured by highly successful films structured almost entirely around celebrations of Australianism. The next six or seven years of the New Australian Cinema profited from this groundwork in that films produced during this time have been able to take for granted many of the images and perceptions of Australia previously forefronted, to find their narratives in microviews of Australia rather than in macroviews, and to offer oppositional or critical images of Australian society. *Silver City* falls into this category.

Basically, however, *Silver City* is a story of illicit and ultimately failed love. In that regard it is a very simple and undemanding story. It is elegantly photographed, at times achieving a real beauty that is never simply aesthetic but always practical, even heavily realistic. But many of the potential social implications in the narrative—its period and its location in Australian history—are allowed to slip by. The suggestions of increasing anticommunist hysteria that was to culminate in an attempt to ban the communist party in Australia are raised fleetingly but allowed to disappear below the surface of the love story. (Comparison with *Newsfront* is instructive in this regard.) The very xenophobia of the Australians, which might have proved an interesting area of examination, is lost through the crude characterization and stereotyping of them. Lost, too, is any real suggestion of the parallels between the immigration hostel and the concentration camps of Nazi Germany with which many of these Polish "new Australians" were only too familiar.

Primacy is given to the love story—which is curiously lacking in any real sense of passion or emotional involvement. *Silver City* maintains a sense of distance both from the passions of its principal characters and from the history and sociology of the period. Given the topicality of the question of immigration to Australia in the 1980s (related to Asian immigration, but with arguments couched in the same terms as those of the 1940s), *Silver City* might have been expected to "grasp the nettle" a bit more firmly. It retains elegance at the cost of remaining aloof from commitment.

Squizzy Taylor 1982

Director: Kevin Dobson.
Producer: Roger Le Mesurier.
Screenplay: Roger Simpson.
Director of Photography: Dan Burstall.
Editor: David Pulbrook.
Production Designer: Logan Brewer.
Music: Bruce Smeaton.
Sound: Phil Sterling.
Cast: David Atkins (Squizzy); Jacki
Weaver (Dolly); Kim Lewis (Ida);
Robert Hughes (Harvey); Steve Bisley
(Cutmore); Cul Cullen (Stokes); Alan
Cassell (Brophy); Michael Long
(Piggott).
Production Company: Simon Le Mesurier
Films.
Running Time: 105 minutes.

STORY

Melbourne, 1919: Squizzy Taylor, a small-time criminal, attempts a robbery with an accomplice but is frightened off by a group of locals. On the instruction of Henry Stokes, a local crime boss, Squizzy conducts a burglary with Stokes's rival, Whiting, and then informs the police. Whiting's partner, Snowy Cutmore, retaliates by brutally assaulting Dolly, the prostitute Squizzy pimps for. Seeking revenge, Squizzy sets off a gang war. He takes over the gambling and prostitution rackets and becomes an important crime figure. His empire begins to crumble after he meets and marries Ida Pender. Cutmore begins to threaten Squizzy's operation. Corrupt detective Brophy arranges, with the connivance of Squizzy's henchmen, to get Squizzy and Cutmore together, and both are killed in a shootout that follows.

COMMENT

It is difficult to get enthusiastic about either Squizzy Taylor the historical figure or *Squizzy Taylor* the film ostensibly based on him. This lack of enthusiasm for Squizzy Taylor as he really was seems to have been shared by the makers of the film: they display a certain reluctance to try to turn him into a cinematic hero. To make a celluloid hero out of the facts of the real Squizzy Taylor would be rather difficult—given that the real-life Taylor was a pimp, an informer, a petty thief, a coward, and a braggart (not that the truth has ever been of great concern in the cinema). But in this film most of these undesirable attributes (and a few more besides) are revealed—hardly the stuff of which heroes, even Australian heroes, are made.

Nonetheless, the film maintains an ambiguous attitude toward the characterization of Squizzy Taylor. He is portrayed as a handsome (if short) young man, with a romantic image in relation to the girl he eventually marries. The treatment of this romance could have come straight out of a Hollywood film of the 1930s or 1940s (even if it is a little more graphic) and is not negated by a rapid cut from the scene of the physical consummation of their relationship to an image of an entirely unrelated corpse. The romance has the effect of humanizing Squizzy, but only in the way characters on the silver screen are defined as human.

On the other hand, writer Roger Simpson and director Kevin Dobson also take some pains to show the less attractive characteristics of Squizzy. This lack of a clear-cut sense of how the audience should respond to the character of Squizzy Taylor further compounds the episodic and incomplete structure of the narrative. The film offers no insight into the rise, and very little into the fall, of Squizzy Taylor. His relationships with women, with his criminal associates, and with the police are merely hinted at or covered in a few lines of dialogue.

The film spends too much time trying to turn itself into Melbourne's answer to Sydney's *Caddie* (an attempt that is rather more successful in *Kitty and the Bagman*). Although set in Australia's "other" city, *Squizzy*

Taylor, like *Caddie* some eight years previously, spends too much time presenting an accurate period reproduction and not enough time on story. There is a plethora of vintage cars, steam trains, trams, and horse-drawn vehicles, and not a few scenes (in Princes Street, The Exhibition Hall) that serve no dramatic function at all. *Squizzy Taylor* fails to engage because it fails to be one thing or the other. It neither overromanticizes as in *The Man from Snowy River* nor creates a portrait of a vicious little thug (which could have worked if we think of Martin Scorsese's films of unsympathetic protagonists: *Taxi Driver* [USA, 1976] or *Raging Bull* [USA, 1980]). There is a lack of psychological insight into the character of Squizzy, which cannot be rectified by assuming that an Australian audience at least knows a larrikin when it sees one. (Larrikins may be embodied in Australian cultural mythology, but more insight than this is required to stimulate that hidden cultural perception.) Nonetheless, the film unconsciously reflects the ambivalent cultural attitude to the larrikin: he is admired for possessing and demonstrating certain Australian traits (attitudes to authority, independence, mateship of a sort), but he is also condemned when these attributes become too antisocial.

Squizzy Taylor is neither tragedy—the character of Squizzy is not developed enough to sustain a sense of a tragic fall at the end—nor comedy—Squizzy is not a sufficient figure of ridicule. Nor is it romantic melodrama or historical biography. It lacks dynamism and structure; pretty photography and the most convincing period reconstruction in the world cannot disguise the film's narrative weaknesses.

In one way *Squizzy Taylor is* interesting: the historical period in which it is set. The interwar period has been ignored by Australian film with a few notable exceptions: *Caddie, Kangaroo,* and, to an extent, *Phar Lap.* The reason the 1920s and 1930s have been ignored—by a cinema devoted to period nostalgia—is related to the historical fact that during this time the fragile consensus of Australia's cultural identity was severely tested. *Squizzy Taylor* is only peripherally interested in this; but it does, in an indirect way, explain why and how a two-bit hoodlum like Taylor could become a minor folk legend, with a romanticized and fictionalized version of his life being made so many years later.

Stanley 1984

Director: Esben Storm.
Producer: Andrew Gaty.
Screenplay: Esben Storm.
Director of Photography: Russell Boyd.
Editor: Bill Anderson.
Production Designer: Owen Williams.
Music: Bill Motzing.
Sound: Mark Lewis.

Cast: Peter Bensley (Stanley); Graham
Kennedy (Norm); Nell Campbell
(Amy); Michael Craig (Sir Stanley);
Max Cullen (Berger); Joy Smithers
(Patty); David Argue (Morris); Susan
Walker (Doris).
Production Company: Seven Keys.
Running Time: 103 minutes.

STORY

Stanley Dunstan, threatened with institutionalization by his fabulously wealthy father Sir Stanley, decides to become "normal" by finding the most normal family in Australia and living with them. He moves in with the Norris family (Norm, Patty, Morris, and Doris), gets a job as a shoe store clerk, and begins a painfully normal courtship of Amy, the girl from the employment bureau. Sir Stanley sets loyal retainer and ex-detective Berger on Stanley's trail. It soon becomes apparent that the Norris family are far from normal; all turn to Stanley for help, and his wealth enables them all to make the necessary changes in their lives. Realizing that there is no such thing as "normality," Stanley carries Amy off on a white charger.

COMMENT

Arguably, suburban Australia deserves all the satire that can be heaped upon it, but since *The Adventures of Barry McKenzie* it has received little overtly comic attention in the New Australian Cinema. There have also been relatively few serious attempts to come to grips with Australian suburbia either: while narratives often take place in inner cities, the sprawling suburbs that are the physical reality of twentieth-century Australia tend to be absent from the New Australian Cinema.

Stanley attempts to redress this imbalance. The very premise of its narrative is that "normality" is to be found in the typical suburban home with the typical Australian family—and that this "normality" will prove to be a site of comedy and mild satire. In the end, the film must

Stanley. National Film and Sound Archive/Seven Keys Films.

discover its comic inspiration in reversing the obvious—the Norrises' normality is all facade—but while the pretense lasts, suburban Australia (brick-and-tile homes, bowling clubs, shopping centers, garden gnomes, barbecues) provides a suitable target for sending up. If anything, *Stanley* errs on the side of moderation in its ridicule; the script lacks the subtle cruelties of Barry Humphries' vision of suburbia as refracted in *Barry McKenzie*.

Perhaps wisely, *Stanley* finds other comic inspiration after suburbia-as-joke has been plumbed sufficiently to exist as a humorous backdrop for much of what follows. The focus of the narrative of *Stanley* is, of course, its eponymous hero—a rarity in the New Australian Cinema, a picaresque hero, a suburban Tom Jones, whose naiveté hides a natural cunning and a certain cynicism behind his Candide-like innocence. But despite this, Stanley is unlike Barry McKenzie or even Alvin Purple: he is not obviously an ocker or indeed a larrikin. In dominant cultural terms, Stanley is an outsider coming from an ultrarich family. This makes his search for normality (assumed to be in suburbia) both possible and plausible—a "typical" Australian would not have been looking for "normality" in the first instance, especially not in suburbia.

Because of Stanley's "alien" status, the character shows few of the

traits that are assumed to be typical of Australian humor: laconic inverted witticism, vulgarity, insult, the sense of the ridiculous masquer-
ading as normal. Indeed, the film itself might be said (beyond its interest in suburban lifestyles as objects of comic attention) to show little
that is instinctively Australian in its comic invention. It is not hard to
imagine *Stanley* translocated to an American location, for example (although it is perhaps a little difficult to imagine quite so passive-seeming
a hero in an American film). Like other clown-heroes in the New
Australian Cinema—Barry McKenzie, Fatty Finn, Ginger Meggs—
Stanley is a winner. But unlike the others, who win as a result of native
traits (in other words, the attributes that define them culturally as
Australian), Stanley wins because he has the money to buy the necessary changes and eventually to buy the woman of his dreams (who,
incidentally, is no more "normal" than anyone else of Stanley's acquaintance).

Stanley's heroic qualities (other than an unexpected ability at un-
armed combat briefly displayed) thus serve more as a catalyst than as a
creator or instigator of situations. It is not quite clear to what extent
Stanley's apparent successes at manipulation are merely good luck or
the result of others using him as a sounding board to reach their own
decisions (not unlike Chauncy Gardener in *Being There* [USA, 1979])—
indeed many of Stanley's dialogues with others (especially with Norm)
consist of a simple parrotlike repeating of the anodyne rather than any
intellectual involvement with the conversation. While Barry McKenzie
may function at a level just above the moronic, he does have a personality of his own. It is difficult to determine whether Stanley's lack of
personality is the result of deliberate search for normality (and repression of his own quirky nature) or whether he in fact has no personality.

Stanley, as one of the few ventures of the New Australian Cinema into
light comedy (it cannot, in the final analysis, really be said to be satire
along the lines of *Don's Party* or the *Barry McKenzie* films), deserves
attention and not a little praise. It is somewhat uneven—the comedy
varies between near satire and slapstick at times, between farce and
wit—but even given this instability of comic style, it is pleasant in its
unpretentiousness and often quite funny.

It is perhaps not true to say that it leaves Australian suburbia reeling
from the force of its attack; in this it is similar to *Puberty Blues*—and
qualitatively different from *The F. J. Holden.* Nonetheless, there is

nothing like the sense of affection for the suburbs one finds in American movies.

Starstruck 1982

Director: Gillian Armstrong.
Producer: David Elfick, Richard Brennan.
Screenplay: Stephen MacLean.
Director of Photography: Russell Boyd.
Editor: Nicholas Beauman.
Production Designer: Brian Thomson.
Music: The Swingers, Tim Finn, Jo Kennedy.
Sound: Phil Judd.

Cast: Jo Kennedy (Jackie); Ross O'Donovan (Angus); Pat Evison (Nana); Margo Lee (Pearl); Ned Lander (Robbie); Melissa Jaffer (Mrs. Booth); John O'May (Terry Lambert).
Production Company: Palm Beach Pictures.
Running Time: 105 minutes.

STORY

Jackie Mullens wants to be a rock star—to the dismay of her mother Pearl and the other members of the irregular family who run the Harbour View Hotel, Sydney. With the help of her fourteen-year-old cousin Angus, Jackie is a hit at talent night at the Lizard Lounge and spends the night with Robbie, leader of a rock band called the Wombats. At her cousin's insistence, Jackie performs a death-defying stunt that leads to an appearance on *Wow*, a television rock show hosted by pop music guru Terry Lambert. The appearance does not include the Wombats. Her punkish energy is muted by television. Angus is still determined to get Jackie and the Wombats into the New Year's Eve rock concert at the Sydney Opera House and to win the $25,000 prize—which will save the pub. After sneaking in, Jackie and the Wombats win first prize.

COMMENT

Although it is difficult to doubt the energy of filmmakers in Australia—over 350 feature films in less than twenty years—not all that many films actually reflect this energy within their own construction. *Starstruck* is one such exception. Despite the excesses reported under the

10BA financing arrangements, films that use Hollywood genre formulas are also not all that common in recent Australian cinema—with
the possible exception of horror films. Since 1970, and prior to *Starstruck,* there has been only one other film that is unmistakably a musical, the rock film *Oz* (a play on the frequently used diminutive for
Australia and also a borrowing from *The Wizard of Oz*).

Starstruck revives a traditional formula that has supported the film
musical since the 1930s—in fact, two formulas: saving the family business and making it in show business. But it does so in an unquenchably
Australian way—no concessions to the possibility of an international
audience here. Icons (especially the Sydney Harbour Bridge), language, humor, and characters are all thoroughly Australian. Much of
the comedy is uniquely Australian: it is difficult to believe that a non-
Australian audience is likely to make much sense of a remark like "I
wouldn't give this to a Jap on Anzac Day." In this, *Starstruck* shares
much with *The Adventures of Barry McKenzie*—a refusal to "culturally
cringe" or play down Australian colloquialisms or avoid jokes that are
comprehensible only to an Australian audience for the sake of overseas
sales. *Starstruck* enjoys an unrelieved sense of fun that runs to lunacy—
but highly diverting lunacy, if not as inventive as *Barry McKenzie.*

Whether there is serious purpose behind the jokes and the music (of
which there is a great deal) is debatable. Since this is director Gillian
Armstrong's second feature film, following *My Brilliant Career,* it is not
surprising that many have tried to see thematic continuities. It is possible to argue that *Starstruck,* like Armstrong's earlier film, does offer as
central protagonist a young woman attempting to realize aspirations to
personal achievement against a background of unsympathetic environments and demanding relationships. But this analysis should not be
taken too far. The film will not bear the moral weight critics would like
to place upon it. Thus, despite some apparent similarities, this is not
one of the "growing up" films that are so abundant in the New Australian Cinema; nor does it rate comparison with other city films that have
as narrative structures women fighting their way to positions of relative
strength or power within a male-dominated society. *Starstruck'*s true
points of comparison with the New Australian Cinema are the *Barry
McKenzie* films (at least at the level of comedy), and, outside the New
Australian Cinema, the Hollywood musical and its descendants.

It is better to consider it a late, and distinctly antipodean, entry into a cluster of musical films personified by Richard Lester's Beatles movies, *A Hard Day's Night* (Britain, 1964) and *Help!* (Britain, 1965), or John Boorman's *Catch Us If You Can* (Britain, 1965), or Bob Rafelson's film with the Monkees, *Head* (USA, 1968). Mixing the 1960s frenetic quality of those films with more recent trends in videos, *Starstruck* sits comfortably in such company. If ambition occasionally outreaches performance—particularly with the Busby Berkeley–style number in a hotel-top swimming pool—exuberance pardons momentary lapse. Despite its borrowing from so many sources, *Starstruck* is one of the most Australian of recent films and simultaneously the most Australianized of borrowed genre formulas.

It is odd that Jackie's career (and, to a lesser extent, her life) is run by Angus. In other words, the focus of the film is on a controlling male figure. But *Starstruck* differs from other "growing up in Australia" films in that Angus is not, like other male protagonists of such films, growing into the status quo. The film indeed divides its attention between Jackie and Angus; if either can be said to grow up, it is Angus who grows from a precocious schoolboy to a sexually active adolescent in the course of the film. There is a suggestion that his whiz-kid activities on behalf of Jackie are a form of sexual signaling and sublimation—excluded from the final concert, he compensates through sexual intimacy with an usherette—and his objections to Jackie spending time with Robbie are not simply based on business considerations. Sex is strongly on the agenda of *Starstruck* in all sorts of forms and is frequently seen as a barrier to appropriate behavior. Jackie abandons Angus, Robbie, and the Wombats because of a crush on Terry, who turns out to be gay. Pearl, Jackie's mother, nearly loses the pub due to sexual infatuation with Angus's father. The growth of Angus is associated with sexual direction and release, Jackie's with sexual control.

Stir | 1980

Director: Stephen Wallace.
Producer: Richard Brennan.
Screenplay: Bob Jewson.
Director of Photography: Geoff Burton.
Editor: Henry Dangar.

Production Designer: Lee Whitmore.
Music: Cameron Allan.
Sound: Gary Wilkins.
Cast: Bryan Brown (China); Max Phipps (Norton); Dennis Miller (Redford);

Gary Waddell (Dave); Michael Gow   Production Company: Smiley Films.
(Andrew); Phil Motherwell (Alby); Ray   Running Time: 100 minutes.
Marshall (Chalmers).

STORY

Habitual criminal China Jackson exposes the brutal treatment of prisoners after a sit-in at Katunga Jail. Caught shoplifting, he is sentenced
to another term at Katunga. His return is watched by Norton, a warder
who took part in the brutal beatings after the sit-in but whose conscience is troubled. Conditions at Katunga under its incompetent governor have worsened since the sit-in. A full-scale riot breaks out. The
prisoners, having effectively destroyed the jail, surrender. As they are
brought out for transport to other prisons, the prisoners have to run a
gauntlet of baton-wielding warders. Norton, whose attempts at reconciliation with Jackson have brought him into conflict with his fellow
warders, brutally beats Jackson and has to be dragged off to avoid
killing him.

COMMENT

Films of social comment are not unknown in recent Australian cinema;
films without the rose-tinted refraction of romance are, however, few
in number.

Stir is one of the few. It is a brutal film, depicting a brutal world from
which nearly all the remaining vestiges of human dignity have been
swept away. It is a world in which those in positions of power and
authority (warders) have resolved collectively to maintain their position by violence and by humiliation—but mainly by violence, which is
random, arbitrary, gratuitous, and unrelenting.

Stir is based on an amalgam of writer Bob Jewson's own experiences
as a prisoner, the events of a prison riot at Bathurst jail, and the
documents of the enquiry into the riot at Attica prison in the United
States. Except for brief precredit sequences and the last few shots of the
film, the entire action takes place within a fictional but not-far-from-
the-facts Australian prison.

Stir makes few concessions to normal narrative film conventions and
takes on something of a documentary feel at times—a feeling that

might have been enhanced had Stephen Wallace permitted a greater sense of the minutiae of prison life to be seen. There are no characters with whom the audience can develop any real or lasting empathy. This is of course deliberate on Wallace's part. He is content, even determined, to show Katunga prison as it is, to show the destruction of human dignity that the system attempts without providing the audience with the easy conscience-salving "out" that these are terrible things to happen to "good" men (that is, romanticized characters in a fictional narrative) but probably deserved in the case of "real" criminals.

Jackson, the most central character in the narrative, does little to invoke the audience's admiration or respect. He is not a good man trapped by the system; he is a bad man trapped by the system—and that is what makes *Stir* all the more terrible. He is sullen and inarticulate; as his rejection of Norton's conscience-stricken attempts to apologize for and to explain the psychology of the warders' brutal reaction to the previous sit-in reveals, Jackson is beyond reason and beyond redemption. The system has been too successful. Implacable hatred has been built into Jackson and his only response is violence as if by instinct.

Yet it is the members of the convict community who appear to be reasonable, acceptable human beings when compared with the "screws." The warders, with the exception of Norton, are shown to be sadists to a man. Although Norton's key speech to Jackson (which comes well into the film) provides motivation for the warders' actions (fear: "We are only in control because you let us"), the film has from the outset determined the audience's response to the warders by their brutal actions.

Character development is very slight; situation development is all. But it is here that the film's basic flaw is most obvious. It is difficult to get any sense of the nature of the grievances that the prisoners feel other than the general sense of inhuman treatment. There are few specific incidents that in themselves add up to an explicable climactic riot. Wallace seems more concerned with reactions than with actions or with theme than with narrative. The tension, felt rather than understood, that builds up to the riot is also dissipated by Wallace dwelling too long on some of the scenes of the rioting. The tightly disciplined cinematography to this point is lost. Wallace may have intended the *mise-en-scène* to reflect the same momentary euphoria of the temporary freedom of the prisoners as they destroy the prison buildings. But relaxing the *mise-en-scène* relaxes the grip the film has on the audience; without the usual narrative identification with character, the audience is distanced from events—including the random shooting—until the conclusion.

For the most part, however, *Stir* is a relentless and tightly constructed film that makes no concessions to romance, to easy identifications, or to the moral judgments of the audience. The men depicted are criminals, duly tried and justly convicted. But they have a right to retain their dignity as human beings. In the end, *Stir* convincingly argues that dignity can only be maintained by forcing the establishment to respond with hatred and with violence. This becomes the way in which the prisoners define themselves as individuals and as a group. *Stir* is a grim, pitiless film that reflects an attempt to drive head-on into a social reality that is unusual in recent Australian cinema.

That social reality inhibits any real sense of *Stir* dealing with mythical aspects of Australia. Cultural specificity is at once obvious and deliberate through character, location, and attitude—but it is so for the purpose of social comment and not national identification.

Storm Boy 1977

Director: Henri Safran.
Producer: Matt Carroll.
Screenplay: Sonia Borg.
Director of Photography: Geoff Burton.
Editor: G. Turney-Smith.
Art Direction: David Copping.
Music: Michael Carlos.

Sound: Ken Hammond.
Cast: Peter Cummins (Tom); Greg Rowe (Michael); Gulpilil (Fingerbone); Judy Dick (teacher); Tony Allison (ranger).
Production Company: South Australian Film Corporation.
Running Time: 87 minutes.

STORY

Michael, a ten-year-old boy, lives with his reclusive father Tom in a shack on the edge of a nature reserve. He meets Fingerbone, an aboriginal, living in the reserve. Two hunters, illegally shooting in the reserve, are frightened off by Fingerbone but only after they have killed the parents of a trio of newly hatched pelicans. Despite Tom's objections, Michael raises the pelicans to maturity. Their voracious

Storm Boy. National Film and Sound Archive/South Australian Film Corporation.

appetite for fish leads Tom to insist that they be returned to the wild. They are released but one, "Mr. Percival," returns to live with Michael and Tom. A storm threatens a fishing boat at sea, but Mr. Percival is able to carry a line out and the men on board are rescued. Mr. Percival is killed when the same shooters return, but Fingerbone shows Michael that life goes on through some newly hatched chicks. Tom decides to move to town so that Michael can go to school.

COMMENT

Storm Boy is one of the New Australian Cinema's early successes, a good film and a popular one. Like many other films of the time, it is based upon a well-known novel—although not on this occasion a period/ historical novel. While this may have assured a degree of acceptability to the film as certified family entertainment, and indeed a favorable disposition toward a well-loved story, *Storm Boy*'s success as film is a consequence of its own qualities as much as of marketing. The relative lack of success of its stablemate *Blue Fin* demonstrates this.

Although *Blue Fin* would seem to have rather more story than *Storm Boy,* the latter is the more satisfactory work of cinema. The narrative is less "busy." For example, characters have little to say: Tom is taciturn almost to the point of noncommunication (ironically, one of the few times he does speak at length leads to Michael's running away from home), and Michael tends to be a mute observer. By the same token, the film is content to let the narrative speak for itself rather than spell itself out through dialogue. It is not really a narrative that demands dialogue.

Story Boy is, indeed, one of the few films of the New Australian Cinema that actually demonstrates a mystical union of man and landscape—and then not simply through the presence of an aboriginal character (as in *Manganinnie* and *Walkabout*). Other films have suggested the positive influence of the bush upon men (and occasionally women: *We of the Never Never*), although the positive results of this influence have generally been gained through an adversarial relationship that forges the character of the men/women. Some films have reinforced the view of the basic malignity of the bush. But the landscape (not merely the geographic formation of the land and the vegetation, but the skies, the weather, and the quality of the light as well) in *Storm Boy*—admittedly not the traditional bush landscape, being on the edge of the ocean—is not included for its mythic resonances or as visual support for the thematic exposition of the narrative.

In a real sense the landscape of *Storm Boy* is a character in the narrative, both a passive and a reinforcing character, and in a curious way functions almost like a Greek chorus: the many moods of the Coorong (where the film was shot and where the narrative is actually located) act as commentators in an aesthetic sense on the actions of the drama. This may not sound different from the way in which landscape is used or presented in other Australian films; but the difference, if slight, is important, a consequence both of the unusual nature of this particular landscape and of the relations of the other characters to it.

The character of Fingerbone, the "renegade" aboriginal, is important in the way in which the landscape operates in the narrative. Mythically (and in reality) aboriginals have a closer (and different) connection with the landscape than white Australians (whose mythology, as we have seen time and time again, is one of confrontation and conflict with the land/nature). Fingerbone can thus, without the need for elaborate narrative exposition, represent a mystical figure whose "natural" place within the landscape serves to initiate Michael (Storm Boy as he is named by Fingerbone) into communion with nature, thereby justifying the many sequences of Michael (and the pelican) situated within the landscape. Fingerbone thus functions as a transitional figure between landscape and man. It is Fingerbone who brings Michael (man) and Mr. Percival (nature) close together in a mutually fulfilling relationship. His function as catalyst is social as well as natural: through his mediating presence, Tom and Michael are brought closer together—although, ironically, the function of their closer relationship is to remove them from their physical intimacy with nature. Importantly, Fingerbone's mystical function is not given the qualities of the supernatural—in contrast with the aboriginals in *The Last Wave* (which uses the same actor in a key role).

Storm Boy, for or because of its modesty, remains one of the most satisfying films of the New Australian Cinema. It may be somewhat open to a charge of romanticism and indeed at times resembles a children-and-animals story of the *Black Beauty* or *Lassie* type, but to its credit it avoids sentimentalization. Its absorbing of the landscape into the narrative provides an object lesson on how the landscape might be utilized in films—a lesson that has not always been learned by other filmmakers of the New Australian Cinema.

Street Hero 1984

Director: Michael Pattinson.
Producer: Julie Monton.
Screenplay: Jan Sardi.
Director of Photography: Vincent
  Monton.
Editor: David Pulbrook.
Production Designer: Brian Thomson.
Music: Ian Morrison, Les Barker; Ross
  Wilson, James Black, David R. Pepper;
  Del Shannon; Garth Porter; Todd
  Hunter, Johanna Piggott, Marc Hunter;
Leo Sayer, Vini Poncia, Sharon O'Neill;
  Bruce Smeaton.
Sound: Gary Wilkins.
Cast: Vince Colosimo (Vinnie); Sigrid
  Thornton (Gloria); Sandy Gore
  (Bonny); Bill Hunter (Fitzpatrick); Ray
  Marshall (George); Amanda Muggleton
  (Miss Reagan); Peta Toppano (Vinnie's
  mother).
Production Company: Paul Dainty Films.
Running Time: 100 minutes.

STORY

Vinnie is an alienated teenager caught between school, the attractions of the underworld, and the wish to be a professional boxer. Bonny

Rogers, the music teacher, and Gloria, Vinnie's girlfriend, persuade him to join the school band. He returns home from a country band tour to find that his stepfather has attacked his mother and killed himself. Vinnie seeks refuge with Bonny, but she eventually suggests that he needs to find another place to stay. He takes this as another betrayal. Vinnie rejects the overtures of the local Mafia and declares his love for Gloria. They accept the need to make their own way in the world.

COMMENT

It is all too easy to see *Street Hero* as a sequel to *Moving Out:* directed by the same director, written by the same writer, and starring the same main actor. The narrative is placed in a comparable milieu, and the thematic concerns are very similar. *Moving Out* is simpler, more observational, and engages attention not through narrative style but through simplicity and realism. It is a documentation of an inevitability. *Street Hero* does not share the same sense of inevitability: the central structuring device of its narrative is choice. Vinnie is faced with an overwhelming number of choices: becoming a member of the Mafia, pursuing professional boxing, school, music, a relationship with Gloria, his family.

Some of these are not logical alternatives, but the film offers them as such and in so doing creates an episodic structure that makes it difficult really to accept the narrative being unfolded. A plethora of dramatic possibilities for Vinnie are strewn about the narrative. Mafiosi, gambling dens, drugs, and corrupt police are mixed with school and family. There is family conflict within a situation of a brutal stepfather, beaten and cowed mother, and adoring siblings. There are the confrontation with unfeeling teachers, the school band, the country trip, and a set-to with local yokels. There is the girlfriend planning to live in France with her mother. There are boxing and the relationship with the grizzled old trainer. Throughout, Vinnie wanders through the plot, his confusion shared with the audience.

In *Street Hero*, Michael Pattinson has adopted a deliberately exaggerated artificiality—not only in the drama but in the *mise-en-scène*. Presumably deliberately aiming for a youthful audience, the film takes on in parts the appearance of the video. The set of "the Street" in particular is designed in hyperrealistic style (not unlike some recent films like *Streets of Fire* [USA, 1984] or *Absolute Beginners* [Britain, 1986] or in a different way the Australian film *Rebel*). But not all the action takes place in the street, and the scenes of school (with the exception of the band rehearsal area) and of the home are clearly real locations. The narrative constantly slips register from the heightened realism of some scenes to the muted reality of others. And the film is not served by an unfortunate tendency toward exaggeration and caricature of peripheral characters.

Street Hero has too much of an eye to an American market, and its representation of school existence is too much like that found in a large number of high school movies made recently in Hollywood. The presence of the Mafia is perhaps too American as well (although organized crime, of course, exists in Australia). The film does represent a ringing of some minor changes on the conventions of the "growing up in Australia" film. It is contemporary in setting (so is *Puberty Blues*) and narratively located at the fringes of society (so is *Fast Talking*). It offers the protagonist a wider choice of social conditions to oppose. But Vinnie's movements, like those of the male protagonists of other "growing up" films, are toward a bourgeois status quo rather than away from it.

Vinnie gradually comes to terms with his adolescent angst, and this is more the root cause of his failure to "fit" anywhere than the otherwise impressive catalogue of social and emotional situations that might have been to blame. Thus, rather too cutely, *Street Hero* suggests that a little true love and a little appreciation of his hidden fine (middle-class) qualities are all that Vinnie needs to become an ordinary member of Australian society. In passing, the film fails to make this fate a particularly attractive one.

A point of departure for *Street Hero* within the formula of "growing up in Australia" is precisely that it is accomplished through a (conventional) romantic coupling. In nearly all the films that explore this theme through a female protagonist, romance may be desired but emotional involvement is at the same time seen as personal entrapment. The male protagonists of these films, less concerned with the need to find freedom outside social convention, nonetheless also avoid emotional involvement (at least with a woman). The convention by which the sexually attractive if rather inarticulate Vinnie and the beautiful Gloria face the happy ending in each other's arms is not a convention of the Australian cinema—indeed it hardly ever happens no matter what the narrative or theme may be. Conventional romance, and especially teenage romance, is not an active presence in the Australian cinema—and this lack suggests a very real cultural perception that is hardly ever identified let alone defied in Australian films.

Street Hero compares favorably with other adolescent films; if its plot is overrich with drama and incident, that is a pleasant contrast to the paucity of imagination of other films.

Strikebound 1984

Director: Richard Lowenstein.

Producer: Miranda Bain, Timothy White.

Screenplay: Richard Lowenstein.

Director of Photography: Andrew De Groot.

Editor: Jill Bilcock.

Production Designer: Tracy Watt.

Music: Declan Affley.

Sound: Dean Gawen.

Cast: Chris Haywood (Wattie); Carol Burns (Agnes); Hugh Keays-Byrne (Idris); Rob Steele (Charlie); Anthony Hawkins (sergeant); David Kendall (Birch); Marion Edward (Meg).

Production Company: TRM Productions.

Running Time: 101 minutes.

STORY

After a lockout at the Sunbeam Colliery the miners of Korumburra in Southern Gippsland (Victoria) go on strike. Wattie Doig, a member of the Australian communist party, works with others to organize the miners in order to make the strike a success. Agnes, Wattie's wife, a member of the Salvation Army, is at first embarrassed by her husband's militancy but later throws herself into organizing a women's auxiliary in support of the striking miners. The mine owners import scab labor, and the atmosphere in the town becomes tense. The miners sabotage the mine pump, then barricade themselves in the mine, resisting all attempts by the police to remove them. They gain considerable publicity and after two and a half days come back out of the mine. Six weeks later, the company agrees to the men's demands.

COMMENT

Overtly political films are rare in the New Australian Cinema. This does not mean that the films are "ideology-free": like all cultural products, Australian cinema has been very much informed by the dominant cultural ideology. Fewer films have attempted to question Australian history or society at a political level. Political cinema has tended to be located on the fringes of Australian cinema; to be the province of "experimental" filmmakers rather than finding a niche in mainstream cinema production.

Strikebound thus stands out because it is, first and foremost, a political film dealing with political issues with both a social and a socialist consciousness. It does not use history in a romantic way or, importantly, to support the existing dominant mythic perceptions. Indeed, it challenges those perceptions at the level of acceptance of Australia as the "lucky country" as a result of "natural" and historical conditions. If Australia is the lucky country, *Strikebound* states quite clearly that it has won that status through hard-fought battle—not battles with the bush, the environment, the external conditions, but political, social, and class struggle. *Strikebound* continues matters implied in *Sunday Too Far Away* but obscured by that film's emphasis on romanticizing the shearer as a mythical creature rather than as an Australian working man.

Richard Lowenstein's approach to the material is radically different from that of any other Australian film. Although a certain tendency toward what has been called a documentary or docudrama approach has been noted in regard to many Australian films, particularly those designated social realism, it is fair to note that this documentary style is perhaps characterized by a certain sense of distance or of observation rather than participation that informs many productions. Occasionally, it is possible to speak of a neorealist style or aesthetic in Australian film. *Strikebound,* however, is much more pronounced in its documentarylike aesthetics. The "feel" of the film is, however, very similar to *Harlan County, U.S.A.* (1977), a documentary shot in a striking coalfield in America. To what extent the makers of *Strikebound* might have been influenced or informed by *Harlan County, U.S.A.* is impossible to state. What seems rather more likely is that the conditions of the struggle and the nature of the participants were so similar despite the distance of forty years and tens of thousands of miles that the actual subject determines, even dictates, the approach taken by both films.

Strikebound is not documentary—everything that takes place has been created for the camera. In this regard, it is aesthetically much closer to Ken Loach's *Days of Hope* series for British television, in particular the episode that deals with a miners' strike in the coalfields of northern England. Indeed, the two films are uncannily alike in appearance and structure. Both have the same mixture of actors and nonactors; both are constructed around the dictates of historical actuality rather than the usual conventions of narrative cinema; both are cinematically created with "natural" rather than "naturalistic" images; and both see minutiae as more important than larger issues. *Strikebound* differs from *Days of Hope* in that it is more "written"—or at least gives that impression—and focuses slightly more on particular individuals. But, as with *Harlan County, U.S.A.*, there is an extraordinary sense of the manner in which history repeats itself: these struggles are almost identical in every respect.

There is no romance or romanticizing in *Strikebound*. Much is taken for granted or simply presented as it is. Small matters (such as the way Wattie and Agnes simply "inherit" the neighbor's child) are given without much emphasis or explanation. But the film does not eschew characterization—less true of Wattie than of Agnes, who undergoes the greater changes throughout the struggle. It also is not devoid of humor. It does not draw the relative positions of striking miners, scabs, and police in simple black and white terms. But there is no doubt where the film stands on the issues.

Strikebound is one of the most exciting films of the latter stages of the New Australian Cinema in that it shows both a strong sense of commitment and fearlessness in being innovative. But it has not to date inspired any further uses of Australian history to reveal the actuality of social existence in contradistinction to the overall romantic/ nostalgic project of the use of Australian history in the New Australian Cinema.

Summer City | 1977

Director: Christopher Fraser.

Producer: Phil Avalon.

Screenplay: Phil Avalon.

Director of Photography: Jerry Marek.

Editor: David Stiven.

Art Director: Jann Harris.

Music: Phil Butkis.

Sound: Bill Pitt.

Cast: John Jarratt (Sandy); Mel Gibson (Scollop); Phil Avalon (Robbie); Steve Bisley (Boo); James Elliott (Father); Debbie Forman (Caroline).

Production Company: Intertropic Films.

Running Time: 89 minutes.

STORY

A week before his wedding, Sandy is taken for a last fling by his friend
Robbie: a trip up the coast with two of Robbie's mates, Scollop and Boo.
Sandy's middle-class, educated background immediately leads to tension between him and the ockerish Boo. They arrive at a small country
town on the coast. Robbie, Boo, and Scollop go to the local surf club
dance. Afterward, Boo seduces Caroline, the fifteen-year-old daughter
of the caretaker of the caravan park they are staying at. As they move
further up the coast and off the beaten track, the car breaks down.
Sandy attacks Boo when he hears Boo boasting that he was out with
Sandy's fiancé the night before they came away for the weekend.
Caroline's father tracks them down and kills Boo before being killed by
Sandy in self-defense. Sandy is later acquitted.

COMMENT

If there is one thing that youth films as diverse as *Summer City, Puberty
Blues,* and *The F. J. Holden* (and others) demonstrate, it is an emptiness
at the heart of the seemingly carefree, hedonist subculture of the
young in Australia. Sometimes this emptiness is shown to be social and
environmental, as in the case of the endless and meaningless rounds of
drinking and emotionless sex in *The F. J. Holden;* sometimes the emptiness is a consequence of socially determined gender roles and peer
group norms, as in *Puberty Blues;* and sometimes the emptiness simply
seems to be there, unavoidable, and by no means alleviated by sex or by
beer. Arguably, there is a resonating hollowness at the center of Australian culture as a whole, a vacuum that is somehow part of the very
conditions of existence there.

Summer City may well have not intended to reflect this essential
emptiness. Indeed, it may well have aimed to offer a positive view of
the surfing subculture. But what has resulted is a film that does not
simply show a certain mindlessness through a storyline involving four
youths presumably out looking for adventure, but also suggests that
this mindlessness is endemic. No character seems to have any real sense
of life. Scollop is probably the closest to having some connection with
the conditions of his existence. As Sandy says of his surfing, Scollop
and the sea seem to be one. But Scollop is totally unable to articulate

what surfing might mean to him and unable to offer any argument to counter Sandy's sterile proposition that "surfing has no security." The sequences of surfing perhaps serve as a counterpoint to the middle-class morality and empty ethics that Sandy espouses or to the ockerish, macho womanizing of Boo.

Summer City, although informed by a certain affection for its young characters, does not allow them to develop because it never really knows what to do with its own narrative. While the opening credits establish the time as the 1960s, it is difficult to determine just what is achieved by placing the film in that period. Admittedly, it may provide a little understanding of the naive, wowserish attitude of Sandy (which contributes considerably to the tragedy); by suggesting that the past was not better than the present, *Summer City* may indeed be a rare example of the reversal of the nostalgic tendency of the New Australian Cinema.

The ultimate climax of the story, the death of Boo, is brought about not simply by the insane actions of the father of the fifteen-year-old girl he has seduced but also by Sandy's priggish attitudes toward sex. The implication, then, is that in a more open society (i.e., the 1970s) this tragedy would not have taken place. Far from harking back to simpler times that are by inference better, *Summer City* finds little to be nostalgic about in the 1960s. Despite the humor, the weekend trip is tinged wih horror throughout, which manifests itself at the climax with two sense-less deaths.

Summer City also reverses another consistent perception of the New Australian Cinema: it does not find country life preferable to urban life. While not actually condoning Boo's sexual involvement with Car-oline, through early scenes providing Boo with his sexual image the film does imply that his actions would hardly have brought about such a violent consequence had they taken place in the city.

Summer City offers an interesting opportunity for conflict in philoso-phies between two characters who are defined (as far as the meager characterization permits) as middle-class on one hand (Sandy) and larrikin/ocker on the other (Boo). Neither is particularly admirable or yet devoid of attractive characteristics. The prologue and epilogue may suggest that Sandy is the narrative center, but for most of the film Boo is more prominent. Boo has some of the attractiveness of the larrikin, but there is a distasteful edge to his boastfulness and his goading of

Sandy. This potential clash of cultures might have provided a thematic coherence, but the film is reluctant to explore it in depth.

There is about *Summer City* a feeling of the amateurish enthusiasm associated with student films. When this is combined with a narrative that seems unable to decide whether to concentrate on melodrama, observation, or simply being a skeleton on which to hang a surfing movie, the result is confusion no matter what the intention of the makers was.

An opportunity to say something meaningful about cultural reality in Australia seems to have been largely lost. This is a pity, because films that challenge the prevailing form of youth movies in the New Australian Cinema—that is, "growing up" films that suggest an optimistic future through the presentation of a nostalgically observed past—are rare. *Summer City* contains implications and suggestions but in such confusion as to render them obscure.

Sunday Too Far Away | 1975

Director: Ken Hannam.
Producer: Gil Brealey, Matt Carroll.
Screenplay: John Dingwall.
Director of Photography: Geoff Burton.
Editor: Rod Adamson.
Art Director: David Copping.
Music: Patrick Flynn.
Sound: Greg Bell.

Cast: Jack Thompson (Foley); Reg Lye (Old Garth); Max Cullen (Tim); John Ewart (Ugly); Peter Cummins (Arthur); Robert Bruning (Tom); Ken Shorter (Davis); Lisa Peers (Sheila).
Production Company: South Australian Film Corporation.
Running Time: 94 minutes.

STORY

The remote country pub in Gimal is the gathering point for shearers "between sheds," including Foley, a gun shearer just back from the coast. Former shearer turned contractor Tim King manages with Foley's connivance to trick some shearers into working for him on his first contract at a remote sheep station. Foley finds his position as gun shearer challenged by an outsider, Arthur Black. Days of the same back-breaking toil turn into weeks, and boredom begins to stretch relationships. Old Garth, an alcoholic shearer, dies. The shed is fin-

ished, and the shearers go on a spree just as it is announced that the
Arbitration Court has decided to drop the shearers' prosperity bonus.
A strike follows, and Foley leads the striking shearers in a brawl with
imported scabs at the pub.

COMMENT

Sunday Too Far Away was the first film of the New Australian Cinema
(ignoring for a moment the "hybrid" *Walkabout* and *Wake in Fright*) to
demonstrate the photogenic possibilities of the Australian landscape,
the manner in which that landscape—rich with mythic significance—
could be used in the exploration of the film's themes and as a meaningful part of the narrative structure. *Sunday Too Far Away* makes full use
of the landscape (including the buildings of the sheep station and
Gimal as much as the bush itself) in creating and maintaining the
atmosphere and the mythical potential of the narrative.

Except for *Gallipoli*, *Sunday Too Far Away* is a strong contender for the
most Australian film of the New Australian Cinema. It addresses the
most potent cultural myth: the bushman legend. Its narrative is totally
informed by the parameters and the criteria of the legend; like *Gallipoli*, it might have stepped fully formed from the collective cultural
consciousness of white Australia. For this reason it is possible to argue
that *Sunday Too Far Away* does not really have a story as such. It is rather
a narrative that works closer to documentary conventions than to those
of the fictional cinema.

Sunday Too Far Away's structure consists of chronologically ordered
episodes from seven weeks with a shearing team rather than a narrative that has a beginning and an end brought about logically by a series
of causes and effects. The central character of Foley acts as a link for
the events of the overall story as such; his narrative function is more as
a focus than as an *actant* in a drama.

Sunday Too Far Away is uncompromisingly Australian: location, situation, and characters display little or no concession to the possibility
of an (uncomprehending) international audience. This is not to suggest
that the film is incomprehensible to audiences outside Australia, merely
that it is an extremely vivid and introspective demonstration of key aspects of the Australian mythos. The film reveals in precise detail the
conditions of the bush worker that gave rise to the definition of the

quintessential Australian character: remoteness, lack of material comfort, hard work leavened only by occasional bouts of hard drinking and reckless gambling. But two aspects of this ethos are emphasized over all others: competitiveness (linked with special ability) and mateship. These two attributes may seem contradictory but are in fact complementary. The competition between Foley and "Black" Arthur to be gun shearer shows both of these. Arthur is actually an outsider, not really a mate as such (and it is significant that he does not stay and show solidarity with the other shearers when the strike begins). But the competition between Foley and Arthur is central to the experience of the shearing shed as the film presents it. It is by no means insignificant that Foley loses the contest. Australian cultural heroes are inevitably losers.

It is because defeat is so much part of the Australian experience (real or mythically defined) that the concept of mateship is so important. Mateship emphasizes loyalty to mates and to the codes of the group, solidarity with others of like mind or in like conditions. But, as *Sunday Too Far Away* demonstrates with the attitude of the other shearers to Barry, mateship can also mean hostility to those who show interests outside the group or whose actions are at odds with the consensus of the group. Nonetheless, it is the attractive solidarity of the group of shearers, rendered more attractive by their humor and their loyalty (not infrequently shown as class loyalty as much as simple bonding—and as such different from the male-bonding concept of mateship in *Gallipoli*), that is the central theme.

Sunday Too Far Away does mateship a service: it does not present it as the inevitable corollary of ockerism. While the image of the average/typical Australian is very close to that of the ocker (so close that precise differentiation is difficult), there is little about the characters of this film that would label them as ockers. This may well be the result of the lack of characterization that the documentary style of the film imposes.

There is a lack of self-consciousness about *Sunday Too Far Away* that is the consequence of its being the first of the period/nostalgia films of the New Australian Cinema. Indeed, its success no doubt led to the desire to find other films constructed around the same notions of Australianness. But if *Sunday Too Far Away* led to the period films that dominated Australian cinema for the next six or seven years, it also suggested at the same time the value of social realism as a mode of representing Australia on the screen.

Travelling North 1987

Director: Carl Schultz.

Producer: Ben Gannon.

Screenplay: David Williamson.

Director of Photography: Julian Penney.

Editor: Henry Dangar.

Production Design: Owen Paterson.

Music: Alan John.

Sound: Syd Butterworth.

Cast: Leo McKern (Frank); Julia Blake
(Frances); Graham Kennedy (Freddie);
Henri Szeps (Saul); Michelle Fawdon
(Helen); Diane Craig (Sophie).

Production Company: View Films.

Running Time: 95 minutes.

STORY

Frank, an irascible widower, retires unwillingly from his job in Melbourne and with Frances, a widow some years younger, heads north to live in tropical Queensland. Her two married daughters are unhappy about their mother leaving, especially with Frank. The house in Port Arthur seems a tropical paradise, despite their privacy being disturbed by an unanticipated overfriendly neighbor, Freddie. Frank's health deteriorates with the onset of heart disease. Frances is torn between Frank's demands and those of her daughters in distant Melbourne. After an argument, she returns to Melbourne, but Frank, recognizing his need for her, proposes marriage. They are married in Sydney and return to Queensland, where Frank dies soon after.

COMMENT

Australia perceives itself to be a young nation. Demographically and politically it is; culturally it is—and it isn't. Much of its culture is derived from older European cultures; but Australia has expended considerable energy on constructing a culture that is significantly its own. The New Australian Cinema has not particularly emphasized youth compared with (recent) American cinema, but the number of "growing up in Australia" films is nonetheless noteworthy. Far fewer are "growing old in Australia" films. In comparison with American cinema, there is no consistent subgenre of "age" films such as those starring George Burns, Art Carney, or the late Ruth Gordon, or as demonstrated in the recent *Cocoon* films (USA, 1985, 1988).

Narratives in which the elderly are central characters and aspects of growing old are central themes are extremely rare in the New Australian Cinema. While Australian films seldom conclude with messages of hope and optimism—fatalism is deeply entrenched in Australian culture—they seldom engage the realities of old age. Death of the elderly is occasionally present, but such characters are usually peripheral and their deaths are relevant only as they affect central (younger) characters.

Travelling North stands apart from the mainstream of the New Australian Cinema in this regard at least. At the same time it does not indicate that there is anything especially culturally specific to growing old in Australia, except in terms of the geographic dislocation brought about by the couple's move to Queensland after Frank's retirement. In this they are enacting a dream and occasionally a reality that is common to many who live in the southern parts of the continent: moving to Queensland, a place of tropical warmth and sunshine, the rough equivalent of moving to Florida for many retirees in the United States. The myth of Queensland as an alternative utopia, an escape from the mundane realities of urban and suburban Australia, has particular potency; it can be seen operating in this mythic manner in *Blood Money* (1980) and in a short film that addresses this obsession directly, aptly titled *Queensland* (1976).

Travelling North continues the close involvement in the New Australian Cinema of writer David Williamson but brings him back full circle to adapting his own theatrical dramas for the screen (cf. *Don's Party, The Club*). The strength of Williamson's dramatic structures is evident: *Travelling North* shows no signs of having been arbitrarily opened out cinematically. Instead the tropical landscape of Queensland seems perfectly natural to much of the drama and not simply a photogenic setting for action and dialogue that might just as easily have stayed indoors. At the same time, the landscape does not seem to have a function beyond description of setting—unlike its role in many other Australian films. In other words, the landscape does not become a character in the drama affecting the actions or determining, in full or in part, the outcomes.

Geography, however, does play its part to the extent that distance and isolation (constants of the Australian experience) are issues within the drama of the conflicting family/personal demands placed upon

Frances. In a contemporary story, distance and isolation cannot have quite the same impact as in a period narrative; airplanes and telephones cannot be ignored in the 1980s, even if economic circumstances may limit their use. Nonetheless, separation from a rather emotionally and physically demanding family is a point of dramatic conflict.

Travelling North is removed from the bitterly comic and incisive views of Australian culture and social mores of earlier Williamson writing (*Gallipoli* seems to have been a watershed for him in this regard) and is interesting for its examination of the possibility rather than the impossibility of "real" relationships between men and women, especially when compared with *Petersen* and *Don's Party.* Elements do remain, however, of the distance that Williamson sees as inevitable between men and women in Australia.

The obvious comparison with the American film *On Golden Pond* (USA, 1981) is instructive, revealing the differences in outlook, attitude, and expression of personal and emotional matters between the two countries. The expression of emotion in *On Golden Pond* seems overheightened to an Australian audience (even with its familiarity with American popular culture); the naturalistic rendering of the relationship in *Travelling North* is much more in keeping with how people do behave. *Travelling North* jerks fewer tears than *On Golden Pond.* This is not simply the difference between soap opera sentimentality and some perceived realism but a fundamental difference in cultural perceptions as to what is appropriate in dramatic renderings of personal relationships.

Undercover 1983

Director: David Stevens.

Producer: David Elfick.

Screenplay: Miranda Downes.

Director of Photography: Dean Semler.

Editor: Tim Wellburn.

Art Director: Herbert Pinter.

Music: William Motzing.

Sound: Peter Barker.

Cast: Genevieve Picot (Libby); John Walton (Fred); Michael Pare (Max); Sandy Gore (Nina); Peter Phelps (Theo); Andrew Sharp (Arthur); Wallas Eaton (Breedlove).

Production Company: Palm Beach Pictures.

Running Time: 100 minutes.

STORY

The 1930s: Libby, sick of her life in the small country town of Mudgee, leaves for Sydney and gets a job with a firm making women's foundations, run by Fred Burley. Burley imports a promotions expert from America, Max Wylde, whose American brashness brings him into conflict with Libby. Burley throws himself wholeheartedly into promoting the idea of a campaign to "Buy Australian Made." Burley's new youth products, designed by Libby, are running into sales resistance because they are not large enough to fit all women. Libby's boyfriend Theo, jealously misconstruing a kiss he witnesses between Libby and Fred, nearly brings about the collapse of the "Buy Australian" promotion. Libby prevents Burley from resigning by publicly explaining the truth. Max and Libby are reconciled.

COMMENT

Undercover, made as late as 1983, exhibits a nostalgia as deep and unquestioned as that of any Australian film that had gone before. This nostalgia is determined by a number of the narrative situations: based upon actual events of the 1930s in Australia, these situations raise (but fail to develop in any way) interesting parallels between Australian society in the 1930s and in the 1980s. But the mood of the film does not encourage such parallels. The film is clearly sentimental about a postulated era when society was simpler; while admitting that the times may have been tough, the solution was obvious: wholehearted enthusiasm for "getting stuck in."

The nostalgia of *Undercover* is, however, tempered by the ambiguity that informs the narrative at almost every level. The film is not even clear about where its narrative focus lies (not an uncommon problem with Australian films). Is the focus on the fictional personal history of Libby McKenzie or on the actual personal history of Fred Burley? At a number of points the narrative shifts between these two, raising one and then the other as the central figure of the narrative. While both may be cast in the mold of the little Aussie battler, their respective sex and position make this mythic function quite different in its implications depending upon which of the two is taking the dominant role.

This strictly narrative confusion arises through the film becoming

Undercover. National Film and Sound Archive/Palm Beach Pictures.

bogged down with plot, or more accurately with multiple plots. *Under-cover* is top-heavy with stories. The film starts as Libby's personal journey of self-discovery, a search for independence and an awakening, but becomes instead Fred Burley's fight for Australian national pride (against a hastily constructed conservatism). The two stories do not in fact run parallel to each other or comment upon each other, but intertwine at times and exist separately at other times. These ambiguities are narrative or dramaturgical and may indicate a certain confusion on the part of the writer and director as to what they were actually doing with the material.

Rather more interesting is the film's ambiguity in its view of Australians and Australianism. First, and rather obvious, is the introduction of the character Max, the American public relations promoter. In this, there are intriguing parallels between *Undercover* and *The Coca-Cola Kid:* the American expert who has come to tell the Australians what is wrong and how to cure it, and the relationship between the American and an Australian woman. While neither film is shaped by a simple Australian/American opposition in which America is seen negatively, America is nonetheless the butt of humor (through comparison and through exaggerated stereotyped cultural perceptions) in both. Yet both films demonstrate genuine admiration for aspects of American culture as well. There is certainly no sense in which these films exhibit anti-American sentiment in the same way that many New Australian Cinema productions exhibit anti-English feelings.

Second and more significant is *Undercover*'s ambiguous attitude toward Australian patriotism and to Australianism itself. The narrative makes central Fred Burley's enthusiasm and fight to achieve pride in Australian-made products. This device provides much of the drama in the central part of the film. But it is undercut in two ways. First, John Walton's manic portrayal of Fred tends to make the character look, if not actually psychotic, at least obsessive, pompous, and even occasionally ludicrous when extolling the virtues of "Australian made." Second, the emphasis on the "Great White Train" taking the propaganda to the "real" Australians (as always, those who live outside the large cities) is undermined by the representation of these Australians living in small towns as ignorant, naive, unsophisticated, and comic.

From the outset, *Undercover* in a few brief images gives a very rapid impression of the unattractiveness of country town existence, an impression it makes no attempt to correct but indeed confirms several times later. Other contradictions exist. Why, for example, is Libby permitted to be shown demonstrating her freedom by throwing her corset from a train window and then spending the rest of the film designing and making the selfsame instruments of female oppression?

Undercover is an enjoyable film, but it is more interesting as a film that indicates that, by the mid-1980s, the New Australian Cinema needed to evolve in different directions, away from prettily pictorial stories steeped in rose-tinted nostalgia and away from thoughtless presentations of unimpeachable Australianness.

Wake in Fright (USA: *Outback*) 1971

Director: Ted Kotcheff.
Producer: George Willoughby.
Screenplay: Evan Jones.
Director of Photography: Brian West.
Editor: Anthony Buckley.
Art Director: Dennis Gentle.
Music: John Scott.
Sound: John Appleton.

Cast: Gary Bond (John); Donald Pleasence (Tydon); Chips Rafferty (Jock); Jack Thompson (Dick); Peter Whittle (Joe); Sylvia Kay (Janette); Al Thomas (Tim); John Meillon (Charlie).
Production Company: NLT Productions/Group W Films.
Running Time: 109 minutes.

STORY

John Grant, a teacher at a one-man school in the remote outback, stops overnight on his way to Sydney for the holidays at the rural mining center of Bundanyabba. Here, introduced to the town by the local policeman, Jock Crawford, Grant loses his money in a two-up game and, broke, is gradually drawn into the beer-lubricated, stifling, and aggressive hospitality of the "Yabba." He goes on a drunken and horrifyingly brutal kangaroo hunt with two locals, Dick and Joe, and the enigmatic Doc Tydon; the night ends with Grant being drunkenly sexually assaulted by Tydon in his broken-down shack. Grant tries to hitch a ride away from Bundanyabba, but, misunderstanding a truck driver, finds himself back in Bundanyabba again. He attempts to shoot himself. After recovering, Grant returns to his isolated school.

COMMENT

Wake in Fright is a cinematic trip into hell. It is a horror film, not within the traditional Hollywood genre this time, but in a uniquely Australian manner. It turns the tables upon the dominant Australian mythology with a vengeance and not merely questions cultural perceptions but shatters some of them—or comes close to it. No other Australian film offers such a savage indictment of a great number of cherished cultural perceptions.

Mateship, probably the single most defining mythic characteristic of Australians, is devastatingly revealed to be based not upon genuine concern for another but upon an aggressive demand that common perceptions and common social activities be shared without question. Ostracizing outsiders (those who deviate from the group norms) has been seen in other narratives—for example, *Sunday Too Far Away*. Where *Wake in Fright* differs is in the extremely distasteful way in which insistence on conformity is enforced. Mateship is inseparably associated with a concept of hospitality that refuses to allow any individual the right to decline an invitation or, more importantly, to refuse a drink. This film does not attack mateship and hospitality directly. Instead it demonstrates that, taken to extremes, these admirable social attributes become social and personal tyrannies. The refusal of hospitality is the greatest sin, and refusal is, in any case, almost impossible.

Although it is a narrative and cinematic journey into hell, *Wake in Fright* does not totally destroy these Australian myths. The trip to hell is a personal journey undertaken by one man, John Grant. Through this focus, the film implies that hell is not inevitable but individual. John Grant is a man who is not able to withstand the agents of the dehumanizing effects of the outback. Clearly, Grant's sensitivity is a narrative device to be used in contradistinction to the foul yobbos who populate the Yabba. But equally important is the fact that his civilization, his education, and his middle-class background and morals are defenseless in the face of the very conditions of life in the outback. Indeed, these are the very things that make Grant's experience a trip into hell; the locals clearly are able to make adjustment to the material and social conditions of their existence.

This is not to suggest that the environment is totally responsible for Grant's fall and that the people of the Yabba are not really part of it. They are part of the outback as much as the desert dust and the blazing sun. They are, beyond any measure of doubt, the "ugly Australians," and it cannot be argued that they do not exist or that they are gross exaggerations. But *Wake in Fright* is not concerned with the reality of character; it is concerned with the reality of experience. Grant's journey to hell (and back) may be, of itself, fiction bordering on fantasy, but it has elements of reality.

It is here that *Wake in Fright* reveals that it is firmly grounded in Australian mythology. One thing that the myths of Australia have taught Australians is that the bush, the outback, is not simply a brutal environment but a brutalizing environment. It is the bush that makes men like Dick and Joe and is even partly responsible for degenerates like Tydon—although he is an outsider, an educated city man. Tydon is the most narratively complex: he serves as guide to hell, as an example of where Grant may be headed, and as an outside voice that can, and does, explain the how and why of the Yabba and its denizens. It is the bush that makes these men (and the one woman given any narrative space) the way they are. If the civilized Grant and Tydon cannot withstand its malevolence, why should it be expected that others can?

Wake in Fright is a film built upon impressions, and in that is comparable with *Walkabout*, a film made at the same time and under similar conditions of production. Both these films, in different ways, do not in fact go beneath the surface of their observations. *Wake in Fright* offers a view of the outback as hell on earth, *Walkabout* a view of the outback as a lost paradise. This is not so much total contradiction as the selection of different impressions. Both are accurate; neither is complete.

Wake in Fright does offer a truthful view of Australia—even if that view is from one perspective only. It is *Barry McKenzie* without the humor. Horrific as the film is, it is too crude in its portrayal. The crudity is essential to the narrative, but it carries observation to exaggeration. Made somewhat later, the film might well have served as a useful corrective to the oversentimentalized views of the bush that have dominated Australian film since.

Walkabout 1971

Director: Nicolas Roeg.

Producer: Si Litvinoff.

Screenplay: Edward Bond.

Director of Photography: Nicolas Roeg.

Editor: Anthony Gibbs, Alan Patillo.

Production Designer: Brian Eatwell.

Music: John Barry.

Sound: Barry Brown.

Cast: Jenny Agutter (girl); Lucien John (white boy); David Gulpilil (aboriginal boy); John Meillon (father).

Production Company: Max L. Raab–Si Litvinoff Films.

Running Time: 100 minutes.

STORY

A father drives his children out into the desert and attempts to kill them before killing himself. The children, a sixteen-year-old girl and a six-year-old boy, start to walk aimlessly in search of civilization. Running out of water, they meet an aboriginal youth and follow him on his walkabout. As they approach civilization, the sexual tension between the girl and the aboriginal boy climaxes in a courtship dance by the aboriginal, which is not understood by the girl. The aboriginal youth kills himself, and the girl and her brother find their way to a mining settlement. Eventually, the girl returns to the city and marries, but she is left curiously disturbed by her memories of the experience.

COMMENT

Walkabout is not really an Australian film at all. It was funded with American money, written by a British writer, and directed by a British

Walkabout. National Film and Sound Archive/Fox Columbia Film Distributors.

director. It demonstrates so completely an outsider's response to Australia that its very shape and structure throw into relief the reflections, representations, and images of Australia offered by genuinely native productions.

Walkabout displays a far greater obsession with the Australian landscape than any Australian film. More than in *Burke and Wills* or *Picnic at Hanging Rock* or *Razorback* or *The Man from Snowy River,* the landscape in *Walkabout* is a character in the narrative. Indeed, the landscape is more than a character, more than a visual expression of the film's themes; the landscape *is* the film. Its brooding presence—beautiful, awesome, changing, and ancient—dominates the film to the extent that the narrative (such as it is) and themes are swamped by it. The presentation of the bush is as an actual conscious entity rather than as an amphitheater for human and nonhuman dramas. Without negative intent, it is possible to claim that *Walkabout* resembles a giant travelogue or even a catalogue of the wonders of the ecology of Australia.

Walkabout is no simple celebration of the landscape. It is a reaction to it, the cinematic representation of the outsider's awestruck incapacity really to come to terms with or satisfactorily define the landscape itself and the outsider's reaction to it through criteria derived from other experiences and other cultural perceptions. The film represents, albeit through a modern medium, the precise response that the first white explorers and settlers of Australia had to its alien and wonder-filled landscape and ecology. The eye that created *Walkabout* is the eye of the outsider.

It has been argued that white Australians are outsiders even after two hundred years of "possession." This status is, nonetheless, structured into a mythic and cultural perception of Australia. And this perception (or complex of perceptions) informs many of the films of the New Australian Cinema. Roeg, in *Walkabout*, is outside these cultural perceptions as well. It may be that this has allowed him to turn an "unclouded" lens upon the Australian landscape, but it has also meant that *Walkabout* is a film constructed not of insight as many have claimed (insight, for example, into the disparity between technological white man and natural black man) but of impressions.

These impressions make themselves felt in the film not simply through the stunning and mystical images of the landscape itself (although these are important) but through many of the incidents and situations scattered through the film that seem to have no thematic attachment: the weather team in the desert; the aboriginals making plaster of paris artifacts; the random appearance of a team of buffalo hunters; the existence of the nearly abandoned mining settlement itself. These and other scenes or actions seem to be responses to the unusual, the picturesque, the unexpected, but they do not seem to be integrated into an understanding of what (if anything) they all mean when placed together. Arguments that *Walkabout* explores the difference between the white occupation of the landscape and the aboriginals' partnership with it lack substantiating evidence from the film itself.

Impressions are the basic structuring principle of *Walkabout*, all worked without a great deal of credibility into a narrative that is almost immaterial. But it must also be admitted that through the eyes of Nicolas Roeg, these are not "mere" impressions: they reverberate with awe and with wonder, and with the sense of inarticulateness in the face of the staggeringly bizarre and mystical landscape. Less important than what Roeg may say about the/his Australian experience is what he is unable to say. Overall the images, the narrative situations, and even the few characters who people his film reflect a surface rather than an understanding. If this is what Roeg is saying, it may be true that white Australians are inappropriate to the landscape; but Roeg's reaction is too sentimental, too idealistic, too utopian, and too ignorant of the irreversibility of history. The aboriginal may represent a finer, nobler response to the ecology, but white Australia cannot simply fold its tents and steal away because its culture is less able to come to terms in a natural sense with the bush.

Walkabout serves an important function in the New Australian Cinema, not only demonstrating the immense photogenic value of the landscape but demonstrating so clearly an alien view of the landscape, a view that has the consequence of throwing Australian cultural perceptions of the bush into stronger relief.

Warming Up 1984

Director: Bruce Best.
Producer: James Davern.
Screenplay: James Davern.
Director of Photography: Joseph
  Pickering.
Editor: Zolst Kollanyi.
Art Direction: Michael Ralph.
Music: Mike Perjanik.

Sound: Ross Linto.
Cast: Barbara Stephens (Juliet); Henri
  Szeps (Peter); Queenie Ashton (Mrs.
  Marsh); Adam Fernance (Randolph);
  Lloyd Morris (Ox); Tim Grogan
  (Snoopy).
Production Company: JNP.
Running Time: 90 minutes.

STORY

Juliet Cavanagh-Jones, fed up with her sports-obsessed lover, leaves Sydney with her ten-year-old son Randolph (Andy) for Wilyunyah, where she has bought a ballet school. She has hardly arrived before she causes all manner of chaos. Juliet commences her ballet lessons in the sports-ground hall but soon runs afoul of Peter Sullivan, local police sergeant and coach of the football team. In secret Juliet gives some of the footballers ballet training to improve their movements and the team (the Wombats) win for the first time in two years. When Peter finds out about the lessons, he sulks. By now in love with one another,

Juliet and Peter continue to fight. Eventually both modify their positions on machoism and settle down to what promises to be a stormy romance.

COMMENT

Seldom has there been such a sustained attack in the Australian cinema on the macho male image as in *Warming Up*. It is, however, an attack carried out with very light artillery indeed and at a target that proves to be a very superficial view of machismo, defined in this film as being obsessed with playing football (in particular) and sport (in general), drinking in "men only" bars, and being emphatically opposed to anything as image-damaging as ballet and serious music. As such, the film leaves the dominant cultural myth of the Australian male largely intact, offering, for example, no challenge to mateship.

The location of the narrative of *Warming Up* in a small(ish) country town serves a number of purposes. It isolates the action from the possibility of other influences, other points of view, and other philosophies diluting the straightforward antagonistic relationship between macho man and liberated woman. It re-creates the dichotomy of country and city and offers another view of the disruptive effect of outsiders (i.e., people from the city) on the country way of life, clearly shown to be healthy and desirable (for the most part). Most importantly, however, by placing the actions of the narrative in a small rural town, *Warming Up* is able to raise (and use) all the cultural perceptions and beliefs about small towns to the advantage of the narrative. Thus the conservatism (real or imagined) of rural Australia allows a greater focus upon and sending up of the essentially reactionary nature of the macho image. The egalitarianism of rural Australia enables the narrative to avoid charges of elitism or of directing its attack upon a particular class.

It is no accident either that the heroine is a woman from the city. A country woman could not achieve the fundamental shake-up of prejudices (sanctioned by tradition) that Juliet achieves. This is demonstrated by the fact that Mrs. Marsh, who has lived in Wilyunyah all her life and appears to have the same view of men as Juliet, has not achieved anything like the collapse of patriarchal values in fifty or sixty years that Juliet does in a few short weeks. City women in Australian cinematic narratives are strong, resolute winners.

At the conclusion, *Warming Up* cannot fully deliver what its initial premise promises: a fully argued dismissal of machismo. While it may be able to find comedy in machismo's excesses, it does little more than dent the outer shell of the cultural image of the Australian male. It does not attack any mythic dimensions of the image and indeed suggests that, while men may be ludicrous in denying the place of less macho activities (dancing, playing the violin), a boy's true destiny is nonetheless to grow up to play football—and ballet may in fact have a use if it helps him to play football better. Thus Andy is not permitted to be interested in ballet for its own sake or even to enjoy ballet but only to continue with ballet rather than hurt his mother's feelings. The film shows its true colors in this regard with the final football match, which the Wombats win by executing ballet routines on the field. The intended farcical comedy of this sequence confirms that for men to "do" ballet is just silly and undercuts any suggestion that ballet would really help men to play football.

Warming Up is rather like *The Best of Friends* (1982) in that it is another rare attempt at the screwball comedy. As in most films of this genre, the narrative revolves around the sexual sparring between a woman and a man. The character of the woman nearly always depends upon her "usurping" to some extent male prerogative—being aggressive, pushy, extroverted, and so forth. But the man only occasionally takes on "female" attributes—weakness, introversion, indecision, and so on. If at the end of the narrative the man is permitted some apparent victory—usually accomplished by "taming" the woman in some way— the basic narrative structure allows the woman considerable dramatic power and she generally gets the better of the man throughout. For these reasons, it is hardly surprising that screwball comedies are not too frequent in the New Australian Cinema. In *Warming Up*, the battle is carried into the domain of men. For this reason it occasionally transcends the basic premise: "wouldn't it be funny if footballers did ballet."

It possibly was not the makers' intention to do more than use these two cultural opposites (it is difficult for an Australian to think of anything less masculine than a man who does ballet) to create some comedy. But in the context of the Australian film, particularly the number of city films that have strong and successful female protagonists, *Warming Up* does set up some interesting reverberations. These do not resound enough to shake any entrenched cultural myths, and the film depends upon an understanding of those myths for its very narrative construction.

Weekend of Shadows 1978

Director: Tom Jeffrey.

Producer: Tom Jeffrey, Matt Carroll.

Screenplay: Peter Yeldham.

Director of Photography: Richard Wallace.

Editor: Rod Adamson.

Art Director: Christopher Webster.

Music: Charles Marawood.

Sound: Ken Hammond.

Cast: John Waters (Rabbit); Melissa Jaffer (Vi); Wyn Roberts (Caxton); Barbara West (Helen); Graham Rouse (Ab); Graeme Blundell (Bernie); Bill Hunter (Bosun).

Production Company: Samson Films.

Running Time: 94 minutes.

STORY

A small rural town is disturbed by the murder of a local farmer's wife. A Polish farm laborer is suspected when he is found to be missing. A manhunt is organized and all the town's men join in "for a bit of fun." The local police sergeant, Caxton, is determined to capture the wanted man alive for personal reasons. The "village idiot," Rabbit, is driven to volunteer by his wife, who desperately seeks social approval. The manhunt quickly begins to go wrong as Caxton proves unable to command the men properly. After a night in the bush, not aware that the real murderer has been caught elsewhere, the men catch up with the fleeing Pole. Inflamed by drink, they disregard Caxton and begin to torment and beat the unfortunate man. Rabbit shoots him, claiming that "a man is not an animal to be hunted."

COMMENT

Once again, small-town Australia comes in for a hammering in *Weekend of Shadows;* comparison can be made with *Wake in Fright, The Cars That Ate Paris, Break of Day,* and *The Settlement*—even *Dimboola,* while affectionate, is far from flattering in its view of the "typical" Australian small town. It seems inevitable that most extended representations of rural towns in recent Australian films are negative. It may be that small

Weekend of Shadows. National Film and Sound Archive/Samson Productions.

towns offer a reduced theater in which all the evils attributed to the city are more obviously on display. *Weekend of Shadows* maintains the general representations of ignorance, vulgarity, xenophobia, brutality, and bigotry that the films noted above have displayed. (But it should be noted that this particular view of small, isolated rural-based communities is not a cultural preserve of Australia—similar representations are noticeable in American films and occasionally in British films.)

Weekend of Shadows, nonetheless, is an interesting film that might well have been a compelling one. It is a pity, therefore, that it does not live up to the promise of its material, which suggests that it has something important to say about Australia and Australians. This is not to say that this message is lost, just that the film is muted where it should be strident and, conversely, obvious where it should be subtle.

The film's theme combines two ideas that are closely linked: the brutalizing effect of the bush and ingrained Australian xenophobia. The hunted man is suspected for no better reason than the fact that he is an outsider (both to the town and to Australia); his guilt or otherwise is not at issue. The brutalizing effect of the bush is, however, presented equivocally. Rabbit, an inside-outsider, has not been dehumanized as have the others. The effect of the bush is therefore not unavoidable or universal. This suggests something more deeply embedded and more disturbing in the Australian psyche—an aspect of the condition of being Australian that cannot be attributed solely to environment: an unsettling thought that *Weekend of Shadows* does not expand upon.

The central narrative core (Rabbit's story, to put it simply) is well handled for the most part, gradually building (through flashbacks) to the situation where his final action of shooting the tormented, hunted man is both explicable and inevitable without being expected. The other narrative (of the policeman Caxton) is, by comparison, clumsily handled. It is overemphasized, with too many scenes in which his motivation (which after all is not complicated or inexplicable) is reiterated through dialogue. The enveloping view of the conditions and attitudes of small-town Australia reflects both these treatments: it varies from the understated and subtle to the blatant. This imbalance is disturbing: too often the film states (and overstates) where it should simply imply—and this is frequently the consequence of inadequate characterization.

Rabbit's story and Caxton's story share the common theme that both men are motivated by their respective wives (a commonality that is driven home by several sequences of less-than-subtle intercutting). The characters of the wives are given too little room to develop a sense of dimension beyond their obsessive need to find outlet through the "success" of their husbands. Vi, Rabbit's wife, is slightly more developed but this is because the narrative gives more space and time to her history as it is relevant to Rabbit's character. But, like Caxton and the men of the town, these two women are one-dimensional. Thus characters run the risk of stereotype or of simply being differentiated for the purpose of the thematic explorations of the film. Indeed, Rabbit is the only character of any complexity—ironically, because it is his "simplicity" (which borders on slow-wittedness) that saves him from having much to say, which determines that the meaning of what he does say must more often be implied than simply and directly understood.

Like *Wake in Fright*, *Weekend of Shadows* is less than convinced that the banding together of men who share certain common conditions of existence—mateship, in other words—is inevitably a desirable thing. Here a common humanity is displayed more as a common inhumanity. Objection to authority (in the form of the policeman Caxton) is rendered as surly stupidity or as the (very real) possibility that the law will get in the way of a little fun at the expense of some unimportant outsider. The picture *Weekend of Shadows* paints of Australian males in a group is not a pretty one. It is an image of a mob insecure in its own identity and turning that insecurity on any who seem to fall outside its own narrow definition of acceptable in-group behavior. In this it touches a raw Australian cultural nerve, one not often exposed in quite this way. *Weekend of Shadows* is a film in which theme dominates drama but one in which intriguingly suggestive thematic material remains underexposed.

We of the Never Never 1982

Director: Igor Auzins.
Producer: Greg Tepper.
Screenplay: Peter Schreck.
Director of Photography: Gary Hansen.
Editor: Cliff Hayes.
Production Designer: Josephine Ford.
Music: Peter Best.
Sound: Laurie Robinson.
Cast: Angela Punch McGregor (Jeannie);

Arthur Dignam (Aeneas); Tony Barry (Mac); Martin Vaughan (Dan); Donald Blitner (Goggle Eye); Sibina Willy (Bett-Bett); Tommy Lewis (Jackeroo).
Production Company: Adams Packer Film Productions/Film Corporation of Western Australia.
Running Time: 121 minutes.

STORY

Jeannie, newly married to Aeneas Gunn, travels with her husband to the remote outback of the Northern Territory, where Aeneas is manager of the Elsey, a huge cattle station. Jeannie's arrival causes dismay among the white stockmen, but she gradually wins them over through her calm acceptance of the hardships of the "Never Never" and her unfailing good humor. Jeannie befriends the aboriginals who camp around the homestead and champions them against the racist attitudes of the men. She cannot prevent one, Goggle Eye, from being "sung to death" or the orphaned half-caste child Bett-Bett from going walkabout. Aeneas contracts fever and dies despite Jeannie's nursing. Bett-Bett returns just as Jeannie is facing the future alone.

COMMENT

We of the Never Never may be seen as a narrative alternative to a postulated continued history of Sybylla from *My Brilliant Career*. If Sybylla had chosen to marry Harry Beecham, then her existence might well have become that of Mrs. Jeannie Gunn in the later film. Once again a mild form of contemporary feminism is presented, although here the feminist theme is demonstrated through unthinking male chauvinism rather than outspoken female objection to social repression. Jeannie does not object to being a wife (with all the social conventions that position entails) but rather objects to the men's objections to her.

This is a much more powerful theme in the cultural sense than feminism. Jeannie's presence is, quite simply, an intrusion into the male preserve of the outback, that mythical place where the true Australian (male) is forged and formed. Jeannie represents a threat to the mythical ethos of the bushman. *We of the Never Never,* therefore, contains the threads of cultural contradiction. If a (mere) woman (and a city woman at that) can not only survive but thrive in the bush, this threatens the image of the bushman on two fronts: either the bush is not as powerful as the myths would have it or women are stronger than the myths would permit them to be.

This contradiction (which is not, of course, a new one) was resolved historically by the creation of a new myth of the bush: the pioneer myth, which permits the place of women in the bush. *We of the Never Never* is almost the classic telling of this legend. It decentralizes the place of the bushman (in this case, the stockmen on the Elsey) and places narrative emphasis on the "boss" (the manager, Aeneas—significantly, not the owner) and on his wife. Certain attitudes that might be considered defining in the bushman legend—chauvinism, racism— are undercut and challenged, in order to be replaced by "permission" for the place of women and a more liberal outlook.

Overall, *We of the Never Never* touches upon a number of possible themes—aboriginals, feminism, destruction of the environment—but it explores none of these dramatically or in depth. They exist, as do many of the narrative situations, as isolated incidents, touched upon but never developed.

We of the Never Never completes, as it were, a collection of films that address, directly and classically, one of the dominant legends of Australian cultural mythology. Thus, *Sunday Too Far Away* tells the myth of the bushman; *We of the Never Never*, the myth of the pioneer; and *Gallipoli*, the Anzac legend. For this reason, if no other, *We of the Never Never* is an important film. Sadly, it does not match up to the other members of the trilogy or indeed to *My Brilliant Career*, with which it also deserves comparison. The film does demonstrate yet again the enormous visual power and appeal of the Australian landscape (especially when rendered in wide screen); indeed, *We of the Never Never* is even more visually striking a film than any of the others. In terms of drama, though, the film is sadly lacking. By avoiding the romanticism of *My Brilliant Career*, *We of the Never Never* has also made itself devoid of satisfactory narrative structure. It is little more than a series of set pieces that have little sense of narrative trajectory. Even characterization is left stranded: there is no real sense that Jeannie undergoes an awakening of consciousness as a consequence of her experiences. She seems just as capable of handling the conditions of her existence and her misfortune at the beginning of the film as at the end.

This curious lack of narrative passion may simply be because the telling of the legend was somehow deemed to be sufficient to make the film interesting. If this is so, it is an ample demonstration of why this legend does not retain the cultural potency of the bushman myth or the Anzac legend (both of which focus on men almost exclusively). In the absence of narrative drama the *mise-en-scène* is raised to higher dramaturgical levels than it can sustain. There is no doubt that the bush is shown to be more spectacular, more exciting, in *We of the Never Never* than in most other films of the New Australian Cinema. But the characters who populate this bush, white or black, male or female, seem somehow irrelevant to it. The bush is neither malevolent nor beneficial, it simply is. It does not have moods so much as changing beauty, and this is curiously at odds with the mythic perception of the bush itself (note in this regard *Picnic at Hanging Rock* or *Razorback*, for example) or the role of the bush in the other myths.

As a late entry into the period/nostalgia category, *We of the Never Never* contains just about all the conventions of the formula—picturesque setting, historical location, emphasis on character rather than action, application of dominant images of Australian identity—but its curious aridity as a film suggests that this particular spring had run dry by the time of its production.

Winter of Our Dreams 1981

Director: John Duigan.

Producer: Richard Mason.

Screenplay: John Duigan.

Director of Photography: Tom Cowan.

Editor: Henry Dangar.

Production Designer: Lee Whitmore.

Music: Sharon Calcraft, Graham
   Lowndes.

Sound: Lloyd Carrick.

Cast: Judy Davis (Lou); Bryan Brown
   (Rob); Cathy Downes (Gretel); Baz
   Luhrman (Pete); Peter Mochrie (Tim).

Production Company: Vega Film
   Productions.

Running Time: 89 minutes.

STORY

Lou, a prostitute, is disturbed by the death of Lisa, a girl she knows slightly. She meets Rob, an ex-boyfriend of Lisa, who claims to be writing, as a consequence of Lisa's suicide, an article about what happened to the "protest generation." Lou begins to identify with Lisa, especially when she finds her diary and reads of Lisa's infatuation with Rob in the late 1960s. Rob now lives in middle-class comfort with his wife Gretel. Lou is attracted to Rob, although he does not reciprocate. She breaks her heroin habit by going cold turkey at Rob's house and later moves into Lisa's old apartment, setting it up so she can meet Rob more equally. Rob's offhand breaking of a meeting that Lou has assiduously prepared for shows her how foolish her infatuation is but at the same time provides her with the strength to make a fresh start and control her own destiny.

COMMENT

With his previous film *Mouth to Mouth* director John Duigan demonstrated a keen eye and feeling for the minutiae of life as it is lived on the periphery of society. (Indeed, he also demonstrated this same capacity with the unfairly maligned *Dimboola*, in which the small rural town in Australia is equally socially peripheral.) In both *Mouth to Mouth* and *Winter of Our Dreams*, Duigan is concerned with emotional commitment, most particularly with the failure of emotional commitment. Not that Duigan suggests that successful commitment will solve all problems: quite the contrary—he realizes that commitment will bring as

Winter of Our Dreams. National Film and Sound Archive/John Duigan.

many problems as it solves. Nonetheless, he does suggest that, first and foremost, individuals need other individuals in whom they can place their emotional trust. (This theme recurs in Duigan's 1987 film *The Year My Voice Broke.*)

This notion is demonstrated in the negative, as it were, in *Winter of Our Dreams.* Despite the fact that Lou is on the screen in nearly every scene, it is the character of Rob that is central to the theme. For it is Rob—and his inability to relate to the women in his life, past and present—who is the destructive agent in the histories unfolded by the narrative. Although it is never fully explained, it is at least suggested that Lisa's suicide is due in part to Rob, even though they separated some ten years ago.

The extent of Rob's emotional handicap, or rather emotional sterility, is revealed through his relationships with three women: Lisa (revealed through her diary, which is read by Lou), his wife Gretel (who, under the facade of honesty, seeks sexual satisfaction outside her marriage), and most cogently with Lou. Of these three, only Lou "outgrows" Rob.

Winter of Our Dreams is, moreover, a complex film of many levels explored through relationships. Each of the women within Rob's orbit has another relationship—with the important exception of Lisa. Gretel has a relationship with Tim, a student of hers from the university; Lou with Pete, another creature of the social edge. These relationships reflect upon the central character of Rob in interesting ways: Tim is if anything an apprentice Rob and he offers Gretel no real alternative; Pete is little more than a boy and like Lou is one of the lost souls of society. But crude as Pete may be with his punk hair, earrings, and tattoos, he is more human, more sympathetic, than the cold Rob. This is in keeping with a sense of disenchantment with middle-class existence that appears in both contemporary stories (e.g., *Don's Party*) and historical stories (e.g., *Kangaroo*). While a real sense of a working or lower class would be contrary to the egalitarian myth of Australia, Duigan and some others find the disadvantaged and/or disenfranchised in society more interesting and more "alive" than those of the somnolent suburbs. In the end, though, Lou must detach herself from both Rob and Pete and seek new, more meaningful relationships. Like many female protagonists of the Australian cinema, Lou is able to find herself and find a mode of satisfactory functioning *without* men. (Men in the Australian cinema, on the other hand, seem to need men in order to function.)

Winter of Our Dreams is a type of film that was all too rare in the New Australian Cinema at the time: a personal film with a sense of commitment, and not merely to the box office. John Duigan may not be the most obviously cinematic director working in Australia. That said, his use of the techniques of cinema is unobtrusive but appropriate in *Winter of Our Dreams;* he allows the film's material to carry itself and is not afraid to edit for thematic reasons rather than simply for the story itself. His is, however, a cinema of personal vision.

Duigan's next film, *Far East* (1982), showed if anything a movement in another direction: the story seems to have overwhelmed any sense of thematic exploration. Duigan's directorial career (like that of most Australian directors) has been rather eclectic in terms of material and type of film—although he has written most of the films he has directed. Overall, his personal films—*Mouth to Mouth, Winter of Our Dreams, One Night Stand,* and *The Year My Voice Broke*—have been more successful cinematically than his excursions into genre films: *Dimboola* and *Far East.*

Winter of Our Dreams is not a flawless film, but its sincerity of purpose and its central acting performances make it a most satisfying one. Released at a time when the period film was still the prestige form of production of the New Australian Cinema, it demonstrated that contemporary urban Australia not only provided subjects for study, but provided subjects that demanded study.

The Year of Living Dangerously 1983

Director: Peter Weir.
Producer: Jim McElroy.
Screenplay: David Williamson, Peter Weir, Christopher Koch.
Director of Photography: Russell Boyd.
Editor: Bill Anderson.
Art Director: Herbert Pinter.
Music: Maurice Jarre.
Sound: Gary Wilkins.

Cast: Mel Gibson (Guy); Sigourney Weaver (Jill); Linda Hunt (Billy); Michael Murphy (Pete); Bill Kerr (Henderson); Noel Ferrier (Wally); Paul Sonkkilla (Condon); Bembol Roco (Kumar).
Production Company: Wayang Productions.
Running Time: 105 minutes.

STORY

Correspondent Guy Hamilton arrives in Indonesia on his first overseas assignment. He is befriended by the Chinese-Australian cameraman Billy Kwan, who intuits in Hamilton a quality for compassion he wishes to foster. Billy also introduces Hamilton to Jill, a diplomat with the British Embassy, and covertly works to bring about a romantic relationship between the two. When Jill tells Guy of a secret cable about a possible communist uprising, Guy's journalistic instincts overrule his emotional attachment to Jill. Billy feels betrayed first by Guy and then by President Sukarno and attempts a futile protest but is killed by the secret police. The uprising fails. Djakarta is plunged into chaos. Guy bluffs his way onto a plane and is reunited with Jill.

COMMENT

Peter Weir is possibly the best-known Australian director, and his film before this one, *Gallipoli*, is probably the closest to an enduring classic so far produced in Australia. Yet, coming after *Gallipoli, The Year of Living Dangerously* is something of a surprise. It seems to have deserted completely the interrogation of Australia (its culture, its social conditions, its myths) present in Weir's films from the outset. Its setting (Indonesia in 1965), its examination of a political conflict enacted in a cultural context far removed from Australia, and its essential narrative structure of a love story all seem to make the film a total change of concerns and preoccupations for Weir. Australia is left further behind in Weir's next films, all made in the United States (*Witness* [1985]; *The Mosquito Coast* [1986]; *Dead Poets Society* [1989]; *Green Card* [1991]).

There are, however, links between this film and his earlier work. The sense of an ineffable supernatural force governing many of the actions of his protagonists flows through Weir's films. The epitome of this is *Picnic at Hanging Rock,* but it is present in the other films where it varies from a sort of mystique (mateship in *Gallipoli*) to premonition (in *The Last Wave*). In *The Year of Living Dangerously,* this supernatural force is symbolized by the *wayang,* the Indonesia shadow puppets, and the suggestion of Billy Kwan not simply as guide but as puppet-master controlling the destiny of Guy and Jill. In this Billy is a figure not far removed from Chris, the aboriginal in *The Last Wave.*

As in *The Last Wave,* the central character is an outsider, slightly alienated from the culture in which he finds himself. Whereas David Burton, the barrister in *The Last Wave,* was born in America, Hamilton's cultural alienation is much greater as a European in Asia. (It is tempting to see Hamilton as a metaphor for Australia, a European nation geographically in Asia, but it is a metaphor difficult to sustain.) Weir is more interested in the response of the outsider to these forces; in *The Last Wave* Burton's response comprises the whole narrative trajectory toward an ultimately unsatisfactory climax. In *The Year of Living Dangerously,* Weir has retreated from both extreme narrative exiguity and unresolved climax, but perhaps retreated too far. The conclusion would seem to permit Hamilton to obviate whatever responsibility he might have for coming to terms with Indonesia and the strange forces that are at play by allowing him simply to retreat into a conventional romantic coupling and a "happily ever after" ending.

In so doing, however, *The Year of Living Dangerously* also differs from Weir's previous films in that it permits its protagonist a degree of autonomy in his final actions. If there is a linking theme in the Austra-

The Year of Living Dangerously. McElroy & McElroy.

lian work of Peter Weir it is connected with a sense of powerlessness. From *The Cars That Ate Paris* onward, the narratives have been structured around a sense of inexplicable (or at best inarticulated) forces driving the protagonists on. (This is also true in some of Weir's American films: it is certainly a subtext in *The Mosquito Coast.*) In *The Year of Living Dangerously,* these elements are partly personified in Billy Kwan, but even he is eventually the victim of forces that he cannot fully comprehend. Guy Hamilton, in boarding the plane, is permitted to escape from these forces; no other Weir protagonist has such a narrative choice.

It is instructive to return to the fact that this film is set outside Australia. The sense not of predestiny so much as of factors beyond the control and even comprehension of men (and women, as in *Picnic at Hanging Rock*) is also closely allied with Australians' mythical conception of themselves and their country. Escaping from Australia (at least figuratively and imaginatively) with *The Year of Living Dangerously* may have permitted Weir to escape this mythical predilection.

In a strange way, this also allows *The Year of Living Dangerously* to be seen as Weir's most complete film to that point in his career—that is, it has a conclusion (rather than simply finishing). It is perhaps ironic that so many reviewers objected to this conclusion, accusing Weir of falling into romantic cliché. But it is better to see the final sequences of the film as a coda: the true ending is not Hamilton's escape but Billy Kwan's death. Although Hamilton is driven by forces he does not understand, the audience is clearly required to see them as the machinations of Billy; the forces that drive Billy are less easily given even metaphoric form, and Billy's oft-quoted "What then must we do?" is probably closer to the film's philosophic core. In the lack of any answer, in the fact that Guy Hamilton avoids any responsibility for attempting to address the question, and indeed in the seeming hopelessness of actually arriving at an answer, this film is linked with Weir's earlier work, especially with *The Last Wave*.

Appendix I. Title Changes

Occasionally, for reasons known only to those responsible, Australian films have had their original title altered for release in the United States. All references to films within these pages use the original Australian title. To help locate films known by other titles in the United States, the following list shows the American title of films that have entries under an unfamiliar (Australian) title.

U.S. TITLE	ORIGINAL TITLE
A Cry in the Dark	*Evil Angels*
Outback	*Wake in Fright*
The Road Warrior	*Mad Max II*
Test of Love	*Annie's Coming Out*

Appendix II. Index of Directors

This list includes only films with individual entries within these pages. It is not a complete list of the credits of the named directors.

ARMSTRONG, GILLIAN
My Brilliant Career, Starstruck

AUZINS, IGOR
We of the Never Never

BARRY, IAN
The Chain Reaction

BERESFORD, BRUCE
The Adventures of Barry McKenzie, Barry McKenzie Holds His Own, Breaker Morant, The Club, Don's Party, The Fringe Dwellers, The Getting of Wisdom, Puberty Blues

BEST, BRUCE
Warming Up

BOURKE, TERRY
Little Boy Lost

BREALEY, GIL
Annie's Coming Out

BURSTALL, TIM
Alvin Purple, Attack Force Z, Eliza Fraser, Kangaroo, The Last of the Knucklemen, Petersen

CAMERON, KEN
Fast Talking, Monkey Grip

CLIFFORD, GRAEME
Burke and Wills

COX, PAUL
Kostas, Lonely Hearts, Man of Flowers, My First Wife

CROMBIE, DONALD
Caddie, Cathy's Child, The Irishman, The Killing of Angel Street, Kitty and the Bagman

DAWSON, JONATHAN
Ginger Meggs

NOYCE, PHILLIP
Heatwave, Newsfront

OFVEN, CHRIS
Oz

PATTINSON, MICHAEL
Moving Out, Street Hero

POWER, JOHN
The Picture Show Man

QUINNELL, KEN
The City's Edge

RICHARDSON, JOHN
Dusty

ROEG, NICOLAS
Walkabout

RUBIE, HOWARD
The Settlement

SAFRAN, HENRI
Storm Boy

SCHEPISI, FRED
The Chant of Jimmie Blacksmith, The Devil's Playground, Evil Angels

SCHULTZ, CARL
Blue Fin; Careful, He Might Hear You; Goodbye Paradise; Travelling North

SHARMAN, JIM
The Night the Prowler

STEVENS, DAVID
The Clinic, Undercover

STORM, ESBEN
In Search of Anna, Stanley

THOMS, ALBIE
Palm Beach

THORNHILL, MICHAEL
The F. J. Holden

TRENCHARD-SMITH, BRIAN
BMX Bandits

TURKIEWICZ, SOPHIA
Silver City

WALLACE, STEPHEN
Stir

Glossary

The Australian version of English, like English transported to many other parts of the globe, developed its own idioms and vocabulary. Since this book deals with a popular culture form that in many cases uses the vernacular, the comments herein have occasionally used "Australianisms" where this seemed appropriate. In the interests of clarity, definitions of some of these terms are provided below.

The author has spent the greater part of his life hearing and using vernacular Australian. These definitions are the result of his familiarity with the idiom and the nuances of its various usages. An introduction to the extent and diversity of Australian English may be found in Lenie Johansen, *The Dinkum Dictionary: A Ripper Guide to Aussie English* (Penguin Books Australia, 1988) and G. A. Wilkes, *A Dictionary of Australian Colloquialisms* (Fontana, 1978).

Aborigine/aboriginal. A descendant of the original or "native" human inhabitants of Australia who arrived and lived in Australia some thirty to forty thousand years before the arrival of the first Europeans a mere two hundred years ago.

Anzac. Derived from the acronym ANZAC for the Australian and New Zealand Army Corps, the term became the generic noun for Australian soldiers in World War I. Occasionally used since for any Australian soldier. The day set aside for remembrance of the fallen in that and subsequent wars became known officially as Anzac Day.

Battler. An accolade applied to an individual who faces up to the difficulties of life in Australia without flinching, complaining, or giving up. Often used in the construction "little Aussie battler," in which it is implied that the individual has little recourse to resources other than the human spirit and Australian character.

Bush. Both a generic term for anywhere geographically outside the city and a perception of the mythical power of the landscape and the environment in forming the Australian character. In the latter usage, the bush is the single most important determining factor in Australian cultural identity.

Bushranger. An outlaw, often an escaped convict, who preyed on travellers in the bush and occasionally robbed banks and wealthy landowners.

Chunder. To vomit. The origin is unknown and the explanation offered by *Barry MacKenzie* that it was a shortened version of the warning "watch under" given by seasick immigrants about to throw up over the ship's rail, while entertaining, is unlikely.

Civvy street. Civilian life.

Cockies. Originally a derogative applied to small farmers in the late nineteenth century. (See Selection below.) More recently the term is applied to any farmer.

Country race meeting. A social occasion in a rural town or village that is centered around horse racing but during which people from surrounding districts often travel considerable distances not merely for the races but for other social events such as dances.

Cultural cringe. A term first used by nationalistic literary critics who wished to champion Australian culture and were dismayed by the tendency, particularly in the arts in Australia, to devalue anything Australian as inferior to anything from Europe.

Didgeridoo. An aboriginal musical instrument consisting of a hollowed piece of wood several feet in length that is blown through, producing a deep rhythmic resonance.

Digger. A slightly outdated term derived from the gold rushes in the late nineteenth century but which did not come into common use until the First World War. It refers to the ordinary Australian male but implicitly recognizes his qualities as a "dinkum" (see below) Australian. Once used interchangeably with "mate" as term of friendly address.

Dingo. Native wild dog believed to have been introduced by the aboriginals. Dingoes can be domesticated but are often still considered vermin in sheep-raising districts.

Dinkum Aussie. Dinkum means honest, sincere, trustworthy, and in this construction is an accolade recognizing these qualities together with the essentially Australian character of the individual referred to. Dinkum also means simply the truth. Sometimes rendered as "fair dinkum."

Dreamtime. From the mythology of the aboriginals referring to the remote past in which the earth, the animals, people, and so on, were formed, a time in which spirits took corporeal form. The time of aboriginal myths and legends.

Fair go. An expression that recognizes the egalitarian nature of Australian cultural identity by insisting that all individuals have a right to fair and reasonable opportunities or conditions. In an associated usage, the exclamation "Fair go!" can indicate that a listener believes s/he is being told an exaggerated or untruthful bit of information.

Famous Five. A group of children, the protagonists of a series of books written by English author Enid Blyton. The books were popular reading for several generations of Australian children, particularly at a time when the "cultural cringe" (see above) made Australian children's literature hard to locate. The Famous Five were all thoroughly English and middle class, and the themes and morals of the stories reflected this.

Garden gnomes. Small concrete statues usually in the form of a gnome or elf intended as garden ornaments.

Get stuck in. To go to work with energy to improve a situation (usually but not necessarily a bad situation), often as an alternative to complaining about it.

Gun shearer. A top-rate shearer; that is, the best, or fastest, shearer on a team of shearers. To "ring the shed" means to shear more sheep than any other shearer working in the shearing shed at the same time. By ringing enough sheds, a shearer earns the reputation of being a gun shearer.

Jackeroo. Roughly speaking, a stockman or cowboy (if working with cattle). Usually the individual is working temporarily as a stockman and is either a visitor (often from England or the city) or is training for station management (see Station below).

Larrikin. Originating in the late nineteenth century, a larrikin was a delinquent or hooligan, often a member of a "push" or street gang, and sometimes of a criminal bent. The term retains something of its antisocial meaning but has taken on the qualities of independence and antiauthority of the true Australian and is frequently used as a term of admiration.

Little Aussie battler. See Battler above.

Mate/mateship. Mateship is the core of Australian national identity. Forged originally in the harsh conditions of a new and hostile environment, the bush (see above), mateship places loyalty between men above all other personal qualities. (The sexist nature of Australian culture has only recently admitted women into this mythic perception.) A mate is closer than a friend, closer even than a wife (although occasionally a wife can be a mate in this sense). Also a general form of address for men and, more lately, women.

Ocker. The quintessential, "typical" Australian male. The term was originally a pejorative with implications of vulgarity, crassness, sexism, and boorishness. It retains the sense of ordinariness in terms of straightforwardness and lack of sophistication but has now become a positive image of typical Australianness.

Outback. Another name for the bush (see above). It implies more remote regions, generally beyond that suitable for agriculture; the wilder, harsher regions of Australia.

Pom/pommie. A generic term for anyone British, and particularly English. Similar to the American "limey." It may be used affectionately, neutrally, or derogatorily. In the latter sense it is usually accompanied by an adjectival expletive.

Selection. A nineteenth-century term referring to a homestead farm "selected" or simply taken up from land in the bush previously not deemed by the government to be owned even when a squatter (see below) had occupied it.

She'll be right. An expression of reassurance which reveals the entrenched Australian attitude that things will work out for the best, that elaborate planning or overconcern and fuss are unnecessary, that close enough is good enough.

Sing to death. From aboriginal mysticism or spiritualism. They believe that a death spell or curse can be placed on an individual by singing him or her to death. The singing is usually carried out by a "kadaycha" or magician.

S.P. Bookie. An illegal bookmaker who operates off the race track. The initials "S.P." stand for "starting price"—the final and official odds at which a horse starts a race determine the payout (if any) rather than odds quoted at the time of the wager.

"'Spiflicate" the poms. To beat the English at cricket. Possibly an incorrect usage in the film *Fatty Finn* as the usual meaning of 'spiflicated is intoxicated.

Sports-ground hall. A pavillion located on the playing field in a rural town. Generally an all-purpose room or set of rooms used by different local groups, often with a kitchen for social dinners and dances.

Squater. Originally in the nineteenth century an individual who simply squatted on or laid claim to a large tract of virgin bush and then raised sheep on it. Now a wealthy pastoralist (someone who raises stock), generally having social power and sometimes political influence in addition to wealth.

Station. A ranch or extensive pastoral holding where sheep or cattle are raised.

Swaggies. Tramps or hobos but without the negative connotations of these terms. Men who carried their essential belongings, especially a "swag" or bedroll, with them through the bush, taking work or charity where they could.

10BA Financing. A way of raising essential funds for a film production, so called because of the particular section of the Australian Tax Act (10BA) which permitted the investor to write off his investment at variable rates against his taxable income and to claim further concessions on any taxable profits.

Walkabout. The European designation of the (to European minds) puzzling habit of aboriginals to simply leave wherever they might be and, usually by themselves, walk off into the bush, returning often many months later. Since aboriginal belief systems are strongly associated with aspects of the landscape, these "walkabouts" may well be a form of spiritual pilgrimage.

Wowser. Generally a teetotaller or someone who believes in temperance, but also a person who is seen as wanting to keep others from having a good time by insisting that a strict code of usually religious-based morality be applied to everyone. In other words, a spoilsport.

Select Bibliography

I am particularly indebted to the editors, writers, and contributors of *Cinema Papers*, 1974–1989. Despite its own ups and downs, *Cinema Papers* has provided a consistent source of information and comment on the New Australian Cinema almost from the beginning.

Until recently, serious scholarship on the New Australian Cinema was hampered by lack of studies of the industry itself during the period since 1970 and by lack of analyses of the films that constitute its product. In the last few years, fundamental steps toward addressing both these aspects (but especially the first) have been taken by Susan Dermody and Elizabeth Jacka with the publication of a trilogy on the New Australian Cinema: *The Screening of Australia, Volume 1: Anatomy of an Industry* (Sydney: Currency Press, 1987); *The Screening of Australia, Volume 2: Anatomy of a National Cinema* (Sydney: Currency Press, 1988); and *The Imaginary Industry: Australian Film in the Late '80s* (Sydney: AFTRS Publications, 1988).

Although nearly all the entries in this book were written before the publication of Dermody and Jacka's works and were not altered as a result of reading them, I acknowledge a debt of gratitude to their lucid analyses of the shape and background of the New Australian Cinema.

Of particular reference value as well have been John Stewart, *An Encyclopedia of Australian Film* (Sydney: Rigby, 1984); Andrew Pike and Ross Cooper, *Australian Film 1900–1977* (Melbourne: Oxford University Press and the Australian Film Institute, 1980); and David Stratton, *The Last Wave* (Sydney: Angus and Robertson, 1979).

The opinions in this book are my own, but I occasionally checked them against the opinions of others (although I seldom changed mine as a consequence). In this regard I must also acknowledge Scott Murray (ed.), *The New Australian Cinema* (Melbourne: Nelson, 1980); and Sandra Hall, *Critical Business* (Sydney: Rigby, 1985).

The complete history of the Australian cinema is yet to be told. In addition to the three books by Dermody and Jacka, I must acknowledge my use of the work begun in this area by the late Eric Reade, *History and Heartburn: The Saga of Australian Film, 1896–1978* (Sydney: Harper and Row, 1979), and earlier books, and by Graham Shirley and Brian

Adams, *Australian Cinema: The First Eighty Years* (Sydney: Angus and Robertson and Currency Press, 1983).

Prior to the birth of the New Australian Cinema, it was said that Australia had the most-written-about nonexistent cinema in the world. The twenty years of the New Australian Cinema have radically altered that equation; but the amount of writing about the Australian cinema (old and new) has also increased impressively over the same two decades. An excellent, if still select, bibliography is available in Albert Moran and Tom O'Regan (eds.), *The Australian Screen* (Ringwood, Victoria: Penguin, 1989), which also contains some insightful articles on aspects of the New Australian Cinema.

My understanding of Australian culture owes a great deal not only to having been born in Australia and living most of my life there but also to several key writings: Donald Horne, *The Lucky Country: Australia in the Sixties* (1st ed., Ringwood, Victoria: Penguin, 1964; 2nd ed., 1971); Russel Ward, *The Australian Legend* (2nd ed., Melbourne: Oxford University Press, 1965); and Richard White, *Inventing Australia: Images and Identity 1688–1980* (Sydney: George Allen and Unwin, 1981).

OTHER REFERENCES

Carroll, John (ed.). *Intruders in the Bush: The Australian Quest for Identity.* Melbourne: Oxford University Press, 1982.

Clancy, John. "Film: the Renaissance of the Seventies," in Carroll (ed.), *Intruders in the Bush.*

Dermody, Susan, John Docker, and Drusilla Modjeska. *Nellie Melba, Ginger Meggs and Friends: Essays in Australian Cultural History.* Melbourne: Kibble Books, 1982.

Fiske, John, Bob Hodge, and Graeme Turner. *Myths of Oz: Reading Australian Popular Culture.* Sydney: Allen and Unwin, 1987.

Rowse, Tim, and Albert Moran. "'Peculiarly Australian'—The Political Construction of Cultural Identity," in Sol Encel and Lois Bryson (eds.), *Australian Society: Introductory Essays.* 4th ed. Sydney: Longman Chesire, 1984.

Turner, Graeme. *National Fictions: Literature, Film and the Construction of Australian Narrative.* Sydney: Allen and Unwin, 1986.

Ward, Russel. "The Social Fabric," in A. L. McLeod (ed.), *The Pattern of Australian Culture.* Ithaca: Cornell University Press, 1963.

About the Author

Neil Rattigan grew up in Perth, Western Australia, where he began making amateur films with friends as a teenager. Later he studied film and television at the Western Australian Institute of Technology and the University of London and received a Ph.D. in film studies from Northwestern University in the United States. In addition to teaching film and television at several colleges and universities in Western Australia, he has reviewed films for the Australian Broadcasting Corporation.

DH

791.
436
294
RAT